Andrea di Robilant

LUCIA

Andrea di Robilant was born in Italy and educated at Le Rosey and Columbia University, where he specialized in international relations. He lives in Rome with his wife and two children and works for the Italian newspaper *La Stampa*.

ALSO BY ANDREA DI ROBILANT

A Venetian Affair

LUCIA

LUCIA

A VENETIAN LIFE
IN THE AGE
OF NAPOLEON

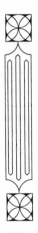

Andrea di Robilant

VINTAGE BOOKS

A DIVISION OF RANDOM HOUSE, INC.

NEW YORK

FIRST VINTAGE BOOKS EDITION, FEBRUARY 2009

The Library of Congress has cataloged the Knopf edition as follows:
di Robilant, Andrea.
[Lucia in the age of Napoleon]
Lucia : a Venetian life in the age of Napoleon / by Andrea di Robilant.
p. cm.
Includes bibliographical references and index.
1. Memmo Mocenigo, Lucia, 1770–1854.
2. Upper class women—Italy—Venice—Biography.
3. Venice (Italy)—Social life and customs.   4. Venice (Italy)—History—1787–1866.
5. Venice (Italy)—History—French occupation, 1797.
6. Europe—History—1789–1815. I. Title.
DG678.43.M46D5 2008
945'.311082092—dc22
[B]   2007042430

Vintage ISBN: 978-1-4000-9511-7

Author photograph © Elizabeth Stokes
Book design by Anthea Lingeman

www.vintagebooks.com

Printed in the United States of America
10 9 8 7 6 5 4 3 2 1

For Alessandra

Contents

Plates

Acknowledgements

The decisive impulse to write about Lucia came from Nancy Isenberg, Professor of Literature at Rome University; this book would not have seen the light without her persistent encouragement. A number of other friends offered their generous and sometimes crucial help along the way. Giulia Barberini, director of the Museo di Palazzo Venezia, shared with me her knowledge of the extraordinary *palazzo* where Lucia lived when her father was the Venetian ambassador in Rome. Wendy Roworth, professor of art history at the University of Rhode Island, helped me locate the long-lost portrait of Lucia by Angelica Kauffmann in Buckinghamshire. Benedetta Piccolomini proved a most enthusiastic guide during our exploration of what remains of Alvisopoli. In Austria, the kind and tenacious Clarisse Maylunas led me to Margarethen Am Moos during a rainy excursion in the countryside south of Vienna. My research took an entirely unexpected direction with the discovery of Lucia's secret lover, Maximilian Plunkett—a discovery which would certainly have eluded me but for the steady prodding of Anne-Claude de Plunkett in Paris. A final tassel in the reconstruction of Lucia's affair came from the ever generous Marco Leeflang in Utrecht. Iain Brown and his staff could not have been kinder in helping me with the Byron papers at the National Library of Scotland in Edinburgh. And I am very grateful to Simon Houfe and Alvise Memmo for allowing me to reproduce Angelica Kauffmann's portrait of Lucia and the miniature of Lucia and Paolina as young girls.

Maps

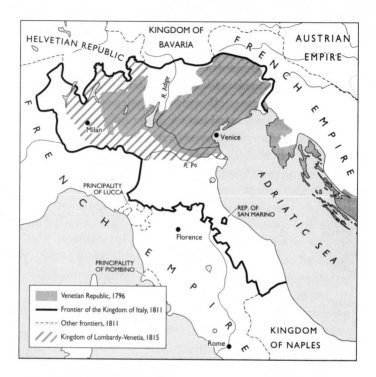

The Venetian Republic, 1796
——— Frontier of the Kingdom of Italy, 1811
- - - - - Other frontiers, 1811
/// Kingdom of Lombardy-Venetia, 1815

The Venetian Republic, which had developed over the course of a thousand years, came to an end with the Treaty of Campo Formio, signed on 17 October 1797 by the French and the Austrians. Venice passed under Austrian rule, but in 1805 it became part of the Kingdom of Italy, a pro-French puppet state. Austrian rule was re-established after Napoleon's fall in 1814.

The families of Lucia and her husband were firmly rooted in the heartland of Venice and the Venetian *terraferma*. The key locations mentioned in the text are shown here.

Prologue

When I was growing up I sometimes heard my grandfather mention Lucia Mocenigo, my Venetian great-great-great-great-grandmother, who was known in the family as Lucietta. Her name usually came up in connection with Lord Byron, to whom she rented the *piano nobile** of her *palazzo* during his scandalous time in Venice. I learnt more about her many years later, while doing research on her father, Andrea Memmo, whose epic love story with the beautiful Giustiniana Wynne in the 1750s was the subject of my last book, *A Venetian Affair*. But it was not until a recent chance encounter brought me face to face with a ten-foot-high marble statue of Napoleon Bonaparte that my interest in Lucia deepened.

The statue, wedged into a corner, faces a damp wall in the *androne* of Palazzo Mocenigo, the venerable old *palazzo* on the Grand Canal which once belonged to my family. The emperor is clad in a Roman toga. His left arm is extended forward, as if he were pointing to a luminous future, though in fact he stares vacuously at the peeling wall in front of him. A mantle of dark grey soot has settled on to his shoulders, and a slab of roughly hewn marble links the raised arm to the head, giving the statue an unfinished look. It is hard to imagine a more incongruous presence than the one of a youthful Napoleon standing sentinel in that humid hallway to the sound of brackish water slapping and sloshing in the nearby canal.

---

* In Italy a *palazzo* is a substantial building, usually the home of an important family or institution. The principal rooms occupy the *piano nobile*, on the first or second floor, while the water-level entrance is called the *androne*.

Alvise Mocenigo, Lucia's husband, commissioned the statue in the heyday of Napoleon's Empire. It was intended to be the centrepiece of a vast utopian estate he built on the mainland. The statue, however, was not delivered until after the emperor's downfall. By then Alvise was dead, and Lucia, not quite knowing what to do with such a cumbersome and politically embarrassing object, stored it in the entrance hall of Palazzo Mocenigo, exactly where it stands today.

The statue is all that remains of our family possessions in Venice. In the 1920s and 1930s, my profligate grandfather, having inherited the Mocenigo fortune, sold the *palazzo* and all its art treasures to finance his high-flying lifestyle. But he was never able to get rid of the marble Napoleon, which continued to languish in its corner untouched. Not long ago, while visiting Venice, I ran into the manager of Palazzo Mocenigo, which is now divided into apartments. Signor Degano looked at me as if I were a ghost from the past. It was quite understandable: not only do I carry the same name as my grandfather but the telephone line at Palazzo Mocenigo is still registered, strangely enough, under the name of Andrea di Robilant, even though my family has not lived there for more than fifty years.

After a few polite exchanges in the glaring sun of Campo Santo Stefano, Signor Degano reminded me that we were still the legal owners of the statue of Napoleon and asked me what we intended to do with it, adding that the various owners of the condominium would be quite happy to see it stay as it had been a part of the *palazzo* for so long. I said I would let him know and we parted. I stayed in Venice an extra couple of days to try to sort things out, though I realised there were few options, and none of them particularly appealing. The statue was officially *notificata*, which meant it could not leave the country, and would therefore be very difficult to sell. I couldn't take it home with me, of course, because I had no space for it. Besides, the thought of facing the grumbling owners of the *palazzo* in a tense condominium meeting was definitely off-putting. The thing to do, I concluded, was to leave the statue where it was and let matters take care of themselves, much as Lucia had done two centuries earlier. But in the course of my brief and fruitless dealings, I paid secret visits to the marble Napoleon, letting myself into the garden of Palazzo Mocenigo and hurrying to the hallway before suspicious tenants caught sight of me. It was hard to resist the peculiar spell of the statue as it lured me back to an age of great turmoil.

When Lucia was growing up in the 1770s and 1780s, the Venetian Republic had long been in a slow and steady decline, weakened by ossified political institutions and a closed, extremely inbred, ruling class. But on the surface, life went on pleasantly enough, much as it had for many years. There were no wars, the economy sputtered along and the Carnival season seemed to last a little longer every year. The thousand-year-old Republic appeared to be immutable; certainly nothing foreshadowed the cataclysmic events that lay ahead. The taking of the Bastille in 1789 reverberated in Venice like a very distant rumble late on a golden afternoon. But of course the storm eventually made its way across the Alps, and when the young Bonaparte led his army into northern Italy in 1796, the Venetian Republic quickly crumbled, vanishing into the vortex that engulfed all of Europe during the following two decades.

The man who had brought such devastation to Venice now stood in the shadows of Palazzo Mocenigo, frozen at the height of his glory. During one of my furtive visits, it occurred to me that this long-neglected statue of Napoleon provided a very tangible connection to Lucia and her world, which I was now loath to let slip.

My quest was lucky from the start. Among my late father's papers I found a neatly tied bundle of very touching love letters Lucia wrote to Alvise during their engagement. But it was thanks to a second, much larger trove of letters found in a small public library in Bergamo—letters written to her sister Paolina over the course of five decades—that Lucia came to life more fully against the fast-changing social and political landscape of the times.

Naturally, the more I learnt about Lucia, the more I longed to know what she had looked like. In several letters written to Alvise when she was still only sixteen, Lucia mentioned sitting for Angelica Kauffmann, the eighteenth-century portraitist then living in Rome. I consulted Kauffmann specialists and none had ever heard of a portrait of Lucia. But after scouring the catalogues and ledgers of the main auction houses I found myself once again on the trail of my spendthrift grandfather, who, it turned out, had inherited the painting back in 1919, along with all the contents of Palazzo Mocenigo.

He first tried to sell it at Christie's in 1931, during the Depression. The painting did not fetch the high reserve price he had set and was "bought in." It was not surprising: my grandfather had chosen the worst possible moment to sell a painting. I pictured him making the rounds of the other auction houses, canvas under arm, in order to pay his expensive bills at 3 Albermarle Street, the elegant London town house where he lived at the time. Eventually, he left the portrait of Lucia with Sir William Agnews, of Agnews & Co., and it was not until five years later, on Christmas Eve of 1936, that Sir William was able to actually sell the picture for a modest sum. The buyer was Sir Albert Richardson, an eclectic architect and collector known in London's artistic circles as "the Professor." He made a down payment of £20 on an agreed purchase price of £160, which included a drawing by the Dutch artist Johannes Bosboom. The Professor hung the painting by the fireplace in the dining room of his Georgian house in Ampthill, Bedfordshire.

The painting now belongs to Mr. Simon Houfe, the Professor's grandson, who has made it his mission to preserve his grandfather's house and art collection. In January of 2005, while in England over the Christmas holidays, I arranged to see the portrait with a Kauffmann expert, Professor Wendy Roworth, of the University of Rhode Island, and took a train out to Bedfordshire. Mr. Houfe, a very amiable man in his sixties, greeted us warmly in front of his house, and took us straight in.

The interior had the appearance of a country museum that had been untouched for many years. Mr. Houfe had laid out a plate of ginger biscuits and cups and saucers. "Will it be coffee or shall we go straight to the painting?" he asked. "The painting!" Professor Roworth and I cried. Mr. Houfe grinned and led us to a large, sunlit room on the ground floor. The walls were covered with

English landscapes, portraits and equestrian paintings. A number of architectural drawings were also in view, and several eighteenth-century miniatures. A great gilded harp stood in one corner, next to a Merlin pianoforte dated 1786. Straight ahead, to the left of the unlit fireplace, in the spot where Mr. Houfe's grandfather had placed it seventy years before, was the glowing portrait of Lucia.

I had, by then, become quite familiar with Lucia and her world, having read several hundred of her letters. But seeing her for the first time, as a blossoming young woman, caused my heart to miss a beat. I had travelled from Italy to see what Lucia looked like, and I was prepared to be more than partial in my judgement. But her warm seductiveness took me completely by surprise. The delicate rosy skin, the pomegranate lips, the generous bosom, the long auburn curls that followed the line of her beautiful gold earrings: every detail gave off a sense of youthful voluptuousness. And her eyes, of a blue so deep as to seem nearly black, drew me to her with a strange intensity. Her profile was far from perfect. Yet even the slight protuberance at the tip of her delicate nose— a trait that so reminded me of her father, Andrea Memmo—did not diminish her beauty but gave it more character. Professor Roworth, meanwhile, was eagerly taking pictures and pronouncing the portrait to be one of Kauffmann's very best.

Mr. Houfe proceeded to give us a guided tour of the house, but I was a very distracted visitor, and at each opportunity I snuck back to the dining room for one more glimpse of Lucia. "I was so pleased to be able to re-unite you with your ancestor in this house," Mr. Houfe said kindly as we bid each other goodbye. "It was a very interesting event, and I hope it is not the end of the story."

At the empty railway station, as I waited for my train back to London, I drifted back to the floating white muslin with which Ms Kauffmann had delicately enveloped Lucia. I missed her already, and in a moment of fancy I wondered whether a million tiny particles had not travelled across time and space to dance in Mr. Houfe's dining room that morning.

LUCIA

Chapter One

ROME

In the winter of 1786, Andrea Memmo, the Venetian ambassador to the Papal States, was visiting Naples with his daughters Lucia and Paolina during the Carnival season, when he received a dispatch from Venice that he had been waiting for anxiously. Alvise Mocenigo, the only son of one of the wealthiest and most powerful families of the Venetian Republic, agreed to marry Memmo's oldest daughter, fifteen-year-old Lucia.

Memmo was an experienced diplomat and he knew this letter was only the first step in what promised to be a long and difficult negotiation. Alvise's personal commitment was no guarantee that the proposal would actually go through, for he was on very bad terms with his father, Sebastiano, and did not get on much better with the rest of his family, whose approval of the marriage contract was indispensable. The Mocenigo elders were irked by Alvise's marital freelancing. Moreover, they did not favour the prospect of an attachment to the declining house of the Memmos, which had been among the founding families of the Venetian Republic back in the eighth century, but whose finances and political power had been waning for some generations. Still, Memmo felt Alvise's letter was a promising start, and he was confident in his judgement that the twenty-six-year-old scion of Casa Mocenigo was a son-in-law worth an honest struggle. "For some time now he has shown real promise," he had explained to his closest friends, "and as I flatter myself of foreseeing the future, I know my daughter will be well taken care of."[1] The wisest course, he had concluded, was to cultivate Alvise directly, encouraging him to correspond with Lucia over the heads of the surly Mocenigos (it was Memmo who had convinced Alvise to go ahead and declare himself for Lucia). Meanwhile, he was going to exercise the full panoply of his diplomatic skills in an effort to bring Alvise's family over to his side; marrying Lucia off without the consent of the Mocenigos in a clandestine ceremony was out of the question.

The small travelling household in Naples was already dizzy with excitement when Memmo, still clutching Alvise's letter, summoned Lucia to his quarters. It was not clear to the rest of the family what the mysterious dispatch contained exactly, but it was plain to all that it must carry portentous news. Lucia entered her father's room anxious and short of breath. Thirteen-year-old Paolina followed, her eyes already swelling with tears of antici-pation, while Madame Dupont, their beloved governess, stood discreetly in the background. After revealing with appropriate solemnity the content of the dispatch, Memmo read out a draft copy of the marriage contract. He then handed to Lucia a sepa-rate letter in which Alvise, who was marrying for the second time, introduced himself to his young bride-to-be. He professed to remember Lucia from earlier days in Venice, though in truth he could only have had a vague recollection of her as a little girl. Lucia did not have any memory at all of Alvise. Standing in her father's study, she must have struggled to conjure up an image towards which she could direct the rush of confusing emotions.

Alvise's declaration called for an immediate reply. Memmo startled Lucia a second time by asking her to write to her future husband at once, and without his help. He would read the letter over, he assured her, but she had to set it down herself, letting her heart speak out and never forgetting to use her head. Lucia obedi-ently retired to her room, and in her neat, elegant handwriting, penned her first letter to Alvise, a letter so poignant yet also so thoughtful and mature that it deserves to be quoted in full:

> My most esteemed spouse, my good father having informed me of your favourable disposition towards me, and having told me of your worthy qualities, I will confess to you that in seeing myself so honoured by

your letter, and having been informed that you have agreed to the marriage contract which my own father read to me at length, I felt such agitation in my heart that for a brief moment I even lost consciousness. And now that I am writing to you I am so troubled, my father not wishing to suggest even one convenient word to me, that I feel embarrassed to the point that I don't quite know how to express myself. I thank you very much for the kindness you have shown me, for the good impression you have formed of me and which I shall endeavour yet to improve by the proper exercise of my duties. I know my good fortune, as well I should, and I will strive to become worthy of it. I am certain that my father, and indeed my loving uncles, in carrying forth this marriage, have had my happiness in mind, which means that in you I shall find all that a spouse may desire. I do not have the strength to say more, except that I have no other will than that of my father's, nor do I wish to have one, just as in the future I will only wish to have yours.[2]

It would have been pleasant to linger in Naples—the seaside gaiety of this port-city so reminded the Memmos of Venice. They had been feted with lunches and dinners in the homes of the Neapolitan nobility, they had visited the porcelain factories at Capodimonte, gone out to Pozzuoli to view the antiquities, made a tour of the Catacombs and had walked through the magnificent stables of King Ferdinand IV, the primitive but jocular monarch known as *Re Nasone*, King Big Nose. On the night of the *gran mascherata*, "the great masquerade," the king had spotted Lucia and Paolina in the packed crowd at Teatro San Carlo and had thrown handfuls of coloured confetti at them, giggling and clapping his hands when the two girls had thrown some back at him. Circumstances, however, had suddenly changed, and Memmo was anxious to return to Rome to push the deal on Lucia's marriage forward before it lost momentum. Lucia, too, longed to be back in Rome, at the Venetian embassy in the Palazzo San Marco, among her things and in the company of her friends. Each additional day spent in Naples made her feel a little more unhinged. Her father had explained how complicated the negotiations might prove, going so far as to admit to Lucia that the deal was not yet sealed because of the opposition of the Mocenigos. With trepidation, she now wrote to Alvise beseeching him "to come to terms with your family before any official notice of our wedding is published . . . I must confess that I would be extremely mortified if your family did not acknowledge me as your very obedient and affectionate spouse."[3]

Memmo drove out to the royal palace at Caserta to take formal leave of the king of Naples and his touchy Austrian wife, Queen Maria Carolina, as soon as it was convenient to do so without giving the impression of a rushed departure. Meanwhile he sent a small portrait of Lucia to Alvise. He had wanted to have a new miniature painted in Naples, but there was not enough time to arrange a sitting. So he sent an old one, of Lucia as a little girl, causing his daughter considerable discomfiture. "For heaven's sake, don't trust that picture," she pleaded with Alvise. "My father had it painted years ago in order to take it with him to Constantinople. You might find me changed for the worse when you see me, and I wouldn't want to suffer such disadvantage after a possibly favourable judgement on your part."[4]

Finally, on 11 March, Memmo, Lucia, Paolina and Madame Dupont crammed their luggage in a rented carriage and headed north for Rome, leaving the hazy silhouette of Vesuvius behind them. "There I hope to receive your portrait, and there, I'm afraid, mine will be painted," Lucia wrote spiritedly to Alvise in a note she dashed off before leaving.[5] She was already addressing him as her *amatissimo sposo,* her beloved spouse.

Although not yet sixteen, Lucia was already a young woman of uncommon poise. As the older of the two sisters she had taken on quite effortlessly some of the duties and responsibilities that would have been her mother's as the wife of the ambassador. Five years had gone by since Elisabetta Piovene Memmo had died in Venice of a "gastro-rheumatic fever," leaving her two young daughters, ten and eight, stunned with grief. Elisabetta had been ill for some time. She was a frail woman, who suffered nervous breakdowns and often took to her bed. She drank vinegar every morning for fear of putting on weight and developed what the doctors described as "a bilious temperament."[6] When she died, Memmo was in Constantinople, serving as ambassador to the Porte. He sailed home utterly distraught, a widower with two young daughters to raise.

Lucia and Paolina's education had been somewhat haphazard during his absence. The girls were taught basic reading and writing skills, they received piano and singing lessons, learnt a little French, but their schooling was unimaginative and perfunctory. Elisabetta became less reliable as her health declined, and the two sisters fell increasingly under the authority of their strict grandmother, Lucia Pisani Memmo, who lived upstairs from them at Ca' Memmo, the family *palazzo* on the Grand Canal, and who was more interested in developing her granddaughters' manners than their intellect.

Ambassador Memmo, a learned and widely read man with a considerable knowledge of history and philosophy and an abiding passion for architecture, embraced the opportunity to educate his daughters, in part because he had been an absent father. "My girls are still a little rough around the edges," he confided to his friends, "but under his care they would surely become "very beautiful and very educated."[7] He did not want to stay in Venice after the death of his wife because it would only sharpen his misery. So he welcomed his appointment to the ambassadorship in Rome, where he moved with his daughters in 1783, at the age of fifty-four.

Life in the papal city offered Memmo a nice change of pace after his very active and distinguished career in the service of the Venetian Republic. He needed "distractions to preserve [his] health," he claimed, and these he certainly found, throwing himself in the arms of lovers, young and old, and thanking his "amiable sluts" for breathing new life into his otherwise "moribund cock." He also indulged in the pleasures of a good table. "My appetite thrives and I am an excellent companion at dinner."[8]

Although he took his pleasures, he did not neglect his duties as a father. His best time, in Rome, was the one he spent in the company of Lucia and Paolina, who blossomed, he said, "thanks to their excellent French governess and to my own efforts." His daughters were indeed much admired and Madame Dupont's "unequalled vigilance" helped to preserve their innocence. "Perhaps even excessively," quipped Memmo, the aging libertine, to Guglielmo Chiarabba, his agent back in Venice, "since it does not seem to me they have the slightest desire to be attractive to men."[9]

In Lucia's case, things were rapidly changing.

After a four-day journey from Naples across the Pontine marshes, the mud-splattered carriage rattled into the courtyard of Palazzo San Marco, the stately residence at the end of the Corso that had served as the Venetian embassy for more than three centuries.* When Memmo had arrived in Rome he had found the building in great disrepair—further evidence of the Venetian Republic's economic decline. The foundations were sinking and wide cracks in the wall zigzagged across the faded frescoes. Many rooms were so damaged they were uninhabitable and had been closed off. It was impossible to restore the *palazzo* to its former splendour, and hard enough to keep appearances up to an ac-

---

* It was a truly imposing palace. Built at the end of the fifteenth century by Cardinal Barbo, a wealthy Venetian, it was the first example of a Renaissance *palazzo* in Rome, with its tower and crenellated walls still conjuring the fortress-like buildings of an earlier age. When Cardinal Barbo was elevated to the Holy See as Pope Paul II, the palace became the papal residence. In 1564, his successor Pope Pius IV ceded it to Venice with the proviso that it would pay for the upkeep. Thereafter, it served as the residence of the Venetian ambassador, though a wing of the *palazzo* was reserved for the Venetian cardinals living in Rome—a condominium-style arrangement that led to endless bickering between successive generations of ambassadors and cardinals over such mundane issues as who should pay for the maintenance of the joint staircase and the courtyard.

ceptable standard. Memmo complained to Chiarabba that the Venetian Senate provided a mere 500 ducats a year "to keep this old and worn-out machine on its feet."[10] He would have needed at least ten times as much to keep up with his flamboyant neighbour and old friend, Cardinal de Bernis, the French ambassador. Memmo was also expected to cover his living expenses, but the family income from his estates in the Veneto was down to a trickle. As a result, he lived in what he plaintively referred to as his "immense *palazzo*" in a state of constant penury, fretting over every little expense. His table was so frugal that even his staff complained of the scarcity of food in the house. He closed down the stables and drove around town in a rickety old carriage he had bought second-hand from his predecessor. He quickly gave up the idea of renting a summer villa in the hills south of Rome, as most other ambassadors did, and in the hotter months he was reduced to cadging invitations if not for himself, at least for Lucia and Paolina. He assured Chiarabba that he entertained as little as was possible without being pointed at all over Rome to his disadvantage.

What Memmo dreaded more than anything was the expensive custom of illuminating the facade of the *palazzo* with torches on feast days and special occasions. He cursed each time a European court announced the birth of a royal newborn, and his weekly dispatches to the Venetian Senate were replete with requests to relieve him from these costly *illuminazioni*. The Senate's replies were almost always negative. Eventually, he decided to stop illuminating the *palazzo* "unless the Senate specifically orders me to do so."[11]

It was on account of his financial worries that, three years after arriving in Rome, Memmo still had not made his *ingresso*, the elaborate and very expensive ceremony during which an ambassador presented his credentials to the Pope. Memmo had calculated his *ingresso* would cost him at least 700 ducats, a sum he could not possibly have come up with except by means of an extravagant loan or a lucky turn at the Lotto, which he played every week. Pope Pius VI, an energetic, cultivated man, had grown fond of Memmo and his family (both Lucia and Paolina received the sacrament of confirmation from him at the Vatican), and he took a lenient view of the matter, hardly pressing his friend at all. But the issue did not cease to worry Memmo, who continued to come up with original excuses to postpone the event, hoping to drag his feet until it was time to leave for his next post.

His plan, while in Rome, had been twofold: to prepare the ground for his next and possibly last career move—which would guarantee him a respectable status in Venice despite the economic decline of the family—and to find good and possibly wealthy husbands for his daughters. He had achieved the first objective the previous year, in 1785, when, to his own surprise, he was elected to the post of procuratore di San Marco, the second most prestigious position in the Venetian government after the one of doge. "I cannot deny that I am much obliged to my Venetians," he conceded, "not just for having contributed in such high numbers to my exalted nomination but for the warmth they have shown me." Indeed, many who had voted for him felt he was a strong candidate to be the next doge. Memmo must have grinned with satisfaction as he watched from his crumbling *palazzo* in Rome events take such a favourable turn for him up in Venice. "Oh my, we might yet see Memmo doge," he observed. True to himself, he quickly added: "Let us go slowly. I will have to see whether I can afford it, and I suspect I won't be able to."[12]

Memmo next turned to his eldest daughter's future. Initially, he had set his eyes on Alvise Pisani, a wealthy cousin of Memmo's on his mother's side. He thought he had the deal wrapped up only to see his two impoverished brothers, Lorenzo and Bernardo, scuttle it for fear they would end up having to contribute to the dowry he had agreed to pay. Memmo took "the loss of this great fortune" in stride, and decided to make one more attempt at a high-profile match for Lucia. If that too failed—he said—he was going to take the less exalted but simpler course of marrying both his daughters "to a pair of Memmo cousins" from a lesser branch of the family tree, and bring them all to live under one roof at Ca' Memmo. "They will keep the name they were born with, and they will have food on their table. For the rest, fate will provide."[13]

For some time he had had his eye on Alvise Mocenigo, who had survived a difficult childhood and an even more turbulent youth to become a handsome, self-assured young man, endowed with the intelligence and the political skills necessary to embark on a promising career in government. The fact that Alvise belonged to one of the wealthiest and most prestigious Venetian dynasties made him an even more attractive choice. But it was a risky one as well, on account of the young man's troubled relationship with his family. Sebastiano Mocenigo, Alvise's father, was a moody, complicated man, whose history of homosexuality had caused grief and embarrassment to the family. Casanova, who met him when he was ambassador to the Spanish Court in the 1760s, writes in his memoirs that his "Greek friendships" were well known in Madrid. He was later appointed ambassador to France and he was briefly arrested in Paris "for displaying his dissolute behaviour against nature in public."[14] The political clout of the Mocenigos was such that Sebastiano, despite his tainted reputation, obtained the coveted post of ambassador to the Habsburg Court in Vienna. Empress Maria Theresa, however, put her foot down, warning the Venetian authorities that Sebastiano was *persona non grata* in the Austrian capital. The scandal was in the open and the Republic, which was especially sensitive to its relations with Austria, could no longer turn a blind eye to Sebastiano's unacceptable behaviour. In 1773, the Inquisitors had him arrested for "libidinous acts against nature." The trial brought out all the more lurid details of his personal life. He was found guilty and imprisoned in the gloomy fortress of Brescia, where he remained confined during the following seven years.

Alvise was thirteen years old at the time of Sebastiano's imprisonment. From Brescia, his father arranged to have him sent to Rome, to study at the Collegio Clementino, a venerable boarding school founded by Pope Clement VIII in 1595. It was a lonely, unhappy time for Alvise, and though he did his best to sound cheerful, his letters to his father and to his mother were filled with the bitter melancholy of a sensitive boy far away from home— and a broken one at that. Unlike the other boarders, he did not return home during the long summers. The priests who looked after him tried to improve his spirits by taking him on an occasional trip to Tivoli or the port of Civitavecchia. His mother, Chiara Zen Mocenigo, wrote brief, monotonous letters to her son, enquiring about his health and little else. His father sent him chocolate, coffee and pocket money from prison in Brescia. The gifts were appreciated but they did not assuage the resentment that was building up in his young heart.

When Alvise was eighteen and his education at the Collegio Clementino was drawing to a close, his father wrote to tell him that the time had come "to choose a wife," and that, "having consulted the Golden Book"—the official ledger of the Venetian nobility—he had "taken aim" at the daughter of Pietro and Morosina Gradenigo, "a family with an excellent reputation, nobly governed and very fecund." As for the coveted bride, Sebastiano added with enthusiasm, she had "good size, good looks, good health and good manners."[15] Alvise was taken by surprise by his father's proposition, and he slowed things up by saying he wished to come home first to see his family, and then make a decision about taking a wife. Timing was crucial in marriage negotiations, and Alvise's attitude was not helpful. The Gradenigos looked elsewhere, and the deal quickly fell through, to Sebastiano's irritation.

Alvise returned to Venice feeling embittered and rebellious but also very confused. He travelled to Brescia to visit his father, whom he had not seen in five years, but their meeting in the bleak prison-fortress did not bring them any closer. Back in Venice he fell under the spell of his uncle Giovanni Mocenigo, Sebastiano's older brother and the titular head of the family. Giovanni persuaded Alvise that, for the sake of the Mocenigo dynasty, he should marry his own daughter Pisana—Alvise's first cousin. Sebastiano, still confined in Brescia, reacted furiously, but he had little control over family affairs. The marriage was forced upon Pisana, a spirited hunchback whose heart belonged to another young patrician; but it was never consummated. Shortly after the wedding, Pisana ran away from Palazzo Mocenigo leaving this note behind:

> My Alvisetto, adorable cousin, you of all people will not be surprised by my decision to leave you in order to give my reasons to a judge competent in these matters. I have voluntarily shut myself in a convent. You were well aware that I did not marry of my own free will, and you even complained about that. Now you too will be able to make your case. You will receive my petition to nullify our marriage. Please accept it with the forbearance worthy of your noble soul.[16]

The judge ruled in favour of Pisana, handing down a decision that reflected the growing opposition in Venetian society to marriage contracts that were enforced against the will of the participants. But Alvise did not accept the ruling with the equanimity Pisana had hoped for. Enraged by a decision that defied the will of the family and made him feel personally humiliated, he fled from Venice, "that fatal place where malice persecutes me" and in those "desperate and painful" first few weeks and months, he wandered in the fields and woods of the vast Mocenigo estates on the mainland, moving from one farmer's house to the next in search of shelter and food. He failed to report to duty in Vicenza for his first government assignment. Instead, he travelled to Udine, and then, against his father's specific orders not to leave the Republic, he slipped abroad, forsaking his monthly stipend. "From the age of twenty-five until my death I will devote my life to country and family," he wrote to his father before disappearing. "I have turned twenty-one, and I have four more years of freedom. Must I forsake these too?"[17] For the next three years he travelled from place to place, living on the generosity of friends and hocking the occasional piece of family jewellery he had taken with him. He was spotted in Toulon, Marseilles, Genoa, Livorno, Florence and Bologna, among other places. As promised, he made his way back in 1784. Upon entering Venetian territory, however, he was arrested and jailed in the fortress of Palma for having defied orders to go to Vicenza three years earlier. His father interceded, and a few months later the doge granted him an official pardon and he was released. Alvise arrived in Venice a changed man: he had matured, he had grown ambitious and he was determined to serve the Republic to the best of his ability. Although the sombre side of his personality still lurked in the background, he became more sociable and learnt to pursue some of the lighter pleasures of life. Very quickly, the most prominent members of the Venetian oligarchy began to take notice of him.

Among them was Memmo, who, though living in Rome, was very much in touch with what went on in Venice. He nimbly stepped in with the idea of marrying his eldest daughter to this promising young bachelor who, though penniless, was sure to inherit a very large fortune in the not so distant future. True, he had had a troubled past. "To that kind of Mocenigo, a light-headed, inexperienced youngster, abandoned by his father and always criticised by him, I certainly would not have offered the hand of my daughter, even if he was going to become four times richer than he will," Memmo wrote to a friend. But Alvise had grown up and changed for the better, his early tribulations having made him a stronger man. It is possible that Memmo saw in Alvise parts of himself as a young man, open to the ideas of the Enlightenment, interested in a career in diplomacy and showing every sign of wanting to serve his country well:

> He has already changed his style of life and sees only good people . . . He continues to study methodically even at twenty-six. He is very knowledgeable about agriculture, for which he seems to have a sublime talent, and he's not a man who is easily fooled. He seeks only the company of respectable ladies, he is generous without excess, and he is sweet and very respectful, and he cuts a good figure without covering himself with ornaments.[18]

Memmo moved quickly to forestall other interested parties. In early 1785, he and Alvise signed a preliminary contract without consulting with the Mocenigos. The deal fixed Lucia's dowry at 43,000 ducats. It was, on paper, a respectable sum, in line with general expectations. However, because Alvise was entering the deal behind his father's back, he was not likely to have any money of his own to pay for an adequate wedding, nor would he have the means to support Lucia decorously. Memmo therefore agreed— and this was the addendum that made it possible for Alvise to accept the deal—to pay Alvise 500 ducats a year until the death of his father, when he would inherit a considerable portion of the Mocenigo estate. Memmo did not have the money to honour the deal, but he did not worry. "It seems impossible that I shouldn't find it on the basis of a signed contract . . . There are many rich Venetians who need to earn four per cent on their capital or the cash they keep in their jewel cases," he told Chiarabba, his agent.[19]

Sebastiano was angry when he found out his only son had entered into a marriage agreement behind his back. Alvise defended his decision: "Such a noble marriage can be the beginning of a new life for me," he explained, adding peevishly that "in accepting, I imagined I would be meeting the wishes of father and family." Sebastiano was not moved: under the circumstances he would not give his approval, adding that he needed at least a year to reflect on the matter, all the more so since he and Alvise were still embroiled in a complicated legal tangle regarding an inheritance they both claimed. "The last thing I expected," Alvise answered with disappointment, "was for my good father to begin a discussion about my future with all this legal talk."[20]

It was a less than promising start. Memmo decided to deal with the cantankerous Sebastiano last, concentrating his effort on getting Uncle Giovanni and the rest of the Mocenigos on board. The strategy seemed to work and after a year of blandishments and reassurances, Memmo and Alvise both felt it was time to act. In January 1786 Memmo made a 5,000-ducat down payment on Lucia's dowry to the Mocenigos; a few weeks later Alvise's official agreement to marry Lucia reached the Memmos during their sojourn in Naples.

Word of Lucia's impending marriage had already spread in Rome by the time the Memmos returned from their Neapolitan journey. Naturally, members of the household at Palazzo San Marco had been the first to know. Abbé Sintich, Lucia's tutor, congratulated her warmly upon her arrival, followed by Memmo's faithful secretary, Abbé Radicchio, the house manager, Signor Ceredo, Zanmaria the cook, down the line of maids to Zannetto Organo, Memmo's young footman, who had been little more than a boy when they had all travelled down from Venice three years before. In her room Lucia found a pile of letters and notes from friends and relatives. To her relief, her father dispensed her from replying to every one, as it would have taken too much time away from her lessons with Abbé Sintich. But Lucia was soon overwhelmed by a stream of visiting Roman ladies, some of whom came to embrace the father as much as the daughter—according to Memmo's own count, he was happily involved with no fewer than six of them at the same time.

All this attention unsettled Lucia. "The causes of such a triumph certainly have more to do with you than with me," she wrote to Alvise with modesty. "How many compliments I have received! And why? Because fate has decreed that I should have an excellent gentleman like you for a husband." Would she be up to the daunting task ahead of her? "I do not doubt you have many good qualities . . . I only hope that patience be among them, so that you may tolerate those defects which I will strive to eliminate as quickly as possible by following your loving advice."[21]

It was not enough to feel every day the anxiety of marrying a man she had never seen; she also had to contend with the depressing thought of being unwanted and unloved by her new family. The Mocenigos' immediate disapproval of the marriage and Sebastiano's outright opposition to it caused Lucia much pain. She begged Alvise to be more conciliatory, to cede ground in order to find peace:

I heard about your family's wrath, for which I am so
sorry . . . I beseech you to use respect towards your
father and your uncle so as to calm them down. Give in
to some of their demands so that we may live in tranquillity . . . I pray to God that all these problems I have
caused may be resolved before our wedding takes
place.[22]

On 1 April 1786, a full five weeks after learning the name of the
man who was to become her husband, the small portrait of Alvise
she had been promised finally arrived with the morning courier.
She rushed to her room "blushing," she later confessed to Alvise,
and sat there gazing at the small image: it was a portrait of him at
sixteen, a handsome youth with a broad forehead, who looked
mature even at such a young age. "Everyone assures me you look
very much the same ten years later and this rather startles me,"
she said, openly flirting with him for the first time. "I can assure
you that I am very pleased with it." Lucia was so transfixed by
this image of Alvise that it took her some time to realise there was
another miniature attached to it. It was a twin portrait of herself,
which Alvise had had copied from the old miniature Memmo had
given him, and embellished. It showed a beaming Lucia holding
in her arms a bouquet symbolising their betrothal. "You could
not have had a kinder thought," she wrote back, very touched.
"And the bouquet could not have been richer or more beautiful."[23] She resolved to wear the twin miniatures around her neck
at the large dinner her father was planning in honour of the Duke
and Duchess of Cumberland.

Meanwhile, Lucia's portrait, which Alvise was waiting for with
equal impatience, was lagging behind. She had begun to sit for
Remondini, a Genoese portraitist in vogue among the Roman
aristocracy, after returning from Naples. But she had interrupted
the sessions because a nasty sty in her right eye had puffed up her
cheekbone, slightly disfiguring her, and giving her a terrible
headache. As soon as she recovered, Remondini disappeared.
Memmo sent a servant looking for him, but the man had vanished
mysteriously and in fact never returned. The portrait was left un-

finished. Lucia, worrying she might give Alvise a false impression of her, was loath to send him a picture that in some parts did not even look like her. She finally relented under pressure from her father. She explained to Alvise:

> Most esteemed spouse, there were good reasons not to send you a portrait in which much of the contour of the head had yet to be completed . . . I could be very sorry should I appear to be more beautiful than I am, or more ugly for that matter . . . But in the end what I most cared for was that it be truthful as a whole, and I think it is. My father is satisfied, except for the colour of the hair, which is certainly not mine . . . If only we had had time for a couple more sittings, the result would have been superior. In my haste to satisfy your desire, I have taken a substantial risk . . . You will observe that I asked to be painted holding a small portrait of you in my hand. It is to remind you that nothing occupies me more than the original article represented in that small frame.[24]

Alvise was delighted with the unfinished portrait and told Lucia how beautiful she was "with words that could not have been kinder or more obliging." The veil that had kept them invisible to one another, adding mystery and anxiety to their long-distance relationship, had been shed. Now both of them held an image on which to fix their thoughts. Their letters became more personal, more intimate, and Lucia must have felt a very sensual pleasure as she began signing off with expressions like "Your most trusted friend," "Your most beloved wife" or "Your loving spouse." She told Alvise: "I want to give myself over to my husband."[25] She did not yet abandon herself entirely to her fantasies because of "the bad situation" between Alvise and his family; but Alvise's letters, which she read in the privacy of her own room, clutching his small portrait, bolstered her confidence. He promised her their marriage would be based on love, but also on truth and loyalty, all the time reminding her that he was marrying her at his own initiative, not because of a family arrangement. There would be no secrets between them, no hypocrisy. And they would never cease to respect and to care for each other in the face of life's tribulations. Lucia was touched by his words. "Your wisdom about the maxims one should uphold in marriage gives me great comfort," she wrote. "It makes me hold you in ever greater esteem."[26] She dwelled on the example of her own parents:

> I will always remember how, despite their age difference, and their different character, and circumstances and education, my mother and father learnt to love each other, and to be always happy together even in adversity, except, as my poor mother used to say to us, at the time of separation, when they were torn by the feeling they might never see each other again.[27]

The weather had warmed since the family's return from Naples. Roman spring was bursting everywhere. From her window in Palazzo San Marco, Lucia could see the flowering wisteria climb around the large marble columns of the main loggia. In the courtyard below, water splattered gaily in a fishpond surrounded by palm trees and laurel hedges. Although Alvise was far away, Lucia felt his presence more strongly each day. She longed to be close to him, to touch him. His letters became an instrument of pleasure. "The longer they are, the longer I feel near to you," she told him tenderly. "My feelings for you are certainly not lesser than those you profess having for me, and I cannot wait to prove it to you with greater freedom."[28]

Memmo could not have been happier at the way Alvise and Lucia were getting to know each other by correspondence. His dealings with the Mocenigos, on the other hand, were more frustrating. They were raising objections about Memmo's ability to honour the marriage contract—legitimate objections, one might add, for rumour had it in Venice that Memmo had accumulated enormous debts during his tenure in Rome. The rumours were exaggerated by interested parties, but money, as Memmo well knew, was a serious problem. "I wouldn't want us to fall on our backside at this crucial point, making a ridiculous spectacle of ourselves and jeopardising my daughter's future,"[29] he told Chiarabba. But it was not just the money: the Mocenigos were raising issues of lineage that infuriated Memmo. There had been a Memmo doge as early as AD 979, well before the Mocenigos had even appeared in Venice! "I honestly cannot imagine what they can object to," he said in exasperation, "apart from the fact she wasn't born a Mocenigo."[30]

Memmo had to guard himself from his own brothers, who were constantly pulling the rug from beneath his feet, making it all the more difficult for him to carve out a decent dowry from a much reduced Memmo estate. And Alvise, with all his haste, was proving a less effective ally than expected. "He is young and wants everything at once, whereas I know that on every issue I must move only if we are sure to be on firm ground," he told his agent. Memmo conceded he was not entirely blameless, especially during his early approaches, "when I operated as if Alvise did not have a father or an uncle." But Alvise had shown himself quite "incapable of dealing with his family," and Memmo "absolutely" insisted on "reconciliation with the Mocenigos."[31]

The deal needed more work, and Memmo instructed Lucia to return to her old routine—not exactly the easiest thing, given the circumstances. She resumed her grammar and composition lessons with Abbé Sintich, her French lessons with Madame Dupont, and her lessons of philosophy and architecture, which Memmo supervised. The days were now longer. If Lucia finished her morning classes early, she and Paolina and Madame Dupont would sometimes go out for a walk at the edge of the city, towards the Roman ruins along the Appian Way, or else in the direction of the Vatican, in the hope of catching sight of the papal cavalcade. The afternoons were usually devoted to music and singing and to social visits. The girls also took riding lessons at the Villa Borghese. Before their trip to Naples, Memmo had escorted Lucia to dinners and balls; but after receiving Alvise's marriage proposal, he curtailed her evening engagements. Occasionally, she was allowed to go to the nearby Teatro Valle, the only theatre where the family kept a box.

Memmo seldom entertained at home for he was too mindful of the expenses. But he occasionally gave a lavish dinner to acquit himself in one go of the many he had enjoyed during the year. He had opened up Palazzo San Marco to honour King Gustav III of Sweden, for example, and he had thrown a memorable ball for the Duke and Duchess of Curlandia. Now Memmo decided to give a dinner with dancing and musical entertainment on Easter night, in honour of the Duke and Duchess of Cumberland. It was their second visit to the Eternal City. The duke had come to Rome in the 1770s with his morganatic wife Lady Anne Luttrell, much to the irritation of his brother, King George III. Back then Pope Pius VI had received the duke, but he had only agreed to meet Lady Luttrell in the papal gardens as if by chance. Now, ten years later the duke was back in Rome with his travelling court, and with Lady Anne firmly established as the Duchess of Cumberland (this time the Pope granted her an official audience). They rented a *palazzo* on Via Condotti, just off Piazza di Spagna, an area known as the English ghetto on account of the many *milordi inglesi* who took lodgings there during their Grand Tours. The Cumberlands spent extravagant sums of money, commissioned paintings from Italian and foreign artists, and worked their way through the palaces of the Roman aristocracy.

Memmo applied himself with special diligence to give his guests an evening worthy of their rank. Palazzo San Marco was scrubbed from top to bottom. The cracks in the wall were filled in or camouflaged. For once he did not penny-pinch in brightening up the building: two rows of torches were laid out to illuminate the facade. Memmo ordered bushels of oysters and fresh fish from the Adriatic, the choicest meats, his favourite cheeses from the Veneto and the best ices in Rome. The Map Room, originally the largest room in the *palazzo*, was divided in two rooms. The several hundred guests were to gather in the smaller one for the reception, and then move into the larger one, the *sala del camino grande*, for dinner. Musical entertainment, followed by dancing, was to take place in the adjacent ballroom. Rather than hiring musicians and singers, Memmo prevailed upon his daughters to organise an after-dinner show with the help of their ballet teacher, the formidable Madame Viganò, who managed the Teatro Valle and therefore had a number of dancers and singers on hand. "God help us!" Lucia wrote to Alvise with trepidation on the eve of her show. "If only my husband were here, I would surely dance more happily than I will!"[32]

The evening was a great success, and a personal one for Lucia and Paolina. The Duchess of Cumberland was so taken with their ballet that she begged to see it again. As a result, all the Roman ladies asked the two sisters to repeat the performance in their palaces. If they did not come, the Marchesa Massimo warned, she would be forced to cancel her dinner for the duke and duchess! Lucia related her adventures with amusement to Alvise. For her, the high point of the evening had not been the ballet at all. "I wore your portrait upon my breast for the first time in public," she confessed. "Everyone loved it and commented on how magnificent you looked. They even went so far as to praise your taste in the choice of the small frame."[33]

The duke and duchess became very fond of Lucia and Paolina, and they took them along wherever they went. The duke only liked to dance with them, while the duchess took it upon herself to improve the girls' halting English. Lucia was frustrated by her lack of progress in the language everyone wanted to learn in Rome. Her conversations with the duchess had only made her more aware of how much practice she still needed "to express myself better and improve my pronunciation." With difficulty, she could get through a book in English:

> But it is one thing to understand a passable amount of what one has read, and quite another to understand what the English are saying when they talk to you, or for that matter to actually speak it ourselves. The two of us haven't got very far, and I fear we never will.[34]

She knew Alvise too had tried to learn English, in Venice, and had given up; but if he desired to do so, they could try to learn it together once they were married. "It's a very difficult language, and I honestly fear I shall never learn to speak it well, but if you should have some extra time available to resume this fruitful occupation, then I will make a special effort to improve my own skills."[35]

Lucia often fantasised about her future life as Alvise's wife, and tried to imagine him in Venice by piecing together the bits of information that came her way. Apart from the letters she received every week from him, she culled useful nuggets from visitors who came down from Venice—Venetian senators who were friends of her father, for the most part, or else foreigners who had been to Venice on their Grand Tour and were visiting Rome. The conversation among these dinner guests at Palazzo San Marco often touched on Venetian affairs, with the inevitable digressions about Alvise, his past vicissitudes, his prospects as a politician—he had his eye on the position of Savio di Terra-ferma, the traditional stepping-stone for ambitious young Venetians embarking on a political career. Lucia was touched to hear how Alvise always rushed to retrieve her letters from the courier; about the inspired toasts he had given to her health in a number of assemblies; about the pleasure he derived in hearing people speak well about "the woman he had not seen and did not know, and yet had chosen as his eternal companion." But she warned him not to rely too much on hearsay. She pointed out she was not a woman who sought the limelight or thrived in society:

> I much prefer tranquillity, and I like to lead a with-
> drawn life unless there is something beautiful or
> worthwhile to see . . . so that I have never really given
> much attention to appearances and ornaments, nor
> have I endeavoured to impress people with endless
> chatter—the way some young ladies do, and are criti-
> cised for it.[36]

Lucia wanted to bring happiness "in a life that has suffered its share of misfortune" and she was ready to do her part in full so as not let Alvise down. "I will take care of my duties to make sure that this time you will not be disappointed," she wrote, bearing in mind his catastrophic earlier marriage to his first cousin, Pisana.

"I pray to God that ill fate will turn to good fortune, and that I will contribute to a happy change rather than making your life less bearable."[37]

Her letters could easily have been written by someone older and wiser than a girl her age. Alvise was often startled by what he read, and in the name of that honesty that he hoped would always prevail in their marriage, he asked her whether someone was watching over her shoulder when she wrote to him. Lucia was flattered and faintly miffed. She had little experience in the art of letter-writing, having so far corresponded mostly with her aunts and uncles. When she wrote to Alvise, she drafted a rough copy to correct mistakes and preserve a record of their correspondence. That was why the letters were so neat, she confessed. Not even Abbé Sintich was allowed to help her:

> I wouldn't hide anything from my dear husband: I write them myself, and no one is allowed to read them, except my Father, who sometimes helps me find the right word, but usually has no time or patience . . . and will leave in place a piece of writing that I myself dislike. He always warns me not to bother him with my requests, adding it doesn't matter if one writes badly to one's husband.[38]

No amount of fine writing on the part of Lucia, however, could conceal the fact that the fruitless negotiations with the Mocenigos were taking their toll on her. Although she put on the best possible front, she admitted feeling "very afflicted" because she seemed to be "everyone's target," as if she were "the principal reason" for the impasse even though she was in no way at fault. "Only the steadfastness you have demonstrated so far," she confessed to Alvise, "prevents me from feeling even more distressed than I am."[39] Her father had promised her "this painful situation" would not last much longer, but she was unsure, and she entreated Alvise over and over not to be stubborn with his family for the sake of their future well-being. "I do not doubt your efforts to give me full satisfaction. If I badger you so," she explained to him on one occasion after he had reacted defensively, "it is only because of my strong desire to accelerate our destiny . . . By cultivating your family and lowering your expectations just a little, we might actually reach a good conclusion."[40]

In speaking with such firmness, she was probably influenced by her father, who felt Alvise had to do everything in his power to appease the intractable Sebastiano and obtain his approval of the wedding. There was talk, in the absence of such approval, of a marriage by proxy, which meant Lucia would remain in Rome for the foreseeable future. Another possibility suggested by the Mocenigos was to go ahead with the wedding, after which Alvise and Lucia would settle in with Memmo—a proposition Memmo did not even take into consideration as it would have added a new burden on his depleted finances. "These Mocenigos will use anything as an excuse to slow things up!"[41] he blurted out in exasperation.

One problem, however, was entirely of Memmo's making. Overly confident in his ability to stage-manage the situation, he deliberately described Alvise to Lucia as less handsome than he was "so that she will find him more so upon laying eyes on him." And unbeknownst to poor Lucia, he described her to Alvise "as heavier than she is, so he will find her less so."[42] Memmo's deception backfired for it sparked a rumour in Venice that Lucia had grown enormously fat, and he had to stay up late at night writing to friends back home in order to undo the damage he had caused. "On the topic of my daughter's fatness," he told one of them, "I assure you it is pure slander generated by nothing but envy. I promise you Lucia will be the most beautiful bride imaginable."[43]

The idea of going through with the wedding without the full consent of Alvise's family worried Lucia. The hurried, semi-clandestine marriage ceremony that was sometimes mentioned as a possibility had no appeal for her. She did not want to begin her married life with a dark cloud hanging over her young family, and she urged Alvise again and again "to demonstrate his affection to people he should respect in any case, even though they are not what you would like them to be."[44]

There was little to distract Lucia from the frustrating pace of events now that she was no longer allowed to go out in society much. Occasionally, Memmo took his daughter to an opera by Cimarosa, the favourite in-house composer at the Teatro Valle. Lucia accepted Princess Borghese's invitation to a dinner al fresco on the Pincio, followed by fireworks and musical entertainment. But the moment gambling tables were brought out, she headed home with Paolina and Madame Dupont. She attended only one public event: the unveiling of the Great Bell of Saint Peter's, a colossal work in bronze that had cost the life of Luigi Valadier, the celebrated goldsmith who created it.

Pope Pius VI had commissioned the great bronze bell in 1779, to replace the one that had cracked a few years earlier. Valadier designed what was arguably the largest bronze bell ever built. It was three metres high and two and a half metres wide; its circumference was nearly eight metres, and it was decorated with beautifully detailed friezes. The technical complexity of melting such an enormous and yet very delicate object, not to mention the huge cost overruns, finally overwhelmed Valadier. He committed suicide by throwing himself in the Tiber before he could finish it. His son, Giuseppe Valadier, completed the work within a few months. He built a wooden fortress on wheels in which the bell was transported from the foundry in Via del Babuino to Saint Peter's Square. As it travelled across the city, the bell rang loudly, attracting cheering crowds along the way. In the atrium of the basilica of Saint Peter's, Lucia watched Pope Pius VI bless the mighty *campanone*. "It is a true wonder," she reported to Alvise, "for its size, for its sound and for all its intricate *bas relief*." She saw it as a good omen. "Let us pray to God that the nasty climate hanging over us will soon change."[45]

By the end of June, encouraging news arrived from Venice. Alvise had finally begun to heed Memmo's advice to seek an accommodation with his family, and his efforts had improved the atmosphere notably. Memmo's own blandishments to the Mocenigos and the sheer lack of solid arguments to oppose the marriage helped as well. Seizing the momentum, Memmo urged Alvise to behave towards his father "with the prudence and respect required at this moment."[46]

Sebastiano's assent to the marriage arrived at last on the morning of 1 July, nearly five months after Alvise had formally proposed. On a hunch, Lucia rushed out of Palazzo San Marco when she heard the courier Nullo had arrived at the station, dragging Paolina and Madame Dupont with her. They ran into Signor Nullo, who was coming to deliver the important dispatch in person. Breathless, they returned home and went immediately to Memmo's apartment. "We couldn't resist closing ourselves in my father's room," she told Alvise. "Some of us cried, some of us couldn't catch their breath, some of us couldn't say a word." After all that had passed, Lucia had not anticipated the warm feelings expressed by her future father-in-law in his letter. "How could we not be utterly surprised at the manner with which he addressed my father, and the generous words he used with me," she wrote to Alvise, at once relieved and elated at how the situation had quite suddenly turned in her favour. "He knew what I had gone through. Moved by delicate, humane feelings, he encouraged me with overflowing words, lifting me from gloom to happiness." This old man, who had been so mean to her future husband and so hostile and strange to her, seemed so transformed and so clearly on her side that Lucia already felt "attached to him by the most respectful affection." Such was her joy that even if he should again give her "displeasures" in the future, she was ready to "forgive all."[47]

Lucia was especially happy to receive a warm letter from Chiara, Alvise's mother, who had remained in the background all this time and about whom Lucia had heard only good things. Chiara wrote:

> My dear child, if I could have listened only to the voice of my feelings, I would have explained long ago to you, my lovable Luciettina, the pleasure and happiness I felt upon first hearing that you might become my daughter . . . Now that I bring together at last my love for you as a mother with the interests of the family, I have not allowed a moment to pass before assuring you of my jubilation . . . and the sheer joy of express-

ing to you my feelings . . . Consider me your mother
for I shall always look upon you as my daughter.[48]

These tender, heart-felt words were what Lucia had secretly
hoped for. She yearned to find in her future mother-in-law some
of that maternal love she had lost as a little girl, when her mother
had died so suddenly. Chiara had wanted to let Lucia know she
understood that yearning. "Surely your unequalled mother will
take the place of mine," Lucia confided to Alvise. She went even
further, fantasising about how her marriage to Alvise, which had
caused such bad feelings, would help bring the fractious
Mocenigo family together. Was it too much to hope that they
could all live together?

> How wonderful it would be if the family lived under
> the same roof, ate at the same table . . . I'll say no more.
> The skies have cleared and heaven is now clement with
> me, and I hope it will not abandon me.[49]

In her letters to Alvise, Lucia had always made a point of reminding him, delicately, that until matters were settled, her father
remained her only guide. After receiving Sebastiano's letter, she
began in earnest her journey into the sphere of influence of the
Mocenigos. "I shall do everything my husband asks me to do,"
she now promised Alvise. "You will be my guide in everything."
Barely sixteen years old, she was ready "to become a true
Moceniga." She may well have felt a voluptuous pleasure in
finally giving herself over to Alvise. His age and experience
added to her sense of security. "The fact that you are ten years
older than me," she admitted, "is another good fortune."[50]

Alvise encouraged her to think ahead about their life together
in Venice. The idea of living with his parents, which Lucia had
broached in a moment of enthusiasm, did not appeal to him at all.
Besides, there was plenty of space in Palazzo Mocenigo for the
young couple to have their own, comfortable apartment. Reno-
vations would soon be under way, Alvise informed her, and she
should send him her ideas about their living arrangements, as

well as any special request she might have. Lucia, unused to this kind of responsibility, was embarrassed by all the fuss. "Apropos *palaces* and apartments," she wrote back, "I tell you with the greatest sincerity that I would suffer to see too much being done for my sake." Besides, she would always be more interested in the people living in the house "rather than in all the beautiful furniture."[51] But since Alvise had asked, she thought she might put in at least one request that was sure to make her life more comfortable: "All I really wish is to have a few small rooms *de retraite* just off the main bedroom, where I might write or paint without fear of messing up or dirtying [the apartment]."[52]

The journey back to Venice was delayed until after the summer. The Senate instructed Memmo to wait for his successor before leaving Rome. And the new ambassador, much to Memmo's irritation, was taking his time winding his way down from Venice with his wife and retinue. Memmo had never quite gotten used to "the deadly heat that springs from the earth" during the summer in Rome, which he found "much more unbearable" than in Venice. "The air is literally on fire," he complained to his agent, "and in order to breathe you must lock yourself up even more than in winter."[53] Palazzo San Marco was surrounded by three large squares that turned hard and dry "causing everyone to eat a lot of dust." His neighbours "tormented" him and pressed him to cover the scorched earth with gravel, like everyone else did. But that was yet another expense Memmo would not put up with, especially now that he was preparing to leave.

Society life ground to a halt in July and August. The Corso was deserted most of the day. The great palaces emptied as the Roman nobility retreated to their summer villas in the hills south of Rome, where the temperature was several degrees cooler and a pleasant breeze blew in from the Tyrrhenian Sea. But renting a villa was a luxury Memmo could not afford. "Too much money for the sake of a little coolness," he grumbled. To alleviate the tedium of those long summer days, Memmo organised a day-trip with the girls and Madame Dupont to the waterfalls at Tivoli. He took them on a picnic by the Roman pool at Hadrian's Villa. And he found some respite from the heat during their frequent excursions to the early Christian catacombs on the Appian Way, just beyond the southern city gate. In the evenings, Memmo gathered the few friends who were still in town for a light dinner at home, followed by ices and a little musical entertainment, usually provided by Lucia and Paolina. On one of these intimate occasions, Lucia, feeling playful, appeared among her father's guests wearing a bracelet with an image of Sebastiano on her left wrist and one with Memmo's image on her right wrist, and with the miniature of Alvise resting as usual upon her breast. "You won't believe the things I sometimes put on,"[54] she wrote to Alvise.

That summer the artist Angelica Kauffmann was among Lucia's favourite companions. Memmo had commissioned her to paint a formal portrait of himself clad in the traditional red brocade robe of the Procuratore di San Marco, to take back with him to Venice. He took the opportunity to commission twin portraits of his two daughters as well, in order to have a family set. Kauffmann's studio was on the Via Sistina, just off the church of Trinità dei Monti. A number of painters and sculptors had recently moved into the area from Piazza Farnese, and Kauffmann, then at the top of her fame, was very much at the centre of this thriving community of artists. The large house she lived in with her husband, Antonio Zucchi, was filled with sculptures and busts and classical paintings. It was a lively and welcoming haven for fellow painters and writers, dealers and travellers, and for the more adventurous members of the Roman aristocracy and the diplomatic corps. The studio, stacked with canvases and cluttered with easels, brushes, jars and powdered pigments, was at the end of the house, overlooking an unruly garden. Memmo often made the short trip from Palazzo San Marco to the atelier in Via Sistina with his daughters, and he encouraged Kauffmann and her husband to take Lucia and Paolina to visit the studios of their artist friends.

One August afternoon, the antiquarian Johann Raiffenstein joined Kauffmann, Zucchi, Lucia and Paolina, and together they braved the heat to go see the new painting everyone was talking about in Rome. It was by Jean-Germain Drouais, the twenty-three-year-old protégé of Jacques-Louis David. He had won the

Prix de Rome and had installed himself at the French Academy. Some critics thought his talent surpassed that of his famous mentor. The large canvas he had just completed depicted the Roman general Marius, wrapped in a scarlet robe, as he stared down at the soldier who had come to murder him in prison after the battle of Minturno. It was a stark, powerful picture in the neoclassical style, which clearly owed a great deal to the influence of "Monsieur David." Lucia was struck by the fact that Drouais had reached such a level of artistic maturity at his young age.[*] "The great Marius is able to confound and send away the soldier who has come to kill him with no other weapon but the sheer strength and authority of his figure," she reported to Alvise. "The general seems to be saying: 'You would dare to kill Marius?' It's a powerful image, and a very beautiful one."[55]

Alvise read Lucia's Roman chronicles with pleasure. It was a way for him to feel close to her as he travelled from Venice to the Mocenigo estates on the mainland, checking on the late summer harvests. And yet he could not help notice that Lucia still remained slightly aloof. True, she filled her letters with declarations of love and devotion to him, and of loyalty to his family, but beneath the surface of her entertaining anecdotes, she kept a reserve about herself. When he prodded her to open her heart to him she was caught somewhat off guard. She turned to her father, but to no avail. So she told Alvise that if she seemed reticent it was because she feared creating excessive expectations. Why live in a dream world while they were still strangers "and then risk falling all of a sudden from on high?" While Alvise wanted her to be more expansive, she remained cautious about expressing "those feelings which I still can't quite explain, given that all I know about you comes from a small portrait, from the flattering reports of others, from the very interesting things that you write to me and from the good things you do." All of this, she said,

---

[*] Goethe, also in Rome at the time, was impressed by the painting, and by Drouais's work in general, and was among those who felt the pupil had surpassed the master. Drouais's death in 1788, at the age of twenty-five, shocked the artists' colony in Rome; his distraught fellow students erected a monument to his memory in the church of Santa Maria in Via Lata. *Marius at Minturnae* is now in the Louvre.

has encouraged me to hold you in esteem and to love you and to be grateful to you. It could be that I feel even more, but I don't know for sure as I have no experience in these matters. I hope, for many good reasons, that I will adore you, for this is the way it should be. But give me time, and if it will happen, and no doubt it will, then my deeds will tell you even better than my words.[56]

Lucia was startled by her own candour.

I don't even know how I could have said as much, and I assure you that no one else has tampered with this letter. My father told me: "I don't want to be involved in this, just speak with your heart." So I consulted my heart, and this is what came out, and I don't even know if it's right or wrong . . . Enough now, I hope you will soon be at the end of this eternal wait and that I will have the very fine pleasure of seeing you at last to tell you in person how much I wish to be your loving and loyal spouse.[57]

At Palazzo San Marco signs of the Memmos' impending departure were everywhere. "People are busy filling trunks, carrying furniture down stairs, beating nails into crates and boxes," Lucia wrote to Alvise with excitement. "Everything now tells me I will soon be leaving."[58] On 1 October, the new Venetian ambassador finally arrived in the vicinity of Rome, and the Memmos drove out to greet his convoy in a rented carriage drawn by six horses. They moved out of the *palazzo* and went to stay temporarily at the house of a Venetian friend next to the Ghetto. Memmo introduced his successor to Roman society even as he tried to sell him his furniture and silverware to reduce his debts.

As Lucia was making her last courtesy rounds, she received another jolt from Alvise. How should they meet, he wanted to know. Should they plan it or did she want him to surprise her by turning up unexpectedly somewhere along the way? Lucia did not hesitate: "I choose the latter course, even if it is the most dangerous."[59] Would it be Padua, she wondered dreamily, or perhaps Ferrara? What if Alvise were to journey as far south as Bologna? The waiting game had a new element of suspense.

Memmo had wanted the return journey to Venice to be something of an educational trip for his daughters. He had planned to visit Tuscany extensively, in order to observe from up close the innovative changes introduced by Grand Duke Leopold in agriculture and public administration; he had also arranged to spend some time in the duchies of Modena and Parma. But the long-delayed departure from Rome had forced him to curtail their itinerary rather drastically, leaving only a much reduced stay in Florence. Although Memmo was anxious to join Alvise in Venice to help and advise him on the details of the marriage, he lamented the brevity of their stop in Tuscany even more than his daughter suspected. "I love Florentine women," he wrote wistfully to a friend in Florence. "How will I ever be able to gain your lovable ladies' confidence in such a short time, let alone have any luck with them? I'm afraid it will be the same as with the gorgeous Neapolitan women, whom I met and admired and even fondled a little, before being forced away from them at the ripest moment."[60]

Before leaving Rome for her surprise encounter with Alvise, Lucia took care of her personal appearance and hygiene. She went to the hairdresser and had two teeth pulled out "to clean up my mouth." Her wisdom teeth were also bothering her, she reported candidly, "but the dentist has assured me that they won't play any of their usual tricks on me."[61]

By early October, only one thing remained to be done before leaving. Pope Pius VI had to return Memmo's credentials—an awkward task since Memmo had never made his *ingresso* and so had never formally presented those credentials. There was a further delay, just long enough for the Vatican to make its displeasure known to the Venetian Republic. But the Pope did not want this issue to mar his friendship with Memmo, of whom he was genuinely fond. He granted a long and very satisfactory audience to the whole family, which left a lasting impression on

Lucia. "We were told the Pope never has such long conversations with women," she wrote to Alvise. "He asked us many kind questions, and even spoke to me about you. I really couldn't have wished for more."[62]

In the previous nine months, Lucia had thought so much and so hard about Alvise, alone at night in bed or else gazing at his picture during the day, that he had become a very familiar presence in her life, even though his image remained necessarily blurred since she had never seen him. Or had she? The closer she came to meeting him, the more she felt she had met him before. It was a strange sensation. Was it a distant, dreamy fragment of her childhood memory or perhaps an illusion generated by her long wait? "I feel as if I will not be meeting you for the first time," she ventured, "but I am not able to explain to you when or where I first saw you. The faster I reach you the happier I'll be to see you, to talk with you, and to feel that happiness I yearn for—provided we will like each other . . . Will I find a note from you in Florence?"[63]

At last the Memmos left. It was the end of October and the weather had turned rainy and cold. They travelled up the Cassia, the old Roman road that was little more than a trail of mud and water, stopping the first night in Bagnaia, near Viterbo. Memmo complained about the perpetual rain even as he wrote detailed instructions to Chiarabba from his rocking carriage. Lucia was to be taken to a convent, where she would remain with her sister until the wedding. Memmo had concluded this was the most convenient solution since he would no longer be living at Ca' Memmo, the old family home on the Grand Canal, but on Saint Mark's Square, in one of the comfortable houses that were made available to the Procuratori di San Marco. Meanwhile, rooms needed to be prepared for the night of their arrival, relatives to be informed, food to be purchased, gondolas to be readied. "We shall be no more than twelve to fourteen for supper on our arrival as I want the girls to go to the convent that same evening. Adieu, my friend. I feel I can already touch Venice."[64]

Alvise, meanwhile, had crossed the Apennines under rain and

sleet to surprise Lucia in Siena, a city he loved. They met on the evening of the second day of the Memmos' journey north. Did their first encounter rise to their best expectations? Did those expectations fall "from on high," as Lucia feared could happen? There are no letters by either Lucia or Alvise describing the moment they had waited so long for. But Memmo made sure the event was recorded. "The bride and groom have met," he solemnly announced to Signor Chiarabba. "And they are both happy with each other."[65] The next day they travelled to Florence, where they took rooms at the Locanda Vannini, on the Lungarno. The few days Alvise and Lucia spent together in Florence were very happy. They explored the city in a state of tender inebriation, taking walks up to the great villa at Poggio Imperiale, gazing at the sculptures and bronzes in the Galleria, visiting collections of pictures.

Alvise left on a rainy morning. There were no tearful good-byes: he slipped out of town leaving an affectionate note behind. If Lucia was hurt she did her best not to show it. She protested:

> Well done, Mister spouse! You dump me right when we are having our best time together without even a word of warning? I forgive you because I understand. But it doesn't mean your absence is less painful to me now that I have enjoyed your dearest, sweetest company . . . I thank you for everything, and at this anxious moment I can only wish you a safe journey, hoping God will protect you from the rain and other more dangerous hazards.

Florence seemed empty without Alvise. "It was strange to revisit some of the same places we went to without the company of my dear husband," she wrote to him the first night they were apart. "I was assailed by such stirring memories. Enough now, when shall I see you again? It is all I can think of." She was sharing the hotel room with her sister, the person she had been closest to all her life and from whom she would soon be separated.

Paolina doesn't want me to write any more, she says she wants to sleep . . . After all that has happened, will I be able to sleep? I don't think so. Not until I will be sure that you have safely arrived in Bologna and then in Ferrara and after that in Padua and finally in Venice . . . Adieu my beloved husband.[66]

Chapter Two

PALAZZO MOCENIGO

Lucia woke up in her sunlit bedroom at Palazzo Mocenigo. Her chambermaid, Maria, brought her a silver tray with a cup of hot chocolate and a note from Alvise. He was in the habit of leaving very early in the morning for a busy day of work, and though he usually took care to leave an affectionate line or two for his wife, she never quite knew when he might reappear. At times it was only a matter of a few hours before his gondola came gliding to the *riva* of the *palazzo*, but often enough he simply vanished, as he had done on that rainy morning in Florence, leaving only vague hints as to his whereabouts and when he should be expected home. The house messengers and gondoliers, however, always knew where to find him. So Lucia sent off a brief reply to his note: "I am just getting up, my beloved . . . Love me and come back to me quickly . . . I feel so lost when you are away from me."[1]

They had been married over a month, but Lucia still felt very disorientated in the sprawling Palazzo Mocenigo. Upon returning to Venice after her four years in Rome, everything had seemed so immediately familiar to her: the shimmering profile of the palaces, the noisy traffic on the water, the raw smell coming up from the canals as the tide ebbed and flowed. So it was somewhat unsettling to be living in such a vast and mysterious house, where so many generations of Mocenigos had lived and died, and not at Ca' Memmo, the smaller, more intimate *palazzo* further up the Grand Canal, beyond the bend of the Rialto, where she had grown up and which she had always considered her home.

On the evening of the Memmos' arrival in Venice after the

long journey from Rome, Lucia was whisked off with her sister to Santa Maria della Celestia, a fashionable convent next to the church of San Francesco della Vigna. Every day, she received a stream of chattering relatives in the parlour; when Alvise's handsome face appeared through the wooden grid, she was always overcome by a flush of excitement. But the Mocenigos continued to hold up the contract and Lucia had to remain in the convent longer than expected.

The difficulties came, as always, from Alvise's father, the moody, unpredictable Sebastiano, who suddenly refused to give the marriage his final blessing after promising he would. Memmo guessed this new delay had something to do with the fact that Giovanni Mocenigo, Sebastiano's older brother, was very ill: after his death, Sebastiano would become the titular head of the Mocenigo family, and would therefore be able to put a personal stamp on the marriage contract.

Weeks passed with no final settlement in sight. Memmo waited "philosophically," as he liked to put it. Alvise stopped by the convent in between sessions of the Senate and business meetings for visits that always seemed too short to Lucia. She reprimanded him gently "for those brief minutes you spend with me that do not satisfy me." He was often distracted, in a hurry to leave, and though she understood he was a busy man with increasing responsibilities, she found his "indifference" wounding. "I have wanted to complain about this to you," she confessed in a note she slipped to him through the grid, "[but] when I see you, my heart is overcome by such turmoil that I grow ever more desperate." She feared Alvise's comings and goings might be a foretaste of their future life together. "For pity's sake," she begged him, "allow me to spend as much time as possible with you in the future and to always accompany you on your trips."[2] Alvise sent her magnificent clothes, bouquets of fresh flowers, baskets of fruit and silver cups brimming with delicious ice creams, but as much as she appreciated these gifts, they did little to assuage her anxiety.

Giovanni Mocenigo died at the end of February 1787. As Memmo had predicted, Sebastiano, now the head of the family, announced he was removing his last reservations. At his insistence, however, a new contract was drawn up and Memmo had to agree to pay Alvise a monthly stipend until he inherited the Mocenigo fortune upon Sebastiano's death. The contract was signed at the end of March, a few days before Lucia's seventeenth birthday. In mid April the dressmakers made their first appearance at Celestia and a festive atmosphere filled the convent. Lucia's residual reserve dissolved completely. "How strongly I wish to tie the knot that will join me to my adorable husband and allow me at last to tell him 'I love you' again and again," she wrote to Alvise, beaming with anticipation.[3]

On a sunny morning in early May, five months after entering the convent, she bid farewell to the nuns, and stepped into the bridal gondola in the full regalia of a splendid Venetian bride, her silk dress studded with gems and lined with tiny white pearls. The wedding cortège glided slowly up the Grand Canal, spawning a long swath of colourful boats of different sizes. Along the waterway, the crowd clapped and cheered—*Evviva la sposa! Evviva la sposa!* (Long live the bride!)—while loaves of bread and flasks of wine from the hills of Friuli were handed out to the populace. The parade passed beneath Palazzo Mocenigo, decked out with banners flying the family crest—two roses against a white and blue background—then moved upstream past the Rialto bridge, to the old church of San Marcuola, in the square adjacent to Ca' Memmo, where Alvise and Lucia were married. After the ceremony, Memmo hosted a lavish banquet at which the newly-weds were toasted with poems and accolades. As the feast wore on, he rejoiced at the success of his tenacious diplomacy. "There is no more perfect marriage," he proclaimed, "than the one between my daughter and Alvise Mocenigo."[4] Alvise led his bride on to the master gondola of Ca' Mocenigo and together they glided back down the Grand Canal to their new home.

Palazzo Mocenigo was made up of three connected palaces facing south at the point where the Grand Canal begins its final turn before heading towards the Basin of Saint Mark. The palaces were built in the fifteenth and sixteenth centuries, during the heyday of the Republic, and were renovated many times. As a result, the various facades formed a disharmonious but impressive whole that reflected the family's steady accretion of money and power over the course of six centuries. It was an intimidating world for a seventeen-year-old bride to enter, filled as it was with the mementoes of a rich and often glorious history. The Mocenigos had given seven doges to the Republic, and Mocenigo admirals and diplomats had helped to expand and protect the Venetian Empire. Room after room was filled with venerable trophies: a picture of a famous battle scene, a *corno dogale* (doge's cap) under a glass casing, the rusty scimitars wrested from the Turks. In the years of Venice's decline, the Mocenigos were among the few great families that had managed, through marriages of convenience and land acquisitions on the mainland, to hold on to their fortune and actually increase it. By the end of the eighteenth century they owned immense estates in the provinces of Padua, Rovigo, Verona and in the northern region of Friuli. Their yearly income was well over 100,000 ducats, making them one of the five richest families in Venice.

The aggregate wealth of the 200 or so families inscribed in the Golden Book of the Venetian patriciate, on the other hand, had suffered steady erosion. Many of these *nobili*, or patricians, were so impoverished that they had long ago lost their palaces, and were housed and fed in special wards funded by the government. By the 1780s the oligarchy which had ruled Venice for nearly a thousand years had become ossified and terribly in-bred, too weak and brittle to face the powerful winds of change that were gathering force in France and would soon bring down the Republic of Saint Mark. In the early 1760s there had been a timid attempt at reform, aimed at broadening the base of political power to make the system more democratic, but the dominant conservative families had been quick to quash it. Instead of allowing new blood and energy to breathe life into its decrepit body, the oligarchy chose to remain a closed, withered caste. A few wealthy families continued to ensure their pre-eminence through patronage, corruption and inter-marriage. And the

Mocenigos were certainly among them—of their seven doges, three were elected in the eighteenth century.

Alvise and Lucia's apartment at Palazzo Mocenigo was on the mezzanine floor and looked directly out on the Grand Canal. It was spacious and elegantly furnished, with sunlight streaming in from the large windows over the water. There was a bedroom, a library-studio, a drawing room, a dining room and a small study adjoining the bedroom where Lucia could write and paint and take lessons—Alvise had granted her special request. The chambermaid, Maria, and the rest of the small staff lived in the servants' quarters in the back. The apartment was quite independent from the rest of the house, a safe harbour, as it were, in the much vaster universe of Palazzo Mocenigo, with its grand staircases, its endless halls, its numerous apartments distributed on four floors where a crowd of Mocenigo relatives lived on more or less friendly terms.

It is easy to see how Lucia could feel lost in those new surroundings. She had hoped Alvise would be her guide and protector, but he was seldom at her side, always rushing to a function, a business meeting and other, more mysterious encounters. His elusiveness unsettled her from the very start of their marriage. The letters and notes she wrote to him those first few weeks of their life together are those of a very young wife in love with her husband, who wants to make him happy more than anything else in the world, and yet struggles to find her right place in his life. "My most beloved Alvise, it seemed to me you were not in your usual sweet humour when you woke up," she wrote to him one morning. "I am a little worried as I am unable to trace the cause of this change." She felt observed by the family yet also isolated, and she spent a good portion of the day wandering through the *palazzo* in the hope of suddenly coming upon Alvise, or walking down the steps to the docking on the Grand Canal where her husband's gondola was usually moored. "Your Lucietta will be waiting for you around two o'clock at the *riva*," she would scribble tenderly, only to receive an apologetic note back from Alvise saying he had been delayed at the Senate. One day, as she walked by a room where Alvise was receiving one of his agents, she stifled the impulse to walk in, but she could not resist dashing off a note to him as soon as she reached her apartment: "It is a cruel thing to pass by one's husband and not be able to stop to see him and hug him . . . Come home quickly." She sometimes wrote in French, perhaps to make her complaints sound more light-hearted: "I wanted to begin by scolding you but I am unable to scold my dear husband; I will only say this: my heart ached when I did not find you home, I wish to see you as soon as possible and I kiss you with all my heart."[5] During the first months of her marriage, Lucia did not have the comfort of Paolina's company. Memmo planned to marry his youngest daughter off to Luigi Martinengo delle Palle, scion of a well-known family from Brescia, so he left her in the care of the nuns at Celestia while he negotiated the contract. Paolina was not yet fifteen and her father worried about the risks of an early pregnancy. He felt it would be "another two years before she can give birth without danger";[6] so he pressed matters to finalise a settlement with the Martinengos while setting a later wedding date. His finances were so depleted, however, that he was forced to give away Ca' Memmo, the venerable family *palazzo* on the Grand Canal, as part of Paolina's dowry. He moved into the comfortable residence on Saint Mark's Square that came with the position of procuratore di San Marco. He planned to open up the elegant *saloni* only for occasional entertainment, and live cosily in the smaller apartment on the mezzanine floor, where he now hung his large portrait, flanked by those of Lucia and Paolina, all of which had just arrived from Rome having been "excellently painted by my excellent Kauffmann."[7] It was shaping up as a perfect cocoon for his old age.

In many ways the three Kauffmann paintings captured a family scene that already belonged to the past. Memmo was a loving, devoted father, but the future of his daughters, which had been uppermost in his mind, was less of a worry now that Lucia was married and Paolina was on the way to the altar. Indeed Memmo briefly contemplated the idea of getting married himself, with

Contarina Barbarigo, a life-long friend and lover; but the two of them squabbled over the marriage arrangement and nothing came of it. So Memmo went back to his numerous lady companions. "I am still oppressed by beautiful women," he confided to a friend with gleeful incredulity:

> In lieu of a cock that is no longer as hard as I wish it to be, I have very hard fingers with which I can happily satisfy all my crazy girls . . . Alas they all want to fall in love with me but I don't want to hear anyone talk to me about love or faithfulness. I've gone back to what I once was . . . I want as many women as I can have and would be bored to death if I only had one.[8]

As he vigorously chased his youth, Memmo, who was nearing sixty, also kept his eye on the doge's rapidly declining health. The idea of crowning his political career with the ducal cap flattered his vanity. "I am complimented at all times as [the doge's] much desired successor," he noted proudly.[9] In Lucia's new world, however, Alvise was now the ultimate authority; and his stature, both within the Mocenigo family and outside, was growing fast. Sebastiano, his father, was still the head of the family. But he was an old man in poor health, with an unsavoury past. Alvise, on the other hand, was gaining confidence and respect among his peers. He was elected Savio di Terraferma, a political office with supervisory responsibilities on the mainland. It was a prestigious appointment for a young patrician who wanted to pursue a career in government. Alvise was also earning a reputation as an able administrator with a keen interest in the development of modern agriculture. And as the only male heir of the Mocenigo dynasty, he was already looked upon as the de facto representative of the family interests within the Venetian oligarchy.

The pressure on Lucia to ensure the future glory of the Mocenigos by producing a healthy baby boy started immediately. Chiara, Lucia's mother-in-law, lived in her own apartment in Palazzo Mocenigo, and often dropped by to keep her daughter-in-law company, staying on for a cup of chocolate or a lunch *à deux*. On such occasions, it was never very long before she turned to her favourite subject. Indeed it sometimes seemed it was her *only* topic of interest. Lucia wondered whether Chiara had been made to feel the same pressure from the Mocenigos when she was a young spouse. The survival of the dynasty had depended on her as well, and she had acquitted herself by giving birth to Alvise. Even though she had had a stressful life with her husband, suffering in silence as he humiliated her and made a fool of himself in the main courts of Europe, she had never lost her deep sense of loyalty to the family she had married into. Over and over, during her visits and in her notes and letters, she impressed upon Lucia the urgency of giving Alvise a son.

Alvise too was evidently keeping up the pressure: a month after the wedding, Lucia, barely seventeen, was already pregnant. It was a difficult pregnancy from the start and she was unwell for most of the first three months. The physical discomfort was made even worse by all the fuss her new relatives created around her. She missed her intimate conversations with Paolina. Most of all, she missed the comforting company of her mother, whose fading memory she now cherished even more lovingly than in the past.

The pain became more severe as the summer advanced, and by early August Lucia had her first miscarriage. Memmo, feeling his daughter's pain but well aware of the unpleasant suggestions that came with an aborted pregnancy, remarked with sadness that the loss of the child was the only blemish on an otherwise exemplary marriage.

When the family pressure on Lucia resumed in the autumn, she was in many ways a changed woman, as if the miscarriage had put her life into sharper focus. Her letters to Alvise show that she had shed much of her shyness, and gained a greater sense of purpose and resolve. She was going to work even harder at loving her husband and giving him a son. True, she still spent most of her time with her maid, Maria, giving half-hearted instructions to the staff and waiting for her increasingly busy husband to come home. But now she ventured out to the theatre and visited childhood friends from before her Roman years. She also became more demanding and more passionate in her love notes to Alvise. "A dangerous wind has been blowing for the past half hour and I hope this means you have decided not to travel [to the mainland]," she wrote to her husband at the Senate. "My dearest Alvise, give me this great token of your love: arrange matters in such a way that I shall see you at the theatre tonight and I assure you that you will make my happiness." How exasperating it was, she wrote to him another day, that Alvise was conducting business "in this very same *palazzo*" and yet "we cannot see each other and kiss." And yet another time: "Oh please wrap up your endless talks and come rejoice in the presence of the one who loves you with all her soul." To her delight, she noticed her sweet calls were often effective: Alvise would steal away from his endless chores and duties, suddenly appearing at the *riva,* and Lucia would have her treasured moment of triumph. There was a new playfulness between them, as when, shortly after an amorous encounter, she sent an envelope to Alvise containing a square piece of paper no bigger than a stamp on which she had scrawled in tiny writing and in French—the language of love and mischief:

> *Aimez-vous Lucille?*
> *Elle vous adore* *[10]*

By the end of the winter of 1788, less than a year after the wedding, Lucia was pregnant again. Her mother-in-law started to hover while the family circle tightened around her. This time Lucia felt more in control of herself, and happy, although her happiness was tempered by the experience she had had only a few months before. She took the greatest care to carry out as best she could what she now accepted as her highest duty: "My beloved husband, rest assured that I am taking every precaution I can to make our happiness even more perfect, and I move about as little as possible."[11]

By late spring, the crucial first three months had passed with

---

*Do you love Lucia? She loves you.

no sign of danger, and Lucia, having obtained a green light from the family obstetrician, felt confident enough to travel out to Dolo, a lovely village on the river Brenta where the Mocenigos and other patrician families had summer houses. Lucia spent her days quietly, getting herself acquainted with the house. Le Scalette was a Renaissance villa, long and narrow, situated on the bank of the river and separated from the clear, slow-moving water by a pathway that led directly to the village half a mile away. In the back of the house was a formal garden with box hedges and potted lemons and decorative statues. Beyond it, fields of wheat and maize extended inland as far as the eye could see. Lucia had the house cleaned and scrubbed from top to bottom, she brought paintings from Venice with which to redecorate the bedrooms, she stocked up the kitchen with supplies of coffee, sugar and flour and had Alvise send more silverware. To better enjoy the cool, she had the dining table moved out to the loggia, which overlooked the Brenta on one side and the garden on the other.

Once the house was in order, she rested and nursed her growing belly. She embroidered shirts for Alvise, played cards, took slow walks to Dolo, stopping at the busy coffee house where other holidaymakers gathered for a little gossip. She paid visits to her neighbours and made a point of cultivating Mocenigo friends and relatives who lived close by. Her mother-in-law frequently came to see her from nearby Padua, bringing baskets of fresh fruit and vegetables. Lucia sometimes asked her father, who was also in Padua for the summer, to come over for lunch so he and Chiara could entertain themselves by talking about old times while she played lady of the house. "I want to describe to you the meal I gave your mother and my papa today," she wrote proudly to Alvise, listing the items on the menu, which included "rice with quails, red meat, cutlets with sauce, mushrooms in casserole, fresh vegetables, salami, salad . . ."[12]

Alvise came and went. In the course of the summer he visited the Mocenigo estates, checking on the crops, going through the accounts, settling disputes among the farmers. But he was also busy with his new duties as Savio di Terraferma: touring government houses, hospitals and technical schools where he gave speeches, spoke to the teachers, encouraged the students and gave out prizes. On occasion he travelled to Verona, where his father, to everyone's surprise, had been appointed governor—his first assignment after the long period of confinement in Brescia. Sebastiano had worked hard behind the scenes to be readmitted into active political duty. "We will see his resurrection after all,"[13] Memmo noted wryly, not realising he would soon regret that very "resurrection."

Sebastiano's acrimony towards Alvise softened, at least for a while, and Lucia was "very disappointed" not to be able to travel to Verona to take advantage of this rare "moment of peace between my dear husband and his father." She longed to be with Alvise but she did not want to weigh on him. "Tonight I will savour the only good thing I have left: to dream of you and think of you all the time . . . Adieu my dearest one. I want to give you a kiss even as I write you this letter. So here it is, where I mark this dot • Adieu my love."[14]

Alvise's complicated relationship with Sebastiano reminded Lucia how fortunate she was that her husband and her father got along so well. Memmo had a soft spot for Alvise and he supported his budding political career. He had watched him grow increasingly alienated from the obtuse conservatism of his own family. In spite of his brooding, introverted personality, Alvise was fast becoming something of a rallying figure in the reformist camp, and Memmo felt that if the Republic was ever to revive its fortunes it would be thanks to progressive young men like his son-in-law. In turn, Alvise saw Memmo—one of the few survivors of a band of reformers who had come of age during the heyday of the Enlightenment—as his political mentor. He sought his advice and cultivated his friendship. And of course it warmed Lucia's heart to see the relationship between them blossom. "However, to make me completely happy," she warned her husband, "you must assure me that all of this is not on my account but rather because you truly wish to consider him both a friend and a father."[15]

In the same way, she hoped Alvise would be a friend and a father "to our own dear son, who is still so tiny and yet, with his little movements inside me, bids me to tell you that he hugs you very hard."[16] Those eager "little movements" continued through August then gradually ceased. Alvise rushed back to Le Scalette as soon as he received news that his wife was again in pain. By the time he arrived the sadness in Lucia's stunned gaze confirmed his worst fears. Memmo arrived from Padua to be with his daughter. "My good girl has had a second miscarriage," he wrote with a heavy heart. "She is recovering after the usual pains."[17]

Lucia's recovery was in fact much slower than her father had anticipated. Two miscarriages in a year had taken their toll on her, undermining her self-confidence and throwing her into a period of depression. Memmo suggested Alvise take Lucia on a long trip: it was sure to distract his daughter and could turn into a useful educational experience for his son-in-law. As soon as Lucia was well enough to travel, they left for Tuscany, staying first at the Bagni di Lucca for a restorative water cure, then moving on to Pisa, Livorno and Florence, where Alvise was able to have a first-hand look at the economic progress achieved under Grand Duke Leopold of Tuscany, younger brother of Emperor Joseph II of Austria. As he followed their journey from a distance, Memmo remarked proudly that his son-in-law "could not be a better husband to his wife, whom he adores and who loves him back."[18]

Alvise wanted to continue the trip as far as Rome and possibly even Naples. He was keen to visit San Leucio, the model community King Ferdinand IV—who had thrown confetti at Lucia and Paolina in Naples—had built around a flourishing silk factory near the slopes of Vesuvius. However, the trip had to be cut short. The political scene in Venice was in turmoil. Worst of all, tensions between the Mocenigos and the Memmos had suddenly flared.

While Alvise and Lucia were still in Tuscany, the health of

Paolo Renier, a corrupt and unpopular doge, rapidly deteriorated. Aspiring candidates for the ducal throne began to campaign behind the scenes, including Memmo, who prowled around the Senate with the assurance of an old cat. "People say the Doge will soon be dead and that I will be elected to replace him," he boasted, adding he would run only if he were spared the need to spend "the usual grandiose sums of money, which I do not have."[19] He wanted to run as the candidate of a reformist coalition. But if the election became a costly contest in which the candidate with the most money had the best chances, he would withdraw.

From the beginning, the campaign took a promising turn for Memmo. There was a fairly widespread perception among the more enlightened Venetians that the Republic had reached a critical point in its drawn-out decline, and that the coming election was going to be of great importance—a last chance, as it were, to set the stage for those elusive yet long due reforms that might reverse the downward spiral. The sprawling bureaucracy had to be streamlined. The powerful, over-privileged guilds that were stifling trade had to be confronted. On the mainland, the modernisation of agriculture, the one development that showed real promise, had to be encouraged and accelerated. And it was also urgent to lift Venice's overseas dominions from their wretched backwardness—the province of Dalmatia, on the opposite shore of the Adriatic Sea, was so poor it had become an embarrassment for the Republic.* But nothing would change if the oligarchy itself did not change by opening itself up to families of more recent wealth which rightly clamoured for representation. Memmo, a true child of the Enlightenment who had devoted his public life to the improvement of government, was keenly aware of what needed to be done. The like-minded patricians who saw him as the best hope to rejuvenate the sclerotic Venetian State, stepped out of the shadows of inertia to rally around him. They

---

* Memmo worked tirelessly in the Senate to improve living conditions in that blighted region and was able to push through a package of agricultural and administrative reforms in 1791.

were a larger number than expected, and the conservative camp was taken by surprise. "We'll see a Memmo elected doge after all!" the candidate chirped.[20] Then a challenge arose from a completely unexpected quarter.

Sebastiano Mocenigo, galvanised by his political "resurrection" in Verona, brazenly decided to play for the highest stakes. He knew he had but a few years to live and this was the last chance he would ever have to be elected doge. On the face of it, it looked like an impossible challenge, but this quirky, contorted man had often deluded himself in the past. If Memmo intended to run without spending a ducat, Sebastiano, on the other hand, intended to plunder the Mocenigo fortune now at his disposal, in order to win the contest. He moved back to Venice and began to plot his campaign from a *casino* he had in a back street behind Saint Mark's Square, with the help of a few fellow conservatives who thought a rich Mocenigo could well block the rise of Memmo. Memmo himself was completely taken aback by Sebastiano's challenge. He recoiled at the idea of running against a man "in whose house I have a daughter," and hoped the strong opposition to Sebastiano would force his rival to withdraw. Sebastiano's surprise candidacy had indeed generated quick opposition, and serious worry for the disrepute he would bring to the office. Sebastiano, however, was obstinate. He knew he could count on support from the families in Verona, a city whose political importance was growing. He promised money to impoverished patricians who had lost everything but their voting rights, and spread the rumour that he intended to create a slush fund worth 30,000 ducats to spend during the campaign. Those rumours produced the intended result. As one informer told the Inquisitors, "the opposition of many patricians to Sebastiano Mocenigo is melting by the hour."[21]

When Alvise and Lucia arrived in Venice after their long trip south, the doge, though in agony, was still alive, but the city was already divided in two camps. The coffee houses and wine shops were filled with political chatter. Figurines with caricatures of the two candidates circulated from hand to hand. Satirical epigrams such as this one were posted on the walls near Saint Mark's:

Memmo wants to be doge without spending a lira,
Shrewdly he distributes his bows for free . . .
And would you believe who else
Now strives for the Ducal crown?
Bastian Mocenigo, who governs Verona
And brought Venetians such disrepute
With his terrible vices,
Enough to horrify any man of good sense,
Let alone a good Christian . . .[22]

Doge Paolo Renier died on 13 February 1789. The authorities did not divulge the news, not wishing to disrupt the Carnival, but word spread quickly among the ruling families and the campaign went into full gear. According to Memmo, "all the people in authority bluntly intervened to convince Mocenigo to withdraw . . . but he remained obstinate and followed no one's advice."[23] Sebastiano promised up to eight silver ducats to impoverished patricians for their vote. He ordered that bread and wine be handed out at all the ferry stops along the Grand Canal and coins distributed in the Mocenigo neighbourhood of San Samuele. He was so sure of victory, it was said, that he had already given orders to deck out as many as sixty-four ceremonial vessels for the splendid cortège he was planning for his accession to the ducal throne.

Alvise watched with great discomfort as his father made a spectacle of himself instead of staying quietly on the sideline, grateful that the Republic had allowed him back into the fold. He feared Sebastiano's unreasonable bid would stain the family reputation precisely at a time when he was trying to restore the prestige of the Mocenigos; he worried, too, about the effect of his father's antics on his own career. If his father persisted in his design, Alvise would have no choice but to stand by him in the name of the family, and participate in an electoral struggle against Memmo, the "friend and father" with whom he felt a much greater political affinity.

Government informers making the rounds of taverns and coffee shops picked up rumours about Alvise's "hesitancy" and his "wariness at taking a firm stance" in favour of his father. This factor, more than any other, changed the dynamic of the contest. Alvise was not a novice: he was a rising political star and the future standard-bearer of the Mocenigos. His vacillation cast a pall over Sebastiano's candidacy, which collapsed like a pack of cards. On 2 March, the death of Doge Renier was finally announced. A day later, an informer reported that there was "universal silence around Sebastiano Mocenigo's candidacy and all the people close to him stay away from those discussing the matter." The following day another report stated "there are no more meetings in Sebastiano Mocenigo's *casino*. One only hears the complaint of those patricians who won't be receiving their money." By 7 March, the candidacy was dead, and Sebastiano was "in a state of great affliction on account of the insuperable difficulties he encountered."[24]

Even though Sebastiano lost his bid, he inflicted serious damage on Memmo, who was unable to turn the situation to his advantage. The conservative patricians who opposed him quickly put forward a new candidate, Ludovico Manin, a weak and ineffectual man from a very wealthy family in Friuli. It was an uninspiring, uncontroversial choice, and on 9 March, four months before the taking of the Bastille in Paris—the first of a series of events that would ultimately have a catastrophic impact on Venice—Manin was elected doge.

If Memmo was disappointed at having been outmanoeuvred in a game at which he usually excelled, he did his best not to show it. "I am at peace with myself," he assured his friends, even as he blasted the obtuseness of his fellow politicians. But Memmo's peace of mind did not last long for he soon had to put all his energy in salvaging Paolina's marriage contract with the Martinengos, which was suddenly thrown into jeopardy when the Inquisitors put Luigi, the future groom, under house arrest for licentious behaviour. While his family was negotiating in earnest with Memmo, Luigi had started a very public and scandalous relation with another woman—"a Roman slut," Memmo noted in disgust. The matter would have been best left to the families to solve, but the Inquisitors, with their obsessive inclination to interfere in private matters, took it upon themselves to have Luigi arrested. Despite all the effort he had put in the transaction, Memmo now realised he might well have to annul the marriage contract. But Luigi, "that great ass," was putting on a pathetic show, claiming to be devoted to Paolina. "He raves deliriously about wanting her back and promises all kinds of things," Memmo complained.[25] To make matters more unpleasant, the Martinengos, who had already taken possession of Ca' Memmo and had begun to refurbish it even though the wedding had not yet taken place, were faced with the prospect of having to give it back. So they demanded that Memmo reimburse at least part of the 10,000 ducats they had spent on house improvements.

Meanwhile, what to do with Paolina? She was still confined at Celestia with the nuns, but now Memmo was forced to consider bringing her to live with him in his alcove at Saint Mark's Square if the marriage fell through—a solution he was not happy with because he felt increasingly protective of his new privacy. Despite his best efforts to resist emotional attachments, he was in fact succumbing to the charms of a young woman. "In love at sixty? Yes sir!" he admitted. Her name was Dinda Petrocchi Orsini and she was only twenty years old. Memmo had met this enticing young beauty in Rome when she was still unhappily married. "Now she has fled from the arms of her husband to fall into mine," he grinned.[26]

Alvise emerged from the 1789 election with his prestige unscathed by his father's debacle. Indeed, he was now regarded as the de facto head of the family, if not formally, at least from a political standpoint. Not yet thirty, he was a player to be reckoned with. His speeches at the Senate had enhanced his reputation as an able and even inspiring young politician. Inevitably, his increased responsibilities—both on the family front and the public one—weighed on his relationship with Lucia. But she was fast learning the rules of the game. She was, after all, the daughter of one of the most respected statesmen in Venice, and she had experienced first-hand the demands a political career placed on the family. "I console myself with the thought that you are happy to stay long hours at the Senate," she assured Alvise without a trace of irony, "since you have a real love for the affairs of your fatherland."[27]

Lucia, meanwhile, worried about fulfilling her own task. To improve the chances of a successful pregnancy, Alvise thought it would be useful for Lucia to continue the water cures she had begun in Lucca during their trip to Tuscany. He sent her to spend the summer in Valdagno, a fashionable little town north of Vicenza, at the foot of the Alps. Valdagno was set in a region Lucia remembered well from her childhood summers. When her father was away in Constantinople, she spent the hottest months with her mother at Castel Gomberto, the country estate five miles down the road from Valdagno that belonged to her mother's family, the Piovene. Castel Gomberto was a handsome neo-Palladian villa with a formal garden, a long rectangular fishpond and a huge elm tree that provided a refreshing shade in July and August. It was a warm, friendly house, filled with sweet memories of her mother. Thus Lucia's dread of being separated again from Alvise for weeks at a time during her stay in Valdagno was mitigated by the prospect of frequent visits to Castel Gomberto to be with her Piovene uncles and aunts.

Lucia took rooms at the Casa Valle, a comfortable house in the main square of Valdagno, with a fenced-in rose garden in the back whence a path led directly to a little house at the source of the curative waters. Lucia's days revolved around the schedule that had been arranged for her by the local doctor to fortify her body in order to carry her next pregnancy to its conclusion. "My health is good," she dutifully reported to Alvise after settling in. "The water cure is following its course and the doctor seems pleased."[28]

In the afternoons, when she did not ride a carriage to Castel Gomberto, she explored the trails in neighbouring woods, taking walks, she wrote to Alvise, "which I cannot wait to show you."[29] Occasionally, a football game was organised in the town square to amuse the summer residents or a travelling theatre company might put on a show. The surrounding mountains were known for the great variety of their mineral ores. They attracted geologists and amateur collectors of rocks and gems from inside the

Venetian Republic and abroad, and the mineral collections on display in several curiosity shops were the principal attractions in Valdagno. In the evenings, visitors came by Casa Valle to exchange niceties, and brought a bouquet of freshly cut flowers, a plate of figs or perhaps a basket of mushrooms from the nearby woods. Lucia often put together a round of *tombola*, her favourite society game, though "I lose most of the time," she complained to her husband, "without even the comfort of hearing you read out the numbers with your usual grace."[30]

During those summer evenings at Valdagno the talk often drifted to the extraordinary events taking place in Paris. France's absolute monarchy had effectively collapsed after the storming of the Bastille and the establishment of the Convention to draft a constitution. Naturally, these dramatic developments were also at the centre of animated discussions back in Venice, where conservative patricians expressed their alarm while the more progressive-minded Venetians followed the beginnings of the French Revolution with the hope that the winds blowing from Paris might ultimately have a beneficial influence on the old Republic as well. Alvise, a devoted reader of Montesquieu, Diderot and Rousseau, kept Lucia abreast of the news. His comments on the situation unfolding in France were sympathetic but cautious—he was not a revolutionary, either by temperament or political conviction.

Lucia knew the discussions taking place in Venice made it more difficult for Alvise to journey out to Valdagno, but in her reveries she imagined him riding his carriage into the little town. Every jingling bell made her blood rush and her head turn. "My darling Alvise, it is so hard to be away from you! I cannot help feeling envious each time I see a married couple." But as the summer wore on, the chances of luring him there grew increasingly remote. "Tomorrow an aerostatic balloon will lift off from our garden," she announced as a last resort. "I don't know what else to offer to encourage you to come . . ."[31]

The one thing that kept her spiritually connected with Alvise that summer at Valdagno were the books that he recommended to her. At his suggestion, she read *La Nouvelle Héloïse*, the epistolary novel by Jean-Jacques Rousseau published thirty years earlier yet still very popular. The book tells the story of two star-crossed lovers. In brief, Saint-Preux, a middle-class tutor, falls in love with Julie, his aristocratic pupil, who in turn falls in love with him. It is an impossible passion. Julie is promised to another man of her same station, whom she marries out of a sense of duty. Saint-Preux leaves on a long journey abroad, but eventually returns and is engaged as tutor of Julie's children. Everyone seems content in this ménage. Beneath the surface, however, the echoes of the earlier passion still reverberate, and Julie realises, as her death nears, that she has never stopped loving Saint-Preux. "You can imagine how eager I am to read it after the description you gave me of the writer and the theme of the book,"[32] Lucia wrote to Alvise as she delved into the thick 800-page tome.

There are many ways to read Rousseau's classic novel. Tearful readers across Europe were certainly captivated by the sheer power of the passion between Saint-Preux and Julie, and the sexual tension underlying the book. And one can easily imagine Lucia in bed, propped up against her cushions, reading by candlelight into the night. Of course, unlike Julie she was in love with her husband. But she yearned to be loved back with the same intensity, whereas Alvise's long absences left her unsteady—a feeling that was no doubt enhanced by the difficulty she was having in giving birth. "Please love me, Alvise," she pleaded touchingly. "If only you knew how deep my feelings for you have reached inside my heart you would understand why I believe I have a right to demand equal love in return."[33]

By the end of August, as the temperature finally cooled a little and the countryside around Valdagno took on a golden hue, Lucia realised that Alvise was not going to come out to see her. In her last letter from Casa Valle before returning to Venice she made no effort to conceal her disappointment:

> I received your latest this evening: very nice letter, amusing, filled with interesting news, and I thank you. But how is it that there is not the slightest word about a visit here, nor do you mention the love you said you

felt for me. Oh God, forgive me if I sound reproachful, but you surely realise that the thing I am most interested in is also the thing I most lack. This is the cause of my bitterness. You won't like this letter—how could you?—but you can forgive my sincerity.[34]

Lucia heard that Alvise, back in Venice, was gambling at the Ridotto, the famous gaming-house closed by the Inquisitors back in the 1770s and now open again and attracting crowds of derelict patricians, ruffians and cheats. Gambling was a real scourge among Venetians. Countess Rosenberg, Memmo's first love and life-long friend, had written an essay describing the ravages of this addiction, which had deeply affected Lucia.* Alvise admitted to her that he played cards for money and was not always lucky. "I am very disturbed by these continual losses," she wrote back in alarm, reminding him that until his father died they only had a relatively small stipend to live on.

You know we have little money. I don't expect you to force yourself away from the gaming table but don't go anxiously looking for it either. Let conversation be your entertainment of choice, and for God's sake always keep that nefarious thought of "earning one's money back" as far away from your mind as possible. Forgive me if I insist in giving you this advice: I do it only for your own sake.[35]

Alvise was also spending some of his time—Lucia seems to have been unaware of this at the time—in the arms of Foscarina, the beautiful wife of a well-known Venetian senator. Foscarina was, by her own definition, "the most open-minded authority in the art of seduction." Whether she seduced Alvise or he seduced her is unclear. In any case, while Lucia was away taking the waters, they began a light-hearted affair made of intimate con-

---

* The essay was published in a collection by Countess Giustiniana Rosenberg, *Pièces morales et sentimentales* (London: J. Robson, 1785).

versations and furtive encounters. Their love notes were more practical than passionate. "My dearest Eige"—this was the nickname Foscarina gave Alvise—"my husband is at home and it would be unwise to receive you here now," read one. "Drop me a line tomorrow morning and we shall arrange to see each other," read another. On one occasion she sent word to him that she was alone at home all evening "so choose the time that is most convenient for you." In the beginning she treated Alvise's occasional lapses—a missed appointment, an unanswered note—with deliberate levity. "If I were one of those women who take the affairs of the heart seriously, then I should have reason to quarrel with you," she once reprimanded him gently. "But it is of little importance to us, so let us laugh about it—we can't go wrong . . . And let us keep trading our little confessions. The freshness of our conversation will continue to amuse us."

It did not amuse them for very long. Foscarina liked to conduct her affairs efficiently and she quickly lost patience with Alvise's disappearing acts. "After receiving two passionate notes from you, I waited for you like an ass until eight o'clock," she wrote in anger, "thinking that if you couldn't come you would at least send word, out of politeness if not affection." The affair got out of hand. She accused Alvise of "running around too much and getting very little done, at least as far as I am concerned." During one of their earlier, sweeter encounters, Alvise, in jest, had slipped off Foscarina's wedding band and taken it home. Now she demanded to have it back, and she asked for all her letters as well. "I'll send you my manservant and as soon as he returns, I'll send him back with all your notes, which I have already gathered . . . Let us put an end to this story and let us stay friends . . . Adieu, and remember my wedding band."[36]

Alvise never returned Foscarina's letters—Lucia found them years later among his private papers. It is unclear whether he ever even gave the ring back. "I am still waiting," an exasperated Foscarina complained some time after the end of their affair. In any case it was over by the time Lucia returned to Venice after her summer in Valdagno.

In September, preparations began at last for Paolina's wedding. Memmo, still frolicking happily in the arms of the beautiful Dinda Orsini, now a fixture in the family, had managed to disentangle the imbroglio with the Martinengos, making it possible for the chastened groom, Luigi, to marry his youngest daughter. Lucia was happy to have her sister just a short gondola ride away, at Ca' Memmo, the old family *palazzo* that now belonged to Paolina's in-laws. And no one was more pleased than Lucia to hear, a few months after the wedding, that Paolina was expecting a child. Yet as the pregnancy progressed, it is difficult to imagine that Lucia did not also feel a growing sense of emptiness in her life. She certainly did not resign herself to childlessness, but the thought of that empty crib at Palazzo Mocenigo must have made it hard to keep her anxiety at bay.

Alvise's frustration at not yet having an heir was deepened by his dissatisfaction at the way his father, Sebastiano, was running the family estate. Alvise was now responsible for the day-to-day management of the immense properties on the mainland and he received an adequate though by no means generous salary on which he and Lucia lived. But Sebastiano kept his son on a very short leash and this made for constant attrition between the two. Unlike his father, Alvise had a true passion for agriculture, or, as Memmo once said, a "talent for growing things." He was fascinated by the development of new crops, the problems of irrigation, the possibilities introduced by machinery. He toured the country fairs and read the increasingly influential agricultural magazines.

The Venetian mainland territories stretched all the way east to the duchy of Milan and included the fertile plains along the river Po. The agricultural revolution that was taking place there was as advanced as it was in England at that time, and it was transforming the Venetian economy. Vast tracts of desolate, marshy land in the Po delta were being reclaimed; new fertilisers and new crops were increasing yield and variety; the development of mechanical equipment was lowering production costs. To men like Alvise, the future of the Republic depended on how quickly and efficiently the agricultural revolution would spread. But his father was of another generation. He was not interested in modernisation. Much to Alvise's dismay he seemed content to exploit the land inefficiently and with minimal effort, leaving everything in the hands of incapable and often dishonest agents. The result was wastefulness on a grand scale, and a decline in income so rapid that Alvise, who would soon inherit the family holdings, realised it might lead to financial catastrophe in a matter of a few years. However, he knew that he would never turn his old father into a champion of agricultural reform and that their relationship was too encrusted with bad feelings for the two of them ever to work together in harmony. Sebastiano, on his part, viewed Alvise's attempts to introduce improvements as the encroachments of an ungrateful son on God-given parental rights. "What truly pains me," he told Alvise, "is that I cannot even invoke the duty of a son, because I would not be listened to. Even worse, I would be treated with disdain and scoffed at, this being the manner in which sons treat their parents today."[37]

By the spring of 1790 Alvise had had enough and he took a decision that had a far-reaching impact on his life. Using the name of a conniving friend, he secretly leased from his own father a vast tract of marshy land that belonged to the Mocenigos. The property, Molinato, was 1,800 hectares in all, and it sloped from the hills of southern Friuli down towards the Adriatic Sea, near the town of Portogruaro. It was a relatively small portion of the Mocenigo land holdings, but large enough to grow extensive crops once the land had been reclaimed. When Alvise signed the lease, the property was still mostly made up of soggy marshes filled with natural drainage and overflowing canals from neighbouring properties.

The lease started on 1 August 1790. That summer, Alvise took Lucia to visit Molinato under the scorching sun. They reached the property by sailing up the small canals that criss-crossed the wetlands along the coast. Lucia was stunned at the sight of such a wild and inhospitable territory. At the centre of the property was a forlorn hamlet inhabited by a few wretched families—sixty people at the most, including women and children. They were desperately poor, had a sickly, yellowish complexion and stood in the mud with their swollen bellies, swatting flies and staring at the newcomers. The air was so unhealthy that the agent Alvise hired, Checco Locatelli, obtained in writing that he did not have to live in the filthy hamlet; he would settle in Cordovado, a village inside the ruins of a Roman army camp some five miles up the road, where the Mocenigos owned a farmhouse.

Alvise did his best to reassure Lucia. He had already planned an elaborate drainage system to reclaim the marshes. He would settle the land by bringing in more labourers with their families, increase the livestock (there were fewer than a hundred scraggy cows), and plant rows of willows and poplars and vineyards until Lucia would no longer recognise the place. If the land proved productive, and the income increased, then he would make even larger investments, and maybe one day build a whole town on those very bogs, something along the lines of San Leucio, the model estate created by the king of Naples and about which he had heard so much. He envisioned an ideal rural community inspired by the progressive philosophers of the Enlightenment yet adapted to a rapidly changing economic environment; a modern agricultural and manufacturing centre with proper housing for the workers and their families, schools and training facilities, and good health care. But all that was in the future, when they would have more money at their disposal. For the time being, and given the small resources he could count on, Alvise developed a short-term plan with Locatelli: they were going to plant wheat, rye and sorghum on the drier fields further away from the coastline while they started to drain the lower marshes. This would allow them to raise cash and offset the cost of the lease, of digging canals, of new machinery and stock.

Despite her initial dismay, Lucia agreed to stay on for a few months and she set to work with pioneering spirit. Alvise was often away, meeting suppliers, calling on middlemen and visiting fairs. Lucia, meanwhile, reorganised the house, which had been left in a state of semi-abandon by Alvise's father. She replaced all the rusty and "completely useless" appliances—the old stove, the water tank, the laundry basin, the casseroles and pans. She started keeping accounts and discovered she was good at cutting expenses. She also learnt to manage a much larger staff than the one at Palazzo Mocenigo or the summer villa on the Brenta. It was not always easy. The old caretaker, for one, was a hot-tempered man who drank and cursed, and resented the new occupants of the house. He did not get along at all with the house manager and threatened to kill him several times. Lucia confronted the caretaker sternly, obtaining a promise from him "that he will not abuse [us] with either words or deeds." Locatelli, the experienced agent of the estate, warned Lucia that the caretaker was not to be believed. But she worried, correctly, about the consequences of sending him away. "If I left this man with no food and no place to go he might well become desperate and take revenge upon those who caused his ruin," she wrote to Alvise. In the end she followed her instinct: she did not send the man away, and it does not appear he caused her further trouble. But it was during such tense moments that she most missed her husband, "wishing [your] return for a thousand reasons."[38]

Lucia had rarely felt so isolated as during those first months at Cordovado. When she was frantic for company, she rode her carriage to Portogruaro, an attractive little town with a bustling waterfront just off the main square where one boarded the *burchiello*, the water ferry to Venice. But she usually stayed at home, catching up on the reading she had planned for herself. Alvise had given her a beautifully bound two-volume French translation of Daniel Defoe's *Robinson Crusoe*. In truth, the choice had left Lucia a little baffled, as her interests ran in a different direction; but it occurred to her, only partly in jest, that Molinato was her desert island and that she might draw strength from Crusoe's ingenuity. Another novel she had enjoyed after *La Nouvelle Héloïse* was Countess Rosenberg's *Les Morlacques*, a romantic tale of love and death set in the rugged mountains of Dalmatia. She was keen to have a copy with her at Cordovado and told Alvise to send one up from Venice. "You might ask Papa to lend us one of his," she added, knowing her father kept several copies of Countess Rosenberg's books at home.[39]

Although Lucia enjoyed novels, she was also interested in books on the education of children. She had brought with her from Venice Madame de Genlis's *Le Siècle passé*, a book on the teaching of history. Madame de Genlis, whom Lucia would meet and befriend years later in Paris, was a prolific writer and educator. She came from an impoverished aristocratic family in Burgundy and had become quite a celebrity in the Parisian salons thanks to her wit and distinguished manners. Appointed governess of the Duke of Chartres's daughters, she handled herself so well that she was promoted to governess of his sons, one of whom was the future king, Louis Philippe. What most intrigued Lucia was how Madame de Genlis revolutionised traditional teaching methods, drawing her students out and engaging them in a dialogue. She taught botany during walks in the garden and in the countryside; she taught history with the help of magic lantern slides to make the lessons more vivid and entertaining; she taught literature by staging small plays and organising readings. Her progressive thinking had led her to welcome the fall of the absolute monarchy in France despite her links to the royal house, and to throw in her lot with the Girondins, the moderate party that was soon to be overpowered by the more militant Jacobins in Paris. In the isolation of Cordovado, this whiff of subversion must have made Madame de Genlis's books even more exciting.

Lucia put in a number of other requests for educational books to Alvise, should he find himself "with a little extra money in his pocket." One in particular she hoped he could purchase for her was *Instruction d'un père à ses enfants sur la nature et la religion*, by Abraham Trembley, a Swiss naturalist known in scientific circles for his studies on the fresh water polyp—the hydra—which he believed to be the missing link between the animal and the vegetable world. Trembley, who was influenced by his fellow countryman Rousseau, later became an educator and a philosopher interested in the connections between nature and human development. His two-volume work was written in very simple, "elementary" prose, Lucia explained to her husband. The first volume dealt with natural history, biology and geology; the second one focused on ethics and physics. Despite Lucia's painstaking instructions, Alvise managed to send her the wrong book, and though she was "quite grateful" to see that he had "so promptly tried to please" her, she told him frankly, and with a touch of irritation: "It's not the book I wanted."[40]

Lucia's sudden interest in pedagogy reflected a change in her feelings about motherhood. Heretofore she had seen it essentially as a duty she had to fulfil. A fully matured woman of twenty-one, she now had a strong, natural desire to have a child. In the autumn, she left Cordovado with a new determination. She was going to do everything in her power to avoid another miscarriage, and she was going to be ready when her child was born: ready to love him, to nurture him, to raise him. She visited Doctor Calvi, a respected obstetrician in Padua. He recommended repeated immersions in cold water to fortify her constitution, so she asked Alvise to send a large wooden wash-tub directly to Le Scalette, their villa on the banks of the Brenta.

All during the spring and summer of 1791 she stayed at Le Scalette, devoting herself to her daily ablutions. "I fervently hope they will have a positive effect," she wrote to Alvise. To increase her daily exercise, she took regular walks to the village of Dolo and to the Tiepolos and Grittis, who lived down the road. She took up riding again for the first time since her lessons in Rome at the Villa Borghese, and she asked Maria, her maid, to send her riding clothes up from Venice, including "boots, fustian trousers, scarlet bodice, black cummerbund, corset, girdle and my round, cloth riding hat." The evenings at Le Scalette were quiet: a game of cards, a piece of music at the clavichord, the occasional *tombola* with the staff. She gently complained about Alvise's absences: "If only you were here with me, my sweet . . . Do not abandon me so frequently; I never married to live in such a cruel condition."[41]

Memmo was a frequent guest that summer, checking on his daughter's health and bringing news of Paolina, who was nursing a healthy baby girl, Caterina, nicknamed Cattina. Le Scalette was a house he knew very well. Thirty years earlier, Countess Rosenberg, then still Giustiniana Wynne, had spent a summer there with her mother and her siblings (they had rented the house from the Mocenigos), and Memmo, then a bachelor, had snuck in and out of the house to meet with the young woman he loved so passionately. Now Countess Rosenberg was dying of cancer in nearby Padua and a distraught Memmo wanted to be close to her. He visited her often, and Lucia sometimes went along, shocked to see her father's first love so "infinitely degraded."[42] The countess died in August, and Lucia could not help noticing how her father too had aged during the summer, often complaining about his splitting headaches, his bad circulation and the gout that tormented his feet. Although Dinda Orsini, his young lover, still provided some consolation to him, their ties were gradually loosening.

The news from France occupied much of the conversation at Le Scalette. The Constituent Assembly drafted the Constitution, but King Louis XVI, unwilling to accept the end of absolute monarchy, secretly fled from Paris and headed for the northern border. His aim was to march back into France with the help of the Austrians and re-establish his rule. But he was recognised in the town of Varennes and brought back in ignominy to the Tuileries, losing the little loyalty he still had among Parisians. He and the Queen, Marie Antoinette, were placed under house arrest, while a stream of émigrés fled from France and pressed foreign rulers to intervene militarily.

Emperor Leopold II of Austria, whom Memmo had met when he was still Grand Duke Leopold of Tuscany, was especially concerned about the turn of events in France because Marie Antoinette was his younger sister. He was travelling through Padua that summer, on his way to Vienna with his other sister, Maria Carolina, Queen of the Two Sicilies, and her husband, King "Big Nose" Ferdinand IV. The question on everyone's lips was whether the emperor, who had been on the throne but one year, was going to declare war against France. "There are some here who believe he is ready to wage it," Lucia reported to Alvise in Venice as the Senate made preparations to receive the emperor. "But others feel he will think twice about intervening as long as his sister is in the hands of the rebels."[43] A few weeks later,

Leopold issued the Declaration of Pillnitz, enjoining other European countries to restore the French monarchy with the force of arms.

During the course of the summer, while Lucia was at Le Scalette taking her cold baths, it was Alvise's turn to succumb to the beguiling Dinda Orsini, whom he had met on several occasions in the company of his father-in-law. He courted her discreetly, obviously aware he was endangering not just his marriage but his relationship with Memmo; Dinda resisted him at first, even as she acknowledged her tenderness for him. "There is no doubt that both you and I feel something that goes beyond friendship, but I don't want to go looking for what it is," she said, wary of an affair that could lead to trouble if it were discovered. But Alvise pressed ahead, sending her flirtatious notes and unabashed declarations of love. "Oh God, how does one answer when you speak to my heart so firmly and obligingly," Dinda asked, while making sure the fire of their budding passion was well stoked.

Despite his feelings for Dinda, Alvise evidently complied with his marital duties during his sporadic visits to Le Scalette because by the end of the summer Lucia was pregnant again. Among the first to congratulate her upon her return to Palazzo Mocenigo in the autumn was her mother-in-law, Chiara. "I hope your health is perfect," she told her, adding frankly that she should "take care to do all you need in order to become a mother, thereby consoling this family which sees in you its only means of survival."[44]

Upon learning his wife might yet give him an heir, Alvise returned to the family fold, giving Lucia the kind of attention she had always asked of him. Dinda expertly withdrew from the scene, not without reminding Alvise how right she had been to resist his courtship.

> I dare not imagine what you would be going through now had I taken advantage of our blind passion . . . My dearest Alvise, I swear to you that I have been a tyrant to myself in this story, but now that I see you happily at the side of a wife, and one so highly esteemed in our

country, I am proud of myself . . . Adieu, my
Mocenigo, and for pity's sake burn all these letters of
mine.[45]

At the end of the third month the familiar pains in her lower
abdomen started again and within a few days Lucia had her third
miscarriage. This time the experience was physically and men-
tally debilitating. An air of gloom spread in the house. Her
mother-in-law lamented "the doleful circumstance" that was
blighting her son's marriage and invited Lucia to seek strength in
religion, "from which we must always expect the best."[46] Lucia
tried to pull herself together, but her heart was broken. At a time
when she most needed Alvise, he was again running away from
her. "When we are not together," she wrote to him, "your letters
are the greatest comfort to me. I have written to you every day
yet I have received only one letter . . . Think about this. I ask that
my love for you be fully returned."[47] If Alvise had to be on the
mainland much of the time, as he claimed, why could she not
join him in Vicenza, in Padua, wherever he pleased? Alvise was
evasive. There never seemed to be enough time.

The truth was simpler and more terrible. After the miscarriage, the "blind passion" between Alvise and Dinda, long frustrated, exploded with full force, taking on the pace of a frantic
affair. Despite Dinda's repeated entreaties, Alvise never destroyed the evidence of their secret relationship, which they con-
ducted between Venice, Padua and Vicenza in the winter and
early spring of 1792. "Tonight we cannot see each other, but I'll
be at our usual place tomorrow evening at six o'clock, I give you
my word," reads one of the fragments that has come down to us.
"I beg you not to come here," reads another. "Find the most
secret alcove where we can meet, then write to me and send your
note by means of our usual gondolier." From Padua, Dinda
wrote: "God knows when we shall be able to see each other
again. For the time being I cannot leave and will be here for
another month at least. I will keep you up to date. Please make
sure no one sees my letters in your house because my handwriting is well known by all the people around us." A month later she

was back from Padua and staying, of all places, at Ca' Memmo, from where she dashed off this note:

> I want to see you. I must tell you something and you must come without fail. You can come here. Nobody suspects we are lovers and you will surely find a pretext to come. After all, it's just a visit . . . Adieu, Dinda.[48]

Alvise received the note at Palazzo Mocenigo as he was preparing to leave for the mainland. He wrote back saying they could meet at his house later on: Lucia would be at the theatre with her sister, Paolina. That evening, Lucia went to the theatre thinking Alvise had already left town. When she arrived, she noticed one of the gondoliers from Ca' Memmo dropping off her sister. This is Lucia's account of what followed, from a letter she wrote to Alvise recapping the events of the day:

> The gondolier tells me he has just seen you and that you are still in Venice, in our heretofore beloved home . . . I inform my sister, who was already in her box, that I will avail myself of her gondolier . . . I fly home . . . What happened next I cannot even begin to repeat, and in any case we both know it well enough, even though we clearly see the matter from two different perspectives.[49]

What the scene was like at Palazzo Mocenigo and how Alvise explained why he was alone in the company of Dinda when Lucia arrived—these remain unanswered questions. All we can infer is that the affair became known and that it caused the first serious crisis in their marriage. Lucia did not indulge in self-pity for it was not in her character, but in the next days and weeks she felt deeply humiliated at having to suffer in silence "unending expressions of sympathy." Everyone had envied her marriage, she noted angrily, yet she "had been living in the most unenviable position for the last four years, nine months and fourteen days."[50]

It is hard to gauge how close Alvise and Lucia came to breaking up their marriage, or if such a possibility was even discussed.
If it was, one may assume that Memmo—who was by then
entirely over his own infatuation with Dinda—stepped into the
fray to comfort his daughter and salvage a union he had worked
so hard to bring together. Certainly Lucia did not have any
options of her own as long as Alvise wanted the marriage to continue, and he did. His relationship with Dinda, as far as we know,
came to an end. He and Lucia resumed their life together, but the
scar on their marriage bore witness to a serious wound.

To encourage a reconciliation, Alvise organised a long summer journey through Carinthia, Bavaria and the Rhineland, all
the way to Vienna. Emperor Leopold II had died unexpectedly in
March after reigning less than two years. Alvise and Lucia would
arrive in the Habsburg Empire in time for the coronation of the
new emperor, Francis II, who was already at war with revolutionary France. Alvise was keen to stop in Vienna to study the
new Austrian government up close. But there was a more personal reason for visiting the capital on the way back. Alvise
wanted to get the best possible medical advice with regard to
Lucia's difficulty in carrying forth a pregnancy, and there was no
greater authority at the time than Giuseppe Vespa, a Tuscan
doctor whom Emperor Leopold had brought with him from
Florence two years earlier and had appointed official obstetrician
of the Imperial Court. If anyone was going to help Lucia give
him an heir, Alvise felt, it was Doctor Vespa.

Chapter Three

VIENNA

On a sunny morning in mid June 1792, Alvise and Lucia left Venice and headed for the Alps. Their aim was to reach Frankfurt on the Main, deep into the Habsburg Empire, in time to attend Emperor Francis II's investiture. They took the familiar road that led from Padua to Vicenza and on to Verona, then they turned sharply to the north, travelling along the western shore of Lake Garda until they crossed into the southern tip of the Austrian Empire. The road threaded its way along the river Adige to the wealthy city of Bolzano, and continued to climb through the quaint towns of South Tyrol, where the air tingled and the snow-capped Dolomites glistened like giant meringues rising high above the thick alpine forest. Once over the mountain pass, they descended to Innsbruck and moved on, across the green valleys of northern Tyrol and southern Bavaria, reaching Munich by early July. They had been on the road for nearly three weeks but they did not pause, continuing their northward run and covering another forty posts in five days. When they finally arrived in Frankfurt, exhausted but exhilarated by their journey, they were only a few minutes late: the city gates had just been closed as the imperial procession was already heading for the cathedral, where the bishop was to bless the emperor. Undeterred by the frowning German guards, Alvise and Lucia pleaded and haggled and brought out any number of impressive-looking letters of recommendation until they were allowed into the city through a side street, and were instantly swallowed up in the festivities.

Lucia had read in her guidebook, Caspar von Riesbeck's pop-

ular *Voyage en Allemagne,* that Frankfurt was a rich town where
Calvinists, Lutherans and Catholics lived together in bustling
harmony—"the only imperial city that keeps all its splendour
and continues to thrive and improve."[1] And indeed the rich
facades of the buildings, the splendid gardens, the elegant carriages, the fine clothes and even the ladies' expensive jewels
showed that Frankfurters knew "how to lay out their money with
taste," as Riesbeck put it. What Lucia did not expect to find on
that particular day, in a city so far away from home, was an
atmosphere that in many ways reminded her of Venice, or rather,
of Venetian festivities. The rowdy crowds and the pageantry, the
sheer excitement in the air: if Lucia narrowed her dark blue eyes
until everything became a colourful blur, she could imagine they
were celebrating a new doge or a new procuratore di San Marco.
"Here, too, fistfuls of coins are thrown about, chunks of bread are
handed out to the populace and fountains of wine are everywhere,"[2] she told her sister, Paolina, who had pressed her to provide her with detailed descriptions of her travels.

Despite the similarities, Lucia added, there were peculiar local
customs her fellow Venetians had never seen. In the centre of the
main square she and Alvise came upon a pile of wheat as high as a
four-storey house. The emperor looked on from a raised arbour
in the shade while an ambassador of the Electorate of Hesse
walked up to the giant heap, filled his cup with grains and came
back to offer it to his majesty as a token of the German princes'
loyalty to the imperial crown. After this very solemn ceremony,
the mountain of wheat was given over to a frenzied mob: men,
women and children threw themselves on the mound, stuffing
their bags with as much grain they could get their hands on.
Within minutes, all the wheat had vanished and the crowd
retreated in an orderly fashion. Lucia compared "the discipline
which prevails in the German throng" to the festive chaos of
Venetian crowds.

Next, her attention was drawn to a simple wooden house that
had been erected in another part of the square. Again, the ambassador walked up to the house and opened the front door: inside
was an ox that had been roasted whole on a great big spit. The

beast was dragged out into the square and cut up into a thousand pieces that were thrown to the crowd. At the same time a band of strong-armed peasants appeared from the side and tore up the wooden house with their bare hands. "Not even the foundations were left standing," Lucia observed in amazement.

That evening, after the celebrations, she and Alvise were to be presented to the emperor and empress. Lucia barely had time to retreat to their lodgings to take a short rest and make her toilette before Mademoiselle Bertin, the celebrated dressmaker who had been in the service of Queen Marie Antoinette and was now attached to the young Austrian Empress Maria Theresa, appeared in their apartment to put the final touches to her evening dress. It was a glittering night, the first of several with the travelling Imperial Court, and Lucia enjoyed every minute of it. "I'm having great fun," she wrote enthusiastically. The black clouds that had gathered over her during the winter were a distant memory. For the first time since they were married, Lucia had Alvise all to herself, and she was happy.

The cheerful twenty-year-old Empress Maria Theresa was half Neapolitan—her father was King Ferdinand "Big Nose"— and she immediately put Lucia at ease by recollecting in her friendly manner their previous encounter in Naples, during the Carnival in 1786. She was glad to have her company, she said, to distract her from the stiffness of her German entourage. "And she repeatedly expressed a strong desire to come to Venice,"[3] Lucia assured Paolina, mindful not to leave her young sister out of her royal banter.

Emperor Francis II was very different from his wife: haughty, cold, and, at twenty-four, older-looking than his age. He was generally considered to be less intelligent and imaginative than his two predecessors, his father, Leopold II, and his uncle, Joseph II. He was certainly more conservative than either of them, and now that the premature death of his father had lifted him to the imperial throne, he was determined to restore the monarchy in France at whatever cost—an obsession that led him very quickly to put himself and the Habsburg Empire entirely in the hands of his bellicose commander-in-chief, the Duke of

Brunswick. In a sense, the French revolutionary government had made things easier for Francis II by declaring war on Austria and Prussia earlier that year. Now the two allied powers were amassing their troops along the Rhine before invading France, and the emperor planned to inspect the troops.

The day after his investiture, Francis II and his vast following left Frankfurt and sailed down the Rhine. Alvise and Lucia latched on to the imperial cortège. They reached Mainz in the evening. The city had been illuminated by thousands of torches. "I danced with the greatest pleasure at a very scintillating ball," Lucia boasted. The next day she and Alvise were among 400 guests at a lunch given by the emperor and empress. Maria Theresa, who loved to dance, seized the occasion to declare she wanted another ball, to be held that very same night. What a dazzling whirlwind it was!

Frederick William II, king of Prussia, made an impromptu appearance among the crowd of courtiers. He too had come to the region to salute his troops before the offensive against France, and was staying in a castle nearby. Unlike his uncle Frederick the Great, Frederick William II was not much of a military man. But he was handsome, intelligent and a great lover and patron of the arts, with a special passion for music. In addition, he spoke Italian fluently, and Lucia was left swooning when he spoke to her in her own language. She later confided to her sister that she got a little carried away, rambling on in Italian with his majesty. She was even tempted to put in a good word for the new Venetian ambassador to Prussia, but fortunately bit her lip. "You know how sovereigns are," Lucia told Paolina knowingly. "It's always a little risky to raise these sorts of issues with them. You never know how they'll react."

From Mainz, the court travelled up-river to Koblenz, where 52,000 Prussian troops were encamped. A small corps of French émigrés who had fled from the Revolution had been integrated into the Prussian army, and the French officers with whom Lucia spoke grumbled and complained about being "entirely encircled by Germans."[4] From Koblenz the imperial train, with Alvise and Lucia bringing up the rear as it were, turned south, towards

Mannheim, where the bulk of the Austrian army, 75,000 men, waited for the emperor. The road to Mannheim followed "the enchanting riverbanks of the Rhine,"[5] and the landscape could not have been gentler or more pleasing. The road itself, Lucia reported, was so well kept and manicured "it rather feels like driving down a pretty alley rather than a major thoroughfare."

In Mannheim, Alvise and Lucia took leave of their imperial highnesses, and headed down the road that follows the Neckar River, stopping briefly along the way to visit Stuttgart and Augsburg. Lucia's trusty guidebook was never far from her. Riesbeck, an engaging traveller who had died at the age of thirty on one of his German journeys, mixed lyrical descriptions with political information, economic facts, social observations and the occasional *chronique scandaleuse* to spice things up a little. His rambling comments were never dull. About Augsburg, for example, he wrote: "Many houses are old and ugly and are built with so little attention to the rules of modern taste," that Johannes Winckelmann, the great neoclassical art historian, "renounced living in Germany after seeing them."[6] From Augsburg the road to Munich went through some of the most primitive parts of Bavaria, "and the country one sees from the road is entirely uncultivated." Every hamlet along the way was full of smelly taverns and drunkards. The Bavarian peasants—this is again Riesbeck writing—were "stout, muscular fleshy and . . . poorly dressed." There were "large puddles before the doors of their hovels and so they were forced to stand on planks."[7] In Munich a packet of letters from Paolina awaited Lucia. News about their father was not good: Memmo's circulation problems had worsened and he was confined to his bedroom, in considerable pain, surrounded by bickering doctors and a gaggle of wailing old mistresses. But there was good news as well: Paolina was expecting another child. Lucia suspected that she, too, was pregnant again, but this time she kept it to herself, choosing to wait until she reached Vienna and spoke to Doctor Vespa before breaking the news.

Paolina's letters were filled with anxious queries about the war, and Lucia filled her in as best she could. The Austro-Prussian forces had by now begun their march towards Paris, with the Duke of Brunswick threatening to destroy the French capital if any harm was done to the king and queen. But his menaces had only inflamed the situation: an angry mob had stormed the Palais des Tuileries and seized the terrified Louis XVI and Marie Antoinette.

By mid August Lucia was anxious to get to Vienna and meet Doctor Vespa, but Alvise prevailed on her to join him on one last side-trip, to the famous salt mines near Salzburg, before reaching the capital. Riesbeck's enticing description of a salt chamber helped to convince her: "Picture yourself in a hall about one hundred square feet, the walls and ground of which are composed of crystals of every earthly colour that reflect the light so wonderfully you imagine yourself to be in some enchanted palace."[8] Leaving the salt mines behind them, Alvise and Lucia travelled through the beautiful lake district until they reached the Danube, with the Styrian hills rising in the background. They followed the river eastward to Linz and made their final run to Vienna, which they reached on 9 September. They had been on the road for nearly three months.

Doctor Vespa was a genial, warm-hearted sixty-five-year-old. He took Lucia under his protective wing and quickly reassured her with his blend of self-confidence and familiarity. The Tuscan doctor was at the peak of a long and prestigious career. In his youth he had studied with André Levret, a pioneering obstetrician who invented the forceps. Having returned to the University of Florence, Vespa published his influential *Treatise on Obstetrics* and encouraged the use of the forceps in Italy. Archduke Leopold of Tuscany appointed him court obstetrician in Florence, and when he succeeded his brother on the imperial throne as Leopold II, he brought the doctor with him to Vienna. After Leopold II's death, Vespa stayed on as court obstetrician, and was now looking after Empress Maria Theresa, who was in the first stages of pregnancy.

Vespa confirmed that Lucia too was expecting a baby. She was in her ninth week and possibly in the most delicate phase of her pregnancy. He told her firmly that if she wanted to have the baby, she had better stay in Vienna under his direct supervision. "He says the climate suits me well, the quiet lifestyle would also help," Lucia explained to her sister, "and he assures me that if I should stay here, the pregnancy would certainly reach a happy conclusion."[9] Lucia, however, wanted very much to return to Venice, especially since her father was not well. She would stay in Vienna with Vespa until the first three months were over, and then decide whether to risk travelling south before the winter set in.

Alvise rented a house at 144 Kohlmarkt, a busy street in the centre of Vienna, and Lucia made herself a comfortable nest. She would have liked to go for strolls at the Prater, visit the porcelain museum and the gardens at the Belvedere, or take a hackney cab out to Schönbrunn Palace, the imperial summer residence that was open to the public. "But Doctor Vespa doesn't want me to move around too much as we are approaching the stage of my last miscarriage."[10] Only once did she defy the doctor's ban, sneaking out one late afternoon to see Wolfgang von Kempelen's latest invention: the wondrous Talking Machine.

Von Kempelen was an intriguing character, a talented inventor with a bit of the prankster in him. He had already wowed the world with a mechanical chess-playing machine—a small cabinet on wheels containing a tiny wooden man wearing a turban, known as the Turk. In reality, a dwarf chess wizard controlled the movements of the Turk from inside the cabinet, but the trick was not discovered until many years later and von Kempelen's machine went on baffling chess players the world over. The Talking Machine, on the other hand, was a legitimate contraption. All Vienna rushed to see it, and Lucia did not want to miss out on the great event. What she saw, as she struggled among the pressing crowd, was an elongated object that looked like a bellows with a keyboard. Inside was an elaborate machine made up of tubes, reeds, wires and a small mechanical device described as a "resonator." The room went silent, von Kempelen sat down to play his Talking Machine, and Lucia was amazed to hear a series of human-like utterances, each connected to the other, and modulated at will by the inventor of this primitive form of synthetic speech.

Despite her escapade, Lucia reached the end of her first three months of pregnancy in fine shape. She now faced a choice: stay in Vienna until she delivered the child, as Doctor Vespa insisted, or risk it and travel home, as she felt inclined to do. Vespa's recommendation made sense to Alvise. And it certainly made sense to Alvise's mother, Chiara, who immediately wrote to her daughter-in-law that she "endlessly applauded" the illustrious obstetrician's advice. "The displeasure in not seeing you sooner," she added, "will be amply compensated by the sheer jubilation I shall feel at the thought of you being solidly and firmly pregnant, without the slightest fear of some ruinous development."[11] But it was not enough to sway Lucia. She wanted to be near her father. And she wanted to be near her sister, whose pregnancy was only one month ahead of hers. Lucia could think of nothing sweeter than the two of them keeping each other company as their bellies swelled, and later nursing their babies together.

It had been some time since the sisters, who had been inseparable during the earlier part of their life, had felt so close. In the past few years, as she coped with her miserable string of miscarriages, Lucia had seen Paolina drift away from her, into her own new family circle. It was easy enough to understand: she had been separated from her beloved older sister at fourteen, she had spent nearly three years locked up in a convent, she had emerged from Celestia to marry a man she became devoted to, and immediately had a daughter on whom she doted. Still, Lucia had counted on more sympathy and attention from Paolina during her difficult times, and she now told her frankly how much she had been hurt when "you did not show me the same tenderness as in the past."[12] Just as frankly, Paolina replied that she too had suffered to see Lucia behave so coldly when Cattina, her little baby girl, was born. To which a miffed Lucia reacted as a firstborn would, rejecting with indignation "the injury you do to my heart, which loved the niece from the very start."

Their correspondence over the summer did much to clear the air and re-establish their old familiarity. "Thank God those endless recriminations are over," Lucia declared, adding with mock pomposity: "My dearest, I'm rather pleased by the new direction you have taken with regard to your affection for me."[13] Their sisterly love, so long neglected, filled them with warmth and joy. "The faith your heart has in my love for you touches me deeply. My greatest pleasure here is to spend my time in your company, writing letters to you."

At the end of October Lucia's mind was made up: she would make the trip to Venice, regardless of what Doctor Vespa thought. "How could I possibly leave you alone in your circumstances? And not to see Papa after such a long illness! Alvise, whose duty calls him back to Venice, would also be far away from me if I stayed . . . I simply cannot resist the temptation any more." She understood what "a risky gamble" she was taking by ignoring Vespa's advice: "If fate wills it, I could well have to renounce for ever the longed for succession. I must do everything in my power to make this family happy, and I would only have myself to blame if it were left without an heir."[14] She knew what was expected of her; the pressure was considerable. Yet she decided to follow her instinct and do what she felt was best for her, which included "having the assistance of the people I love and by whom I am loved during the most interesting moment in my life."[15]

It was all set: she fixed her departure for 20 November and assured Doctor Vespa she would take every precaution during the trip. Once home she would spend as much time as possible in the country, leading a very tranquil life. Doctor Vespa grumbled and growled like an old bear, but as Lucia was adamant he shrugged his shoulders and prescribed bloodletting sessions before the trip. Lucia went shopping for warm clothes she would need during the journey across the Alps. But on 15 November Vespa came to check on her again and showed great alarm. Her pregnancy, he warned, was suddenly at risk again; and she was also very weak. In all conscience he could not allow her to make the voyage back home.

Lucia was crushed. Was Doctor Vespa acting in good faith? Perhaps, but it is at least plausible he made up some medical excuse to prevent her from leaving, possibly in connivance with

Alvise. In her letters to Paolina, Lucia never mentioned any pain or any complications. On the contrary, she wrote over and over again how healthy she felt and how well the pregnancy was proceeding and how excited she was to be going home. "I cannot begin to tell you about this new situation," she wrote to her sister with resignation. "Only you can imagine how I feel."[16]

Alvise returned to Venice, leaving Lucia to spend the winter in her isolated cocoon on the Kohlmarkt. As the freezing Viennese temperatures set in, she retreated to her warm apartment above the street bustle, seldom venturing outside and drifting into a dreamy world of her own where she was free to conjure up her sister's presence. "I spend my time pleasantly building castles in the air with my imagination," she wrote tenderly. "I walk around the house hoping to see you suddenly appear . . . sometimes I imagine you watching over me . . . I know your feelings for me, my dear, and I can assure you mine are the same for you."[17] Lucia admired Paolina's moral fibre and the goodness of her heart, and she was a little in awe of the depth of her spirituality. She remembered her sister having a strong religious sensibility as a young girl. Her long stay at Celestia had no doubt strengthened it. Paolina yearned to devote her life to the poor and the ill. She composed prayers for Lucia, slipping them in the envelope she addressed every week to Vienna. Lucia's religious sentiment was not as deep as her sister's and she did not compose prayers for her, but she sent other tokens of her love that were just as touching. When Alvise headed for Venice, for example, Lucia gave him an envelope for Paolina containing her favourite earrings. "They are not new but are the latest fashion here," she explained to her sister. "I've often used them and it will give me pleasure to think of you putting them to your ears at the same time as I, by sheer force of habit, would think of putting them to mine."[18]

The small staff in the house, a maid and a cook, spoke only German, a language with which Lucia was having a good deal of difficulty. Communications were limited to the bare necessities, thereby increasing Lucia's sense of isolation. The one person who came in and out was Doctor Vespa. He was Lucia's link to the outside world; a benign, avuncular presence. He came by every day to check on how the pregnancy was proceeding, answer questions about what she was going to go through during delivery and illustrate his theories about nursing. The subject matter was endless and Lucia was an eager questioner. But the two also chatted and gossiped, and Doctor Vespa never failed to fill her in with the latest on the state of Empress Maria Theresa's pregnancy. He was happy to dispense medical advice of all kinds, prescribing laurel oil baths for Paolina's frequent blood discharges and aromatic tisanes to reduce her flatulence, special unguents for Alvise's haemorrhoids and balls of opium to ease poor Memmo's pain and give him a chance to rest. Lucia told Paolina:

> Doctor Vespa says opium is the most effective remedy in such cases. Giving him just enough to doze off won't do, I'm afraid. He needs a ball of opium every four hours for it to work. Make sure his swollen parts are kept moist and soft with the proper creams. And remember Doctor Vespa also advises he should be taking a few spoonfuls of China salt. My dearest sister, I know how much you love [our father] and how much you love me, and therefore I beg you to follow these instructions carefully.[19]

It broke her heart not to be with her father.

> Hug Papa for me very, very tightly, and tell him not to worry because otherwise I shall not cease to worry myself. Above all, protect him from ordinary balsams that will only cause more inflammation and prevent other pernicious steps by all those so-called professors who have already been the cause of so many unhappy errors.

Vespa was one of the best-known doctors in Europe and Lucia, quite understandably, fell very much under his spell. Less so Paolina, who often stood her ground in her long-distance disputes with him. The discussion could turn quite heated, with Lucia stepping in to find some middle ground, especially when it touched issues related to childbirth—a field about which Paolina, already a mother, felt women knew more than men ever would, even if they were eminent doctors. Which was the best way to bring a child to life? Doctor Vespa wanted Lucia to deliver lying down in bed "since he strongly feels that it is the safer and more comfortable position." Paolina argued that it was much more natural to deliver "in the chair," that is sitting in a specially designed armchair with a large hole in the seat, and pushing downwards. This way the weight of gravity did much of the work, and the mother had only to help things along. It was, she argued, the more "natural" way to give birth. Vespa replied, through Lucia, that if Paolina wanted nature to do its work properly, it made "more sense to let the baby do most of the effort to come out, instead of making the mother exert herself on the chair, forcing a process that nature might not want to precipitate." Paolina was not swayed, so Vespa took on a more scientific tone to make his point more forcefully. "Child delivery occurs as a result of the contractions of the uterus," he expounded with impatience. If the mother is sitting, she will accelerate the delivery "and the weight of the baby will end up tearing at the uterus." Bottom line: he never, ever, gave the go-ahead to "accelerated deliveries" such as the one Paolina was defending. Paolina insisted that delivering "in the chair" might be increasingly frowned upon in the medical community, but it suited her because it reduced the heavy discharges that had been such a problem the first time around. Not so, interjected Lucia, who valued Paolina's experience but felt she was not in a position to contradict Doctor Vespa. "What do you think was the cause of so much discharge in your case? Precisely the fact that you gave birth in the chair," she told her sister. "It seems obvious to me that all the effort one has to make in that position is likely to produce more consequences than if one is lying horizontally, on a bed."[20]

When the doctor was away attending to his imperial duties an eerie silence filled the house. Lucia heard from time to time the jingle of the sleds swishing below her windows and the muffled tolling of the bells at Saint Stephen's Cathedral. It was freezing cold outside. "Fourteen degrees below zero," she informed Paolina, "and it doesn't look as if the rest of the winter will be any better. The Court is organising sled races all the way out to Schönbrunn."[21] Writing rambling letters to her sister would have provided a comforting distraction had it not been for the anguished thoughts about her father that inevitably found their way into them. Paolina worried about Lucia being alone; Lucia, in turn, worried about the "agitation" Paolina felt "in seeing Papa so ill." According to Vespa, that very agitation was the cause of the "heat rushes" Paolina often complained about. He suggested soothing infusions of sorrel, violets and chicory. "You can water down the herbal solution or even mix it with broth if you like," Lucia added. "And be sure to take it for fifteen to twenty days. It will certainly freshen up your blood."[22]

Vespa offered solace but not much hope for Memmo's condition. The opium he prescribed was a painkiller, not a cure. In December, Lucia's father sounded a little perkier, and was even fantasising, probably just for the benefit of his oldest daughter, that he might be well enough to travel north to see the newborn as soon as the weather improved. "In the spring, dearest Papa, come and enjoy the dry climate of Vienna," she urged him, keeping the fantasy alive. "I cannot tell you how happy I would be if such a project came true. The little baby living inside me returns your greetings by way of kicks and turns."[23] To Paolina she confessed more soberly that being so far away from her father at this time was "the heaviest burden" and she saw "as a gift from heaven" the possibility of the three of them being together again.[24]

Having to rely on the mail for news of her father was tricky. If, for some reason, Paolina's letter from home did not arrive with the weekly post, Lucia had to content herself "with what my imagination will provide," which was seldom reassuring. She asked her sister to write down her father's condition every evening, so she could have a day-by-day progress report when the mail arrived. "It will only take you a minute at the end of the day and you will be doing the most charitable work, I assure you."[25]

At Christmas Lucia was alone, save for a brief visit from trusty old Vespa. It was too cold to go to midnight mass, the doctor told her. She stayed home, holding her growing belly as she stood by the window and watched the snow falling on Kohlmarkt. Her thoughts were fixed on her father. On Boxing Day she wrote to Paolina that the last thing she wanted was for him to tire himself in his effort to reassure her:

> My poor, beloved Papa, in spite of all his pain, he must have thought I would feel anxious without a letter from him. But of course I renounce what brings consolation only to me. I beg him not to weary himself by writing just to satisfy my longing to have news of him. To hear that he is well again is all that my heart desires, so that I may continue to dream of hugging him—and you—somewhere on the way back home.[26]

By January, Lucia was receiving daily accounts from Paolina "that truly make me feel as if I were with you." The general outlook was not discouraging. Despite her entreaties, Memmo sent her a few "very lively and tender lines that gave me real comfort." But the delay caused by the long distance the post had to cover created a false impression. The situation had in fact worsened. By the time Lucia received that last note from her father, he was already dead.

Fearful of the impact Memmo's death might have on Lucia and the baby, Alvise left immediately for Vienna. He had already planned to be with Lucia when she delivered and with that in mind he had obtained a six-month leave of absence from his government duties. Now he hastened his departure in order to be the one to tell Lucia about her father's death. He reached Vienna in less than a week despite a difficult crossing of the Alps in the dead of that frigid winter. The moment Lucia saw Alvise on the doorstep at Kohlmarkt, her happiness was crushed by what she read in his eyes. A feeling of complete devastation swept over her. Memmo had been the pillar of her life ever since her mother had died when she was only a little girl. And the pain was made all the more acute by the guilt she felt for not having been at his side. There were, of course, very good reasons why she had remained in Vienna, but that did not lessen the laceration she felt—and had felt for weeks. "My situation has been so cruel—forced to stay here in order to fulfil my duty as a mother and thus compelled to forget my duty as a daughter,"[27] she wrote to her sister in desperation. Worried about Lucia's health, Doctor Vespa ordered her to stay in bed.

> But all I really want now is to be in your arms, Paolina. Oh God! Please tell me what I must do to stop thinking about dear Papa all the time, because no matter how hard I try, everything reminds me of him and I cannot bear it any more. I was so impatient to come back to Venice with my little baby. Now I can see that coming home will be the most difficult time of my life. And his sweet plan to meet me halfway, to surprise me some-where on my return journey . . . It is lost for ever.[28]

The "oppressive weight" of the loss did not lift for weeks. The pain renewed itself "every moment of the day." And just as Paolina was constantly worried about how Lucia was managing in Vienna, Lucia worried about Paolina's "anxiety" about her. Their only thoughts were for each other. "What will happen to us when I come back?" Lucia asked, as she struggled to imagine her life without the reassuring presence of her father. During his illness, Memmo had tried his best to avoid upsetting his daughters excessively, especially Lucia, who was so far away. He had encouraged them to look ahead, and think of the children they were carrying in their wombs. And in the end "the thought that Papa would have forbidden us to torment ourselves in this way for the sake of our innocent babies," helped Lucia to regain her balance.[29]

As she began her seventh month, Alvise's presence made it easier to focus again on the child she was carrying. Doctor Vespa encouraged him to take his wife out for short walks or for carriage rides around town to get some fresh air and do some shopping: a crib, swaddling cloth, baby clothes, bottles, pans and even a beautiful dummy made of blown glass. So when the sun shone and the avenues glistened in the snow, Lucia, looking quite beautiful in her black mourning *andrienne,* a flowing loose gown, would venture out into the city bustle holding on to Alvise's arm. She was grateful to have him by her side. His leave of absence might slow down his career a little bit, but how would she have managed without him? She was also "quite happy" that Alvise's decision to take a pause in his work had been approved not only by the Mocenigos but by the ruling authorities as well. "I was sure such a friendly gesture towards me, in such a delicate moment for the family, would be applauded by the more sensitive people we know," she wrote to Paolina. "But I also needed to hear the public applause following the inevitable suspension of his civil career, and having heard it, I can now look forward to all the good things his loving care and his experience will provide me with."[30]

Doctor Vespa still came by every day, bringing his usual share of Viennese gossip and the latest news on the empress's pregnancy. In mid February the talk of the town was Maria Theresa's latest escapade to a carnival party dressed up as an oyster-and-macaroni vendor. But apart from the occasional titbit from the doctor, Lucia did not know much about what went on beyond Kohlmarkt. She remained very much confined. Carnival festivities were out of the question, and she agreed to her shopping forays with Alvise mostly out of necessity. She took her mourning seriously, and wore black at home as well.

Her conversation with Paolina—for this is what it was, a continuous, daily dialogue by mail—was really the centre of her life. Lucia informed her sister:

> Doctor Vespa says you will give birth before you think. I don't exactly know when I am due. I am always made to worry. Everyone tells me I should be wary of the eighth month, which, thank goodness, will

soon be over. Meanwhile I've ordered the hard, embroidered mattress we will use when I deliver. I've already hired the woman who will watch my baby. God willing, I'll be well enough to provide the rest.[31]

Lucia felt very strongly about nursing the baby herself. In the past, the infants of the aristocracy had been put in the care of wet-nurses. Lucia's generation, influenced by the new literature on childbirth and childcare generated by the ideas of the Enlightenment, was interested in a closer, more intimate relationship between mother and child. In Lucia's case it was not merely an intellectual point of view. She yearned to breastfeed her child in order to fulfil the maternal instinct she felt growing in her. In this respect, she had a strong ally in Doctor Vespa, who, like many male obstetricians of the time, wanted to reduce the role of mid-wives and wet-nurses—in large measure to enhance his own authority and control. "He is encouraged by the fact that milk serum has started to ooze out of my right breast first," she informed Paolina.[32] Her sister had mixed feelings about breast-feeding her second-born; she remembered it had been a rather painful experience the first time. If she decided to go ahead any-way, she explained, she would probably breastfeed only the first few days, and then pass the child to the care of a wet-nurse. Lucia, under the influence of Doctor Vespa, argued against the idea of switching midway.

> If you are not willing to raise the child with your own milk all the way, then you should think twice since changing to an inferior milk after such a short while would certainly be harmful for the child; and to sud-denly interrupt your breastfeeding after allowing the milk to reach its natural flow would be harmful to you.[33]

As to why this was so, Lucia was forced to admit Doctor Vespa was "rather short on details." Memmo had raised his daughters to be always curious and inquisitive in order to improve their knowledge. But the doctor simply said Paolina's plan was "folly" and that she should not go ahead with it and that Lucia should tell her so. "I asked him if he could explain to me the reason behind his belief, as we are used to doing all the time, but he merely replied that we should just trust him because what he said was solidly grounded."

By the end of March, Paolina, being one month ahead of her sister, was about to deliver at any moment. Lucia was in a state of utter fretfulness. She filled her letters with short, nervous questions. How was Paolina feeling? When did she expect to give birth? Was she in any pain? What had she decided to do about her milk? Was the bloodletting reducing her blood discharges? It is hard to imagine anyone being more anxious over a sister's impending delivery. "Now I'm sure of it," she wrote on 20 March, unable to stand the excitement any longer. "I know you've delivered. But what have you delivered? . . . Oh I am so happy . . . And you are such a strong girl I needn't worry." She assumed Paolina was breastfeeding the first few days, and she urged her once again not to give up. "I would be so happy if you decided to continue giving your own milk to the little baby," she insisted. "It is better for him as it comes from the same body that has already nurtured him. It's lighter, more easily digestible than the one of a stranger, whose milk thickens over time."[34]

It turned out Paolina had not yet given birth when Lucia wrote her this letter but she had by the time she received it: another girl was born and she was christened Isabella, like their mother.*

Despite the fatigue, Paolina made the effort of sending a short note to her sister a few hours after delivery in order to reassure her. In one of those curious double-takes caused by the slowness and irregularity of communications, Lucia could rejoice all over again:

* Elisabeth and Isabel are names of the same saint; Lucia's mother was known both as Elisabetta and Isabella.

Bravo! Hurrah! So, my dear sister, you have happily
delivered and those few lines you sent me gave me infi-
nite pleasure because it means you are in good health. I
am so happy! I hug you with all my heart, and my two
nieces as well. I so much want to see the first-born
again, and the second one, who bears our mother's
name, I will love her so.[35]

Of course, Paolina's husband, Luigi, was hoping for a son, an
expectation Lucia well understood given the pressure she herself
had felt from the Mocenigos. "I too was wishing for a little boy,"
she wrote to her brother-in-law in a consolatory postscript, "but
my prayers will not be useless and you will soon have one, I am
sure."

Lucia was so caught up in the emotional turmoil surrounding
Paolina's delivery that she had managed to put aside momentarily the fears about her own pregnancy. They came back to her
even more strongly now that she was next in line. "I must tell you
what scares me most as my own delivery approaches," she confessed to her sister. "It is the awful pain I will have to endure: it
terrifies me. And I know what a coward I can be in such a situation."[36] Her fear was compounded by the possibility that Doctor
Vespa might not actually be at her side when the time came. After
passing by to see her every day for months, he was now telling
her that since the empress was also entering the last phase of her
pregnancy, he would be on call at all times.

Lucia had seen the imperial carriage passing below her window just a few days before, when the empress had arrived from
the country to spend the last part of her pregnancy in Vienna. "I
actually enjoyed the splendid spectacle," she told Paolina. "The
cortège passed right in front of our house, followed by parents
and friends and twenty-four postilions. The streets and windows
were crowded with people. Everyone applauded and shouted
hurrahs. The trumpets blared. It was all very beautiful and moving." Still, Lucia was "immensely distressed" at the possibility of
not being able to count on Doctor Vespa when she delivered. And
the outlook was not encouraging. "Just yesterday the Empress

told Vespa she had been on the point of calling him the night before. She'd woken up with terrible pains that had forced her to get out of bed and walk up and down the room, though luckily the pain had subsided." Next day, Lucia added with a touch of irritation, the empress felt so much better "she went off to the theatre in an excellent mood."[37]

The Viennese custom, at a time of mourning, required one to wear white in lieu of black after the first six weeks, except for a black veil over one's head. Lucia consented to change her attire with the greatest reluctance. "Our loss has been so devastating," she told her sister, "that I would like my outward appearance to continue expressing my sadness."[38] In her mind, the death of her father was still so indissolubly bound with the birth of her child that she even feared her enduring grief might somehow affect the newborn. She was afraid of pain, but more than anything else she was afraid of giving birth to a weak or diseased child. "I would be utterly crushed if, albeit for a noble reason, the creature I shall soon give birth to were unhealthy." And she revealed to Paolina "that right after our terrible misfortune, I felt the baby trembling as he moved inside me. I hope to God my baby will not have to live in agony."[39]

The regular post left once a week, but Lucia made a point of writing every day, often picking up the letter where she had left it the night before, in order to give her sister a precise account of what she was going through. She registered every movement of the child, checked her nipples for more traces of serum, took down Doctor Vespa's latest advice—when he came to see her. Everything was ready; it was just a matter of waiting with Alvise at her side. "I begin my letter to you today," she wrote to Paolina on 9 April, "even though I might have to interrupt at any moment. Now is when it should all be happening if the counting has been exact. But I haven't felt any of the premonitory signs yet." The next morning, she began: "No news as far as I am concerned . . ."[40] The letter was left unfinished. Later that day Lucia delivered a healthy-looking baby boy who was christened Alvise, and instantly nicknamed Alvisetto to distinguish him from his father.

Alvise was ecstatic and Lucia, though exhausted, was happy and relieved. After six years of marriage and three major miscarriages, she had produced at last the heir the Mocenigos had been anxiously waiting for. Everything had gone well. Lucia had delivered in bed, as planned, and Doctor Vespa had arrived just in time to supervise the delivery and savour his triumph. Lucia recovered very quickly and Vespa dispensed her from lying in the dark the first few days—a practice he often required on the grounds that daylight made it difficult to rest. He decided not to truss up her belly, as was usually done. "If the binding is too tight it prevents the normal functioning of the uterus, and if it is too loose it is useless," he explained. "Besides, it creates excessive heat around the lower parts, which is never a good thing."[41] Vespa made sure Lucia was all settled and rushed off to attend to the empress's needs.

Propped up against a wall of comfortable pillows, Lucia soon picked up her correspondence with Paolina. Alvisetto, she said, was giving her all sorts of satisfactions. He lost his umbilical cord on the third day, which she saw as "a sign of strength and health." Six days later he shed all his milk crusts—another "sign of robustness." The outlook for breastfeeding was promising too:

> I haven't had the joy of giving him my own milk yet but I understand it will happen very soon. The milk we are drawing from my breast we are giving to the wet-nurse's daughter. [In two days] I will put my feet on the ground for the first time, and lie on the chaise-longue while they make my bed up.[42]

As she ended her letter she heard the thundering blast of 300 cannon announcing the christening of Archduke Ferdinand, the son of Emperor Francis II and Empress Maria Theresa. From her bed, Lucia could see the candles the Viennese had put at their windowsills to welcome the imperial heir. She also heard the crowds in the streets below "expressing their joy with boisterous chants"—a little too boisterous for Lucia's taste, as they often kept her awake.

It was not until two full weeks after Alvisetto's birth that Lucia announced to Paolina: "I am nursing my child and I am the happiest woman."[43] When she held her baby boy at her breast and felt him gently tugging at her nipple, she said, her fulfilment was complete. Doctor Vespa came by to check on Alvisetto and monitor Lucia's condition, and resume his cosy chitchat. The empress was having difficulty with her milk. "Apparently she is envious that I am nursing my son," Lucia reported with a hint of mischievous pride. The post brought packets of congratulatory letters from Venice, mostly from Mocenigo aunts and uncles and cousins. And nobody was genuinely more enthused than her mother-in-law, Chiara, who now claimed to have known all along that Lucia was going to deliver a baby boy: "My darling Lucietta, I cannot begin to tell you the joy I feel for this birth which, I can now reveal to you, my soul had presaged. I hope with all my heart that the two of you will remain in perfect health, and no doubt the good blood with which you have imbued your son will ensure this. Believe me, the arrival of this sweet baby has consoled this family, and us parents, no end."[44]

Only echoes of the outside world had reached Lucia during the bitter cold winter. She had been far too absorbed by her apprehensive musings about motherhood to pay more than scant attention to the war of Austria and Prussia against France. Nevertheless, she had been shocked to learn, back in January, about Louis XVI's beheading in Paris. She was also aware, thanks to Doctor Vespa's briefings, of the court's anxiety for the fate of Queen Marie Antoinette, herself a Habsburg and the aunt of Emperor Francis II. The Austro-Prussian offensive against revolutionary France had been repelled during the autumn of 1792. Now, in early spring of 1793, the tide seemed to be turning, with the monarchist coalition gaining victories at Liège and Maastricht, taking control of Holland and pushing the French *armée* as far south as Antwerp, where the attackers were hoping for a breakthrough that would open the field to an invasion of France.

As she nursed Alvisetto in the penumbra of her bedroom, Lucia sometimes heard the bells of Saint Stephen's tolling for the dead soldiers who lay strewn in the muddy fields of Flanders. But otherwise, life at 144 Kohlmarkt went on quietly and uneventfully. Lucia's milk was plentiful, and she spent most of her time with the baby, mired in a jumble of sheets, swaddling cloth, bathing appliances and bottles of essential oils prescribed by Doctor Vespa, who came by to see if Lucia had properly put the baby to sleep, "always on his side." At the end of April, Lucia and Alvise planned to celebrate their sixth wedding anniversary with a quiet dinner at home. "But you won't be here, Paolina," Lucia noted with sadness, "and neither will be the person who is always present in our hearts. So this family gathering won't give me the pleasure it used to give me in the past."[45]

Lucia slowly emerged from her gauzy cocoon. The weather grew mild and signs of spring were everywhere. She and Alvise took Alvisetto for an occasional stroll. The linden trees were regaining their lush foliage and flowerbeds were bursting with bright yellows and reds. It was a different, more vibrant and colourful city than the one she had seen when she had arrived in the early autumn. The latest fashions from Paris were all the rage—Lucia had heard that Viennese women had special dolls clad in Parisian clothes sent to them so as to better replicate the style of the new season. Splendid carriages paraded up and down the cobbled streets. At the Prater, music stands and lemonade booths attracted crowds of young families like theirs.

When Lucia had recovered enough strength, she began to organise dinner parties at home, eight or ten people at the most, "the quality of the guest compensating for the small number of people at the table." These evenings were a welcome diversion—especially for Alvise, who was growing somewhat restless so far removed from the political scene in Venice and from his beloved Molinato. The guests tended to be mostly diplomats and travellers from Italy—Neapolitans, Tuscans, Milanese, and of course every Venetian who came through town. Doctor Vespa, practically part of the family and something of a hero to the Mocenigos, was a regular at these Italian soirées. Lucia was keen to get as much out of him as she possibly could before heading back to Venice. Unguents, potions, infusions, herbal teas: she wrote everything down very carefully, including his latest therapy for increasing the level of iron after childbirth, which she thought would be very useful for her slightly anaemic younger sister. The island of Elba, off the coast of Tuscany, was known for its rich iron ore, and the doctor strongly suggested drinking the water from the river that flowed to Porto Ferraio, the main harbour on the island. A good apothecary in Venice might carry some bottles, Lucia told Paolina. If not, the simplest way was to have a demijohn of the precious water shipped from Livorno and drink two glasses every morning for two months.

In early June, Alvise mapped out their return journey. They would travel through Carinthia, making a stopover in Klagenfurt before crossing the Julian Alps and descending towards Udine, the capital of Friuli, practically in sight of the northernmost Mocenigo estates. From there it would be an easy ride home. Lucia could already see herself in Venice with her sister, nursing Alvisetto on the balcony of Palazzo Mocenigo at one end of the Grand Canal, while Paolina nursed little Isabella further upstream, at the former Ca' Memmo, renamed Palazzo Martinengo. "We shall visit each other all the time and enjoy the afternoon breeze together," she wrote with anticipation.[46]

She was returning to Venice victorious. Her station in society was secure; her rank among her peers considerable. As she pictured herself settling once more at Palazzo Mocenigo, some of the old anxiety came back to her as she worried about the numerous relations living there—many of them quite old and doddering—reacting with impatience to Alvisetto's shrieks and wailings. But her mother-in-law reassured her on that count: "My grandson's loud music will never be unpleasant. It has been a very long time since such a comforting sound was heard in Ca' Mocenigo."[47]

Alvise and Lucia did not arrive in Venice until mid July, after a much longer and rougher journey than expected. The weather was unseasonably cold and the skies were stormy most of the way. It even snowed as they crossed the Alps. Apart from the general discomfort—the constant rattle, the banging on the hard wood—Lucia hardly had time to enjoy the scenery, what with having to breastfeed Alvisetto and nurse him to sleep as their carriage climbed up and down the mountains. By the time they reached Palazzo Mocenigo Lucia was sore, exhausted and sleepless. The absence of her father threw her into deep melancholy, which the sight of Paolina and her two daughters, Cattina and little Isabella, only partially assuaged. She was ordered to bed and the Mocenigo doctors gathered around her prescribing the usual cycle of bleedings. But Lucia feared this perfunctory, all-purpose remedy might reduce the quality of her milk if not even diminish it. Her mother-in-law hovered over her protectively, insisting she follow the house-doctors' advice. "It would be most useful if you had the vein of your arm punctured in order to extract a good four ounces of blood," she advised. As for the milk, Lucia need not worry. "If the blood is taken out while you are breastfeeding, then there is no danger of reducing the quantity of milk you have."[48] Lucia knew there was nothing wrong with her. She was just very tired. All that useless fretting made her feel a stranger in her own house again. She missed Vienna. Above all, she missed the comforting presence of Doctor Vespa.

In only a year the atmosphere had changed noticeably in Venice. All of Europe was at war now, and though the Venetian Republic still clung to its proud neutrality it was slowly being sucked into the vortex unleashed by the French Revolution. Great Britain, Spain and Piedmont had joined the Austro-Prussian coalition, which was routing French forces north, east and south. The French government was also defending itself from a bloody insurgency in the region of Vendée. It looked as if the Revolution were hopelessly besieged. Even the legendary General Dumouriez, the hero of the battle of Valmy, had quarrelled with the politicians at the Convention and had gone over to the enemy. The Jacobins had taken effective control in Paris, expelling the moderate Girondins from the Convention and establishing a Committee of Public Safety, a de facto dictatorship led by Maximilien-François Robespierre, that dragged the country deeper into a spiral of state violence and terror. By the time Lucia arrived in Venice in July, the grisly tales coming from Paris were suddenly brought into focus with the news that Queen Marie Antoinette had not been spared the guillotine. Hundreds if not thousands of French émigrés were roaming northern Italy now in search of a safe haven, and many of them had settled in Venetian territory. Chief among them was Louis XVI's brother, the Comte de Provence, second in line to the throne after the dauphin, the young Louis.

The war was having a profound effect on the political climate in Venice. The Council of Ten tightened its grip and made all decisions largely ignoring the Senate. The State Inquisitors expanded their role in an atmosphere of suspicion and fear. Alvise, who had been on leave to be with Lucia in Vienna, was eager to get back into the political game. He was alarmed by the reactionary turn the government had taken and blamed the old, conservative patricians for seeking cover in the face of turmoil rather than rising to the challenge with a more imaginative diplomacy. But he knew he had to bide his time and not appear callow or over-ambitious. His time would come, no doubt. Meanwhile he sought and obtained the post of captain of Verona—a city where the Mocenigos had maintained strong connections with the local ruling families.

In all the major cities in the mainland territories, the Venetian government traditionally appointed a *capitano*, in charge of security and finances, and a *podestà*, a mayor in charge of justice and local administration. These positions carried prestige, but they also required considerable personal expenditure, and the government was finding it increasingly hard to recruit qualified patricians who were also rich enough to occupy the position decorously. As a result, the military and the civilian ruler were often the same person. This was the case with Alvise, who was appointed *capitano* and *vice podestà*—deputy mayor, the position of mayor remaining vacant during his tenure. He was, in other words, the highest and most visible authority in Verona, headquartered in the Palazzo del Capitano, an imposing early Renaissance marble *palazzo* in the Piazza della Signorìa, where a succession of Venetian proconsuls—including a number of Mocenigos—had lived since Venice had conquered Verona in the early part of the fifteenth century. The appointment was for sixteen months and Alvise installed himself in the autumn of 1793. The province of Verona was one of the richest of the Venetian Republic. Extensive fields of wheat and maize, interspersed with vineyards and olive groves, shaped the gently rolling countryside east of Lake Garda. Rice paddies covered the wetter plains along the river Adige. The mulberry tree was also widely grown, producing the worms for the silk industry that thrived in the area. Verona itself, an old Roman city on the banks of the Adige, had a population of about 50,000. Its military importance, once considerable, had diminished as the military power of the Venetian Republic had declined. But it was a busy commercial centre—the gateway for the all-important trade with the Habsburg Empire—and there could not have been a better vantage point for Alvise, interested as he was in exploring new outlets for his agricultural ventures and experiments at Molinato.

What was a good move for Alvise, though, was not the best arrangement for Lucia, who was just settling back in Venice after a year in Vienna, and was already being asked to pack up and get back on the road. Of course, Verona was not far. In ideal conditions, one could leave Venice at dawn, cross the lagoon and be in Padua by mid morning, take a post-chaise to Vicenza and reach Verona by nightfall. But travel conditions were seldom ideal. Carriages broke down, old beaten-up horses collapsed, and in the autumn and winter parts of the road were often flooded. Besides, Lucia was still on a full breastfeeding schedule, determined to nurse Alvisetto as long as she had milk to give him. The journey from Vienna had been distressing enough and the last thing she wanted was to climb into a carriage with her baby boy, who was not even six months old, and travel to a new city. So she decided to join her husband the following spring, when Alvisetto would be a little more robust, while her husband went ahead.

Somewhat to his surprise, Alvise discovered that the people of Verona had a fond memory of his eccentric father, who had held the same position he now occupied until he had launched his ill-fated candidacy for the supreme office of doge in 1788, only five years earlier. At the time, Sebastiano had celebrated the start of his campaign by distributing large quantities of money and bread among the Veronese and throwing an extravagant ball in the Palazzo del Capitano, where Alvise now lived. The Veronese had given him an equally impressive send-off, with dancing and drinking in the main city square, and fireworks at midnight over the splendid ruins of the Roman arena. The memory of that joyful carousing still lingered in the city and Alvise was warmly received as the son of Sebastiano—something he had hardly expected given his own view of his father.

The Veronese quickly realised Alvise was very different from his father. He certainly seems to have cut quite a figure in his own right in the somewhat provincial atmosphere of local society, the ladies in particular perking up in his presence, perhaps encouraged by Lucia's prolonged absence. He formed several liaisons, none of them of any lasting importance. In fact, every trace of them would probably have disappeared had it not been for Alvise's persistent neglect in destroying the evidence of his secret affairs. Thus one learns of the anonymous wife of a government official who confessed to him she stared "all day at your miniature portrait, isolated in my usual, rigid solitude." Or of the equally mysterious but rather more sanguine Spanish lady who warned Alvise to keep his wandering eye in check "because in matters of gallantry, women of my *nación* do not care for the company of other ladies."[49] Verona, of course, was the city of Romeo and Juliet, but the tone of these letters to Alvise was hardly Shakespearian. It was more like vaudeville in the Venetian province.

His romantic entanglements did not distract Alvise from his official work. From the start he faced a tricky diplomatic controversy with France. Louis XVI's young brother, the Comte de Provence, having failed to obtain a safe passage to Vienna, had fled from Paris and established his headquarters in Verona of all places, where he was attracting an increasing number of French émigrés.* The revolutionary government in Paris was pressing Venice for his expulsion. Alvise's instructions were to mark time using whatever delaying tactic he could come up with. There was no legal ground for the Comte de Provence's expulsion: he led a relatively dignified life in Verona, and the Venetian Republic was a neutral party in the war. Alvise remained on very cordial terms with him: as long as the anti-French conservative European alliance was forcing France on the defensive, there was no need to rush to comply with the request of the revolutionary government in Paris.

Lucia moved to Verona in the spring of 1794. Alvisetto was now a year old and it would have been difficult to postpone her trip any longer without appearing to snub the Veronese. She was reluctant to leave all the same. Her baby boy was neither strong nor particularly healthy. He was prone to catarrh, colds and fevers that kept Lucia in a state of perpetual worry. She wondered whether they had left Vienna too soon. She complained about the humid climate in Venice. She even asked herself if something might be wrong with her milk. The Mocenigos, meanwhile, observed Alvisetto with creeping scepticism, some relatives even beginning to make unpleasant remarks about "Memmo blood" after having praised that very same blood only a year before. Even Chiara, always very protective of her grandson, admitted he was a weak child. "The truth is," she told Lucia shortly before their departure for Verona, "I shall remain in anguish until he has grown a little more, especially every time you set off on a journey."[50]

In Verona, Alvisetto seemed to get stronger as the days grew warmer. Lucia still nursed him and was never far away from him. She would have liked to take advantage of the pleasant weather and parade him in the lively marketplace in *piazzale delle erbe*, or

---

* The Comte de Provence's title was no longer recognised and he was living in exile as the Comte de Lille. After the death of Louis XVI and Marie Antoinette, he declared himself regent for his nephew, Louis XVII. After the boy's death in June 1795, the Comte de Lille became more vociferous in his claim to the French throne, issuing proclamations and mobilising émigré support from his makeshift court in Verona. The French government's pressure on Venice for his expulsion increased accordingly.

visit the square in front of the Roman arena, where the Veronese took their afternoon stroll, or walk along the banks of the Adige, its icy cold water rushing from the snows of the Dolomites towards the Adriatic Sea. But of course the wife of the captain was not free to move about as she pleased; as the first lady of Verona, Lucia was forced to follow a fairly rigid protocol and she felt a prisoner within the grey walls of the Palazzo del Capitano. The view from her apartment was cut off to the right by the Torre Lamberti, the 300-foot-high medieval tower that had served for centuries as Verona's trusty sentinel, and to her left by the gothic spires of the church of Santa Maria Antica. The place was definitely austere.

Lucia stayed but a few months. In the summer she returned to Le Scalette, their villa on the Brenta, while Alvise shuttled back and forth between Verona, Le Scalette and Molinato. Alvisetto was in fine shape during the entire *villeggiatura* (summer season), taking his mother's milk but also eating solids. He ventured about the house and the garden on his own feet, and uttered his first syllables. He played and laughed and basked in his mother's company. In early autumn, they all travelled back to Verona. It was their last stint in the Palazzo del Capitano as Alvise's tenure would soon be over. Lucia did not look forward to spending another winter in those inhospitable rooms, but at least she felt more confident about Alvisetto's ability to endure the cold season.

With the first chills, however, Alvisetto's catarrh began to thicken, and his breathing difficulties started again, with coughing bouts and the inevitable fevers. He ate with difficulty and often refused to take his mother's milk. Lucia held him close to her. She stroked his chest and massaged his spindly legs and arms. She felt the frailty of her little boy at the end of her fingertips. In February the days grew longer and Lucia beheld the first promise of spring in the air. The worst seemed behind them. The winter would soon be over, she told her sister, and Alvisetto was going to be all right. The first couple of years were always the most difficult. It would be easier as time went by. Each day, each week that passed strengthened his chances.

Then the sudden cold spell at the end of February caught everyone by surprise. It all happened very swiftly. Alvisetto's chronic catarrh problems worsened. The infection moved to his lungs. He breathed with increasing difficulty and would not take any food. Soon his body was burning hot. Lucia pressed damp cloths on his face and limbs to cool him down but the temperature would not abate. The doctors insisted on puncturing his veins and the bleedings made him weaker each day. "He is struggling against the illness," a distraught Alvise wrote to his father on 9 March.[51] The little boy fought a few more days but the odds became overwhelming, and he stopped breathing in the early morning on the 12th.

Alvisetto was buried the same day in the church of San Sebastiano, around the corner from the Palazzo del Capitano. He was a month shy of his second birthday.*

The tiny coffin had barely been lowered into the ground in San Sebastiano and covered with a marble slab when Mocenigo family politics took over again. The passing away of Alvisetto meant there was no male heir. Alvise, grief-stricken as he was, moved quickly to reassert control over family affairs, pre-empting those relatives who might be tempted to take advantage of the situation in order to lay their own claim to parts of the estate. As Alvise saw it, his principal liability was his own spendthrift father, who had grossly mismanaged the estate and was sinking deeper into personal debt in order to pursue his extravagant lifestyle. If Sebastiano was allowed to persist along that path, the entire Mocenigo fortune would soon be at risk. Alvise confronted his father, who was in very poor health, and forced him to relinquish control over the estate. In May 1795, only two months after Alvisetto's death, father and son signed an agreement that made Alvise de facto head of the family. He took over his father's conspicuous debts in exchange for complete control of the family holdings. He also agreed to pay his father a yearly stipend of

* Alvisetto's death certificate is in the Libro dei morti in Santa Maria Antica dal 1797 al 1806, in the Archivio storico della Curia diocesana di Verona. The church where he was buried, San Sebastiano, in the heart of Verona, was destroyed by a bomb during the Second World War.

9,000 ducats, a proviso that in the end proved unnecessary: Sebastiano died a broken man a few weeks later.

When the deal between Alvise and his father was made known, Chiara told Lucia she was now "free to move about as you please within the land of the Mocenigos."[52] It was a strange thing to say given what she herself referred to as "the sad circumstances" that had led to the new arrangement. Was it simply an awkward attempt at consoling her daughter-in-law? Or maybe the spontaneous cry of one who had clearly not been able to move around as she pleased in those lands ever since marrying into the family? Whatever the reason for that remark, it is doubtful Lucia paid much attention to it. After the death of her son, she retreated into a stunned silence. Not a single letter from that period has come down to us. Not even a cursory note, nothing at all, month after month, as if a dark chasm had opened up before her and she had fallen deep inside it.

Chapter Four

THE FALL OF VENICE

I n the spring of 1796, Napoleon Bonaparte came charging across the Alps at the head of some 40,000 ill-fed and poorly clad soldiers. His instructions from the Directoire in Paris were to tie down the Austrian army in northern Italy in order to facilitate the main French offensive against the Habsburg Empire along the Rhine. Bonaparte went well beyond his mandate: moving with astonishing speed, he led his ragtag army to a string of spectacular victories, crushing the Austrians at Montenotte, and again, in rapid succession, at the battles of Millesimo and Dego. Then he turned against the Piedmontese, Austria's allies in northern Italy, and defeated them at Ceva and Mondovi. The Piedmontese taken care of, he again set off in pursuit of the Austrians across the plains of Lombardy, routing the enemy at the battle of Lodi. Barely a month after crossing the Alps, the twenty-six-year-old general entered Milan as liberator and set about establishing the Cisalpine Republic. Meanwhile, the shattered Austrian army retreated north and forced its way into the Venetian fortress of Peschiera, the gateway to the Tyrol.

The sudden occupation of Lombardy brought the French revolutionary army right up to the western border of the Venetian Republic. Bonaparte's descent into northern Italy had been so swift, his legend had grown so fast, that the ruling oligarchy in Venice looked upon him with as much confusion as fear. Incredibly, it clung to a feckless policy of "unarmed neutrality," and thus the Republic remained open to an invasion by a force even half the size of Bonaparte's. A feeling of unease settled over the city as the French made repeated forays into Venetian territory and warned menacingly that they would soon be "sipping coffee" in Saint Mark's Square.[1]

Lucia sensed the apprehension that was in the air, but she kept her distance from the world around her. Only a year had passed since Alvisetto's death, and she was still learning to live with her grief. At first the pain had pressed against her heart and seared her lungs to a point where she had only wanted to stop breathing. But it had slowly evolved, changing in intensity and moving inside her, penetrating every particle. Now it seemed to have reached the end of its long mutation. It was not as sharp, and came over her in waves, like fog rolling in, deep and all-encompassing.

Alvisetto would have turned three that spring, old enough to run about the house and gambol alongside his mother in the narrow streets of Venice. When Lucia ventured out of Palazzo Mocenigo, she usually walked over to the church of Santo Stefano for morning mass or simply to sit at the family pew, finding comfort in the smell of incense and the soft-spoken voices around her. Paolina sometimes joined her for a walk. On such occasions, Lucia went to the balcony to watch her sister's gondola make its way down the Grand Canal before mooring at the docking of Palazzo Mocenigo. Together they walked out through the courtyard and into the narrow back-alley behind the *palazzo* that led to the busy streets of San Samuele. At other times, she joined Paolina directly in her gondola and they travelled downstream, all the way to Saint Mark's Square, before stepping ashore for a stroll. During these outings, Lucia remained aloof, taking in only fragments of the conversations she heard. She returned to life little by little.

Alvise rarely went out with Lucia. He had his own way of mitigating the pain for the loss of their son: every day he threw himself into work, hoping to regain a sense of purpose by directing all his energies to serving the Republic. Soon after Bonaparte's invasion of Lombardy, he was appointed governor in Brescia, a gritty manufacturing city in the alpine foothills, near the western frontier of the Venetian Republic. He was to make contact with the elusive French commander-in-chief and gauge his intentions regarding Venice. But he had literally just settled in the Governor's Palace when Bonaparte entered the city and came looking for him on horseback, surrounded by a cluster of prancing young officers in blue uniform.

Alvise later told Lucia that he was surprised by the general's appearance: he was so small and skinny and dishevelled that at first glance he looked like a boy-man, a strangely magnetic creature, very youthful yet astonishingly self-assured. During that first meeting, Bonaparte was "in an excellent mood" and expressed "the kindest feelings" towards Venice. They went for a walk around the *piazza* and talked amicably, while the officers nodded eagerly at Bonaparte's every word, often repeating what he had just said. As the day wore on, however, Bonaparte began to press Alvise for logistical information. He demanded to know why, if Venice was neutral, it had allowed the Austrians to occupy the fortress of Peschiera, a bastion of the Venetian defense system. Alvise reminded him that the Venetian garrison had been forcefully ousted from the fortress by the Austrians, but he made little headway. Bonaparte's earlier, affable mood turned dark. He became irritable, unpredictable: "In a flash, even the most innocent remark turns him into the most ferocious person if he so much as suspects it contains a hint of opposition to him."[2] Alvise became more cautious, making sure he pulled "all the right strings" during their conversations, so as not to upset "this very conceited man who believes he is superhuman." Yet for all his guardedness, he was drawn to the excitement surrounding Bonaparte. He kept the Governor's Palace open day and night. Officers, engineers, food commissars, dispatchers came and went at all hours in an atmosphere of feverish confusion. There was something mesmerising "about these new men, alluring, seductive, teeming with ideas, filled with courage, always on the move, always writing, always singing."[3] He described the French soldiers as "electrified," a new term made fashionable by the progress of electrostatics.

Lucia did not join Alvise in Brescia. Had she been allowed to decide for herself she probably would have gone. She was intrigued by Alvise's reports, by his own mixed feelings about the French, and about their charismatic commander-in-chief. She sensed the energy in his letters, and she thought it would do her good to be more active, to participate in the work of her husband. But he had left Venice at such short notice that they had not had time to make plans to move out together, and now the situation seemed so uncertain as to discourage any decision.

Bonaparte did not stay long in Brescia. Alvise organised a banquet in his honour, to which he invited the local nobility. The wine flowed. The mood was festive. The French generals raised a number of toasts to the Venetian Republic. Bonaparte whispered to Alvise that he was going to stay for a few days, even hinting that he might like to spend the night at the Governor's Palace. But towards midnight he abruptly took leave saying he was returning to his headquarters at the monastery of Saint Euphemia, just outside the city limits. During the night, the bulk of the French forces under the command of General André Masséna lifted camp and moved rapidly north towards the Austrian defence lines. Alvise joined Bonaparte early next morning just as he was leaving town to join his troops. The commander-in-chief assured him he would be back within twenty-four hours, but he did not return. The next day, at the head of his men, he stormed the fortress of Peschiera and crushed the fast-retreating Austrians. Alvise received a dispatch from Bonaparte's chief of staff, General Louis Alexandre Berthier: "We have defeated the enemy and crossed the river Mincio, and are now pursuing them . . . We have mowed down their cavalry and the battlefield is covered with their dead."[4]

Alvise was still in Brescia in early June, when Bonaparte ordered the occupation of Verona, the largest and most important city on the Venetian mainland, in order to protect his line of retreat. General Masséna crossed the river Adige and entered the city unopposed: fearing the French would torch the city, the Venetian commandant decided not to resist. The news stunned Venetians: grabbing Verona was a blatant violation of the Republic's neutrality. The government tried to shake itself out of its long lethargy. Crusty ambassadors went to work in the European capitals. What little remained of the fleet was ordered back to protect the city. Restoration was begun on the old fortifications scattered around the lagoon. A tax was levied on the population. Foreign ships were forbidden entry to the harbour. But these were tepid half-measures which did not really strengthen the Republic and only irritated Bonaparte.

Alvise returned to Venice to argue, with a handful of senators, in favour of quickly raising an army and shifting to a policy of *armed* neutrality. He saw such a step not so much as a last-minute defensive measure—after seeing the French army at close quarters, he was under no illusion about the possibility of Venice winning a war—but as a move that might get the Republic back into the diplomatic game which it had played so expertly in the past. His proposals, however, were voted down; the old Republic withdrew into its shell, burrowing in the brackish waters of the lagoon in the hope that the threat from the mainland would subside.

Bonaparte had received clear instructions from Paris: Venice was a neutral country and he was not to take hostile action against it. But he was determined to chase the Austrians across the Alps and all the way to Vienna before another French general stole his thunder by reaching the Habsburg capital from the Rhine. By seizing Peschiera and occupying Verona he had shown that he was ready to take whatever step he thought necessary to strengthen his position vis à vis the Austrians, no matter what the politicians in Paris had to say. Bonaparte has often been accused of betraying Venice and ultimately causing its downfall. But he never expressed an intention to protect or defend the old Republic, and the accusation of betrayal has always had a hollow ring. He was playing politics on an extremely volatile chessboard and there was just as much improvisation on his part as there was calculation. In the summer of 1796, he still did not know what to do about Venice—though he clearly intended to use the Republic to his advantage in the larger struggle with Austria. As late as July he went so far as to offer the bewildered Venetian government the chance to join him in an anti-Austrian alliance. Had

Venice accepted, it might have saved itself. But the pro-Austrian sentiment of the largely conservative Venetian ruling class prevailed, and the offer was turned down. Already irritated by Venice's feeble defensive measures, Bonaparte took this new rebuff as a personal affront, and his grudge hardened into contempt. For the next few months, he turned his attention to the rest of Italy, leaving Venice to sink in its quagmire.

Alvise and Lucia spent the whole of that summer at Molinato. The estate had lost that air of desolation it had when Alvise had first taken Lucia to see it a few years earlier. Indeed she would have had some difficulty in recognising the place, which was developing very rapidly under her husband's assiduous supervision. Rows of poplars and beeches grew along the ditches and canals that criss-crossed the field in neat, geometrical patterns. There were two large cattle barns to house the expanding livestock and a sheep shed. Seven new farmhouses housed labourers and their families. Molinato had a general store, a tavern and a chapel. Two brick factories were under construction, as Alvise intended to build many more buildings in the years ahead. Lucia wrote to her sister that she had never seen her husband work so tirelessly at improving the estate. During the summer he drew up a new investment plan to reclaim more land and accelerate the pace of cultivation, he oversaw construction of more housing units for the workers, he started building a school for the growing number of children living on the property and he approved the drawings for the town church. Meanwhile, work on the main house proceeded speedily, and plans were now laid for a large park that was to extend from the fruit orchards behind the villa all the way to the small river that formed the eastern boundary of the property. Molinato was no longer just a big farming estate. It was growing into something different from anything Lucia had ever seen: a large, self-sufficient community centred around a functional, well-organised small town. For the first time she wondered whether Alvise's dedication to his ambitious project was not also related to the precariousness of the world beyond it.

Bonaparte, meanwhile, consolidated his position in northern Italy. In rapid succession he deposed the Duke of Modena,

Hercules III, occupied the Duchy of Reggio and formed a confederation of these two cities with Ferrara and Bologna, thus creating a French-controlled puppet state on the southern border of the Venetian Republic. His troops then marched on towards Rome and frightened Pope Pius VI into signing a peace treaty in which he agreed to yield cash, provisions and one hundred works of art from the Vatican collection. In the late summer and early autumn Bonaparte fought back a fresh Austrian offensive in Lombardy, gaining victories at Castiglione, Arcole and Rivoli. The fortress of Mantua, Austria's last bastion in northern Italy, fell in February 1797.

As it happened, Alvise was appointed governor of Udine, the capital of Friuli—the same region in the north-east of the Republic which Bonaparte chose as the staging ground for his final offensive into Austria. As Alvise and Lucia settled into their new quarters, some 70,000 French soldiers marched through town on their way towards the Austrian border. Bonaparte faced a well-entrenched, highly trained army of 100,000 men under the command of Archduke Charles, the emperor's twenty-five-year-old brother. Charles had already defeated the French army on the Rhine a year earlier; now he planned to wrest the rich plains of Lombardy from Bonaparte and bring them back into the Habsburg fold. But in March 1797, Bonaparte crossed the river Tagliamento and took the fortified city of Palmanova. He moved quickly to the north-east, overpowering the Austrian defences and seizing the city of Gorizia. Next, he crossed the Julian Alps at Tarvisio, descended on the Austrian town of Villach and moved on to Klagenfurt and then Graz, where he set up his headquarters. It was an extraordinary run by any measure. In less than three weeks Bonaparte had crushed Charles's well-trained army and taken his troops within a hundred miles of Vienna.

"Limitless luck is surely the guiding star of this French army," Alvise burst out in near disbelief.[5] But a more complicated picture emerged from his conversations with French officers riding in and out of Udine. Bonaparte was tempted to advance all the way to Vienna, but he was deep into hostile territory and stretched very thin. If the local peasantry turned against him, he would be forced to retreat, exposing his men to a furious Austrian counter-attack in northern Italy, with anti-French riots breaking out in the Venetian Republic and perhaps even in Lombardy. "So far his good fortune has exceeded his own expectation," Alvise reported back to the Senate, "but I am told he is hearing many complaints from his soldiers and some of his most trusted generals about the excessive risk of moving deeper into a country where not enough is known of the territory, the language, the people." Bonaparte's brilliant Italian campaign could yet turn into a nightmare and Alvise was hearing that the politicians in Paris were grumbling. "The star of this young general is dimming in the Directoire and I think it unlikely he will risk everything by putting in jeopardy the entire army that has been put in his trust."[6]

In mid April, as Alvise had expected, Bonaparte agreed to a six-day armistice with the Austrians, later extended by another ten days:

> Clearly he is beginning to see the extreme imprudence of his deep advance into Austrian territory. The common view is that, as a result of his position in the field, he will be forced to accept less advantageous conditions for France than if he had stopped on the bank of the Tagliamento.[7]

After a few days of negotiations in the castle of Eckenwald, near the town of Leoben, Bonaparte and his Austrian counterparts reached a preliminary peace agreement. The terms might well have seemed disadvantageous to France, but they were devastating for Venice. According to a set of secret clauses, which Alvise and the Venetian government were unaware of, Austria recognised French rule over Lombardy and the western part of the Venetian Republic. In exchange, Austria obtained control over the eastern part of the Venetian mainland, the Istrian peninsula and the Dalmatian coast. On paper, France and Austria had already carved the Republic in two, leaving to the Venetians a mere skeleton of a state, consisting of Venice proper and a narrow strip of land across the lagoon.

Alvise, meanwhile, faced the daunting task of governing a province that Bonaparte's fraying back-lines were tearing apart. French food commissars raided granaries and flourmills while marauders roamed the countryside, infiltrating small villages and taking the law in their hands. A French army engineer confiscated all the timber in one village, ordered the peasants to build a bridge over the Tagliamento, and then forced them to pay a toll to pass across the bridge. The post system, Alvise lamented, was breaking down because French officers rode horses "to heaven knows where," leaving the stables empty for those coming behind them. He warned the Senate that Venetian authority in Friuli risked a complete breakdown. His anguished pleas fell on deaf ears. The Senate had no money or men to send him, and was incapable of providing any kind of guidance. It sent off perfunctory replies, thanking Alvise, in stolid, over-wrought prose, for his "zeal," his "patriotic fervour," his "unstinting dedication" to the cause of the Republic.[8]

The Republic, however, was already in a state of semi-collapse. According to the news reaching Alvise and Lucia in Udine, the situation in the rest of the Venetian mainland was even more out of control than it was in Friuli. In Bergamo, Brescia and Crema—three cities near the western border—Italian supporters of Bonaparte, instigated by French agents, ousted the Venetian authorities and lowered the flag with the lion of Saint Mark. But these local *coups d'état* did not have the support of the conservative peasantry, whose hostility against the invading French troops only sharpened. French officers and soldiers were taunted and harassed everywhere they went. In the countryside they were often ambushed and killed. News of this random violence against his men enraged Bonaparte, who was still in Austria. He turned against the old Venetian oligarchy in a fury and sent his aide, Andoche Junot, a fiery twenty-five-year-old officer known as "the Tempest," to deliver an ultimatum in Venice. Junot gave a spellbinding performance, spreading terror among the senators as he filled the hall with Bonaparte's own frightening words. Junot read:

> Do you really believe that even as I find myself in the heart of Germany, I cannot obtain respect for the first nation of the universe? Do you really believe that our legions in Italy will continue to endure the massacres that you incite? . . . If you do not disband these groups immediately, if you do not arrest and hand over to me the perpetrators of these assassinations, I will declare war on you.[9]

Stunned by Bonaparte's threat, the government sent two senators, Francesco Donà and Leonardo Giustinian, to the general's headquarters in Austria to assure him of Venice's friendship. But the mission could not have come at a more inauspicious moment, for much of the Venetian mainland was now in open revolt against the French. The climax came in Verona, which had been under French occupation for nearly a year. During the Easter festivities, the peasants coming in from the countryside filled the streets. A band of drunkards picked a quarrel with several French officers. Violence broke out and quickly degenerated into serious street fighting. Fearing the worst, the Venetian representative, Iseppo Giovanelli, stole out of town dressed as a peasant. The city rose against the occupying troops. By the end of the day, the French were driven out of town. Hundreds of dead lay strewn in the bloodied streets and squares. It took three days for General Augier, the French commander, to retake Verona, and several public executions to restore order. The Venetian government immediately denounced the killing of French soldiers, but Bonaparte would have none of it. He vented all his fury on Donà and Giustinian, who had the misfortune of reaching his camp near Graz in the wake of the awful news from Verona. "No more Inquisitors! No more Senate!" he yelled at the two hapless envoys. He was fed up with the treacherous, decrepit institutions of the old Republic, he said. If the oligarchy did not renounce power and proclaim a new, democratic republic, he would behave "like Attila with Venice."[10]

Donà and Giustinian were heading glumly back to Venice when they were intercepted by a messenger bearing more bad news. The *Libérateur d'Italie,* a French lugger under the command of Captain Jean Baptiste Laugier, had approached the narrow opening at the Lido that leads to the Basin of Saint Mark. According to the Venetians, Domenico Pizzamano, in command of the small fortress of Sant'Andrea overlooking the strait, had fired several shots across the bow to remind the French vessel that Venice's harbour was closed to foreign ships, but Captain Laugier had apparently pressed on. The French, on the other hand, insisted he had heeded the warning and was turning away when the Venetians had opened fire. After a short exchange of cannon shots, the *Libérateur d'Italie* had been taken by assault. Five Frenchmen had been killed, including Captain Laugier.

Donà and Giustinian were ordered to turn around and go back to Bonaparte, to explain the circumstances that had led to the killing of Captain Laugier. The Senate, feeling Alvise had "earned Bonaparte's goodwill"[11] in Brescia the year before, instructed him to leave Udine and join the other two envoys on their unpleasant mission. The wandering trio eventually found the French commander-in-chief at Palmanova, an ancient fortress on the road to Austria. The meeting was even stormier than the previous one in Graz. Bonaparte sat in the middle of the room surrounded by French officers who kept interrupting the Venetians and loudly repeating the general's accusations. "He's in an absolute fury," the three envoys reported back to the Senate, "and he will hear no reason. He wants to do away with the Venetian aristocracy, and demands the heads of the Inquisitors for the events in Verona and the head of Pizzamano for the death of Laugier."[12] The envoys made matters worse with a fumbling, last-minute attempt to offer money in exchange for a more benevolent attitude. Bonaparte yelled back that he was not going to give up taking his revenge "for all the gold in Peru."[13]

While Alvise returned to his post in Udine, Donà and

Giustinian travelled back to Venice carrying Bonaparte's new ultimatum: the oligarchy had twenty-four hours to comply with his demands. If it did not, his troops would attack the city. French soldiers were already taking position along the shore facing Venice, while French ships blocked the access to the city from the sea. Venice was trapped, and a feeling of total impotence swept through the old ruling class. On 4 May the Maggior Consiglio or Great Council, the sovereign assembly of the Venetian patriciate, agreed to accept some of Bonaparte's demands by ordering the arrest of the three Inquisitors and Pizzamano. That was enough to obtain a three-day extension of the ultimatum. On the central issue, the dismantling of the oligarchy, the Maggior Consiglio took time. Alvise, Donà and Giustinian were sent off again to make one last attempt at a general settlement with Bonaparte. If the oligarchy was to commit suicide, as the French general was insisting that it do, then let it at least obtain guarantees on the territorial integrity of the Venetian state.

Alvise met Bonaparte alone in Milan on 7 May as Donà and Giustinian arrived two days later. He wrote to Lucia in Venice that the commander-in-chief seemed sincerely glad to see him. Bonaparte was in good spirits, possibly because his wife, Joséphine, after dilly-dallying in Paris during her husband's Italian campaign, had joined him at last.* Bonaparte declared himself pleased that Pizzamano and the three Inquisitors had been arrested, but insisted the oligarchy had to go. Alvise assured him he was there to discuss the issue, and obtained a further extension of the ultimatum to 14 May.

During the next few days the three envoys tried to pin down Bonaparte to a settlement that ensured the survival of the Venetian state and spared the city of Venice a humiliating French occupation. Bonaparte kept changing his mind every day, promising territorial compensation of one kind, retracting, making more promises. As the talks in Milan continued, the situation in

---

* Bonaparte married Joséphine de Beauharnais in a small civil ceremony in Paris on 9 March 1796, two days before heading south to take command of the Armée d'Italie.

Venice unravelled as the government lost control over the city under pressure from French agents and local Jacobins. There was widespread fear of a popular uprising. The most immediate threat was a mutiny on the part of the Dalmatian troops in charge of security. On 12 May the Maggior Consiglio convened in an atmosphere of near panic. The great hall was only half-filled with harried patricians, as many had already left the city. Doge Manin put forth a resolution in which the assembly that had ruled over the Republic for nearly a thousand years abdicated all powers in favour of a provisional government. The balloting took place amid an undignified confusion. Ordinary Venetians gathered outside the Ducal Palace, hardly able to believe the rumours that were circulating. As tensions rose, the commandant in charge of security sailed out of port with his restless Dalmatian troops for fear they should ignite a general revolt. There were parting shots from the boats leaving the Basin of Saint Mark. Inside the Ducal Palace, the patricians mistook the volleys for the start of a mutiny and rushed to pass their death sentence on the Republic: 512 yeas, 30 nays and a handful of blank votes. The balloting was fifty-three votes short of the legal quorum, but evidently it was no time to quibble over formalities.

Two days later, General Baraguey d'Hilliers peacefully occupied the city with 4,000 men, and installed himself in Palazzo Pisani, off Campo Santo Stefano, just a short distance away from Palazzo Mocenigo. He set up a sixty-member provisional government, drawing in large part on Jacobin sympathisers from middle-class professions. He also included eight patricians from the old regime, Alvise being the most prominent among them.

Alvise, however, was still in Milan with Bonaparte, unwittingly putting the finishing touches to a treaty he was signing in the name of a Republic that was already defunct. It provided for the abdication of the patrician oligarchy in favour of a democratic republic and stated that 4,000 French troops were to ensure an orderly transition—all of which had already occurred. The new government was to give high priority to the trials of Pizzamano and the three Inquisitors. Furthermore, Venice was to pay three million lire in cash in three instalments, and provide another three million worth of military equipment, including three warships and two frigates. Finally, twenty major works of art and 500 precious manuscripts were to be shipped to Paris.

This pseudo-treaty signed in Milan had no legal value and the Directoire in Paris never recognised it. Bonaparte, however, brandished it to provide an appearance of legality around the occupation and the plunder of Venice. Alvise returned to Venice on 19 May, exhausted and deeply embittered. He tried to go over the events of the previous days with Lucia and his mother, Chiara, pacing the drawing room at Palazzo Mocenigo like a wounded animal in a cage, but his rage "at the wickedness beyond all measure of the French" kept coming to the surface. He railed against "the destruction of the Republic of our elders"; centuries of history "in which the Mocenigos played such an honoured role." In a single blow, he complained, he had lost "both state and fatherland."[14]

If Alvise was angry at Bonaparte's deception he should have been even more so at his own disingenuousness. Yet as Lucia listened to her husband's lament, she could not help noticing the superior tone in his voice. He sounded more indignant than sad or pained—how was it possible, he seemed to be asking, that his own peers had destroyed the Republic in which his family had had such a large stake? Lucia's Venetian roots went even deeper than the Mocenigos'. The Memmos had been among the founding fathers of the Republic back in the eighth century, when Venice was little more than a cluster of islets in the lagoon. How would her father have reacted to the catastrophe? She had heard people say that if Andrea Memmo had been elected doge back in 1787 perhaps Venice would not have been so weak when Bonaparte arrived on the scene. But if the thought occurred to her now, she did not dwell on it. She knew her father's hopes for Venice had dimmed in his old age; by the time gangrene attacked his body he had lost confidence in the Republic's future. In a way she must have been glad Memmo was no longer there to witness the final collapse.

. . .

Alvise ended the family reunion announcing rather vague plans for the future. What he feared most, he declared, was the confiscation of his properties. Perhaps, in due course, it would be to their advantage to become subjects of the Habsburg Empire; maybe even move to Vienna and transfer to Austria whatever assets could be salvaged. Many Venetian patricians had already done so, having left Venice before the arrival of the French troops. But it would be harder for them because Alvise was perceived as a French sympathiser in Vienna. One reason he was unhappy to discover he had been included in the provisional government was precisely because it was going to reinforce that impression. Still, he had no choice but to accept the appointment. On the positive side, he was going to be in a better position to protect family interests. He intended to sit on the finance committee and do his work quietly.

The new government held its first public meeting on 23 May, in the great hall of the Maggior Consiglio, where the Republic had been voted out of existence only nine days before. It was a chaotic session, interrupted by long-winded speeches in praise of democracy and passionate jeremiads against the old regime. Alvise found the rhetoric and the endless invective discouraging. He had little sympathy for the small group of Venetian Jacobins who had quickly seized control of the Committee of Public Safety, the heart of the government. And the feeling was mutual: as an influential member of the former oligarchy, he was looked upon with resentment and suspicion.

The first order of business was the proclamation of a national holiday: 4 June. For the occasion, Saint Mark's Square was festooned with red, white and green, the new national colours. In the centre of the square a Liberty Tree was erected, and crowned with a Phrygian cap. General Baraguey d'Hilliers, dressed in high uniform, entered the square followed by all the members of the provisional government. The strangely assorted group marched twice around the square before halting at the Liberty Tree, at which point a fiery Jacobin monk, Pier Giacomo Nani, hurriedly recited a Te Deum—Baraguey d'Hilliers felt it would reassure the wary Venetian crowd. Vincenzo Dandolo, the pharmacist who headed the Committee of Public Safety, gave a speech thanking the French for bringing liberty and democracy to Venice. After a three-gun salute, a band struck the notes of the "Carmagnole," a popular song in Paris during the Terror.

Lucia looked on from a distance. The ceremony seemed strained, and the mood of the sparse crowd hovering in the background was anything but festive. A few people started to dance around the Liberty Tree, shouting and making movements that seemed exaggerated. She saw her friend Marina Querini Benzoni, a glamorous beauty a few years younger than her, throw herself into a frenzied dance. She was wearing a light Greek tunic, open at the sides all the way to her hip. Her long braids slashed the air as she threw herself wildly from the arms of Fra' Nani, the monk, to those of Ugo Foscolo, the passionate executive secretary of the municipal government.* The dancing was more and more out of control. At first, General Baraguey d'Hilliers appeared amused, then he grew annoyed. All at once, the scene came to a climax: the wild-eyed Marina tripped and crashed and lay half-naked on the ground. She pulled herself together with the help of a few solicitous French officers, and resumed her dance. By then the *festa* had lost the little steam it had. It was dusk, and candles were lit all around the square, but the evening breeze picked up and in a few minutes put them all out.

Next day, the pro-government daily *Il Monitore* said it was "not surprising the huge crowds that used to fill the square during important festivities" in the days of the old regime chose to stay home this time, given "the secret machinations" of a few patricians and "other enemies of freedom."[15] The municipalists, as the pro-French Venetians were called, naively believed they were building a new, independent state that would, in time, join the Cisalpine Republic that Bonaparte was setting up from his headquarters in Milan. But Bonaparte had little interest in Venice's future. It was a city to despoil before it was turned over to the Austrians. The last thing he wanted was to have Francophile

---

* Ugo Foscolo, a poet and a novelist, became one of the most influential exponents of Romanticism in Italy.

Venetians knocking at his door at a time when he was preparing to sit down with the Austrian plenipotentiaries to finalise the peace treaty.

Venice struggled to survive through the summer of 1797. The government was saddled with a staggering debt inherited from the old Republic. The treasury was empty, trade was dead and the central bank—the Banco Giro—was emptied to pay the first instalment of the three million lire owed to the French. A forced loan was levied on patricians. It was followed by another emergency loan on property, industry and commerce (gold and silver objects were confiscated when there was no more cash). But the economy continued to languish. Venice could no longer count on income from the mainland. The westernmost cities of the old Republic joined Bonaparte's Cisalpine Republic, while closer cities, like Padua, Vicenza, Treviso and Udine, proclaimed their independence from Venice and set up their own provisional governments. As the weeks wore on in an atmosphere of uncertainty and increasing poverty, Venice's territory continued to shrink. French troops took over Corfu and the Ionian islands, the last vestiges of the Venetian Empire in the Mediterranean. Even more devastating to morale in the city was the Austrian occupation of the Istrian peninsula and the Dalmatian coast. The government reacted with disbelief at Bonaparte's acquiescence to this Austrian land-grab. But of course Vienna was merely accelerating a move that had already been agreed to in the secret clauses of Leoben. By the end of the summer all that remained to the Venetians was their city and the coastline areas along the lagoon. The once sprawling Republic had been picked to the bone.

Inside the city, the organised looting proceeded apace. By early September over twenty masterpieces had been selected and packed and were on their way to the Louvre, including eight paintings by Veronese, three by Titian and two by Tintoretto. As many as 470 invaluable manuscripts documenting Venice's early history were shipped. The Sasanian lion of Saint Mark, which had greeted visitors for centuries from the top of the marble column in the *piazzetta*, was pulled down and crated and sent off to Paris. French engineers erected large scaffolding in front of the basilica and lifted down the four heavy bronze horses the Venetians had brought back from Constantinople in 1204.

The sentiment of the majority of the population turned sharply against the French. Venetians had not welcomed the occupying force, and the truculent arrogance the soldiers often displayed made relations steadily worse. Only a diminishing band of municipalists still clung to the illusion that a Venetian state could survive. They repeatedly invited Bonaparte to visit Venice, but he was wise enough to decline, choosing instead to send his wife, Joséphine, in the hope of softening opposition at least as long as French troops remained there.

The art of welcoming foreign dignitaries had been for centuries a matter of national pride with the Venetians, but the coffers were empty and the planning of Joséphine's five-day visit was in the hands of well-meaning but inexperienced officials. Still, the city managed to put on one, last, performance. When her small cortège arrived in the Basin of Saint Mark, Joséphine waved to the crowd assembled in the *piazzetta*. A warm applause broke out. Cheerful gondoliers cried out their welcome. Dozens of colourful Venetian boats escorted her in a spontaneous parade up the Grand Canal to her headquarters, at Palazzo Pisani Moretta, directly across from Palazzo Mocenigo. "She is neither pretty nor young," noted the punctilious *Il Monitore*. "But she is very sweet and attractive and courteous."[16] What she lacked in good looks, Joséphine made up in style and flair and Creole charm. Her natural indolence, her accessible, unpretentious manner, put everyone at ease, including the nervous officials fussing about her.

The next morning, after a tour of Saint Mark's, Joséphine paid a visit to the former Palace of the Doges, renamed the National Palace. In the very hall where the assembly of patricians had once sat, the government was noisily discussing the need to encourage Venetian poets to compose Pindaric odes to reignite the patriotic fervour of the citizenry. Joséphine made her entrance and all rose and applauded as the speaker introduced her as "the wife of our liberator, Bonaparte." She looked lovely as she took a seat in an armchair that was carried forth and placed between the public and the government benches. Her simple white dress brought out her tawny complexion. A light green stole covered her shoulders, and a pretty bonnet gave her an extra touch of Parisian chic. She sat for no more than five minutes, but it was long enough for her husband's supporters to introduce a resolution bestowing on him the title of "Bonaparte the Italian," as the great Scipio had been named the African after conquering Carthage.

General Berthier, Joséphine's escort in Venice, approached Alvise, whom he had met in Brescia the previous year, with a special request: Joséphine wanted very much to see one of Venice's famous regattas down the Grand Canal before leaving, and she wondered whether one might not be squeezed into her programme. Alvise objected that there was not enough time and not enough money to organise a proper regatta. Nevertheless, as soon as Joséphine had left the hall, he rushed to inform his colleagues of her wish. Some replied mockingly that Alvise should pay for the regatta himself, but after a short debate, the majority decided it was Venice's patriotic duty to organise a reduced version of the traditional regatta. Alvise caught up with Joséphine at Palazzo Pisani Moretta. Alas, she had just received a dispatch from Bonaparte asking her to cut her visit short by a day and join him at Passariano, in Friuli, where the French and Austrian delegations were gathering to draft a peace treaty. Could the regatta not be postponed until her next visit, she asked, when she was sure to be in Venice with her husband? Alvise rushed back to the National Palace, where he found the excitement over the regatta was now unstoppable. He had only two days to organise it.

General Baraguey d'Hilliers and his wife, *la Générale*, hosted a ball at Palazzo Pisani. It was a glamorous affair such as Venice had not seen in a long time. Many Venetians were reassured by Joséphine's presence in their midst. It strengthened the illusion that they had found a friend and an ally who would go back to her husband and press the case for Venice. As the wine flowed, a hopeful mood spread among the guests dancing under the great Murano chandeliers. Nobody complained much about the urgent need to find another 4,000 silver ducats to foot the bill for Baraguey d'Hilliers's glittering extravaganza.

That evening Lucia had an opportunity to spend some time with Joséphine. It is easy to imagine how she found her natural charm seductive even as she sensed the vulnerable soul behind it. As far as we know, the two of them got along from the start. It was only a brief encounter during a crowded evening, yet the seeds were planted for a friendship that was to blossom many years later, in Paris, at the height of the Empire.

For the next two days, Alvise worked non-stop to organise the regatta, while Joséphine visited the languishing Arsenale, paid homage to the French fleet anchored off the Lido and sat through a gruesome play at La Fenice about the life of Orso Ipato, Venice's fourth doge, who had his eyes carved out by an angry mob. When she stepped out of the opera house, red, white and blue paper lanterns glowed at every window along the water-ways, and as she crossed the Giudecca Canal to attend a dinner for a hundred guests in the garden of the Pisani summer *palazzo*, the city behind her was swathed in flickering French tricolour.

On her last day in Venice Joséphine woke up to see fifty gym-nasts performing spectacular acrobatic feats beneath her window. It was the prelude to the regatta. Soon a colourful armada of dif-ferent vessels, representing Venice's naval history, glided down the Grand Canal in a dazzling parade as the crowd cheered from the side canals and the windows of the palaces lined along the great waterway. Behind the scenes, General Berthier made last-minute arrangements for Joséphine's journey to Passariano. She was now in a hurry to reach her husband. Before the regatta was over, she slipped away with her party and crossed the lagoon to the mainland.

Joséphine's four-day visit to Venice had a bizarre coda. She was met on the mainland by Dandolo, the president of the Committee of Public Safety, who promised her jewels worth 100,000 ducats if she managed to keep Bonaparte on the side of Venice during his negotiations with the Austrians. Joséphine took him with her to Passariano and convinced Bonaparte to grant Dandolo an interview. The pharmacist made an outlandish offer he was in no position to make: if peace should fail and France were to go back to war with Austria, he said, Venice would provide him with 18,000 men and several million ducats. Bonaparte made a few vague promises to get rid of Dandolo, who misread the situation completely and sent reassuring dispatches back to his friends in the government. Tommaso Zorzi, a wealthy grocer and himself a member of the Committee of Public Safety, also travelled to Passariano, where he presented Joséphine with a priceless diamond ring as a token of the city's gratitude. She introduced him to Bonaparte, who gave Zorzi lunch and walked with him in the gardens of Villa Manin, the estate which belonged to the deposed Doge Ludovico Manin, and which now served as the French headquarters at the peace talks.

Clearly, Bonaparte's supporters in Venice were losing their heads. The growing uncertainty surrounding the peace talks at Passariano was creating a climate of suspicion and fear inside the government. There were rumours of a plot to murder a hundred patricians in their sleep, simply as a show of force on behalf of the most extreme Jacobins. Alvise followed these strange developments with growing dismay. He was further troubled when Bonaparte recalled General Baraguey d'Hilliers up to Passariano. Alvise had grown to appreciate this engaging, energetic soldier who was often easier to deal with than some of his over-agitated colleagues in the government, and who had managed the difficult task of preserving peace in the city. He and *la Genérale* were frequent guests at Palazzo Mocenigo.

Baraguey d'Hilliers's successor, General Antoine Balland, was known as the man who had drowned in blood the Easter uprising in Verona the previous year. He was soon to demonstrate his incompetence in Venice as well. In early October, government informers picked up the rumour that a lawyer by the name of Giovanni Pietro Cercato was conspiring to deliver Venice to the Austrians. When Cercato was arrested, maps, money and false documents were found in his house. "The fatherland is safe," *Il Monitore* proclaimed the next day. "The treacherous plot that was to bloody this city, oppress the sovereignty of the people and leave it in chains at the feet of despots, has been uncovered."[17] But the Committee of Public Safety, already in the throes of collective paranoia, felt incapable of handling the Cercato case, and asked General Balland to intervene. General Balland over-reacted: instead of assessing the seriousness of the threat, he declared a state of siege, suspended government meetings and brought out his soldiers from the barracks. Not satisfied, he announced that he was taking fifty hostages until the matter was cleared. Alvise's name was on the list and that same night, the National Guard went to Palazzo Mocenigo and arrested him. He was taken to the island of San Giorgio, directly across the Basin of Saint Mark, and locked up with forty-nine fellow hostages.

Cercato turned out to be a two-bit schemer with very flimsy connections to Vienna. The conspiracy threat had been wildly overblown. Balland realised his mistake and released all the hostages three days after their arrest. Alvise was relieved to return to Palazzo Mocenigo alive. He was also fuming after such a display of incompetence on the part of the authorities. The next day, at the government's morning session, he insisted that all the hostages receive a complete and public rehabilitation. A motion was approved unanimously, and the hall broke out in applause.

The hopelessly confused state of affairs in Venice—the phoney conspiracy, the state of siege, the taking and releasing of hostages—irritated Bonaparte no end. But more irksome news was on the way to Passariano. Under the aegis of the inept Balland, the municipal government organised a congress of representatives from the former Venetian territories to decide whether to join the Cisalpine Republic Bonaparte had founded, with Milan as its capital. The congress was held in mid October, and the delegates voted unanimously in favour of annexation to the Cisalpine Republic—this at a time when Bonaparte was preparing to hand a large chunk of the former Venetian territories over to Austria.

Bonaparte was furious with Balland for allowing this to happen, and immediately replaced him with the more experienced General Jean Sérurier, a trusted old officer from the pre-revolutionary military school. Sérurier did not come alone: 10,000 French soldiers crossed the lagoon aboard hundreds of transport vessels and took over the city. They were to complete the pillage of Venice's art treasures and ensure, when the moment came, a peaceful transfer of power to the Austrians.

The Treaty of Campoformio, named after a small village near Passariano, was signed on 17 October, the same day Sérurier arrived in Venice. The contents were even more devastating for Venice than the secret agreement reached in Leoben at the beginning of 1797. In exchange for peace and the recognition of the Cisalpine Republic, Austria obtained not just the eastern territories of the former Venetian Republic, but also Venice itself. There was nothing left of the sovereign Venetian state. The details of the treaty were not immediately made public, but chilling rumours quickly spread in Venice, and led to one last desperate attempt to prevent the city from falling into the hands of Vienna.

At the end of October the government held a referendum on independence. Those in favour narrowly prevailed. What remained of the pro-French party decided to appeal above Bonaparte's head, to the Directoire. Dandolo and three fellow municipalists secretly headed to Paris carrying the referendum results, as well as wads of cash with which to persuade the notoriously corrupt Directors. Bonaparte, who was back at his headquarters in Milan, heard about the plan and sent his men chasing after the Venetians. Dandolo and his party were caught before they could reach the French border, and taken to Bonaparte with their hands and feet tied.

The Bonapartists in Venice having lost all credibility, Sérurier asked Alvise to head a five-member commission to liquidate the affairs of the municipal government, shut down *Il Monitore*, settle all outstanding accounts, recall all diplomatic envoys and prepare the city for the arrival of the Austrians. The French occupation force gradually withdrew to the mainland during the month of December, and in early January 1798, Sérurier hauled down the French flag and departed with his staff, to the relief of most Venetians. On 18 January, despite the cold wind blowing in from the Adriatic, an expectant crowd gathered on the *piazzetta* to greet the new Austrian governor of Venice, the fifty-six-year-old veteran field commander General Olivier Wallis. Alvise and his fellow commissioners handed the keys of the city to the general, who proceeded into the great basilica of Saint Mark, followed by Austrian officers in their white uniforms. The Patriarch of Venice, Cardinal Giovanelli, who had looked on with horror as some of his fellow Venetians danced to the Carmagnole around the Liberty Tree only six months before, intoned a Te Deum.

Chapter Five

COLONEL PLUNKETT

G eneral Wallis established his headquarters in Padua rather than Venice so as to have a stronger presence on the mainland. He speedily imposed Austrian rule over the former Republic with the assistance of conservative patricians who had fled to Vienna during the Bonapartist occupation and now had returned to take positions of responsibility in the new administration. Alvise knew all along that his collaboration with the French was going to cost him a period in purgatory; but he had not expected the degree of acrimony he and Lucia were subjected to during the first months of 1798, not so much by the Austrians—in fact relations with Wallis and his wife, Josephine, were friendly—but by those fellow Venetians who had reclaimed their position of privilege under the shadow of the House of Austria. They were ostracised everywhere. Many former colleagues from the Senate stopped exchanging even the most perfunctory greetings with Alvise. Those who mentioned his name, he complained, did so only "to say horrible things."[1] He spent as little time as possible in Venice, visiting one by one all the Mocenigo estates he had necessarily neglected during the last phase of the Republic. Lucia moved out to Padua, where there was less hostility towards her, and settled into the run-down Memmo *palazzo* with Paolina and her four children.* The two sisters had spent some happy times there during their childhood, when their father was governor of the city, and the return to that old family house alleviated the feeling of loss and displacement.

---

* After Cattina and Isabella, Paolina had two little boys, Venceslao and Ferighetto.

At a soirée given by Madame Wallis at the Governor's Palace, Lucia and Paolina were introduced to an engaging Austrian officer of Irish descent, Baron Maximilian Plunkett. Although still in his early thirties, Plunkett was a battle-hardened colonel and one of General Wallis's most trusted military aides. He had come to Italy after the Treaty of Campoformio at the head of the 45th Infantry Regiment, setting up camp near the village of Montagnana, between Este and Padua. He was always rushing in and out of the Governor's Palace, advising General Wallis and staying on for meals and evening entertainment. Lucia was attracted by the mixture of Irish ruggedness and Austrian courtliness. He was not especially handsome, but she sensed the vigour in him, the courage, the discipline. She noticed how his generous character softened the qualities that made him a good soldier: he was warm and charming, and the more they saw each other the more she felt at ease with him.

Maximilian had an unusual background. He came from a prominent Irish family of soldiers, many of whom had emigrated to the Continent over the previous 200 years—at the end of the eighteenth century there were Plunkett officers in both the Austrian and the French armies. Maximilian's father, Thomas Plunkett, had joined the Austrian army as a young man, quickly rising through the ranks to become one of Empress Maria Theresa's favourite generals. His mother, Mary D'Alton, also came from a well-known family of Irish soldiers. Maximilian, one of nine brothers and sisters, was born in Linz in 1768. He was ten years old when his father died. Yet a career in the Austrian army was never in doubt. Still a teenager, he joined the 20th Infantry and went off to fight the Turks in the Ukraine. After the French Revolution, he was transferred to the western front, along the Rhine, and was badly wounded in the battle of Mainz. Promoted to the rank of lieutenant colonel, he took command of the 45th Infantry and joined Wallis's occupation force in Italy.

The company of Lucia and Paolina gave Maximilian a welcome respite from his life at the military camp. He delighted in their bright conversation and bonded easily with both of them. They formed an unconventional trio; when they were not spending the evening at the Wallis residence, they were happy to stroll together down the main street in Padua, look into curiosity shops or savour ices at one of the cafés. Lucia absorbed Maximilian's energy. She felt alive again, eager to be part of the world around her. She had not felt such longing since the death of her son three years earlier, and a sense of gratitude enhanced her admiration for Maximilian. Paolina's presence did not inhibit her: on the contrary, it gave her the strength she needed to embrace her feelings.

Lucia and Maximilian fell in love in the spring of 1798 under the wary gaze of General Wallis and the more benevolent one of Madame Wallis. As a token of her affection, she gave the colonel, as she often called him, a cluster of decorative cordons and tassels she had secretly embroidered during the winter, with which to embellish the flag of his regiment—a gift which moved him deeply, and endeared her to his officers, who wrote her an enthusiastic "thank you" note. Evidently the relationship was widely known about in Austrian circles.

From the beginning of his assignment in Italy, General Wallis had felt it was in everyone's interest to send Alvise abroad for a while, ostensibly to mark Vienna's displeasure at his earlier ties to the French but really more to remove him from a hostile environment. Lucia and Maximilian's burgeoning relationship may have encouraged the general to speed up the paperwork. In June he issued passports for Alvise and Lucia "to take the waters"[2] in Tuscany. It is unclear how much Alvise knew at the time about his wife's romantic involvement—he was seldom in Padua and only for brief stop-overs. In any case, he seemed glad to leave for he was tired of living as a pariah in his own homeland. A period of exile in Tuscany was sure to turn into a useful experience. It would allow him to observe up-close the progress of agriculture in Tuscany and to borrow ideas with which to improve productivity on his own estates.

Lucia was desperate at having to separate herself from the man she was just beginning to love. She was not even sure she would ever see Maximilian again. What if his regiment were transferred before she came back? What he if he had to go back to the front?

How would they keep in touch? As a parting gift, Maximilian gave her a lovely writing set—a small inkwell and a quill made of finely blown glass from Murano. But how safe would it be to write to him?

The Grand Duchy of Tuscany was as pleasant a land of exile as Alvise could have hoped for. In travelling from Venice to the baths in Lucca and then on to Florence, he and Lucia had moved from one Habsburg dominion to another—Archduke Ferdinand being Emperor Francis's younger brother. But unlike the rest of northern and central Italy, Tuscany had remained fairly untouched by Bonaparte's invading armies and the strife that had come in their wake. "One enjoys perfect tranquillity here [in Florence]," Lucia wrote to her sister, longing for news of the colonel. "The people seem delighted with their government and the Archduke is universally esteemed." The inn where they had settled was entirely satisfying: "We have an excellent cook, proper bathrooms and even carriage service."[3] From her room at the Corte d'Inghilterra, she had a full view of the Arno, with the Ponte Vecchio further downstream and olive groves shimmering on the other side of the river, up to the Belvedere.

Alvise and Lucia fell into an easy routine, visiting picture galleries and calling on Florentine friends from their youth. They watched the picturesque boat races down the Arno, which seemed quaint affairs in comparison to the magnificent Venetian regattas down the Grand Canal. "Four little vessels and a rather thin show . . ."[4] Lucia commented. There was something endearingly *passé* in the way the Florentine ladies liked to dress "three years behind everyone else." Some of the clothes she had brought down from Venice were frowned upon as being "excessively jacobinesque"—especially the airy, Grecian-style tunics which became fashionable in Paris during the Directoire, and which Lucia had occasionally worn during the French occupation.

Life was slow yet the atmosphere was cosmopolitan. Florence was a haven for Italian families escaping from either the French or the Austrians. Arch-conservative Roman aristocrats mixed with Bonapartist democrats. The most prominent refugee was Pope Pius VI, who had been run out of Rome by French troops a few months earlier, and was living temporarily in the charter-house overlooking the city. Lucia remembered the elderly pontiff with affection from her Roman days, when he had confirmed her and Paolina in Saint Peter's basilica, and she made a special effort to seek him out. "He lives in the most unhappy state, sustained only by his faith and his courage,"[5] she reported to her sister. But he had brightened up at the memory of his good friend Memmo and was curious to know "how the two of us have done in the world."

Lucia had an ulterior motive in seeking out Pius VI. The convent of Celestia, in Venice, where she and her sister had lived during their childhood after their mother's death and again, later on, as they waited for their marriage contracts to go through, was now off-limits to them as a result of the restrictive policies adopted by the local religious authorities after the arrival of the Austrians. In the face of unceasing turmoil, Lucia was not prepared to lose touch with the one place that had always offered her safe haven. She appealed to the Pope for a special permission to visit the enclosed nuns, and was relieved when he granted a written authorisation to enter the convent once a week. "The permission is for both of us," she informed Paolina. "I couldn't wait to tell you. It has given me such comfort."[6]

The lazy Florentine summer came alive in early August with the stunning news that Lord Nelson had sunk Bonaparte's fleet off the coast of Egypt. After his triumphant Italian campaign, Bonaparte had returned to Paris planning to invade England but had shelved the idea after taking a disparaging close look at the French fleet assembled in the Channel. Instead, he had decided to weaken England by conquering Egypt and threatening the route to India. Soon after his first, successful landing, lack of food and the hostility of the local population had convinced him to set sail again in search of a safer harbour. Lord Nelson had intercepted Bonaparte's dispatch to the Directoire with his new plans. On

1 August he had come upon the French squadron at Aboukir and destroyed it.

It was hard to imagine the invincible Bonaparte stranded in a faraway desert, without a fleet left with which to sail home; but Lucia had, in Naples's minister to Florence, the Duke of Sangro, an excellent source of information (Naples was Lord Nelson's base in the Mediterranean). She filled her reports to Paolina with precise facts and figures, as if only hard news could convey the reality of what had occurred. "The English took nine ships, including a frigate," she wrote in one meticulous account only days after the event.

> Two ships went up in flames and sank, including one which carried all the riches [Bonaparte] had seized in Malta. Only eight French ships managed to get away. But then the Turks massacred the French soldiers as they hit the shore, leaving 4,000 dead in the sand and 1,500 wounded. [7]

With Bonaparte seemingly out of play, Alvise and Lucia became more certain that their future lay in the German-speaking Habsburg Empire. They even embarked on a German-language course. As Lucia explained to Paolina, "[German] will become increasingly necessary to us."[8] Alvise, though talented, showed a singular lack of patience with grammar and put in an average effort. Lucia took the lessons very seriously, but then she had an incentive to learn the language quickly.

At the end of September, nearly three months after she and Alvise had settled in Florence, Maximilian paid a secret visit to Lucia. Preparations were made through Paolina, who had become a fully fledged go-between in the affair. Lucia did not write directly to her lover, and those few notes she received from him she destroyed immediately. Her sister's help was indispensable. It was through her that she sent Maximilian a detailed map of Florence—a copy of the one she used—in order to plan their meetings with the greatest possible accuracy. Lucia's letters to Paolina hint in the vaguest terms that they managed to have a few perfect days to themselves—certainly nothing occurred during Maximilian's stay in Florence to spoil their reunion, and it is possible Alvise was away on a work-related trip somewhere in the Tuscan countryside. In one letter Lucia wrote to Paolina, Maximilian added his own playful note:

> It is from Florence, my dear lady, that I write to you but even as I begin to address you these few words, your sister is already pulling the pen away from my hand. I do want to tell you that I have never been happier . . . If Lucia were not reading these lines I would tell you all the wonderful things she says about you. Forgive this hurried scribble; and tell those adorable creatures of yours I detest them as I detest their mother. Adieu, Madame, someone next to me is forcing me to stop writing, otherwise I would fill all four sides . . .[9]

As the two lovers took walks in the public gardens and visited churches in search of art treasures, Lucia was seeing with new eyes many of the sites she had first discovered with Alvise back in 1786. They made a few purchases together—Florentine fans for Paolina and her two daughters, and a set of paper fish and a rod for the two boys. "The Colonel can teach them how to use the magnet attached to the hook,"[10] Lucia reassured her sister. She added, rather mischievously, that she was showing off her German by whispering a few well-practised sentences to her lover. "But I beg you not to tell a soul about the German lessons I am taking," she insisted, suddenly worried by the possibility that some malicious gossip back in Venice or Padua might draw a connection between her friendship with the colonel and her sudden enthusiasm for the German language. "I wouldn't want people laughing behind my back."[11]

Lucia's happiness was suddenly eclipsed by the news she had long been dreading. Plunkett had kept it to himself all along, so as not to spoil their time together, but at the end of his stay in Florence he confessed that he had been given the command of the newly formed 60th Regiment based in Theresienstadt in Bohemia, and would soon be on his way to Austria to resume fighting the French.

"We shall be losing our worthy friend,"[12] Lucia wrote poignantly to Paolina in her last letter from Florence.

By the end of the summer, Alvise and Lucia were making preparations to leave as well. Alvise, growing restless in Florence, had wanted to spend the winter in Naples, but the arch-conservative Bourbon monarchy denied him passports. Fortunately General Wallis decided his brief exile had lasted long enough and granted him permission to visit his estates on the Venetian mainland. In mid October, Lucia returned to Padua. She was able to see Maximilian again on several occasions during the autumn and early winter before he left.

With Bonaparte still stranded in Egypt, Vienna decided the time was right to strike back at the French and recover its territorial losses in Italy and southern Germany. In January 1799, Maximilian received his marching orders: he was to join forces with General Hotze, in the Voralberg, at the head of two elite battalions from the 60th Regiment. The objective was to take the city of Zurich, a pivotal stronghold for the control of southern Germany. General Hotze, with Maximilian's help, was to protect the right flank of the advancing 80,000-strong Austrian army, led by Archduke Charles.

When Maximilian left Padua, heading for the snow-bound Alps, Lucia was expecting his child. She was only a few weeks pregnant and it is quite possible she did not broach the subject before his departure because she herself was not yet sure of her condition. After the first couple of months, when she no longer had any doubts, communications with Maximilian's regiment were fragmentary at best, and it is unlikely she would have informed him in a letter that had few chances of reaching him and which risked being read by others along the way.

Lucia may well have contemplated seeking the help of an abortionist but it was always a dangerous road to undertake. Besides, the memory of her painful miscarriages, not to mention the death of Alvisetto, probably contributed to push the thought away from her. In the absence of any evidence about how she handled her pregnancy, the simplest explanation seems the truest: she was deeply in love with Plunkett and she decided to have their child no matter what the consequences might be. In any case, she never tried to pass him off as Alvise's issue—husband and wife had probably ceased to be lovers.

Having made her choice, she was relieved to learn that Alvise was about to embark on a long journey abroad. All his adult life he had been trained to govern, to participate in the affairs of Venice. A year had passed since the Austrians had taken power, yet he continued to be isolated. He felt useless, unable to fit in the new ruling class that was being groomed by Vienna. His trips to the countryside became increasingly frantic and soon he was overcome by what he called his *rage de voyager*, his irrepressible urge to travel as far and as long as his heart required. He had experienced such mad wanderlust before in his life, most notably when he had run away from Venice and his family after the humiliating divorce from his cousin, Pisana Mocenigo, and had travelled in Italy and France. This time he conceived a grand journey across the Habsburg Empire.

In late March, when Lucia was already in her fourth month and it was becoming increasingly difficult to dissimulate her pregnancy, Alvise obtained his travelling papers: they stated he was "moving to London with two servants and journeying through Trieste, Lubiana, Graz, Linz, Prague, Dresden, Berlin, Hamburg."[13] It was unclear when he would be coming back. Lucia chose not to tell him she was carrying her lover's child.

It was not a rare thing for married women to have children out of wedlock and there were well-tested ways to give birth discreetly. A pregnant woman might stay on in the countryside long after the end of the *villeggiatura* or she might return to her family of origin for a prolonged stay. Or she might enter a convent "to

1. Andrea Memmo, Lucia's father, was elected Procuratore di San Marco, the most prestigious political office in the Venetian Republic after the one of doge, in 1785, when he was serving as ambassador in Rome.

2. Sebastiano Mocenigo, Lucia's father-in-law, was a complicated man and a difficult father. His rampant homosexuality and outrageous behaviour during his tenures as ambassador to Madrid and to Paris put an end to his diplomatic career: Maria Theresa of Austria refused to accept his credentials as ambassador to Vienna. 3. This ivory miniature of Lucia and her sister, Paolina, when they were little girls was commissioned in the mid-1770s. Their father probably took it with him to Constantinople, where he served as ambassador for four years (1779–82), to lessen the pain of his separation from his two daughters, who remained in Venice with their mother.

4 and 5. Lucia (left) and Paolina, aged sixteen and fifteen, sat for Angelica Kauffmann in the summer of 1786, in the artist's studio in Rome.

6. In the same year Alvise Mocenigo wrote to Andrea Memmo asking for the hand of his daughter Lucia. This is Lucia's reply to her future husband— a man ten years older than her, whom she did not know and who had already been married and divorced.

7. As Venetian Ambassador to Rome, Andrea Memmo and family lived in Palazzo San Marco, the "immense palace." The Venetian ambassador lived in one wing, the Venetian cardinals in the other—an arrangement that led to constant bickering about keys and bills.

8. "I feel so lost when you are away from me," Lucia wrote to her husband, Alvise, shortly after moving into Palazzo Mocenigo, the sprawling family home on Venice's Grand Canal. It was, indeed, an intimidating world to enter for a seventeen-year-old bride, with its grand staircases, its endless halls and its innumerable apartments distributed on four floors, where a crowd of Mocenigo relatives lived on fairly unfriendly terms.

9. A highly symbolic moment in the fall of Venice: the lowering of the four bronze horses from the facade of Saint Mark's Basilica by Bonaparte's troops. The horses, which the Venetians had brought back from Constantinople after the Fourth Crusade, were shipped to Paris and placed atop the new arc de triomphe in the Place du Carrousel.

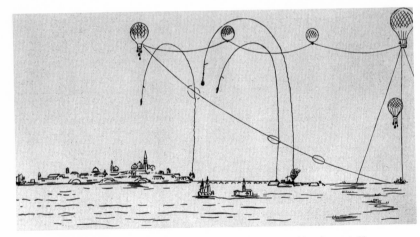

10. During the siege of Venice in 1849, the Austrians dropped bombs carried by air balloons that were strung together by very long ropes. To counter this move, Venetian engineers planned to launch projectiles with ropes attached.

11. Lucia's husband commissioned this statue of Napoleon from Angelo Pizzi with the intention of placing it in the main square in Alvisopoli. Then Napoleon fell and Lucia no longer wanted it. Reluctantly, Lucia had the statue shipped up the Grand Canal to Palazzo Mocenigo. She put it in a shadowy corner on the water-level ground floor, where it stands today.

12. Alvise Mocenigo was especially proud of this etching of Emperor Napoleon and Empress Marie Louise; it was "the first work of art produced at Alvisopoli."

13. The pro-French municipal government established in Venice proclaimed 4 June as a national holiday. The ceremonies were held in Saint Mark's Square. In the foreground, Marina Querini Benzoni, clad in a light Greek tunic, is dancing with Fra' Nani, a priest with strong Jacobin leanings. According to eye-witness reports, there were fewer spectators than those depicted in the painting, and the atmosphere was not cheerful.

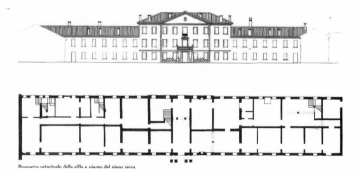

Prospetto principale della villa e pianta del piano terra

14. Facade of the main villa at Alvisopoli and the ground-floor plan. Alvise Mocenigo wanted the main house to be simple, functional and well integrated into the working community. The estate remained in the family until my grandfather sold it in the 1930s. The park behind the villa has survived and is managed by the local branch of the World Wildlife Fund.

15. Empress Joséphine was very fond of this drawing and she gave it to her son, Eugène de Beauharnais. Lucia met the artist David in Paris in 1813 through an old friend of her father. She could see the artist's studio from the window of her apartment.

16. Lucia saw Prince Eugène frequently at the royal palace in Milan when she was lady-in-waiting to Princess Augusta.

17. On one of Lucia's first visits to Malmaison, Empress Joséphine took her upstairs to see her newly refurbished circular bedroom. "It is magnificent," Lucia wrote in her diary. Today it is possible to see the same room at Malmaison just as Lucia described it.

18. In the summer of 1813 Lucia often visited Empress Joséphine at Malmaison, her retreat outside Paris. The decor was very stylish and the atmosphere relaxed. The estate was given to Joséphine by Napoleon as part of their divorce settlement.

19. Lord Byron lived at Palazzo Mocenigo during part of his stay in Venice—here he is seen at work in his study overlooking the Grand Canal. He took a three-year lease at £200 a year—a considerable sum in the Venice of the post-Napoleonic years. His relationship with Lucia, however, grew steadily worse as she proved to be a tough and stubborn landlady.

restore her nerves," as the expression went. Still, the strain on Lucia must have been excruciating, not just because of the daily complexities involved in a clandestine pregnancy but also because of the uncertain future she and her child would face. Was Maximilian coming back from the war? Would she ever have the courage to tell Alvise she had given birth to someone else's child? Would her son or her daughter have to be given away to adoptive parents?

They were daunting questions, which Lucia presumably shared only with Paolina. Indeed, it is hard to see how Lucia could have preserved her secret without her sister's close collaboration. But very few other people knew, apart from her trusted maid, Margherita, and the midwife who was eventually called in to assist her during delivery. It helped, of course, that Alvise was away during this ordeal. But it is unlikely Lucia spent much time at Palazzo Mocenigo at all during her pregnancy. Padua would have been too risky as well. It is possible that she returned to her mother's family estate, Castel Gomberto, north of Vicenza, which she had not visited in nearly a decade, since last taking the waters in Valdagno. There she would certainly have felt protected, in a familiar environment, away from prying eyes. Another possibility is that Lucia made the best of Pope Pius VI's special authorisation to visit Celestia, and spent the latter part of her pregnancy attended by the nuns of the convent which had become, over the years, a second home to her.

At the end of May, six months into her pregnancy, Lucia was relieved to hear from her friends at the Austrian military command in Padua that Maximilian was alive and well. He had found himself thrown into battle as soon as he had joined up with General Hotze's forces in the snowy Voralberg, where the gathering Austrian troops were under the constant fire of General Masséna's soldiers. At the end of the winter, the French had begun their retreat towards Zurich, leaving a sea of melted snow and blood-stained mud in their wake. The Austrians had advanced into Switzerland, occupying the city of Chur, and had continued their pursuit of the French, marching north and taking the French-controlled city of Winterthur, some twenty miles east of Zurich.

According to the battle report now in Vienna's Military Archive, a daring action on the part of Maximilian led to the crucial victory in Winterthur. After a day of fierce fighting, the French began to retreat towards the city, crossing the river Toess. They burnt all the bridges but one, across which the last soldiers scrambled to safety. Maximilian realised the gains of the day would be lost if the Austrians remained stranded on their side of the river. He led a platoon down to the banks of the Toess and followed it downstream until he found a bend where he and his men waded across. In certain points the water rose above their chests and the current was so strong it very nearly took them away. But they managed to reach the other side, climbed a steep ravine and surprised the French rear-guard from behind their lines, capturing the last bridge before it was blown up. Towards dusk the French abandoned Winterthur and began their final retreat towards Zurich.

"We have taken the city," General Hotze wrote in his report, "thanks in large measure to the successful operation carried out by Graf Plunkett at his own initiative and with the help of his excellent troops."[14]

In the early summer, Lucia received a letter from Maximilian telling her he was happy to be alive after falling with his horse over a precipice:

> During the fall I managed to free myself of the stirrups and I landed, miraculously, on soft, marshy ground. I hardly felt the blow. The crowd of people peering down from the roadside were sure I was dead. I returned to our camp and rested. The next day I felt much better and rode from morning until evening to check all our positions.

This rare letter from her lover must have made Lucia very happy, though she told her sister with discomfiture that it was "not enough for Plunkett to face the daily dangers of bloody battles—he also risks his life in deadly accidents!"[15]

Lucia entered the final period of her pregnancy in the summer of 1799, and on 9 September she gave birth to a boy. Two weeks later the baby was christened in the church of Santa Maria Zobenigo, and declared son of parents unknown. However, the name inscribed in the birth registry—Massimiliano Cesare Francesco—left no doubt as to who the father of the little boy was. The Venice Patriarchy, which had control over the birth registry, certainly knew his true identity, and Lucia must have hoped the church would bury this secret as it had so many others. She put little Massimiliano in the care of a warm, friendly woman, Signora Antonia. Nothing else is known about the early stages of Lucia's relationship with her son, though one longs to know whether she made furtive visits to cradle him, whether she nursed him as she had Alvisetto. As in the case of her love affair with Maximilian, she carefully covered her tracks, for she was sure that if the truth ever came out, she would be ruined.

Lucia had only a vague idea where Plunkett was when their child was born. But the military records tell us the story in detail. After the battle of Winterthur, the Austrians advanced towards Zurich and took the city in mid June, opening up the road to southern Germany. Archduke Charles headed towards the Rhineland, while General Hotze and Maximilian remained south of Zurich, waiting for their Russian allies led by General Suvorov to take over their position. The Russians, however, were slow in coming, and all during the summer Maximilian fought to hold the line along the Linthe, skirmishing daily with General Masséna's troops on the other side of the river. When Masséna realised that Suvorov was on his way to join the Austrian contingent, he decided to strike before the Russians' arrival. In the early morning, the French, hidden by the fog rising above the Walensee, attacked the Austrians near the village of Schannis. Maximilian was not with his men but a few miles north, at General Hotze's headquarters in Kaltenbrunner. As soon as he learnt about the butchery taking place at Schannis he rode at full gallop towards the scene. General Hotze went with him, taking a small escort. As they approached the northern shore of the Walensee, the fog became thicker and suddenly they found themselves in a rain of bullets, vainly trying to seek cover from the invisible enemy. General Hotze was killed first. Then Maximilian was hit and fell to the ground, gravely wounded. He died in the arms of one of his soldiers on 25 September, two days after his son's christening at Santa Maria Zobenigo.

The battle raged on all day as the French gained control of the right bank of the Linthe, then lost it, then gained it again. As the two armies clashed, Maximilian's men fought hard to retrieve his body. All day long, as the battle line shifted, they carried the corpse with them and protected it. At the end of the day, the battle was lost. They retreated to the village of Lichtensteig and gave their beloved commandant "a burial worthy of a brave man."[16]

Alvise reappeared in Venice in the late summer of 1801. He had not seen Lucia in twenty-eight months: he knew nothing of what she had gone through during his absence, and he knew nothing of little Massimiliano. For over two years he had zigzagged up and down central Europe, from Dresden to Berlin and all the way to Hamburg, and on to Stockholm, then back down to Brunswick, east to Prague and finally to Vienna. He had never made it to London, but then he had probably never intended to reach England. His itinerary, traceable thanks to brief entries in his diary, looks at first sight like the trail of an aimless wanderer. But closer examination reveals Alvise's design: to make his way gradually to Vienna, gaining familiarity with the political institutions and the sprawling administration of the Habsburg Empire, and collecting useful contacts and letters of recommendation along the way. At the end of his journey he came to a halt in Prague, where he lobbied the Austrian government for a passport to Vienna—evidently the capital was still off-limits to him because of his supposed French sympathies. He bribed an official—he paid a certain Herr Jonek the princely sum of 200 sequins—and after a two-month-long wait, he finally got his passport. "Vienna becomes my fatherland," he wrote in his diary, before heading down to Italy. "I shall buy a house in Austria and bring my family here and settle for good."[17]

During Alvise's long absence, the map of northern Italy had been redrawn in such a way that his estates were now separated by a border. Bonaparte had escaped from Egypt aboard a frigate in the summer of 1799, returning to Paris as a saviour. The corrupt and unpopular Directoire had lost control of the government. Everywhere the Grande Armée was in retreat. The country was in turmoil. Bonaparte became first consul after the *coup d'état* of 18 Brumaire (9 November), and established a de facto military dictatorship. Furious at the way his predecessors had lost "his" rich Italian provinces, he led a new campaign against Austria, driving his men through the Saint Bernard Pass and crushing the enemy in the battle of Marengo on 14 June 1800. Three days later he was back in Milan, the capital of his beleaguered Cisalpine Republic. With the Treaty of Lunéville, he enlarged the Republic to include the river Adige and the city of Verona. As a result, the western Mocenigo estates in the province of Verona were now under French rule, while the eastern estates—Valli Mocenighe, Villabona, Este and Molinato—remained part of the Habsburg Empire.

Alvise decided to sell the Mocenigo estates that were under French rule to raise the necessary cash for a substantial purchase in Austria. However, the legal complications soon confounded him. He abandoned the idea and left the Cisalpine Republic in a huff. The French-controlled territory was in "an appalling state," he wrote in his diary. Bonaparte was "a greatly misunderstood man of evil" who merely wanted "to drain as much money as possible" out of the country. "[Money] is his only goal, his only ambition . . . Everything is in a state of anarchy . . . He destroys all local traditions, banishes religion . . . Nobody is interested in proper administration . . . Instead of putting roots here, the French merely take advantage of the moment."[18] Alvise showed disdain for the Italians in the Cisalpine Republic who had hitched their wagon to the French army. "There is not an honest man to be found in these local committees set up by the government. All they are interested in is their own personal profit." They spent only public money to organise *festas* and to send presents to the French government. "A foreigner travelling through these sad districts in a hurry might draw a different picture," he conceded. "Feasts and spectacles and cries of mirth and long live liberty are everywhere. But who are the actors on this scene? Only thoughtless young men, hiding behind their mighty sabres . . ."[19]

Alvise crossed back into the Habsburg-controlled Venetian territories and put his hopes in the rapidly changing tides of history. "Farewell, my lands," he concluded melodramatically. "If all is temporary, then why shouldn't these [new] borders also be?"[20] He wrote as if he secretly wished Austrian officials would peek into his diary and judge for themselves the extent of his conversion to the Habsburg camp. Alvise was a true chameleon: one only wonders to what degree he was aware of his changing skin, if he was at all.

After the initial shock of her husband's reappearance, Lucia withdrew back into her shell. She had not seen him for so long that he seemed like a stranger to her; and of course there was so much in her own life that she kept hidden from him. How did one resume a marriage after such a long interval and after all that had passed? It was a not a question for which she had a ready answer. Lucia lived in a state of aloofness, waiting passively for her life to lurch forward in a new direction. Several times she told her sister she felt like an "automaton." And so she did not put up any resistance when Alvise, flush with cash from the sale of Villabona, one of the oldest Mocenigo estates, announced they were moving to Vienna. Lucia's heart filled with dread at the idea of leaving her child behind, but still she went about preparing her travelling trunks, and organising the shipping of her winter clothes and of those treasured objects that she hoped would make her stay in Vienna a little easier.

They left Molinato for Vienna on 1 September 1801. The one thing Lucia was not able to face was the separation from her sister. Final arrangements were made in secret as Paolina was staying with them. On the eve of departure, Lucia bid her goodnight standing coldly on the staircase that led to the bedrooms upstairs, forcing herself not to hug her for fear of breaking down. She did not know when she was coming back to Italy—it would certainly be many months before she returned, maybe years. Paolina was her link to Massimiliano; she was the one person with whom she could talk about her son openly and without fear of betraying herself. But she knew that in order to protect her secret she would have to remain silent and never mention him in her letters to her sister—not even to ask what games he liked to play or whether he was eating properly or whether his health was holding up.

Chapter Six

VIENNESE CAROUSEL

The watering season had already passed its peak when Alvise and Lucia arrived in the Austrian town of Baden on 5 September 1801, dusty and exhausted after their long journey from Molinato. They had stopped briefly in Vienna to leave the bulk of their luggage in temporary lodgings before embarking on the final leg to the fashionable resort on the edge of the Wienerwald, two hours south-east of the capital by post. Having travelled from the war-ravaged countryside in northern Italy, they were all the more dazzled by the elegant crowd strolling in the narrow streets. Every year at the end of the summer the emperor and the empress moved to Baden with their large family to take a restorative cure. Viennese society followed, and the Liechtensteins, the Schwartzenbergs, the Furstembergs, the Stahrembergs, the Pallfys, the Lobkowitzes, the Clarys and other grandees of the Habsburg Empire filled the alleys of the thermal station.

As soon as they had settled in their pleasant apartment off the main square, Alvise hurried to purchase tickets for that evening's opera, only to find they had all been sold. After milling about with other disappointed late-comers in front of the theatre, hoping for a last-minute purchase, he glumly made his way back home. Lucia had noticed how even small nuisances of this kind had a way of exacerbating Alvise's persistent feeling of exclusion. Four years had gone by since Venice had become a Habsburg dominion, but his reputation as a *mauvais sujet,* a bad subject of the Empire, still dogged him.[1] He was, however, determined to gain acceptance in Vienna, and he continually reminded

Lucia how important it was to establish good relations with the Imperial Court if they were to hold on to their land in Italy and make Molinato prosper. Moving from Venice to Vienna, making the hurried trip to Baden to catch the end of the season—it was all part of Alvise's effort to establish himself in the Habsburg Empire, which he self-consciously referred to in his diary as his "adopted fatherland."[2]

In Alvise's mind, Lucia, being a more amiable and tactful person than he was, had an important part to play in upholding the good name of the Mocenigos in Austria. A few days after their arrival in Baden, he returned to Vienna to look for a suitable house to move into before winter, and left her to fend for herself until the end of the watering season. To Lucia's chagrin, the handful of Venetian émigrés staying at the resort—most of them conservative patricians who had fled to Vienna after the fall of the Republic in 1797—were of little comfort. They treated her coldly, and many did not even acknowledge her presence when they met her in the street, considering Alvise's collaboration with the French in 1797 as a betrayal of his class. The only matter of any interest to them was whether or not the Golden Book of the Venetian nobility, which Bonaparte had abolished after conquering the city, was going to be reintroduced by the Austrian government. Vienna had yet to reach a decision on this matter and Venetian émigrés, pining for their lost status, felt that Alvise and Lucia's sudden arrival on the scene spelled trouble for their cause.

Fortunately, Lucia ran into some of her old Viennese friends. Her beloved Doctor Vespa, whom she had not seen in eight years, was still in Empress Maria Theresa's service and was in Baden to monitor her eleventh pregnancy! Signor Boschetti, who had come many times to the apartment in Kohlmarkt to arrange Lucia's hair for a small fee when he was a young apprentice, was now the undisputed king of Vienna hairdressers; and he, too, was in Baden, cutting and trimming and powdering the hair of society's best. Of course neither Signor Boschetti nor Doctor Vespa would be able to open the doors of society for her. But they were precious sources of information; and they helped her master the social map of Baden.

Lucia faced an immediate practical problem: in Vienna, and by extension in Baden, it was not proper to be seen in public "in the company of a man other than her husband," as she put it to her sister. Since Alvise was away and the Venetians would not speak to her, she rented a smart-looking horse-buggy to get around town until she made lady friends with whom she could go out.

She quickly became acquainted with the rules and rhythms of social life, pointing out to Paolina the occasional oddity, like the fact that everywhere in the Habsburg Empire one went out for the afternoon stroll at four o'clock, but in Vienna (and in Baden) one went out half an hour later. "At half past six it is time for the theatre, and it is usually over at nine. Then one either joins a small *coterie* or else one goes to one of the larger assemblies, though many simply retire to their homes."[3] Life in Baden had an intimate feeling, very different from the splendour of Vienna. Even the emperor and the empress stayed in a house on the main square that was anything but grand.

Still, the ladies were never casual about their *toilettes*. Within days of arriving, Lucia drew up her first Baden fashion report, noting that "all the dresses have a very high waist, are worn very tightly and have a long train." The popular item of the season was an expensive *bonnet à l'enfant*, so called because it looked like a child's bonnet. Lucia found them rather silly—an outdated throwback to the extravagant bonnets worn by the previous generation. Alvise, after seeing all the ladies wearing one, had insisted she have one too, but she had put her foot down. "They cost a hundred florins each," she told Paolina. "It seemed such a waste of money that I begged him to dispense me from wearing one."[4]

She attended the end of season's *bal masqué*, a festive, informal waltzing party, where the empress mingled in the crowd of masked guests. There Lucia ran into Madame Wallis, whom she had not seen since their days together in Padua. Her husband, General Wallis, had since died, but she was still busy on the social scene and a good friend to have.

Madame Wallis told Lucia that the empress had heard she was

in Baden and had spoken well about her. "She also asked whether I had kept my good looks during all these years," Lucia could not help boasting to Paolina. "Don't tell anyone, I am blushing even as I write this to you . . . But since you are another me, I feel I must keep you informed about what is said of us . . ."[5]

Lucia was soon a familiar figure, trotting along in her buggy on her way to the waters in the morning or taking her ride out at half past four in the afternoon. She began to enjoy exploring the small world of Baden and following its easy routine—it was a way to distract herself from the anxious thoughts about Massimiliano that never left her. The one thing she did not get used to, though, was the sulphurous water she had to drink every morning. It was warm and murky and smelled of rotten eggs washed in chlorine. "Simply bringing the glass close to my lips makes me want to throw up," she complained.[6] Nor was she enthusiastic about sitting with the other ladies in tepid pools of dirty water, especially after finding out that her Austrian companions thought nothing of taking their baths when they were menstruating. "Here women don't really care one way or another," she told Paolina in disgust.[7]

She was happiest out in the countryside, driving her buggy to nearby villages or taking walks in the woods that sloped down to the edge of the town. One of the rituals in Baden was the Monday afternoon excursion out to the gardens of Schonau, the beautiful property belonging to Baron Peter de Braun and his wife, Josephine. Baron de Braun was a very successful impresario who had started out in the business twenty years earlier and had risen to become the director of the Court Theatre. He was by far the most influential person in the world of musical entertainment, and one of the richest. At Schonau, de Braun had turned his flair for entertainment to garden design. He had landscaped his vast estate in the English manner, with rolling hills, leafy groves and natural grottoes. Clear, slow-moving streams connected a network of ponds on which small Ottoman vessels—*caiques*—carried visitors from shore to shore. The focal point of the gardens was the Temple of the Night, a neoclassical building symbolising death, which one reached by entering a maze of underground passages, similar to catacombs, inscribed with maxims for a virtuous life.

A large crowd pressed at Schonau's entrance gate when Lucia arrived there on her first visit. She could not make her way through, but she heard Baron de Braun himself was going to lead a party of dignitaries across the lake, to the temple area. So she walked away from the crowd and over to a wharf where a smaller group of distinguished guests was already waiting for the Baron, ready to take up the seats in a small flotilla. Lucia stepped into the main boat, secured a seat for herself and waited until Baron de Braun appeared. Later, she described the excursion in detail to Paolina:

> The Baron finally arrived, followed by a party of the highest nobility. The large *caique* then sailed across the lake, trailed by two smaller vessels tied together and carrying an orchestra that played music during the brief crossing. We glided straight into a vast cavern hidden behind a sheet of clear, pure falling water. Inside, a crowd of spectators stood watching us from a bridge, under which we passed smoothly. I saw the Emperor and the Empress, the Crown Prince and his sister, mingling among the visitors incognito and watching us pass by. They wore unexceptional clothes and as far as I could see they were not accompanied by any member of the Imperial retinue, nor by any of their servants. Still, I was able to recognise them because I had seen them only a few days earlier. We finally disembarked. [Baron de Braun] held a torch that made light for those in front, while the rest of us stumbled along in perfect darkness. The unevenness of the narrow, tortuous passageway, the sheer number of people pressing against each other, inspired universal silence, and I let myself be carried by the flow until I was seized by nervous giggles. My uncontrolled laughter was all one heard in that gloomy underworld.

Luckily we came to a resting area, with water games and lighting effects produced by artificial fissures in the rocks. Musicians played wind instruments behind a veil of cascading water. Further down the passageway, rest rooms were carved into the limestone and illuminated by lamps of alabaster. The rest rooms were equipped to service twenty-four people of both sexes—here gentlemen and ladies use the same facilities. We continued our journey to the Temple of the Night and were soon enveloped by total darkness, an effect meant to enhance the contrast as we finally reached the temple itself. The building is formed by a circle of columns, sustaining an upper balustrade decorated with cupids. Alabaster lamps in the shape of pyramids illuminate the vaulted ceiling: a deep blue sky, with twinkling stars and a shiny moon. At one side stands a large crater, the Vase of Destiny. It is said that the vase glows in a particular way depending whether the answer to whatever thought is on your mind is yes or no. At the other side is the Book of Destiny, where those who want to question the vase must put down their name. Then a series of mysterious symbols on the ground lead one to the centre of the temple, where the Goddess of the Night stands on her chariot. I've never seen anything in such bad taste as that paltry wax statue being pulled by those scrawny little horses. Baron de Brown [*sic*] should have commissioned a better artist to do the work—Canova would have done a fine job. For a moment I was tempted to let the Vase of Destiny know what I thought about the Goddess of the Night. I caught myself just in time . . .[8]

Lucia emerged from that bizarre netherworld in a daze, and walked up to the main pond. She saw the villa standing on the other side of the water and headed towards it when she suddenly stopped in her tracks: tethered to the mooring near the house, a sleek Venetian gondola slapped and sloshed in the afternoon breeze. What was it doing there? Was this a dream or one of Baron de Braun's fabulous stage tricks? Eventually, a rational explanation formed in her head: the gondola had probably been brought from Venice as a decoration, like the Ottoman *caiques* ferrying the visitors across the ponds. Yet for a long while she could not take her eyes away from that awkward trophy moored, a bit like herself, in waters so far away from home.

That evening, writing to Paolina about her day at Schonau, Lucia dwelt on the strangeness of that moment. For it was not a rudimentary Austrian version of a gondola, she insisted, but "an exact copy of the ones we have back at home." Perhaps for that reason it had taken her so long "to let go of the illusion that I was in a familiar place with you; not in Venice of course, because of the bucolic surroundings, but perhaps somewhere along the Brenta canal."[9] She missed Paolina terribly, and told her how sorry she was to have deceived her the night before her departure. "If I had given in to my feelings and had hugged you tight, you would have guessed the truth," she wrote tenderly. "The coldness I forced myself to display, and which I was so far from feeling, is the true measure of how hard it was for me to leave you."[10]

From the beginning of their stay in Austria, it was clear to Lucia that Alvise had no intention of spending more time in Vienna than was strictly necessary. Indeed, his plan was to travel back and forth between Italy and Austria, but Molinato would continue to absorb most of his energies. Lucia, on the other hand, was to stay in Vienna, set up house with the help of her maid, Margherita, and lay the groundwork for their entrance in society. At the end of September, Alvise took a five-year lease on a pleasant apartment off Saint Stephen's Square, with tall windows and a side view of the cathedral. It was not a grand or showy set-up, but it was elegant and spacious enough that she would be able to entertain adequately when the time was right. Lucia set about her task with diligence, even a certain meticulousness. She hired a cook, who installed himself with his wife; and two more maids,

Teresa and Felicita, to assist Margherita. Checco the groom completed the staff. It felt a little awkward to have so many people working in an empty house, but she reminded herself she was merely planning ahead. Still, she was concerned that she was going to be living much of the time as a single woman in a city which, she soon discovered, treasured family unity—or at least the appearance of it.

Extending the kindness she had displayed in Baden, Madame Wallis went out of her way to introduce Lucia in Vienna. She organised a small birthday dinner at her house. Among the guests were Princess Stahremberg, Countess Maillath, Baroness Zois, Count Moravieff and Duke Albert of Saxony-Teschen, whom Lucia had heard so much about when she was still in Venice (grief-stricken after the loss of his wife, Archduchess Maria Christina, in 1798, the duke had commissioned a large funerary monument from Canova that was on its way to Vienna). These were the first names Lucia diligently wrote down, together with their addresses, in a brown leather notebook that was to become her personal social registry. She used those initial introductions to gain access to other illustrious houses, and planned her courtesy visits dividing the city up by areas and neighbourhoods. She called on an average of two to three houses a day, and always wrote down the address and the date. She drew a map and kept a precise tally.

Anxious to own property in Austria in order to demonstrate his allegiance to the Habsburgs, Alvise purchased Margarethen am Moos, a large estate a few hours south-east of Vienna that looked out on the plains stretching towards Hungary. Lucia was not enthused by what she saw when Alvise took her out to view the property before he left for Italy. The house was damp and austere-looking. The fields around it were soggy and teeming with mosquitoes. The garden had gone to seed long ago. She felt the place had never been happy. In medieval times, she discovered, Margarethen am Moos had been a frontier outpost. For centuries fierce Magyars had crossed the plains to make bloody incursions into Habsburg territory. In fact the main house had originally been built as a castle—a fortified quadrilateral with a tower and a moat and a rickety bridge over the water. The tower had been torn down in the eighteenth century by the Harsch family, the last owners, in an attempt to make the place a little more inviting. The facade was renovated in the Austrian neoclassical style. But the building never quite lost its dreariness.

Lucia tried to make the best of it, reminding herself, and her sister, that Alvise had purchased the estate principally "to satisfy his wish to own property" in Austria. "It is not intended as a country home at all, as Alvise doesn't much like living in the country here."[11] If the estate at Margarethen am Moos was to serve a purpose, apart from making Alvise a landowner in Austria, it would be as a testing ground for crops and fertilisers and planting techniques that might eventually be used at Molinato.

One thing Lucia did not immediately realise, and which she discovered only after Alvise had left her in charge of the place, was that the Harsch family was still waiting to be paid. Alvise had sold part of Villabona to purchase a property in Austria, but in fact he had ploughed a substantial portion of the sale into Molinato. Once in Vienna, he had only enough cash remaining to make a down-payment of 25,000 florins to finalise the purchase of Margarethen. He signed an agreement to pay the balance of 105,000 florins within a year, hoping to raise the sum directly from the revenue of the estate. It was a risky gambit, but Alvise was convinced he could easily generate higher income by digging drainage ditches to improve cultivation, as he had done at Molinato, and by running the farm more efficiently. He drew up a work-plan before leaving for Italy, and instructed Lucia to supervise its implementation until he returned in the spring.

Every year, in late May and early June, Viennese society broke up into small clusters and moved to various summer retreats. Alvise promised Lucia that upon his return they would travel together for a few weeks down the Danube and up the Elbe, into Saxony, before returning to Margarethen for the harvest season. But in the end he backed out, on the grounds that he had too much to do in Molinato. Besides, he had already toured Saxony during his solitary travels across northern Europe.

Lucia decided to leave anyway—the alternative was to sit in a dusty and empty Vienna, or listen to the crickets and toads at Margarethen. In early July she visited Madame Wallis at her house near the thermal baths of Carlsbad, in Upper Bohemia. From Carlsbad, she continued on to Toeplitz, the seat of Prince Clary's summer *palazzo*, where Giacomo Casanova—a close friend of her father's—had been a frequent and popular dinner guest until his death four years earlier. She found the house still rang with echoes of his merry mischief.

Lucia followed the Elbe downstream, navigating through a romantic landscape "dotted with the ruins of feudal castles." Often journeying alone, she kept up her spirits by taking copious notes and writing to her sister about the gardens along the river. "Flowers grow in great profusion and the wild roses and carnations are especially beautiful," she reported. "There are fruit trees everywhere and the fruits are as tasty as they are back home. Flies, too, are as insolent as they are in our parts. I'm losing my patience with them even as I write this letter."[12] She was in Teschen on 7 August, and spent the night "in a magnificent castle on a rock, with a sweeping view of the most enchanting countryside." The next day she arrived in Pillnitz, where she toured the beautifully landscaped gardens at the country estate of Frederick Augustus, Elector of Saxony—those very same gardens, Lucia noted for her younger sister's edification, where the emperor of Austria and the king of Prussia had met in 1792 to discuss "the war against France that eventually led to the downfall of our [Venetian] Republic."[13] In Dresden, she was a guest of the young von Metternichs. Count Clement, at twenty-eight a rising star in Austrian diplomacy, was Vienna's minister to Saxony. He had married Eleanor von Kaunitz, daughter of Empress Maria Theresa's minister, Anton von Kaunitz. Eleanor presented Lucia to court and took her to see the famous picture galleries, the cabinet of antiquities and the porcelain collections. The Metternichs also organised a day-trip to the renowned porcelain factories in

Meissen. Dresden was the first Protestant city Lucia visited. She was fascinated by Protestant churches, which reminded her more of public theatres, with their galleries and parterres, than they did of Catholic churches.

She made her way back to Vienna via Prague, rushing a little as she had been away two months and was tired and eager to be home. She arrived on 4 September, a day earlier than scheduled, meaning to surprise Alvise, who was back in town, and had gone to Prince Colloredo's for an evening of gambling. Lucia told Margherita and the rest of the staff to hide while she waited for him in a dark passageway that led to his apartment. When he returned home he found the house in total darkness. Lucia spoke from her hiding place. "He heard my voice but could not see me, and he was taken completely by surprise."[14] Her childlike delight was a measure of how glad she was to be home with her husband.

Alvise stayed the few weeks that were necessary to plan work at Margarethen. He was not happy with the way the farm was run. The soil was still too soggy in large parts of the estate and he ordered the digging of more drainage ditches. He oversaw the planting of different crops—wheat, barley, alfalfa—in the drier fields further away from the house, and he hired the manager of the local beer factory, Herr Schedel, to run day-to-day operations. But Lucia was to stay on top of things, and keep Alvise informed with detailed reports. She was also to go over accounts, in Vienna and Margarethen, and send balance-sheets at the end of each month. Having given his set of instructions, Alvise was off again, promising Lucia he was going to return in time to celebrate her saint's day on 13 December.

Lucia never openly complained about Alvise's long absences in her letters to Paolina, but traces of her disappointment were just below the surface. "It is very important here in Vienna to display family harmony," she wrote, adding touchingly that "the appearance of it often generates the actual substance: leading the same life, spending a lot of time together—it helps bring two people closer, it helps them join their souls."[15] After all that had passed—the birth of Massimiliano, the death of Plunkett, the shock of Alvise's return, the move to Vienna—Lucia was willing to make a new start with Alvise. By living together in "family harmony" she hoped they might generate "the actual substance."

Was Alvise listening to Lucia? In his diary, he had proclaimed rather emphatically to himself that he was moving his "family" to Vienna. So far, he had moved only his wife. During that first year in Austria, he was with her a mere few weeks; and he was always on the go, always restless, clearly reluctant to put roots in his "adopted fatherland." In the eyes of Lucia, Alvise was still, in many ways, the inscrutable, enigmatic person she had married fifteen years before. So it was not without a certain wistfulness that she set about organising her life in Vienna without him.

Running the households in Vienna and Margarethen, keeping the accounting books in good order and writing her reports to Alvise kept Lucia busy and gave a structure to her daily life. She actually enjoyed working with numbers and discovered she had quite a knack for good management, always looking for ways to run things more efficiently. The memory of her father's uncertain finances during her youth had remained vivid and, perhaps as a reaction, she was generally parsimonious and very meticulous about keeping track of her personal expenses. She liked to follow a general rule she had picked up from Madame de Genlis, her favourite writer, and which she passed on to Paolina: "Divide your monthly stipend three ways: the first for alms-giving and charity, the second for clothes, the third for treats and entertainment such as coffee, tickets to the theatre, ice creams, toys for the children."[16]

When she had time to spare, in between her regular trips out to Margarethen, she ran errands and went shopping for Paolina and her nieces and nephews. She was always wrapping packages of some kind or another to send to Italy—winter boots, clothes, books, toys. She once bought an amusing set of wax ice creams and sherbets for the children. Before sending them off to Paolina, she took the ice creams over to old Doctor Vespa, thinking a practical joke would cheer him up after the mild stroke he had suffered. It did—especially when he discovered she had also brought real vanilla ice cream, which he ate with delight.

In the evenings Lucia often went to one of Baron de Braun's

productions at the opera house. She was usually home for supper shortly after nine o'clock, arriving with her head full of dust raised by the evening traffic of carriages. Before going to bed, Margherita cleaned and combed her hair as they chatted about the day's events.

As the winter season approached, her social schedule grew busier. "I have an assembly with dancing and supping at the Russian Embassy today," she wrote to Paolina, showing off a bit. "Tuesday a ball at Court. Wednesday another ball at the Coblentz's. Thursday I'll be at Count Zichy's and then at Prince Esterhazy's."[17] Lucia discovered how ridiculously difficult it was, in these circumstances, to fix an appointment with Signor Boschetti. "I sent out for him at seven in the morning so that he could fix my hair today but he had apparently left the house at six because he had so many heads to do. His wife said thirteen messengers had come by before mine, and all to no avail."[18] She was grateful to have Margherita.

In general Lucia preferred large events to smaller gatherings because she was freer to leave when she wanted. She sometimes enjoyed the informality of dinners and soirées in private houses, but she seldom found the conversation stimulating. It could also be downright silly, with guests falling off their chairs with laughter for the most trivial reasons.

One evening, at Princess Clary's, the assembled guests were evoking the good times they had had the previous summer at the Clarys' *palazzo* in Toeplitz. Someone mentioned a play they had staged, adding that a Countess Golowkin's acting had been especially pleasing.

"Oh, she couldn't possibly have pleased the public because she is too ugly for words," Count Hohental blurted out, unaware that the gentleman sitting just a few seats away was none other than Count Golowkin.

"Ah, but her ugliness is balanced by her spirit and her amiability," Countess Hohental replied, realising her husband's *faux pas*. But there was no stopping Count Hohental: "My dear, spirit and amiability count for little when one is *that* ugly."

Count Golowkin lamely defended Countess Golowkin: "I agree no one would want her as a lover, but she will do as a wife."

"Oh no no no! Not as wife and not as a lover," Count Hohental insisted, mimicking poor Countess Golowkin's traits. By this time the rest of the assembly was cracking up. Old Prince de Ligne could not hold his giggles any more and hobbled out to the billiard room in a fit of hysterical laughter. Count Hohental, still completely oblivious to what was going on around him, joined the Prince de Ligne and innocently enquired who the tiresome Russian in the drawing room was. "He is Count Go-low-kin," the old Prince stammered, choking on his guffaws. Count Hohental turned red in the face. "Oh my, what a terrible thing I have done! And to think that I am always so careful not to cause the slightest displeasure around me."[19]

Lucia no doubt had a laugh at the expense of the ugly Countess Golowkin. Yet by the time she reached home and sat down to describe the scene to her sister, an unpleasant after-taste had already blemished the pride she had felt at being invited to a soirée in one of the most exclusive houses of Vienna. How easy it was to fall prey to malevolent chit-chat or to be laughed at behind one's back, she wrote, realising that no amount of compliments and fancy invitations were going to protect her from becoming herself a conversation piece—as indeed she was soon to be, and in that very drawing-room at Princess Clary's.

Margarethen became a little less inhospitable after Lucia brought new furniture from Vienna, hung a few Venetian paintings and prints, and substituted the worn upholstery with more colourful fabrics. Her regular tours of inspection at their country estate became welcome pauses from the pressures of her social life. Herr Schedel's wife, Maria, was a big, good-natured woman from a village near Verona, and Lucia enjoyed the long chats with her in the large country kitchen filled with the familiar smells of dishes from back home. Maria baked an excellent *pan casalino,* a bread typical of the Veneto. Lucia pronounced it "as good as the bread at Molinato."[20] She always took fresh loaves of it back to Vienna for her Venetian friends, winning over the more cantankerous émigrés with her deft *pan casalino* diplomacy.

"The milk, the butter, the cream at Margarethen are also excellent," Lucia told Paolina. "I sleep ten hours in a row. I have a good appetite when I am out there, I have a rosy complexion and I feel very well."[21] Indeed, some of her Viennese lady friends said she had changed so much they would not have recognised her as the same person who had arrived in Vienna the year before.

"My grief, too, is finally lessening," she added hesitantly. Three years after Maximilian's death in the early-morning fog of the Walensee, Lucia realised she at last had the strength to look into the eyes of the colonel as he faltered to the ground, bullet-ridden—and hold her gaze. Even the absence of her little boy became a bit more bearable. She missed him terribly, but she did not worry as much about his well-being for she knew that with Signora Antonia he was in the best possible hands.

In Margarethen, Lucia's main outdoor activity was to stand over muddy ditches and supervise work on the large-scale drainage system Alvise had devised. She planned a rose garden around the house that was going to keep her busy in the spring, and a sizeable vegetable patch to supply the household needs in Vienna. She also became fixated with the idea of making money by growing safflower, a plant that produced a red dye much in demand.

Lucia first heard about safflower (*Carthamus tinctorius*) from Doctor Vespa, who in turn had heard about it from Empress Maria Theresa. At the time, safflower was imported mostly from India and Egypt, and was very expensive. But a Tyrolean farmer by the name of Herr Colonna, who was related to a girl employed at the Imperial Palace, discovered he could grow safflower in colder climates too. It seemed a good business opportunity. The empress financed Herr Colonna with an imperial grant worth 700 florins, and the venture took off very promisingly. Lucia decided to get into the safflower business, even though Alvise was sure to react with scepticism. She encouraged Paolina to seize this chance to shore up her own family finances, and sent her two boxes of the precious seeds. "I would be so happy if I could get you to plant at least a field or two . . . It would look beautiful too—a carpet of red powder puffs. And once they wilt you gather the dead plants and sell them to the dyer."[22]

Lucia enjoyed conjuring up schemes to make a little extra money for Paolina and herself. She drew up simple, common-sense business plans that required only minimal investments. Together they purchased a few geese, fattened them at Margarethen and sold them at the local market. With the profit, they bought a piglet that grew into a hefty sow and gave birth to more piglets. They owned a flock of sheep that grazed at Molinato until it was time to sell their wool. "The sow has recovered well," ran a typical update on their small commerce.

> She gave birth to seven piglets, which will soon be able to reproduce. What shall we do next, my dearest sister? I favour selling five of the seven piglets, and keeping two of the females so as to double the size of our business. As for the geese, I would use the profit from their sale to buy another four, unless you feel we can get a lamb for the same price . . .[23]

As the days grew colder and the freezing Austrian winter set in, Lucia reduced her trips to Margarethen. She could see herself staying out there "quite happily, surrounded by snow,"[24] if Alvise were with her and she had friends to visit, or, even better, if Paolina and her children were visiting. But the prospect of being snowbound with the German staff for weeks was not so appealing. So she tucked herself in the town apartment, waiting for Alvise to come up from Molinato. She watched the first snow flurries swirling in the street below her windows. Despite the weather, she kept up her routine of dropping by two or three houses a day, dutifully writing down in her notebook the name of the family and the date of her visit.

In early December, Empress Maria Theresa had her ninth child. She named him Charles, like the emperor's brother, the popular commander of Austria's army under whom Plunkett had fought in Switzerland. It occurred to Lucia that nearly ten years had passed since she had given birth to Alvisetto while across the street from Kohlmarkt, in the Hofburg, the young empress was about to deliver Crown Prince Ferdinand. Since then, Theresa had given birth practically every year, and Doctor Vespa had always been at her side. He had followed this last pregnancy as well. But he was old, he had suffered a stroke, and when the time came to deliver the child, Theresa had called upon the services of a younger obstetrician. The empress had softened the blow by writing a very touching letter which the doctor had read so many times, tears streaming down his wrinkled old cheeks, that he knew most of it by heart. When Lucia went to check on him, he read it to her, "holding it open in his hand but looking at me all the time."

"Dear Vespa," the letter began, "a sense of duty and obedience has forced me to call on someone else on this occasion and God only knows how much I have suffered because of this." The empress went on to assure him that she would not be at ease until she knew he was "happy and at peace." Her greatest wish was to see him again soon, but if he chose not to come to see her after what had happened, at least he should let her know whether he was, in fact, happy and at peace. In the meantime she was pleased to announce to him that as a reward for his long service, the emperor was making him a baron. She signed "your very affectionate Theresa."[25]

For once Alvise kept his promise and arrived in time for Lucia's saint's day on 13 December, only to find he was excluded from the official, ladies-only celebration. The custom in Vienna was for a close friend to give an open-ended lunch party at which lady-guests dropped by to exchange kisses and offer a small present to the honouree. Lucia was feted in the house of Marietta Contarini, a lively, warm-hearted woman, and one of the few Venetians who had welcomed her with open arms when she had arrived in Vienna. Maria was a cousin of Alvise's, and she belonged to an old Venetian family which had given to the defunct Republic one more doge than the Mocenigos—eight against seven. In the old days, this unique ducal rivalry had been taken fairly seriously by the two families. Now, whenever someone brought it up in the conversation, as they did again during the lunch at Marietta's, the story had a bittersweet note.

Lucia needed a little time to readjust to Alvise's presence in the house after his long absences. But in the end she was always glad to have him with her, glad to be escorted out in society or at the theatre. Despite the chilly weather, they took long walks at the Prater, often lunching at the Lusthaus, the imperial hunting lodge at the end of a long alley which had been turned into a pleasant restaurant during the reign of Joseph II. When the first big snowfalls came, the white city became silent save for the muffled sounds of cab drivers and bells ringing. They went to the sled races, and Lucia picked up the habit of rubbing her nose with snow to prevent it from freezing. Apparently, she had seen the Russians do it. Or so she told Paolina.

Baron de Braun's big production of the season at the Court Theatre was Cherubini's *Medea*. All of Vienna turned up for opening night. Lucia, too, was walking a stage of sorts, and she did her best to put in a pleasing performance for her husband. Alvise was impressed at how gracefully she made her way through the glittering foyer, nodding and greeting and often introducing him as she went along. Lucia was much complimented, the production was splendid—a perfect evening, if one of Vienna's renowned pickpockets, mingling among the theatregoers, had not disappeared with Alvise's new embroidered wallet.

On Christmas Eve Alvise and Lucia attended midnight mass at Saint Stephen's Cathedral with the highest-ranking nobility. Next day, her hair still in curlers, Lucia watched from her window as the emperor and empress arrived for Christmas mass. It was a dazzling show, the rich plumage of the mounted imperial guards mixing with the colourful uniforms of a hundred grenadiers. A crowd of onlookers filled the square and waited in silence throughout the mass, until the bells of Saint Stephen's rang out, and Francis and Theresa emerged from the church, waving to the cheering populace. Lucia smiled at the thought of Paolina. "If only you were here with me this very instant," she scribbled to her sister, "watching the Empress surrounded by chamberlains and guards as she steps into the imperial carriage . . ."[26]

In January the pace of social life in Vienna became dizzying, and Alvise and Lucia found themselves in a whirlwind of soirées, assemblies, dinners and balls. "All the houses in Vienna are open to us and I dare say it is impossible to be more ubiquitous than we are," Lucia boasted to Paolina, listing her engagements as much to impress her sister as to keep track of her complicated schedule.

> Sunday we have an assembly at Count Colloredo's, Monday a soirée at Countess Lasranski's, Tuesday an assembly at Count Trautsmandorff's, followed by a coterie at Countess Cageneck's, Wednesday an assembly at the Cobentzels', Thursday an assembly at Countess Lasranski's, Friday a soirée at the Cobentzels', Saturday an assembly at Countess Kollowrath's, Sunday a dinner at Charles Zichy's . . . Next week Duke Albert [of Saxony-Teschen] is giving a ball, and Alvise insisted I buy a new dress for the occasion. Forty sequins![27]

For the first time Alvise and Lucia hosted their own social events as well. The week before Christmas they held an assembly starting around nine o'clock in the evening, after the theatre. Over 300 guests filled their apartment, drinking champagne and picking at the dishes prepared by the French cook with the help of Margherita, Teresa and Felicita. "Your assembly, my dear, is a veritable feast," Princess Stahremberg whispered in Lucia's ear at the sight of the merry crowd.[28] In early January, they had a more intimate soirée, and a week later they hosted a ball—the final step in Lucia's initiation after an apprenticeship that had lasted eighteen months.

Lucia chose her dress with special care. She wanted to look

fashionable without appearing too daring, mindful that Vienna was always at least a season behind Paris. She greeted her guests in a long white taffeta dress, rimmed at the bottom by a silk garland, also white. Over the dress, she wore a white knee-length tunic lined with two stripes of silver. She had long, light grey sleeves and a matching camisole, and wore a string of pearls mixed with Venetian glass beads. Her hair was combed backwards, into a bonnet crowned with a bouquet of large and fluffy white flowers. A light make-up gave her a natural look. "The French call it *couleur intéressante*,"[29] she informed her sister in her next-day report, pleased that everything had gone smoothly and that her dress had been much admired. Was it too extravagant for Paolina's taste? Lucia thought it probably was, given her sister's habit of dressing so unassumingly. "But then we do have different tastes, don't we? I like to be among the first to wear the latest fashion, because it always ends up being adopted by everyone else—especially if it comes from abroad. You, on the other hand, won't even wear a coat if it looks too new. What can I say?" she asked teasingly. "I think you're wrong!"[30]

Alvise had every reason to be grateful for Lucia's success in Vienna. The cloud that still hung over him when he had arrived a year and a half earlier had dissolved thanks largely to her amiable character and her determination. She had restored the Mocenigo name to respectability without appearing eager or calculating, and slowly she had built an ever-larger circle of friends. Her well-worn leather notebook bore testimony to her efforts. By the end of the winter she had paid 114 courtesy visits to all the important houses, criss-crossing the city from Prince de Ligne's modest palace off the Place des Ecossais to Prince Esterhazy's grand estate near the High Bridge over the Danube.

Lucia had also succeeded in the smaller but no less impressive feat of making peace with the grouchy Venetians, including old Francesco Labia, the dean of the émigrés, who had refused to speak to them when they had arrived. "Now he too wishes to be our friend," she noted with satisfaction.[31] The Vienna government decided not to reinstate the Golden Book of the old Venetian nobility after all, but to give out Austrian titles instead, and only after a careful examination of each request. The more nostalgic Venetians felt rather glum about the irrevocable demise of that age-old symbol of the Republic. To cheer them up, Lucia often had them over for a plate of steaming polenta. "All Venetians must know our house is a second home to them,"[32] Alvise proclaimed at one of these gatherings—enjoying his new role as much as his guests were enjoying the tasty polenta he had brought from the mills of Molinato.

Alvise did not really care about the Golden Book one way or another. The Venetian oligarchy was dead and gone, he always reminded Lucia, and there was no point in looking back. His home, now, was Molinato. For nearly a decade he had worked tirelessly to build a modern, self-sufficient community. He had poured huge amounts of money into the project, and had pursued his goal single-mindedly, always putting the needs of the estate above everything else, including the needs of his wife. Of course it was a grand design, the kind of utopian project that was usually the prerogative of wealthy princes and kings. But in a way, that is how Alvise saw himself: the founder of a small, enlightened republic that replaced in his heart the one he had lost. So he felt especially gratified when the Vienna government informed him that the emperor had granted his petition to give his domain of Molinato a new name: Alvisopoli, the city of Alvise.

Alvise returned to Italy at the end of January so he did not witness Lucia's final consecration: her part in the Carousel, the most eagerly awaited event of the season. It was held two days after Mardi Gras, in the Winterreitschule, the beautiful riding school on the ground floor of the Imperial Palace. Twenty-four expert horsemen, selected from the great houses of the Empire, were divided into four quadrilles: two German, one Hungarian and one Polish. In the old days, when the Turks were Austria's greatest enemy, the purpose of the game was to slice off a symbolic Moor's head placed at the top-end of a pole. Now it was a far less gruesome affair. A ring had replaced the head of the Moor, and the real challenge was in performing a dazzling array of figures and sequences. An element of courtly love had also been added. Each horseman invited a dame to the Carousel. At the end of the performance she presented him with a silk scarf: the prize for his ability and a token of her love. *Donner l'écharpe,* the offering of the scarf, had replaced the head-chopping as the highpoint of the event.

Lucia had not anticipated an invitation to the Carousel as it was unusual for a foreigner to be asked. She was very flattered when Count Callenberg, of the Polish quadrille, asked her if she would accept giving the scarf to him. Callenberg had been a close friend and a comrade in arms of Maximilian's, from whom he had taken over command of the 45th Infantry Regiment. In Vienna, he had become a friend and admirer of Lucia. Inviting her to participate in the Carousel was a way for the two of them to celebrate Maximilian's memory—their secret, as it were.

The other dames in the Polish quadrille were Princess Lobkowitz, Countess Lanskranka and Princess Stahremberg, who had so complimented Lucia on the success of her assembly. Lucia was flattered to be the only foreign member of the Polish quadrille, and indeed of the entire Carousel. Later, it occurred to her that in the eyes of Vienna she was perhaps no longer a foreigner at all, now that Venice was part of the Habsburg Empire.

The Carousel was taken very seriously by all the participants. Lucia sensed the tension that was growing by the day. "The horsemen's young wives," she noted, "are exceedingly worried about how their husbands will perform."[33] During the daily practices, the Winterreitschule became society's favourite meeting place, its colonnaded gallery turning into an elegant drawing-room filled with chattering guests. Even government officials and high-ranking ministers dropped by at the rehearsals to catch the latest gossip.

On the day of the Carousel, the hall was packed, the lower and upper gallery overflowing with spectators in their grand gala attire. The emperor and empress took their seats in the imperial stand at one end of the hall. At the other end, four trumpeters entered the arena, followed by a sea of fluttering feathers. The twenty-four horsemen in their flashy uniforms made their entrance into the great *manège,* or riding school, and lined up to salute their dames. The quadrilles broke up into beautiful arabesques with perfect timing and grace. The shiny blues and reds and yellows and greens of the different uniforms created a feast of colours as the horsemen burst into roaring charges and rumbling *contre-danses.* Lucia was overwhelmed by the spectacle. A beaming Callenberg steered his horse towards her, and she rose, lifting and waving the Polish banner. Callenberg then pulled out a scroll and read aloud the sonnet he had composed for her—not the greatest poetry, but an honest effort:

> *The trumpets blare,*
> *The proud horseman*
> *Enters the arena.*
> *He has a natural instinct for battle:*
> *He stiffens his chest, his arms and feet,*
> *And firmly holds his steed.*
> *The memory of ancient feats sharpens his skill*
> *As he dashes the skull to the ground.*
> *The soldier*
> *Can taste victory,*
> *But his heart is not satisfied,*
> *And he stands uncertain.*
> *"Shall I find glory in battle," he asks,*
> *"Or seek my destiny in your beautiful eyes?"* [34]

Lucia handed Callenberg his well-earned scarf. She took the scroll on which the sonnet was inscribed, pressing it to her heart.

That evening, at the *bal masqué* given by the twenty-four horsemen, the guests wore costumes from Valachia, Bukhovina, Morlaquia and other exotic lands of the Habsburg Empire. Only the waiters serving at the tables laden with cakes and pastries and ice creams and candied fruits seemed to have a proper, recognisable uniform. Lucia went as a young Greek from an island in the Ionian archipelago which had long been part of the Venetian Empire. Empress Maria Theresa asked her what she was dressed as. "A Dalmatian," she fibbed, knowing how fond the empress was of Dalmatia.[35] She was dressed as a Greek, but she did not forget she was in the heart of Austria.

Lucia looked forward to spending the summer and autumn in Venice. After two years in Vienna she was curious to see how the city had changed under the Austrians. Alvise was not going to open Palazzo Mocenigo since he planned to be in Alvisopoli most of the time, so she fancied taking a nice apartment in the Procuratie, on Saint Mark's Square, where her father had lived after they had returned from Rome fifteen years earlier. Would it be safe to take Massimiliano there some afternoons? He was going to be four in September. Would she recognise him? Would he remember her at all? For two years she had kept every loving thought about her little boy buried inside her. Now her mind was racing ahead, and she could not wait to hold him in her arms. So it was a shock for her to learn from Alvise that her trip to Italy had to be postponed until late autumn. Her presence at Margarethen during the time of harvest in the summer was required because he had lost confidence in the management there. Lucia accepted with the greatest reluctance—she felt she had done her duty in Vienna for the sake of the Mocenigo family.

There was more bad news. Paolina had recently given birth to another baby girl, Lucietta. Now Lucia learnt that the baby named in her honour had died of pneumonia, the same illness that had killed Alvisetto. She tried to console Paolina:

> My dear sister, think of all the good you have given to that innocent soul who is now in heaven. I cannot stop the tears as I write these words but I do believe them to be true. And I'll go so far as to say that you have now made your offering to the Lord and that you must believe it is for her own good. I know such an effort requires us to stifle our natural feelings, but you are capable of such Christian heroism . . . Remember this, my sister: you must think only about staying strong. You cannot let yourself go, for the sake of the other

children. It is your duty now, and I live in the hope that you fulfil it.[36]

Lucia was quite hard on Paolina, perhaps because she feared her sister, who was the more fragile of the two, was letting herself fall apart.

We all have to walk down the same path, and to let yourself go like this to a loss that is Heaven's will is not a Christian behaviour . . . Don't lose control, don't allow grief to become so overwhelming that it will destroy your health, because you will only hurt those who love you without bringing back to life those who have ceased to be mortals.[37]

Lucia spoke from her own experience, and in the steely words she addressed to Paolina one catches an echo of the struggle with the death of her own son. She warned Alvise that if Paolina gave the slightest sign of illness, she was getting on the first post to Venice, and was going to travel night and day by the Pontiebba road—the shortest route but the roughest—and he should not try to stop her. Her greatest fear was to see her sister succumb to her grief. "If such a thing should occur," she pleaded with Paolina, "I beg you to inform me by special courier, or even better, by sending someone in person."[38]

The summer in Margarethen was stressful enough, what with the staff not getting along, the accounts in disorder, and the German manager utterly unreliable. But the lack of any kind of distraction—no interesting excursions, no amusing guests—made the waiting even more nerve-racking. Lucia did a little gardening around the house, played cards with Margherita, read a new collection of moral essays by Madame de Genlis and ate large quantities of *pan casalino*. Her only break came in September, when she went to Baden for a cycle of mud baths and soakings, but that was hardly much fun: she had her period and did not bother to finish the cure. On her last night there, the empress invited her to her box at the theatre and she was surprised to find herself placed next to the emperor—a seating arrangement that would have made her quite boastful only a few months before, but which she now related rather matter-of-factly to her sister.

Back in Margarethen, Lucia found a letter from Alvise. He urged her to leave for Alvisopoli at once. He gave no explanation for the sudden rush, but his tone was harsh. A feeling of dread came over Lucia as she became certain that there was only one possible reason for such a cold summons on the part of her husband: he had discovered the truth about Massimiliano. During the following days she turned silent and numb as she packed her things. She left Margarethen on All Saint's Day and headed for the mountains. The weather was cold and rainy and she no longer looked forward to the rough journey across the Alps.

Chapter Seven

THE EDUCATION OF ALVISETTO

Lucia returned to Vienna in May 1804, six months after her hurried departure to Italy. As she stepped out of the carriage in front of the house, a little boy, his eyes still puffy from the long journey, clung shyly to her travelling cape. Lucia's maid, Margherita, and the rest of the staff—Teresa, Felicita and Marietta, the new cook—came rushing out to give him a festive welcome. They clapped their hands, hugged him and planted kisses on his cheeks.

Despite being a rather plain-looking four-year-old, Alvisetto (for this was now Massimiliano's name) had a sweet expression and a searching gaze that made him seem somewhat older than his age. At first bewildered by the attention, he eventually joined in the merry clamour, as children do even when they are not quite sure what the fuss is all about. He was escorted to his room, where he found books and toys waiting for him. An extra bed was prepared for him in Lucia's bedroom in case he should be afraid at night.

For a moment Lucia had the feeling she had walked into a different apartment from the one she had left, busier but also brighter and more spacious. Only after settling in did she realise that a row of buildings on the other side of Saint Stephen's Square had been torn down during her absence. There was now twice as much light streaming in through the tall windows overlooking the square.

After a light meal, Lucia took advantage of the fine spring weather to go for a walk with Alvisetto to the Prater. They visited the Carousel and watched the swans. On their way to the ice-cream stand, she recognised Emperor Francis, dressed in tails, taking a stroll with his adjutant, Count Lamberti. A valet was following them discreetly, and she noticed in the distance the anonymous carriage in which they had driven to the park. She had heard about the emperor's occasional incognito walks at the Prater, but to see him materialise so suddenly a few yards away from her gave her a start. Although she had been introduced to him on several occasions, and most recently in Baden, she felt that, given the circumstances, it was inappropriate, even a little foolish, to attract attention to herself with a curtsey. She walked away pretending not to recognise the emperor; after the first turn in the alley, she squeezed Alvisetto's tiny hand and whispered to him who the important man was.

It was late afternoon by the time they walked back home. The sky was dark blue and the air was ripe with the fragrance of spring blossoms. A pleasant evening breeze gathered up and reddened Lucia's cheeks. It felt good to be back in Vienna, walking hand-in-hand with her son as they made their way to Saint Stephen's Square. She took her chance encounter with the emperor as a good omen.

Lucia's worst fear had come true when she had arrived in Venice the previous autumn: Alvise had indeed found out about her secret child with Colonel Plunkett. What really passed between husband and wife—how Alvise confronted her, how she faced the ordeal, what they said to each other—can only be imagined: there is no trace of this crisis in their surviving correspondence. But the story was mentioned in other people's diaries and letters, including this surprisingly detailed one, written to Princess Marie Louise Clary* by her sister Princess Flore de Ligne, who happened to be in Venice at the time of the scandal:

> About a month ago [August 1803] Monsieur Mocenigo comes face to face with a four-year-old boy in some-

---

* See Chapter Six, p. 155.

one's house in Venice; he surmises, he guesses, and in the end he convinces himself that the child belongs to his wife. To be certain of this, he summons her to Venice. She throws herself at his feet, and confesses that the child is the fruit of her attachment to Monsieur de Plonquet [*sic*]. She begs for his mercy and forgiveness. He replies: "This child is yours, but since I am without children, he will be mine. I shall legitimise him and make him my heir." The poor woman falls into the greatest affliction. She tells him such a step will disgrace her for ever, that she won't be able to show her face, that it will cause an extraordinary scandal, etc., etc . . . The furious husband doesn't listen, doesn't want to listen, and threatens a separation if she doesn't consent to all his demands . . . He tells her to go to the judge so that the child can be publicly legitimised. Madame Mocenigo, no longer able to reason, does all her nasty husband asks, and everything happens the way he has planned it. Now the poor woman can't leave the house without being pointed at; as for him, his atrocious behaviour has earned him universal scorn and execration. The whole thing has made an incredible noise here . . .[1]

Did Lucia really throw herself at Alvise's feet begging for mercy? The story making the rounds in Venice was no doubt embellished with details that are impossible to verify. It is certain, however, that after his initial shock, Alvise seized the opportunity to legitimise Lucia's little boy and make him his heir, at the cost of giving false testimony. In an official statement to the Venice Patriarchy, Alvise declared the boy to be his and Lucia's natural and legitimate son, *"esse vere filium naturalem ac legitimum N. H. Aloysius et Lucia Mocenigo."*[2] Next, he had a clerk at the Patriarchy change the boy's baptismal records by wedging the name Alvise in front of his original Christian names (Massimiliano Cesare Francesco). Alvise's deliberate tampering with Church documents did not go down well at the Patriarchy. Church officials knew that the boy was not Alvise's *"filium naturalem."* And evidently the time had passed when a high-ranking patrician could use his influence to make false statements to the Church with impunity—especially one whose reputation in Venice was still tainted by his association with the French. The Patriarchy blocked the legitimisation process stating that "the name 'Alvise' was inserted in violation of the truth and the laws of the synod."[3]*

Alvise brought Lucia and Alvisetto to the safe enclave of Alvisopoli to spare the family further embarassment. Paolina, ever the thoughtful sister, immediately came to visit with her own children so that Alvisetto could meet his cousins. "I am so deeply grateful to you for your show of affection at this moment," Lucia wrote movingly after her sister had left.[4]

After four years spent in near seclusion with Signora Antonia, Alvisetto had a lot to contend with: new parents, a large family and a great deal of attention from everyone at Alvisopoli. And of course his new name—the traditional Mocenigo Christian name, borne by his father, his grandfather and his great-grandfather. Lucia too, had so much to learn, so much ground to make up. It was exciting and overwhelming at the same time. During those first days with Alvisetto there were moments of pure joy and moments when she felt so awkward she could not even find the right tone of voice to use with her son or the proper attitude.

Two weeks after their reunion, Alvisetto behaved badly during his lesson with his tutor—he was learning the alphabet—and Lucia told him he was going to have his dinner alone in his room and not at the table with her. "He started to cry uncontrollably so we left him to himself, thinking it was only a display of anger," she wrote, seeking advice from her more experienced younger sister:

---

* Alvise appealed the patriarchal decree, thus initiating a nine-year-long legal battle with the Church to establish his paternity of Alvisetto. He won the appeal in 1805 but local Church officials took the matter to the Tribunale d'Appello degli Stati Veneti. Alvise pleaded for dismissal of the case but it was not until 9 June 1812 that the issue was finally resolved in his favor through the intervention of Stefano Bonsignore, Bishop of Faenza and Patriarch of Venice.

But the tutor took on a serious expression as he realised Alvisetto was crying not out of anger at all but because he was truly suffering. So he was moved to ask me that I forgive the child, which of course I immediately did. Alvisetto, however, would not stop weeping. Everyone in the house tried to comfort him, but the sobs kept coming and coming. He didn't quiet down until much later, at which point he finished his lesson and, without anyone telling him, he got on his knees and asked the Lord to forgive him.[5]

Every day Lucia picked up new signs of Alvisetto's sensitive nature:

When he passes workmen sweating in the fields he shakes his head and says "poor men . . ." The same thing happens if he sees peasants walking barefoot or with not enough clothes. He feels pain for the suffering of other people. Just the other day the village priest was preparing a show of tricks, and Alvisetto went to watch him get ready. The door to the back room was open and the priest was practising sticking a knife in his hand. He greeted Alvisetto with the thing still hanging from his palm. Alvisetto burst out crying convinced the priest was injured. But although he is sensitive, he is also very courageous, a combination that seems to foreshadow an excellent nature. When he injures himself it is always others who notice because of the bruises. He will say, "It's nothing, I'll never give you worries of that kind." Nothing seems to frighten him. We stopped by a peasant's house where there was music and dancing because one of them had married. Alvisetto loves music and dancing and he was busy watching the *festa*. Suddenly we heard a shot, and then another—the custom on these occasions is to fire pistols out the window. Well, Alvisetto didn't bat an eyelid even though the shots were at very close range. All he wanted to know was how the pistols had fired and whether there would be more shots.[6]

In early April Lucia took Alvisetto with her to the thermal waters of Abano, in the Euganean Hills. She took a cure of mud baths to improve her circulation and invigorate her skin. Alvisetto did his homework in the morning and went out for walks with his mother in the afternoon. He seemed at ease with himself, happy with his new life and growing increasingly attached to his mother. In early May, the two of them finally made the week-long trip to Vienna. "The journey couldn't have been a happier one,"[7] Lucia wrote to her sister as soon as she arrived. "The little one had no trouble sleeping in different beds along the way, and I had taken the precaution of bringing a straw baby-mattress and some covers so that he was able to lie down and stretch his legs and sleep in the carriage as well." Her only worry was Alvisetto's constipation—an ailment with which Lucia was familiar. She prepared a bran-water and sugar solution when they stopped in Klagenfurt, and by the time they arrived home, in Vienna, he was in fine shape, if a little tired.

The news of the scandal surrounding Alvisetto had reached Vienna well before Lucia arrived there with her son. She had no intention of living in seclusion, and was not afraid to "show her face," as Flore de Ligne had written; but she felt a lower profile was in order for the time being. Sadly, the one person whose company she would have treasured, Baron Vespa, had died while she was in Italy. Lucia had so much wanted her old friend to see her boy that she had pictured their encounter many times during the idle hours in the carriage on the journey up to Vienna. It occurred to her that at least poor Vespa was not going to have to fret over the latest imperial pregnancy—for the empress was expecting another child!

Lucia was determined to spend most of her time with Al-

visetto, and to devote herself seriously to his education. He was
three months shy of his fifth birthday, an age at which a boy of his
social class had usually begun to read and write simple sentences
and do basic arithmetic. But his education had been very rudimentary—a fact Lucia had become keenly aware of when
Paolina's well-trained children had visited them at Alvisopoli. "I
know he lags behind his cousins," she remarked defensively. "But
it's really not his fault, poor thing, if he can't yet write."[8] While
they were still in Italy, Lucia had arranged for him to take lessons
to get him in the habit of studying. Now that he was finally settled
in Vienna, however, a more structured education was called for.
Alvise had already mentioned the possibility of sending Alvisetto
to boarding school the following year, when he would be six—a
prospect Lucia considered so awful she did not want to think
about it. Until then, she was going to take matters in her own
hands.

Lucia looked for guidance in the work of her beloved Madame
de Genlis, whose two-volume *Leçons d'une gouvernante à ses
élèves*, published thirteen years earlier, had become a classic text-
book for home-schooling in all of Europe. It was based on her
teaching experience in Paris and London and was really more
useful to the tutor than to the student. A more accessible book for
children was Arnaud Berquin's *L'Ami des enfants*, a collection of
short stories, each one with a specific pedagogical message about
friendship, goodness, honesty, generosity—it was said his stories
were written for children but should be read by adults. Berquin's
book was translated into many languages. The Italian translation
was by Elisabetta Caminer, a Venetian journalist who had been a
good friend of Lucia's father. Lucia had a fond memory of
Caminer, and since she was frustrated in her search for Italian
educational books, she had Paolina send her the Italian version
rather than ordering the original one in French. *L'Ami des enfants*
was actually intended for children a little older than Alvisetto,
who was still struggling with his As and Bs and could not be
expected to appreciate Berquin's moral teachings. On the other
hand, he was certainly ready for *Le Magasin des enfants*, the
pioneering collection of fables by Jeanne-Marie Leprince de

Beaumont, which included the popular "Beauty and the Beast." Leprince de Beaumont, who had tutored upper-class girls in London in her youth, used classical sources to write fables in a language that was accessible to children, and had none of the irony or cleverness associated with the genre. The book had wonderful illustrations, which no doubt helped.

Lucia worked out a routine for Alvisetto. Early morning prayers: Acts, Credo, Salve Regina and Confiteor. Then they read together in Italian—usually a story from Caminer's translation of *L'Ami des enfants*. After that, they looked at German prints and picture books, and she gave him a short piece to memorise. When there was time, she taught him a simple geography lesson about the difference between mountains, plains, rivers, islands and peninsulas, and together they made drawings. As an alternative, she used a new method of teaching geography to children. "First we work on the plan of our apartment," Lucia explained to her sister, "then we draw the plan of the building, and that of the city, then we move to the countryside and work on distances, and so on."[9] Teresa usually took Alvisetto out for a walk in the afternoon and when he returned there was still time for reading and story-telling. His favourite stories, however, were neither the pedagogical tales of Berquin nor the moral fables of Leprince de Beaumont, but the stories from the Old Testament. He often put Lucia to the test. "He'll say: 'Oh mother, tell me the story of the Creation again, or tell me the one about the fall from grace . . .' And you know how few stories from the Scriptures I remember," she reminded Paolina. "I wish my memory would serve me better on these occasions—if only you were here with me to guide me in these matters."[10]

As much as Lucia wanted to be a good teacher to her son, it was not something she was trained to do. Nor did she have Paolina's experience, as she readily admitted. Lesson-time was not always idyllic; she was often frustrated, and there were even bursts of anger on her part—followed by tearful reconciliations. In one typical scene, Lucia lost her patience because Alvisetto was not copying out the letters the way she had told him to. She raised her voice until she was scolding him:

Very quietly he started to cry and wrapped himself around me. "Please don't shout at me," he pleaded. "But I have to raise my voice if you don't copy the letters the way you are supposed to," I replied. "Do correct me, mother, but use a gentler voice," he whispered. And I must recognise there was wisdom in his observation . . .[11]

In fact, Alvisetto was an intelligent little boy, with a logical and inquisitive mind. After his lessons with his mother, he often wandered back to the pantry and held forth among the maids and the kitchen staff, engaging them in rambling conversations and stating his opinions very firmly on everything from the difference between an island and a peninsula to the advantages and disadvantages of confession.

Lucia's involvement in her son's education led her to put some order in her own books, and to get rid of works that were "not suitable for the bedroom of a lady," as she coyly put it to her sister.[12] Despite her scarce knowledge of the Scriptures, she yearned to find a spiritual message in literature that would give her guidance in her turbulent life. Her interest in the important authors of the Enlightenment had waned—she found Voltaire was often too materialistic. And the literature of entertainment favoured by her father's generation seemed excessively frivolous. Still, cleaning up her library was not always simple. It was hard enough to separate herself from the multi-volume memoirs of Maréchal de Richelieu, the prince of eighteenth-century libertines whose amorous escapades had delighted so many readers. But she found it even more difficult to destroy Jean-Baptiste Louvet's *Les Amours du Chevalier de Faublas*, a licentious novel that had been all the rage ten years earlier. She wrote to Paolina:

> I was determined to burn it, but I couldn't bring myself to do it. I had the key to the library in my hand for a month and a half, and I kept telling myself I should get the book out and burn it. Then a young man I met asked me if he could borrow my copy and I

told him I didn't have it—a plain lie. So today I finally
got around to burning the book—to make up for the
lie, of course.[13]

With Alvisetto in Vienna, it was harder for Lucia to run the
estate at Margarethen—and God knows it needed a vigilant eye.
While she had been in Italy, her friend Maria Contarini had
checked on the farm. She had reported that things were going
"very badly" and that bringing any kind of order at Margarethen
seemed "quite impossible." She had mentioned "confusion and
infightings, rivalries and thefts," adding it was hard to understand
who bore the greatest responsibility "as everyone there is equally
implicated."[14]

When Lucia finally went out to Margarethen with Alvisetto,
she found things to be in even worse shape than she had imagined. The new German caretaker, a disabled war veteran who
drank too much, had let the property deteriorate to the point that
"rats have taken over the house, mattresses are full of holes and
everything is in disorder."[15] The garden around the house had
gone to seed. In the fields, the construction of drainage canals had
stopped. The accounts were a mess. Corn and wheat production
was so low that she could not even begin to pay the debt on the
purchase of the estate. In fact, Count Harsch, who had not seen a
single one of the 105,000 florins he was owed, took Alvise to
court. "From a business point of view, things are not at all in good
order," Lucia concluded at the end of her detailed report to her
husband. But she didn't complain, and if she secretly damned
Alvise for investing in such a poor property and then forcing her
to look after it, this never came through in her correspondence.

Lucia hoped that, in the general disaster, her safflower experiment might provide some consolation. But the field she had
planted not far from the house did not look at all as she expected:
the plants had struggled to grow and only very few had the reddish puffs that yielded the desired powder. "Evidently the farmers in charge had better things to do than to keep an eye on such a
silly experiment," she noted with sarcasm. "They simply passed
on the task to hired hands who were less than diligent. The cows

from the adjoining pasture did the rest." She was left with plenty of seeds, which she sent off to Paolina in the hope that she, at least, could make some money off them. "I would be so happy if your investment in the flower business were to be crowned with success."[16]

Lucia's dispiriting report convinced Alvise that it was time to sell the property and move his assets back to Italy. If he could get 200,000 florins for it, he reasoned, he would pay back his debt and still make a profit of 70,000 florins on a property he had owned for only three years. Lucia thought the price much too high as "the improvements made on the property are not so considerable."[17] As she secretly feared, there were no buyers. Alvise fell back on his second option, which was to keep the property and lease it. But even that solution proved elusive. After several false starts, Lucia concluded there was nothing to do but get down to work and give their swampy, rat-infested property another chance.

Lucia dismissed the manager and the accountant. A new team was sent up from Alvisopoli to reorganise the farm and get the accounts in order. The excavation of canals resumed. Alvise invested in a new cotton gin. Lucia cleaned up the house, had it repainted and got the garden ready for planting in early spring. She enlisted the cheerful Maria Contarini to help her improve the interior decoration, and brought furniture from Vienna. She also set up several treadle looms and embroidery frames, and put the women of the house to work, including Maria and herself. They made cotton shirts and camisoles, silk gilets, scarves and handkerchiefs. Lucia often sat up late making embroidery designs, and when she was particularly pleased with one, she carefully traced it on a slip of vellum paper and sent it to Paolina so that she might use it too.

The kitchen, too, was busier, as Lucia tried out new recipes with the help of the cook. She developed the habit of going in to make simple dishes such as veal *gelées* and quiches that she and Maria ate as snacks or light lunches. She tried her hand at desserts, with mixed results, and in the end stuck with her favourite one, a very rich and tasty *crème au chocolat* which she poured into little white and blue porcelain cups and left to cool off in the pantry, where she could easily sneak in whenever she felt a craving.

LUCIA'S CRÈME AU CHOCOLAT

Half a stick of chocolate
Four egg yolks
Four tbsps of sugar
Half a cup of flour
⅙ pint of cream

Chop the chocolate stick into small pieces and mix with two or three tablespoons of cream in a casserole on a low fire until the chocolate has melted. Let it cool for a while so that when you add the egg yolks they won't curdle. Add the egg yolks, the sugar and the flour. Mix and slowly add the rest of the cream. Put the casserole back on the fire, and when it reaches boiling point and has started to thicken, pass the chocolate cream through a strainer and then pour into the cups and let it cool. Makes six cups.[18]

Despite Lucia's efforts to improve life at Margarethen, it was usually a relief to get back to the city, away from the headaches of running the farm. In Maria, she found the close, intimate friend she had always longed for in Vienna. The two became inseparable, running around town like two young girls, and often dragging Alvisetto off with them, to his utter delight. Lucia realised that she had been so wrapped up in Vienna's social life before that she hardly knew the city at all. They went to see the fabulous jewels in the Habsburg Treasury, they visited the celebrated *cabinet de minéralogie,* which reminded her of her summer in Valdagno twelve years earlier, and where she saw "certain rocks fallen from meteorological clouds—rocks that most experts here believe come from the moon."[19] They spent delightful afternoons studying the Renaissance masterpieces in Prince Liech-

tenstein's collection, and made repeated visits to the first kanga-
roo on display in Vienna, drawn by "that bizarre pouch he has in
front of his tummy."[20]

Lucia had seen balloons rise in the air, but never one carrying
passengers. So she was excited about the arrival in town of
Etienne-Gaspard Robertson, the most famous aeronaut of
his time. Robertson was an eccentric and tireless Belgian self-
promoter, who had first gained notoriety in 1796, during the
Directoire, when he had presented the French government with a
plan to send the British fleet up in flames with a giant *miroir
d'Archimède*—an assemblage of mirrors that beamed solar rays
on to a distant object. Eight years later his fame across Europe
was mostly based on his flamboyant balloon flights—he had
recently established an altitude record in Hamburg. In Vienna, he
planned to mesmerise the crowd with his first parachute launch.

It was a beautiful spring day when Lucia and Alvisetto joined
hundreds of Viennese at the Prater to see Robertson float down.
At the last minute, however, Robertson decided to send up his
young assistant, Michaud, while he watched from the ground.
Michaud ascended to an altitude of about 900 feet. The long
silence was broken by a cannon shot—the signal to Michaud that
he had to cut himself loose from the balloon. The young apprentice slashed the ropes, the balloon soared away and for instant Lucia had the impression that the box carrying Michaud
was about to crash to the ground. Suddenly, two parachutes
unfolded—one was attached to Michaud and the other one to
the box—and came down gently (Lucia had read they were made
of silk from Lyon) to a spot that was just a short distance from
where the balloon had risen. The crowd applauded as Michaud
scrambled out of the box. Lucia and Alvisetto walked back home
elated and entirely wrapped up in fantasies about airships and
air-exploration.

Robertson went on to propose to the Austrian government a
scheme for making a tour of the world with the *Minerva*, the fan-
tastic airship he had designed. The balloon, with a diameter of
150 feet, was to be the largest ever made. The ship, decorated
with two giant ornamental wings, would accommodate up to

sixty scientists and carry a weight of 150,000 pounds. Robertson planned a fully furnished observatory, a recreation room for walking and gymnastics, a medicine room, a large store for water, wine and provisions, a kitchen, a theatre, a music room and a pilot's cabin. And for good measure the ship would come equipped with "a small boat in which the passengers might take refuge in the event of the larger vessel falling in the sea."[21]

Roberston hoped to demonstrate that aerial navigation was safer than sea navigation but the government in Vienna was not persuaded, and though it showered him with accolades and gifts, it passed on his offer and politely suggested he go fly his balloons elsewhere.

Alvise planned to join Lucia and Alvisetto in the autumn of 1804. His recent letters to his wife had been affectionate and warmer than usual. He sounded genuinely interested in Alvisetto's health, in the progress of his education, in how he was adapting to his new life in Vienna. So much attention, after all that had passed between them, touched Lucia, and encouraged her to consider Alvise in a fresh light—not as the cold husband interested only in securing an heir, as some people thought of him, but as a deeply scarred man who yearned for the joys of fatherhood. Perhaps Lucia even hoped for a small miracle—that the fruit of her love for another man might rekindle her husband's love for her. For the truth is that she missed Alvise and wanted him by her side. "I so much want to see him," she confessed to Paolina. "It really is ridiculous the way I rush to the window every minute, and ask over and over if someone has heard the postilion blow his hunting horn."[22]

Alvise and Lucia had not seen each other in nearly six months when he finally arrived in early November, and he seemed a changed man. He was no longer irritable as in the past. He did not brood or complain or raise his voice. He showed little inclination to go out in the evening, preferring to stay at home with the family. He was full of attentions for Lucia, and took Alvisetto for a walk every day, often stopping at the sherbet kiosk by the Court

Theatre. He took his new role as father seriously, and showed appreciation for Lucia's efforts in educating their son. Alvise being Alvise, his demeanour with the little boy was usually tempered by a certain rigidity. He was constantly putting Alvisetto to the test, not so much to verify his knowledge in this or that field as to gauge his moral fibre. One day, he promised to take him out for an ice cream. It started to rain, and Alvise said that since he had made his promise but did not want Alvisetto to get wet, he would send a servant to fetch the ice cream for him. "But you should bear in mind that *he* will get soaked on the way," Alvise reminded him. "So it's up to you. Do you still want him to go?" Not surprisingly, Alvisetto meekly answered, "No."

Teresa stepped in to lighten the atmosphere. "You'll see, his heart will be more content than if he had eaten his sherbet."[23]

Another evening Alvisetto was getting ready to go to a children's play. Alvise needled him: why didn't he give up the play and stay home to keep him company? "Alvisetto did all he could to persuade his father to go with him to the theatre," Lucia told Paolina, wondering whether Alvise was not pushing their son a little too hard. "But it was useless, so in the end he said he'd stay at home with his father. He added touchingly: 'nothing makes me happier than seeing my father and my mother with a smile on their face.'"[24]

Despite the rigidities in Alvise's character, he was warming to Alvisetto and enjoyed being with him. In fact it was hard to tell who was happier, father or son, when the weather was good and they could walk hand in hand to the kiosk for their sherbet. Alvise had looked forward to taking him to the sled races, but the winter was very cold, it seldom snowed and very few races were held. On the other hand, it was a great winter for ice-skating, and there was nothing Alvisetto enjoyed more than going with his father to watch the older kids speed by and bump into each other at the rink in the Prater. He also made his formal entrance in society—children's society, that is—by attending his first *bal d'enfants* at Countess Neuwirth's. It was the usual array of odd-looking youngsters. Feisty three- and four-year-olds in velvet suits were thrown in with lanky teenagers in military uniform, all

making their way among columns of tasty sandwiches and a profusion of cakes and pastries. Alvisetto quickly overcame his shyness, piling his plate with delicious food and participating
enthusiastically in all the games. He went home exhausted, and
Teresa assured Alvise that the afternoon had been a triumph.
"Everyone praised him because he behaved very well . . . They
gave him a million kisses when he left, he made friends with all
the children, and danced most of the time."[25]

Lucia enjoyed describing these episodes of family life to her
sister, and despite her occasional reservations about the way
Alvise engaged Alvisetto, a feeling of gratitude towards her husband showed through her letters, mixed with the hope that their
marriage regain some strength and a sense of purpose.

Before the winter was over, Alvise, perhaps remembering how
he had missed home when his father had sent him to Rome to be
educated by priests, gave up the idea of sending Alvisetto to the
boarding school in Pressburg he had been in touch with. He was
looking for a suitable tutor, he announced to the rest of the
family, who would live with them and take charge of their son's
education.

He chose Francesco Vérand, a young man of about thirty,
"very sweet, with excellent manners." He had good references,
spoke French and German well, and drew very beautifully.
Everyone liked him from the start, and Lucia was glad to hand
over to such a charming young man a responsibility she had held
out of necessity. "Oh do say a prayer or two, my dear sister, so
that Alvisetto's first lessons are held under divine auspices."[26]

On his first day Vérand "set about earning his pupil's trust
with the sweetest manners."[27] The following morning he left the
house at nine o'clock next morning, telling Teresa he was going
to the post office and would be back shortly. At midday he still
had not returned. Lucia brought the issue to Alvise's attention.
He reassured her: it was his second day at work and he probably
needed a little more time to move his things to the house. Lucia
went out for a ride in the carriage and returned at three in the
afternoon. Vérand was not at home. Alvise, Lucia and Alvisetto
had a plate set for him at the table and went ahead with their din-

ner. Still no sign of Vérand. Later, they looked through his things, and found a beautiful drawing of a rose he had made for Alvisetto.

The next day, they got in touch with his previous employer, a French lady, a certain Madame Cavanac, but she had not heard from him either. It occurred to Lucia that perhaps Vérand was unhappy with his bed or his mattress and might have gone back to his previous lodgings. So they called on a Madame Lamoine, from whom Vérand had been renting a room while in the employ of Madame Cavanac, but there was no sign of him there either. Alvisetto came up with his own explanation: perhaps Vérand's mother had been ill and, on his way to the post office, he received news that she was suddenly worse or perhaps had died and he was lying in the grass somewhere, stunned by grief.

Alvise and Lucia heard about a carriage crash and they contacted the police. Luckily, Vérand's name was not on the list of casualties, but the police knew who he was because he had recently reported the theft of his purse. Alvise and Lucia made a more thorough search for clues among his things, and found a crumpled letter in which Vérand confessed to being overwhelmed by debt. Alvise made enquiries but no menacing creditors turned up, only a former landlady to whom he owed 400 florins from a time when he had been ill for six weeks—"a perfectly acceptable cause for contracting a debt," Alvise remarked to Lucia. But in his letter, Vérand added woefully that he would rather "suffer a punishment" than carry the weight of his debt.

Alvise's investigation revealed that the young man had no bad habits. He neither drank nor gambled and he was unattached. Everyone described him as honest, upright and devout, and said he had never failed in his duty. "Apparently," a baffled Lucia wrote to Paolina, "his only weakness is his great sensitivity. Madame Lamoine told us that when she informed him of his brother's death he fell to the ground and didn't regain consciousness for three hours. What on earth might have happened to him? Did he seek refuge in a hermitage? Did he join a small religious sect? Or perhaps the army?"[28]

A week after the disappearance, a letter arrived from

Pressburg, a hundred miles east of Vienna. In it, Vérand begged Alvise for his forgiveness. In the stolen purse, he explained, was a letter from his parents explaining they would not be able to help him repay his debt. On the morning he had walked out of the house on his way to the post office he had seen a man by the Danube with his stolen papers, so he had run after him. That was it: Vérand did not explain what had happened next, nor did he give a clue as to his whereabouts.

Two weeks later, a Capuchin friar whom Alvise and Lucia happened to know found Vérand wandering in the streets of Pressburg. He was hungry, poorly clad and with no money. The friar helped him find some food and a shelter, then he informed Alvise, who immediately sent Vérand a hundred florins, not without remarking that it was "quite a sum for the twenty hours he spent under our roof."[29] It turned out to be money well spent. Vérand came back to Vienna, was forgiven for disappearing, and welcomed back into the Mocenigo household. But not as Alvisetto's preceptor. Alvise, impressed by his integrity and his language skills, took him on as his personal assistant. In mid April 1805 he headed back to Venice with his new secretary in tow.

The surprise dénouement of the Vérand affair forced Lucia to resume her role as her son's teacher, which did not make her happy. It was one thing to read a story to Alvisetto or to practise spelling with him or to impart to him the occasional geography lesson, but quite another to be responsible for his formal education. And not so much because she would have preferred to spend her time differently, but because she felt she was not up to the task. She hired Herr Gartner to give Alvisetto German lessons, and he made rapid progress. But he lagged behind in Italian, French and arithmetic, which were Lucia's responsibility. His penmanship, too, was still poor, "but then my own letters are even more crooked than his. He's not learning from the best."[30]

Alvise had insisted, upon leaving Vienna with Vérand, that during his absence Lucia apply for the Order of the Starred Cross, one of the most prestigious distinctions granted by the Habsburg

Court, and one which he thought would nicely complete Lucia's rise in Austrian society. At first she had been reluctant, fearing that such a request would needlessly attract attention and risk exposing her to an embarrassing refusal on the part of the court. But she gradually changed her mind as she learnt that a number of patrician ladies in Venice—including her mother-in-law, Chiara, with whom relations had cooled after the scandal of her love affair with Colonel Plunkett and the birth of Alvisetto—had applied to receive the order. "I feel that at this point I cannot put off making a request myself, all the more so since, unlike most of our Venetian friends, I have actually lived in Vienna for the past few years," she explained to Paolina, begging her "not to say a word" about her step. "The order only proves you are born a patrician . . . though I hear it can be useful if one's children run for offices that require patents of nobility."[31]

Lucia was told by people knowledgeable about these matters that her request would probably be refused the first time around, and accepted the second—it was the usual practice. There was nothing for her to do but wait.

Paolina was hardly in a condition to appreciate the politics of Vienna etiquette. She had never really recovered since the death of Lucietta, and now she suffered from chronic fatigue and diarrhoea, and began to lose her voice. She was under the care of Doctor Zuliani, an old family doctor. Lucia had been treated by him in the past and she did not trust him. She had long concluded that Paolina's chronic ailments were the result of her psychological frailty, and not the reverse, and that the only way to get her sister on the road to recovery was to consider all aspects of her health, including her medical history and that of their parents. Doctor Zuliani was too old-fashioned, Lucia argued, too set in his ways "to get your machinery back in good order." Besides, he was hopelessly out of touch with the "new medicine" being practised in Vienna.

> I used to have the highest opinion of him, but I don't any more. How does he explain the pains in your chest? How does he explain your loss of voice? You

know I believe the weakness of your nerves has a great deal to do with your general debility: to neglect this entirely, as Doctor Zuliani does, and to speak only of diarrhoea, does not predispose me to have much consideration for his ability.[32]

Lucia's reference to the "new medicine" practised in Vienna was a way of introducing her sister to Herr Speck, the medical guru of Viennese society under whose spell she had recently fallen. Doctor Speck was a self-taught medicine man who had picked up much of what he knew while working as a lay nurse in the hospital of Maria Caelis in Rome as a young man. He treated his patients with what Lucia called "tonic remedies," a vague term that covered everything from herbal infusions to natural laxatives. But Doctor Speck's fame rested largely on the "miraculous powders" he prepared for his patients. The formulas varied according to the particular ailment and the patient's constitution and medical history. He never revealed the composition of his remedies, but his devoted followers had a blind faith in his healing powers. The modest apartment out of which he worked was always crowded with society ladies waiting to pick up their little packets—small envelopes, each holding a single dose of the preparation. After one of her regular trips to Doctor Speck's, Lucia wrote:

> We stand by the heating stove in the tiny entrance hall, fill up the living room and often have to spill into the kitchen. He has brought about so many remarkable recoveries here in Vienna that he is looked upon as Aesculapius himself. And I believe in him so much that I take his powders without thinking twice about what he has put in them.[33]

In fact the number of Viennese ladies addicted to Doctor Speck's powders was such that one saw them pulling out their envelopes and swallowing the contents at all hours of the day, in the streets, in the Prater, even at the theatre. Lucia saw Countess

Korolyi, thin as a reed since her husband's death, cross paths with another lady during their afternoon stroll as they both were about to take their powders. "They greeted each other, and with an air of complicity, raised their little envelopes *'à l'honneur de notre Docteur Speck.'* "[34]

In her effort to enlist Paolina, Lucia added the cautionary tale of poor Prince Liechtenstein: "He was gravely ill, Herr Speck got him back in health, he stopped taking his powder, became gravely ill again, and died."[35]

Lucia convinced a reluctant Doctor Speck to prepare a powder for her sister—the doctor did not usually mix a preparation without visiting the patient first. It was reddish, very fine, and each dose looked like a generous pinch of paprika. She sent it off to Paolina, begging her to take it. Paolina had reservations, but she did not want to disappoint her solicitous older sister. "I am not hurt in the least by your hesitation," Lucia reassured her. "By all means, show the powder to a chemist and he'll easily tell you what's in it. Adieu, every day I love you more, and I think you did the right thing not to take Speck's powder without having it examined first."[36]

This medical exchange between the two sisters, stretched over several months, echoed their discussion a decade earlier on the merits of giving birth in the chair, with Doctor Speck now in the role of guiding light in the place of Doctor Vespa. Lucia, ever the older sister, could be very insistent in pressing her point if she believed it was for the good of Paolina. And Paolina, in turn, had developed her own delicate ways of holding her position in the face of Lucia's affectionate encroachments. Her shield, this time, was Doctor Zuliani, who gladly stepped into the breach, stating firmly that Paolina was not touching that reddish powder until Doctor Speck revealed its chemical components. But there the matter stood, for it was suddenly overshadowed by alarming news.

Bonaparte was back in northern Italy and his arrival, Paolina wrote, had everyone saying that the next war would be fought there. If war did break out and borders closed down, how would they stay in touch? Lucia reassured Paolina, mostly to reassure herself:

> What is being said in Brescia about the break-out of hostilities in the near future is being said here in Vienna as well—all one sees at the theatre, these days, are plays with military themes. But I am convinced these fears are groundless and we shall have peace for several more years. The recent wars brought too much suffering for anyone to contemplate a renewal of hostilities. No one is about to close down the mountain passes, no one is about to declare war.[37]

This was wishful thinking on the part of Lucia, for Bonaparte had been stoking the fires of a new European crisis for some time. The Treaty of Amiens in 1802 had brought relative peace to continental Europe, and for two years the first consul had focused most of his energies on domestic affairs, modernising public administration, reforming the judicial system, building up public education and founding the Banque de France. His restlessness abroad, however, remained unabated, and he never lost a chance to push France's borders and exasperate his neighbours, as if peace were merely a continuation of war by other means. In 1804 the British government, fed up with Bonaparte's peacetime expansionism, financed a plot to assassinate him. When the plot failed, Bonaparte declared himself hereditary emperor, ostensibly to discourage further attempts on his life. He was crowned on 2 December 1805 in Paris by Pius VII. Emperor Napoleon set about creating an imperial aristocracy, lavishing high-sounding titles of nobility on members of his family and his most loyal generals. The Cisalpine Republic in northern Italy, the puppet-state over which he presided, became the Kingdom of Italy, and he was crowned in Milan on 26 May 1805. His stepson, Prince Eugène de Beauharnais, became the kingdom's viceroy.

The bulk of the French army was still assembled on the coast near Boulogne, apparently poised for an offensive against

Britain. But Napoleon's presence in Italy for the coronation ceremony suggested he had indeed changed his mind in favour of another continental war—certainly that was what everyone talked about: a new war in northern Italy.

Lucia received fresh news from Antonio Canova, the artist, who arrived in Vienna in mid June to install the mausoleum commissioned by Albert of Saxony-Teschen for his wife, the Archduchess Christina. Lucia had known him for many years and she had him over for lunch, eager to hear the latest from Italy. It was the season of white asparagus, the large, fleshy variety that was so popular with visitors, and Lucia went to the market expressly that morning to buy some. On the way home, she stopped to purchase a special vinegar *aux fines herbes* with which to dress it, and two bottles of white wine from the Rhineland. After singing the praise of the trusty white asparagus, the great sculptor turned to the subject of war. He described the gloom that was spreading back home, the memories of Napoleon's past campaigns being still so vivid among the Italians. Turning to the mausoleum he was working on, a large monument in the shape of a pyramid costing 8,000 florins, he said the expense of bringing the artwork across the Alps in such uncertain times was so high it had put a serious dent in the sum he was taking home.* The great man grouched about working too hard and travelling too much, and in the end he confessed that he had not even begun work on a marble statue of Mary Magdalen that Alvise had commissioned for the new church in Alvisopoli for a fee of 10,000 ducats.[38]

Despite Canova's discouraging outlook, Lucia continued to pray for peace. Austria, she informed Paolina, was preparing three armies: one under the command of the emperor, with General Mack at his side, and the other two under the command of Archduke Charles and Archduke John. "They say that he who

---

* The mausoleum, commemorating Archduchess Maria Christina, is in the Augustinerkirche in Vienna and served as a model for Canova's own funerary monument in the Chiesa dei Frari in Venice.

wants peace prepares for war. Let us hope this proverb will once more be proven true."[39]

The following month, however, Napoleon ordered the bulk of the Grande Armée to redeploy from Boulogne to the Rhine. Austria and its Continental allies—Russia, Sweden and Naples—responded by forming a new grand coalition with Britain. As the storm gathered during the summer of 1805, Lucia and Alvisetto saw the city empty itself. Viennese society broke ranks, and all the great families retreated to country estates scattered about the Habsburg Empire. Only government officials and military officers remained in the capital, preparing the country for war. Lucia felt she had the city to herself. "I hadn't been to the Prater in a long time," she wrote to her sister after a night stroll under a full moon.

> Alvisetto and I walked for hours. We then went over to the Ramparts, and were both so entranced by the beautiful light of the moon that we didn't want to return home. It occurred to me that the same moon was shining over you; but, philosopher that you are, you probably did not even notice her. I pictured you in your room, the blinds closed, with only the light of your candle flickering around you.[40]

Lucia much preferred being in Vienna than in Margarethen. Her trips out to the country, while necessary to keep track of business accounts, became increasingly burdensome. The drainage system still did not work properly, and after every rainshower the grounds around the house remained waterlogged for days, attracting clouds of mosquitoes. "How can we possibly have purchased such a dump?"[41] she asked out of sheer exasperation after arriving at the property one day and finding the house in disorder and the garden so flooded she had trouble getting inside. On that same visit she discovered the caretaker had scabies. She had gone to the kitchen to prepare her usual pots of *crème au chocolat* and had asked the man to stir for her while she went to fetch a cooking implement. "When I returned, I took the wooden spoon from him: that's when I realised. You know how I dread that disease.* The doctor came over and confirmed my suspicions; but the caretaker refused to be taken to the hospital . . . He asked to be let go, and I immediately said yes."[42]

At Margarethen, Lucia was seldom in the mood to appreciate even the sounds of nature. "The toads delight us with their croaking harmonies—the only recognisable noise around here," she sneered. "That, and the hissing of bats." A nightingale in the pheasantry had given her pleasure in the early part of summer. "But now the pheasantry is flooded and the bird has flown away."[43]

Having given up hope of ever cultivating safflower in the swampy fields of Margarethen, she developed a new passion: *Prunus cerasus*, the lovely cherry tree she had originally seen cascading down the banks of the Elbe during her first summer in Austria. She now planted row upon row of *Twieselbeerbaum*† around the house; she pored over German agricultural almanacs to learn all there was to learn about this particular cherry tree; and she spent hours translating the abstruse technical texts into Italian. "It's a good way to improve my German," she remarked. This was the fifth summer in a row she was spending in the "dump," away from her husband.

The growing noises of war soon caught up with her in the country. One day, in mid July, Alvisetto's German instructor came back from his walk to the village and announced that recruiting officers had arrived. "I'd rather not have to witness those poor parents torn from their sons,"[44] Lucia replied with anguish. The mood turned sombre in the house.

"Will they come to separate us as well?" Alvisetto asked his mother later that evening, at the dinner table.

"No," she replied. "We shall always be together."

---

* Lucia had had scabies too, earlier in her marriage, with sores covering her right hand and arm. Alvise once spent the night with her, and the next day, fearful of becoming infected, instructed his manservant, Zuanne, to bring him his wife's nightgown every morning so that he could inspect it. Zuanne later confessed to Lucia, who told the story to Paolina.[45]

† Lucia notes this as the local German word for the tree.

"I feel much better now; I shall eat with greater appetite."

After dinner, Alvisetto walked about the house with his big hat on—a peculiar habit he had recently developed and which his grandfather, Andrea, also had. Lucia watched her son come through the room as she sat at her writing desk. "His blood is truly Memmo blood," she scribbled to her sister. "This thing he has about wearing his hat in the house has become a fixation. No doubt he'd keep it on all day if he weren't made to take it off."[46]

A few days later, Lucia was forced to break the promise she had made to Alvisetto about not leaving him alone: she had to go to Vienna to organise the move to a new apartment, a smaller place but with a nice view of the Danube, which she had let for six months. Alvisetto would not have it. "I am not going to be separated from my mother," he insisted, tears swelling in his eyes. "I will go with you—don't even speak of leaving me here if you don't want to see me cry . . ."[47] With that, he burst into tears.

Lucia stayed in Vienna only the time that was strictly necessary. Exhausted, her muscles aching from moving furniture around, she wrote to Paolina on 7 August: "Our new home is delightful. The river here is at its widest point."[48] She looked forward to moving in with Alvisetto and living there until the end of the following spring, by which time she hoped to return to Italy—provided war did not force her to change plans. While in Vienna, she learnt that she had been awarded the Starred Cross. It occurred to her that she now had a formal tie to the Habsburg Court. But the timing seemed so odd, what with war preparations by now in full swing.

Two days later she was back at Margarethen with Alvisetto. "The Austrian regiments are marching through the fields around us," she reported. "It is said that General Mack is heading for the Tyrol on his way to Italy with His Majesty at the head of 100,000 men . . ."[49] Alvisetto gave his own bit of strategic advice, drawing from his recently acquired knowledge of geography: "I believe the Russians should join the Imperial Army. I have seen on the map that the Russian Empire is very extended and may provide us with many troops."[50]

In fact, the Russian army was already moving west, albeit at a woefully sluggish pace. In mid August, Lucia wrote that "friends who have just come from Russia and have a keen eye for military matters told me they saw 120–130,000 troops marching into Poland."[51] A week later, an Austrian cavalry battalion stopped in Margarethen. Three hundred soldiers camped in the fields around the house. Lucia found Alvisetto playing billiards with a group of officers belonging to General Mack's regiment. The commanding officer said cheerfully that if the boy were old enough he would recruit him. "I shall only go to war to defend my papa and my mama,"[52] Alvisetto snapped back. Everyone laughed, and Lucia let her son bask in the limelight a little longer before taking him up to bed.

General Mack entered Bavaria, France's ally, on 11 September, then moved north, concentrating his troops between Ulm and Gunzburg, on the Upper Danube, about eighty miles east of the Black Forest, whence he expected Napoleon to appear. There Mack waited for the Russian reinforcements marching west from Poland. He estimated Napoleon headed an army of 70,000 men, and he wanted to crush that force before it reached Italy, the presumed theatre of war. Once the Russians joined him, he should easily have the upper hand. But General Kutuzov and his troops were moving too slowly. As Lucia wrote to her sister in mid September, the Russians were still in Polish Galicia.

Far worse was the fact that General Mack had made a terrible miscalculation: Napoleon had chosen to make Germany, not Italy, the main battleground of the new war, and planned to annihilate the Austrian forces before the Russian reinforcements arrived. On 25 September, when he crossed the Rhine north of the Black Forest, Napoleon was at the head of 210,000 men, not the 70,000 General Mack had expected. The Grande Armée wheeled south, then east, and, covering eighteen to twenty miles a day, reached the Danube in only two weeks, moving speedily to General Mack's rear, between Ingolstadt and Donauworth, and cutting his line of retreat.

The Austrian high command, suddenly aware of the catastrophic position of its army, urged the Russians to rush west-
ward. "I hear they are marching at an incredible speed now,"
Lucia reported on 1 October. "Many of the troops travel by cart,
and manage to cover up to 48–50 miles a day."[53] But it was too
late. The French attacked the Austrians during the second week
of October, pushing them towards Ulm, and eventually forcing
the bulk of General Mack's army into the city. On 16 October, the
French artillery opened fire. The Austrian commander realised
his forces would not be able to withstand the siege without the
support of the Russians, who were still a hundred miles away. He
surrendered to Napoleon to avoid the complete destruction of his
army. Some 50,000 Austrians were taken prisoner; the French had
hardly any losses. Napoleon had again humiliated Austria. With
his army practically intact, he made a run for Vienna, and on
13 November, he was sleeping in Schönbrunn Palace, the
Habsburg summer residence near the capital. Emperor Francis
and his court had fled days before. Vienna was entirely in the
hands of the French.

Lucia returned from Margarethen to find the city swarming with
blue uniforms. Her apartment along the Danube was requisi-
tioned. "Nineteen men are camping out in ten rooms,"[54] she
complained, overwhelmed by the chaos in her house. But she was
relieved to find three letters from Paolina, whom she had not
heard from since August because of the disruptions caused by the
war. "At last I have found you again."[55]

Napoleon did not stay in Vienna. After a few days' rest, he was
off to chase the Russians and the rest of the Austrian army. On
3 December, Lucia told Paolina confidentially she had received
"amazing news" that very evening from the battlefront, but
could not share it with her "for fear that our correspondence be
interrupted" by censors. "Peace may already be close at hand,"
she added, biting her lip.[56]

The "amazing news," of course, was that Napoleon had won a

decisive victory against the combined forces of Austria and Russia in the plains around the village of Austerlitz.

Three days later, Lucia was at home discussing the latest events with a few Austrian friends. During dinner, a messenger brought her a note from a French commanding officer returning from the battlefield: General Baraguey d'Hilliers, who had commanded the French occupying forces in Venice in 1797. Having heard Lucia was in Vienna, he was eager to see her and wondered at what time he could visit her. When it became apparent that the general wished to come by that very evening, panic swept the room and the soirée quickly came to an end as Lucia's guests "did not wish to compromise themselves by being introduced to him."[57]

Minutes later, Baraguey d'Hilliers walked into the house exuding all the raw energy that came from a great victory on the battlefield. In the eight years since Lucia had last seen him in Venice, he had become one of Napoleon's most trusted generals. Now he paced across her empty living room, strong and self-confident, filling her in on the details of the French triumph at Austerlitz. As he spoke, images from the past merged confusedly with the present. Lucia's world had been overrun by Napoleon and his armies before. As Baraguey d'Hilliers rushed on with his narrative, she felt her life was about to be transformed once again.

The next day a messenger came to inform Lucia that an entire French squadron had pitched camp at Margarethen. "The captain has apparently taken over my room, while two officers and four *chasseurs* have fixed themselves up in the rest of the house."[58]

Austria renounced all influence in Italy by signing the Treaty of Pressburg. Vienna ceded Venice and its possessions to Napoleon, as well as the German states of Baden, Bavaria and Wurtenberg. "We have peace at last," she wrote to her sister. "This morning a Te Deum was sung in Saint Stephen's."[59]

On Lucia's saint's day, 13 December, Alvisetto woke his mother up with a bouquet of flowers, and recited a few German verses he had memorised for the occasion. It occurred to Lucia that she had made a little Austrian boy out of her son. Now she kissed him on the forehead, and wondered whether his French was fluent enough to hold him in good stead.

Lucia was disappointed but not entirely surprised when Alvise did not come to Vienna to fetch her. In Milan, the young viceroy, Prince Eugène de Beauharnais, was reorganising the Italian Kingdom according to Napoleon's strict guidelines; Alvise felt he had to stay in Italy, in the hope that his past experience with the French would help him secure a prestigious assignment. It was not prudent, he explained, to leave while everyone was jockeying for position in the new administration.

Following her husband's instructions, Lucia rented out the apartment in Vienna for the remaining part of their lease, and organised the sale of paintings, carpets and furniture. She failed to rent out Margarethen, however. Alvise had yet to finish paying for the estate and it made Lucia uncomfortable to leave an unsettled situation behind. She made sure farming schedules were in place and accounts more or less in order before leaving. "It is wise," she told her sister, "to leave [our] affairs in this country in the best possible shape."[60] Thus it was not until the late autumn of 1806 that she was finally able to make the journey back to Italy. She took leave of the emperor and the empress and headed south on a rainy November day—she, Alvisetto and Margherita in the large travelling carriage, with the luggage, and Teresa, Marietta and Felicita, rather cramped, in the two-horse buggy driven by Checco. At a post-station where they stopped shortly after crossing the Alps, Lucia received a letter from Alvise: he had been appointed governor of Agogna, one of the twenty-four departments which now formed Napoleon's new Kingdom of Italy, and she was to join him there as soon as possible.

Chapter Eight

LADY-IN-WAITING

Novara, the capital of Agogna, was a quiet, unpretentious city five hours from Milan by coach, on the way to Piedmont. Alvise set up offices in the newly established Prefecture on the square, and leased the main floor of an elegant *palazzo* owned by Countess Bellini, the local *grande dame,* where he was joined by Lucia and Alvisetto, Monsieur Vérand and the staff (Margherita, Teresa, Felicita and Checco). The district of Agogna was not among the larger or more important ones in the kingdom; Alvise was nonetheless satisfied because he was one of only a handful of Venetians called to serve in Napoleon's government. He threw himself into work, staying at his office late when he was not travelling to the towns and villages under his jurisdiction.

"We have been well received," Lucia wrote to Paolina soon after settling in. "Everyone here seems pleased with Alvise's ability and fairness." It was her own role she was a little uncertain about.

> Initially, I thought we might open our house once a week. [Countess Bellini] assured me she would be the first to come if we decided to receive society. Then I heard the people here don't generally fancy social gatherings so I told the Countess we were not yet ready. Now we tend to spend our evenings at home alone.[1]

What a contrast to life in the Kingdom's capital! Prince Eugène and his young wife, Princess Augusta-Amelia of Bavaria, established a highly structured court at the royal palace in Milan, with rigid rules of etiquette borrowed from the Imperial Court in Paris. There were also suppers and balls in grand Milanese houses. "I hear these soirées can be quite glittering. The Viceroy usually makes an appearance and dances too; not the Vicereine, who has given up these amusements on account of her advanced pregnancy."[2]

There was not much regret in Lucia's comments. Having just completed two exhausting, back-to-back moves, from Vienna to Alvisopoli and from Alvisopoli to Novara, she was content to lead a quiet life with her family now that circumstances had brought them all under the same roof again. Although she and Alvise had been married for twenty years, Lucia had spent many more days alone than in the company of her husband—indeed there were moments when she felt their life together had never really begun. And she did not look forward to the time when she would be summoned to the court in Milan to take on her duties as lady-in-waiting to Princess Augusta—a prestigious assignment Alvise had sought for his wife to strengthen their ties to the ruling family.

Monsieur Vérand was put in charge of Alvisetto's education, the job for which he had originally been hired in Vienna. He wasted little time in expressing his displeasure at how much the boy had fallen behind in Latin and arithmetic, how easily he was distracted, and just how plain lazy he could be. Vérand started to keep a daily record of his pupil's performance and general behaviour in a green and blue booklet known as "Alvisetto's Journal." Once a week, a tremulous Alvisetto took it to his parents so that they might judge his conduct, and discuss it with him. From the start, Vérand was quite harsh in his judgement, filling his reports with epithets like "disobedient," "stubborn," "ill-mannered," "restless" and "capricious." He noted sternly that the boy "laughs out loud without a reason, just like a child."[3]

The parents encouraged Vérand's method because, as Lucia said, "loud reprimands and threats of awful punishments have produced no effects." Alvisetto showed occasional signs of intelligence, she added, "but his mind is always elsewhere and it sometimes takes him three hours to do work that should take him no more than fifteen minutes. It is astonishing how he can seem an absolute prodigy at times, then days and days will go by without the slightest progress."[4]

Alvisetto's uneven results made Lucia anxious. She knew Alvise wanted to send their son off to boarding school at the earliest opportunity, possibly to Paris, in order to acquire a proper French education. The prospect of a separation filled her with dread. The only way to delay Alvisetto's departure, she felt, was to convince Alvise that the child was making progress in his studies. She put her faith in Vérand, conscious of the trust her husband had in him, and the two entered a silent pact to work Alvisetto hard in order to keep him at home as long as possible.

In Vienna, Lucia had grown accustomed to spending a good deal of time with her son, going over his lessons when she was not actually doing some teaching herself. She did not want to give up that part of their relationship entirely. Having relinquished prime responsibility for Alvisetto's general education to Vérand, she nevertheless remained in charge of his religious studies, to make sure, she told her sister, that he received a solid Christian upbringing. Lucia ordered *The Life of Jesus* from a bookshop in Milan, and she and Alvisetto curled up together in bed every evening to read three chapters of the big volume. "I'm finding this book very useful. I had never read the life of Jesus as a whole but only in bits and pieces. In fact, what I knew of it usually came from the study of paintings and sculptures when we were young."[5] On her own, she tackled the multi-volume *Histoire Ecclésiastique*, a heavy-going history of the Church. She also studied the gospel of Saint Paul.

Lucia's decision to take on Alvisetto's religious education

reflected her increasing interest in the sacred scriptures. Her father, who had been such an inspiring intellectual mentor to her and Paolina in their youth, had paid distracted attention to their religious upbringing. Over the years, Lucia had come to regret this lacuna. She believed a deeper knowledge of the gospels and the history of Christianity would give sustenance to a spiritual yearning she felt was growing with time. It is hard to pinpoint the beginning of Lucia's religious awakening: it was part of a general trend sweeping across Europe as a reaction to the secularism of the eighteenth century and the anti-clerical excesses of the French Revolution. Perhaps her embrace of religion was accelerated by the emotional turmoil caused by Alvisetto's illegitimate birth, Plunkett's death, the subsequent scandal and the child's adoption by Alvise. Certainly the letters she wrote to Paolina from Vienna already testified to a strengthening of her faith. But it was in Novara that she started to observe church rituals with great diligence and devotion. Every day, during her first winter there, she got in the habit of bundling up and going off to attend early morning and evening services at the neighbourhood church of Saint Gaudentius—she much preferred the intimacy of the small parish church to the stateliness of the Duomo in the city's main square. She also looked for new places of worship as she explored the city, and she was always eager to join mass in the church of a neighbourhood she was not yet familiar with. In the early spring, when it was warm enough to venture out in the countryside, the long walks she took with Alvisetto and Vérand often turned into impromptu pilgrimages to one of the ancient religious sanctuaries that dotted the hills around the city.

Alvise encouraged these outings. Much of his work as governor of Agogna depended on his good relations with local church officials. Napoleon's first invasion of northern Italy, back in 1796, had been so fiercely anti-clerical it had caused a great deal of acrimony and even violence between the French troops and the local peasantry. The emperor had since made peace with Rome and signed a Concordat in 1801, but relations with the clergy remained tense throughout the Kingdom of Italy, especially in the smaller cities and towns, where the influence of the church was deeply embedded. Alvise soon discovered that the cooperation of parish priests was indispensable in enforcing the conscription quotas to fill the ranks of the Armée d'Italie, the new Italian army Napoleon had placed under the command of Prince Eugène. In return for the priests' help, Alvise obtained an exemption for young married men. This earned him the gratitude of the population.

In March 1807, Princess Augusta gave birth to her first-born, a little girl she and Prince Eugène named Joséphine, like her grandmother. Alvise ordered that the city be illuminated by a thousand torches. The bishop sang a Te Deum in the Duomo. He also agreed to a special request by Alvise: the display of the sacred host to the congregation. It was a notable concession, and yet another example of how relations with the Church were improving in Alvise's district.

As spring turned into early summer, Lucia travelled throughout the region of the Agogna. She crossed wide green valleys, filed through narrow gorges and climbed mountains to visit ancient villages mostly inhabited by women and children, the men having gone over the mountains to look for work in France and Switzerland. The villagers were poor but very dignified. She reported to her sister:

> They survive on a simple diet of chestnuts and milk, yet they have healthy complexion and appear very robust. The women wear unusual and rather beautiful clothes and fix their long hair in elaborate ways. They are very hospitable—and I was very fortunate to make it back home without succumbing to chestnut indigestion.[6]

Paolina was always in Lucia's thoughts during these excursions for she had the most natural impulse to share with her sister everything that was new and strange and interesting. One day, as

Lucia crossed the dry bed of the Agogna, she found a pebble in the perfect shape of a heart. She sent it to Paolina, with these words: "Dear sister, how truly happy I would be if only I could live with you." The dialogue between them never ceased, and made their separation a little more bearable.

At the time, Lucia was under the spell of an unusual book by Madame de Genlis, *Les Savinies*. It was set in an imaginary Swiss romantic landscape and told the story of two sisters who loved each other very much and lived happily together until one of the two was married off. The other sister became twice jealous: first, because her sister now loved someone else, and second, because, in the past, she too had had feelings for the same man. The husband-to-be left town on business, and the future bride, noticing her sister's sadness, got her to speak her mind. Realising she was the cause of her misery, she renounced her marriage and vowed never to see the man again. The other sister blamed herself for confessing the truth and died of grief. The surviving Savinie asked to be buried with her sister, and soon followed her to the grave.

Lucia gave her sister a long, rambling account of the story. She drew a parallel between her love for Paolina and that of the two Savinies, although she quickly added that the comparison referred only to their "happy life together," before the intrusion of the husband-to-be. The moral of Madame de Genlis's tale was clear, she concluded: "Reason must temper even the most innocent love."[7] But a closer reading of the letter makes one wonder whether Lucia was not also making a veiled, perhaps even unconscious reference to Maximilian Plunkett, whom both she and her sister had loved in their own way (Paolina's relationship with "the worthy colonel" remained platonic). After Maximilian's death, Lucia never once mentioned his name in her letters to Paolina—at least not in those which have survived. And writing about the two Savinies is probably the closest she ever came to evoking his memory in her correspondence with her sister.

· · ·

By the end of 1807 the quiet provincial life began to lose its early appeal. Lucia complained:

> We are immersed in permanent fog. I spend all of my time in my room and I am bored to death. Alvise stays all day at the Prefecture and my son is busy studying. During my first year here I explored the city and the region; this year I have nothing left to describe except this one room where I take my meals, I sleep, I get dressed, I read, I write and I receive occasional guests.[8]

Her humdrum days in Novara came abruptly to an end in early January 1808, when, as Alvise had predicted, she was summoned to the court in Milan to take up her duties as lady-in-waiting to Princess Augusta. She hurriedly packed her luggage, bade farewell to her husband, her son and the house staff, and was off to the capital.

Marchioness Barbara Litta, who, as Princess Augusta's lady of honour, was in charge of protocol at the royal palace, warned Lucia to prepare herself for a demanding schedule, especially during those weeks when she would have to be in attendance at the palace from early morning until late at night. She was to draw a monthly salary with which to cover her expenses. The palace that was to house Princess Augusta's twenty-four ladies-in-waiting was still being refurbished, but Marchioness Litta found her temporary lodgings in the house of Countess Cattaneo.

Lucia was immediately caught up in a whirlwind of activity. She rushed to the hairdresser, went shopping for clothes, introduced herself to the other ladies-in-waiting, who, she found out, were all Milanese but a few. She called on the most prominent families in town as well as the foreign dignitaries. And after a few days, the exacting Marchioness Litta was ready to present her to Princess Augusta—who was pregnant with her second child.

Lucia found the princess beautiful and charming. Despite her young age, she was at ease in her important role. She was also very much in love with Prince Eugène and absorbed by family life. When they had married, in Munich, in the spring of 1806—a marriage entirely orchestrated by Napoleon after his resounding victory at Austerlitz—Augusta had been in love with the Prince of Baden, to whom she had been promised, and had thrown herself at the feet of Empress Joséphine, imploring her not to impose the marriage with her son. In the end she had succumbed to powerful reasons of state—Napoleon crowned her father king of Bavaria—but then she had met the amiable Prince Eugène, and had liked him from the start. A year and a half later, with a child in the crib and a second one on the way, they were a handsome, loving couple.

Despite the difference in age—Lucia was nearing forty while Princess Augusta was only twenty-two—they got along well. The problem, she told Paolina one week into her job, was the nature of the work rather than her employer:

> I lead the dullest existence, rushing from my apartment to Court and from Court to my apartment. What does one do at Court? Well, the evenings in which we have *Grand cercle* ("Large Circle") we tend to sit around for about an hour before moving to the gaming room. When the card-playing is over the Princess rises, says a few nice words to us and I run back home as fast as I can. When we have *Petit cercle* ("Small Circle"), only those of us attached to the Court are invited. The evening usually begins with a session of baby-watching: we crowd around ten-month-old Joséphine, Princess of Bologna, as she plays in her pen. Very interesting . . . Then we move on to our usual card games and Madame de Sandizell* serves tea. The Princess chats with us familiarly when the playing is over and then retires, and so do I. This is what my

---

* Madame de Sandizell had accompanied the vicereine from Bavaria and served as chief-of-staff at the Palace, liaising with Marchioness Litta, who was in charge of the Italian ladies-in-waiting.

life is like on Sundays, Tuesdays, Thursdays and Fridays from seven in the evening until about midnight. On Mondays a ball is held at one of the prominent Milanese houses and the Court is present. Which means I have Wednesday and Saturday evenings off. I spent last Wednesday evening sitting alone by the fire; today is Saturday and I'll do the same as I am too exhausted to go to the opera. In fact I'm rather looking forward to going to bed early as I have only just now been informed that, starting tomorrow, I am on duty for the entire week![9]

To be "on duty" meant one had to be in attendance at the palace from the time the princess got up in the morning until she retired at night. So the following morning, a Sunday, Lucia arrived early at the royal palace to breakfast with Princess Augusta. They proceeded to mass, Lucia burdened by the weight of her long, heavy velvet mantle. She was allowed a short break to change into a more comfortable dress, but had to be back promptly at the palace for *Petit cercle*. During the rest of her week, she arrived at the palace at eleven wearing a *déshabillé*. She stayed with Princess Augusta for lunch and accompanied her on her early afternoon walk. "She loves to take long walks beyond the city limits," Lucia noted with slight impatience:

> We're back by four, at which point I'm allowed to go home to change so that I can reappear for dinner on time, usually wearing a round dress. Marchioness Litta has had to reprimand the Milanese ladies, who have been rather negligent about arriving for dinner on time. The reason is that when they go home to change, many are tempted to eat at their own table rather than at Court.[10]

After a gruelling week, always rushing to the hairdresser, changing clothes three times a day, coming home late and getting up early, Lucia was primed for release. At that week's ball, she stayed until half past one in the morning and danced "like I haven't danced in fifteen years."[11]

Lucia did what was expected of her, with diligence and grace; but she found it hard to muster any kind of enthusiasm for her job. She resented being kept away from Alvisetto, who was still in Novara, having enrolled as a day student in the Collegio Gallarino to study Italian, Latin, geography and mathematics. She did not complain to her husband because she feared his irritated reaction. But to her sister she confessed "how really awful this arrangement is for me."[12]

Alvise was determined to send Alvisetto off to boarding school in Paris, for Napoleon wanted the sons of officials in the foreign kingdoms of the Empire to be educated in France. Lucia did not see what good could possibly come from sending her eight-year-old child far away from home. She lost no opportunity to underscore how miserable little boys were in boarding school, reminding her husband that Paolina's two boys, Venceslao and Ferighetto, thirteen and eleven, had sadly lost their natural verve at their school in Padua.

The issue, however, went beyond Alvisetto's education. Since joining the government in the Italian kingdom, Alvise had wholly embraced the Napoleonic cause. His earlier criticism of the French, which he had vented so many times as he struggled to gain the trust of the Habsburgs, was now a thing of the past. Napoleon had brought Europe to his feet. He was creating a new order, a modern society. The future, Alvise was now convinced, belonged to this extraordinary man he had met in Brescia a decade earlier. "I work twelve to fourteen hours a day," he observed, "but it is worth it because I know that I am working for the hero of all time."[13]

Alvise was increasingly confident that the Italian kingdom was going to become an important part of Napoleon's expanding empire; as a result, Alvisopoli would continue to prosper—a model estate in a model kingdom. He saw himself as the founder of a dynasty in a Napoleonic Europe, and he was seized with the notion that Alvisopoli would become, one day soon, an autonomous duchy within the kingdom—with himself as the first Duke of Alvisopoli. To set the seal on his political metamorphosis, Alvise commissioned a monumental statue of Napoleon from Angelo Pizzi, the much admired director of the sculpture department at Venice's Arts Academy, and planned to place it in the centre of Alvisopoli's main square—certainly not in the damp ground-floor hall of Palazzo Mocenigo, where it eventually came to rest.

Alvise grew impatient with those Venetians who felt a nostalgic attachment to the old Republic and who still referred to Venice as their "fatherland." Among them was Lucia. She did not live in the past, as some of the more conservative old patricians did, but she had no sense of loyalty towards Napoleon or to the Kingdom of Italy, and certainly no great love for her duties at court. Lucia still thought of herself as a Venetian, and she felt the deepest attachment to her Venetian heritage. The Republic no longer existed, of course; there was no Venetian fatherland to speak of any more. But it survived as a spiritual place to which Lucia still felt deeply connected. It pained her to hear Alvise say, as he often did, that the Kingdom of Italy was his new fatherland and that he loved it "more than he loves Venice." Although she was wary of "the self-inflicted suffering that comes from standing against destiny," she found her husband's constant praise of the emperor exaggerated and even jarring.[14]

Lucia also cringed at the way Venetian ladies tried to please and befriend their Milanese counterparts, "to tie themselves" to the new kingdom, she noted with slight repulsion:

> How many visits they pay, how many presents they give, how they seek a confidential tone in addressing women they hardly know, even using the familiar *tu*. Wrongly perhaps, I tie myself to no one. I lead a withdrawn life, never going out on those nights I am not on duty at Court. Ah, if only it were a *Petit cercle* of old friends! The thing is that I am nearing forty—and it's too late for me to start all over again.[15]

In the winter of 1809, a year after settling in Milan, Lucia moved into her rooms in Palazzo Visconti with the other ladies-in-waiting who were from out of town. She regretted not having the privacy of her own apartment, away from her colleagues, where she could put up her feet and entertain a few Venetian friends when she was not on duty. But she was also tired of moving her things from place to place: she had lived in four different apartments since arriving in town, "the last one so unbearably smelly"[16] that her clean, freshly painted rooms in Palazzo Visconti were a relief in that respect.

Princess Augusta personally gave Lucia the new uniform she was to wear at court during the day: a long, light-brown smock buttoned tightly around her neck. "Apparently the French word for it is *sarte*," Lucia told her sister, complaining it made her look like a mother superior. "More and more I feel as if I were living in a nunnery."[17]

After serving for two years in Agogna, Alvise was awarded the Iron Cross, an order established by Napoleon to gratify the new elite he was forging in his Empire, in consideration of his administrative achievements in Novara and Alvisopoli. Napoleon also made him a count (a non-hereditary title assigned on the basis of merit), and a senator of the Kingdom, a prestigious but largely ceremonial post. Alvise's senatorial duties often brought him to Milan, but he spent the greater part of his time on his estates. All of his landholdings were now consolidated in one large agency, headquartered in Alvisopoli.

Alvisetto, nearly ten, moved to Milan to be with his mother for a year, before finally going off to boarding school. He had spent a satisfactory year at the Collegio Gallarino in Novara. His teachers were pleased by his effort and he had matured. "He's not as restless as he was when we first moved back to Italy," Lucia noted. "Alvise is also quite happy with his conduct though he would like him to be more dedicated to schoolwork."[18] The plan was still to send him to Paris, but Alvise agreed to let him spend a year in Milan to assuage Lucia's anxiety.

Vérand moved to Milan as well, to supervise Alvisetto's lessons, as Lucia was at court most of the day. She hired a kind, well-mannered Austrian music teacher who turned out to be Carl Thomas Mozart, the eldest son of Wolfgang Amadeus. When his famous father had died, in 1791, Carl Thomas was only six. At thirteen, he was sent to work as an apprentice in a commercial firm in Livorno. His dream, he told Lucia, was to start a piano business, but he had not been able to raise the necessary capital. He had gone back to studying music and for the past four years had made a living by giving piano lessons in Milan. "Of course he's not his father," Lucia told Paolina rather cruelly. "But he's very sweet, plays well enough, and he teaches in German, so Alvisetto can practise the language."[19]

Lucia's life at court resumed its dull and predictable pace after the summer furlough. She continued to do her duty without any special affection for the kingdom she served, and she still kept her distance from the scheming Milanese ladies who hovered around Prince Eugène and Princess Augusta. It occurred to her that the viceroy and the vicereine were probably the people she had grown fondest of in the period she had been in Milan. They were not an especially lively couple, but she came to value their kindness and consideration.

Lucia's relationship with Princess Augusta revolved a great deal around clothes, as the Vicereine was constantly giving her rich gala dresses, more informal round dresses and easy-to-wear *déshabillés* from the best houses in Paris. The fabrics were among the finest, the colours fashionable, the gold and silver linings and bordures always of the best quality. Princess Augusta gave Lucia two or three dresses at a time, and she always remembered her birthday and her saint's day. Lucia loved beautiful clothes and liked to be *à la page*, and of course she had plenty of opportunities to wear her new dresses. But she accumulated so many of them that she did not know where to store them any more. "[The Princess] is so generous with all of us and of course I am grateful for everything she gives me," she told Paolina, "but I have reached the point where a new dress fails to excite much interest in me."[20]

Somewhat to her surprise, Lucia found that clothes were often Prince Eugène's preferred topic of conversation as well. "The Viceroy called me to his room last night," she wrote to Paolina conspiratorially,

> He said: "In the last few days I've looked at many waistcoats and have chosen several for myself. There is one I like especially, and I've ordered a cut of the same fabric for you to make a dress. You know the fashion is now for men and women to wear matching dresses and waistcoats . . ."[21]

The fabric was a beautiful *velours cachemire,* with a flower pattern embroidered in the Ottoman style. Lucia was flattered to be the object of Prince Eugène's attentions, and she enjoyed the light flirtation between them. But she found it odd, and vaguely frustrating, that the Prince did not wish to discuss more serious matters.

Fashion, of course, was what the ladies-in-waiting mostly talked about among themselves and with Princess Augusta during the afternoon stroll or after their game of cards at *Petit cercle.* There were tedious disquisitions on the merit of short sleeves over long sleeves, on the latest designs from Paris, on the colours in vogue that season. Conversation was seldom lively and never brilliant. No one touched politics. Very little was mentioned about art, literature or even music. In the early days of the Cisalpine Republic, when poets and artists had been drawn to Milan by the young Bonaparte, the intellectual life had been quite vibrant. But after the proclamation of the Empire and the transformation of the Cisalpine Republic into the Kingdom of Italy, the monotonous rituals of royal etiquette imported from Paris created a soporific atmosphere.

Milan was an emasculated capital. All the important decisions were made in Paris. Prince Eugène took his orders directly from Napoleon. Members of the government, senators, courtiers: everyone wanted to be in Paris rather than Milan. Carriages with travelling officials crowded the road to France across the Alps that was being enlarged. "There seems to be a permanent migration to the French court," Lucia grumbled. "Every minute one dignitary or another is leaving town with the excuse that he must go fetch his orders."[22]

In 1809, Prince Eugène travelled to Paris to be at his mother's side as she faced one of the most trying periods in her life. Napoleon had made it clear to Empress Joséphine that there would come a time when she would have to step aside and allow him to marry a young European princess capable of bearing him an heir. After ruminating over the matter for many months, Napoleon decided the time for a divorce had come. It was not an easy decision; he remained deeply attached to his wife, even as they saw less and less of each other and other women came into his life. But having learnt that, contrary to what he had long assumed, he was not sterile—at the end of 1806 Eléanore de la Plaigne, one of his lovers, had given birth to a boy named Léon—he now wanted a legitimate son in order to ensure a Bonaparte dynasty. The divorce papers were signed on 14 December 1809, during a tense, tearful ceremony at the Tuileries. Joséphine read a note handed to her by the foreign minister, Prince Talleyrand, declaring that, since she could no longer hope to bear children, in the interest of France she was "happy to offer this greatest proof of her devotion and attachment." The emperor, to the irritation of the Bonaparte brothers and sisters who had always detested her, paid one last homage to the woman "who has illuminated my life for fifteen years and whose memory shall always be present in my heart."[23]

Joséphine retained the title of empress. She was given full ownership of Malmaison, the beautiful country palace outside Paris where she lived, and her yearly stipend rose to a combined three million francs, a huge sum of money even for a profligate spender like her. Behind the scenes, Talleyrand and the interior minister, Fouché, were already putting the finishing touches to Napoleon's offer to marry Marie Louise, the eighteen-year-old daughter of the Austrian emperor, Francis I. The news was leaked to the papers and in early February 1810, Lucia read about it in the Milanese gazettes.

Alvise joined the senate delegation that headed to Paris to congratulate the emperor on his marriage. Lucia was also making the trip: the vicereine was taking all her ladies-in-waiting with her to attend the wedding. At first, the thought of leaving Alvisetto threw Lucia into a state of turmoil. "I am desperate about this sudden departure and I can't wait to be back," she told her sister. "Oh, do write to my little boy, and give him the sound advice you give to your own children. I beg you to take my place in everything while I am gone."[24]

However "desperate" she was, Lucia could not entirely stifle the excitement of going to Paris for the first time. "Ah, Paris! Paris!" she cried out, obviously thrilled and anxious at the same time.

Alvise had been to Paris twice before the Revolution, and he had described the city many times to Lucia. She was familiar with the major monuments and churches and famous landmarks through many Parisian novels she had read—especially those of Madame de Genlis. The Louvre, the Tuileries, Saint Germain, Notre Dame, the bridges over the Seine—were all part of Lucia's mental map of Paris. The more vivid images of this imaginary landscape, however, had come to her from Madame Dupont, her childhood governess, who had enchanted her and Paolina with her wonderful tales of the city where she had grown up. Madame Dupont was still very much part of the family. After Lucia and Paolina were married, she had stayed in Venice, living as lady companion in several prominent Venetian houses. Lucia made a point of giving her a small monthly stipend to cover basic expenses, and she was always happy to see her whenever she was back in Venice. Now she had a mission to accomplish: discover Madame Dupont's Paris. "I should so much like to find the places she often mentioned to us," she told Paolina. "All the names changed after the Revolution and then again with the Directoire and the Empire. But I have her old address and the name of her parish and I shall do my best to uncover the original denominations."[25]

Napoleon and Marie Louise were married by proxy in Vienna on 11 March 1810. Two days later, Lucia left Milan heading west, towards the French Alps. She paid for the trip with her salary. She and Countess Trotti, a fellow lady-in-waiting, shared the travel expenses. They bought a *bastardella*, a sturdy, four-wheel coach hitched to four horses, for fifty-two sequins. There were six passengers in all, as both Lucia and Countess Trotti brought a personal maid (Lucia had Margherita with her) and a servant. It took ten days to reach Paris. The journey went smoothly apart from the discomfort of being piled into a small coach for so long. The snows had melted in the mountains and the new road Napoleon had built over the pass of Mont Cenis was clear—the crossing of the Alps was faster now as it was no longer necessary to transfer to hand-carried *chaises* to get over the pass.

In Paris, Lucia was immediately drawn back into the circle of Italians "who have come here in droves from the kingdom."[26] Prince Eugène and Princess Augusta were there to welcome her and the other ladies-in-waiting, and the travelling Milanese court soon resumed its daily rituals under the watchful eye of Marchioness Litta. Before she knew it, Lucia was getting in and out of round dresses (day-wear), *douillettes* (quilted silk overgarments) and negligees (morning gowns), and following the Princess around, as if she had never left Milan. Prince Eugène, having weathered the stressful divorce between Napoleon and his mother, took a new pleasure in chaperoning his flock of rustling ladies. Each night, he gave out seats in the boxes assigned to him at the Comédie Française. "The choice of plays is horrible, the acting very common,"[27] Lucia opined, after seeing a production of Molière's *L'Avare*—clearly she found it hard to enjoy Paris on such a short leash.

Archduchess Marie Louise, meanwhile, was on her way from Vienna. She stopped frequently along the way to wave at the crowds and reply to all the speeches that were made in her honour. "The word in Paris," Lucia told Paolina, "is that she is poised and quick and wins everyone over wherever she goes." Napoleon was waiting for her at the castle of Compiègne, an hour out of Paris. He supervised the expensive decoration of her apartment and personally chose the works of art that adorned the rooms, including Canova's beautiful *Psyché* about to be kissed by

Cupid. "I hear he is in a complete tizzy over her and frets over a thousand details. He sat at length in the carriage he sent to Strasbourg for her, just to make sure her seat was comfortable."[28]

When the archduchess stepped out of her carriage at Compiègne, Napoleon took her straight to her apartments. To the surprise, and indeed the disbelief of many dignitaries who had come to greet the future empress, they did not emerge until the following day. Having been assured that the marriage by proxy in Vienna was valid in the eyes of the Church, Napoleon wasted no time in putting his feisty young wife to the task.

The following week, their civil marriage was celebrated at Saint Cloud, and the next day they were married in a religious ceremony at the Tuileries, where the *salon carré* of the Louvre was transformed for the occasion in a dazzling imperial chapel. At Napoleon's request, the ritual was the same that had been followed forty years earlier for the wedding of Louis XVI and Marie Antoinette.

The emperor and the empress returned to Compiègne for their honeymoon in a state of complete enthralment—Marie Louise even took to making coffee for her husband every morning and within days she was calling him silly nicknames like "Nana" and "Popo."[29] Napoleon gave every indication that he intended to linger in the arms of his wife at their countryside castle while important state papers piled up in his study. Prince Eugène and Princess Augusta, summoned to Compiègne with the rest of the court, brought their own vast retinue. Lucia felt her cloistered days were back:

> I have been living like a monk since the day I arrived. Our residence has the appearance of a dormitory. The rooms open out on to this long corridor where lonely ladies-in-waiting pace up and down waiting for instructions. We pay each other visits, going from cell to cell. Our schedule is intense and rigid: we cannot leave the house even when we are not on duty all day long. [In the morning] we have breakfast together in the refectory. Then we walk over to the Empress's quar-

ters, and there we wait for their majesties to walk
before us on their way to chapel. We follow the
Empress. But only Princess Augusta, her maids of
honour and those of us who are on duty are allowed to
follow the Empress all the way inside.[30]

Like all Habsburgs, Marie Louise was a fervent Catholic.
Napoleon, anxious to please his wife, showed an unusual devout-
ness during the numerous religious ceremonies that began to take
place at court. A rather startled Lucia, who well remembered
young Bonaparte's early crusade against the Pope when he first
conquered Italy, reported that the emperor "seems completely
absorbed by his prayers." At Marie Louise's request, all meat was
forbidden at court during the week preceding Easter, and
Napoleon extended the injunction to all the restaurants in the
area of Compiègne, to make sure that wily dignitaries did not
circumvent the court's order.

The stay at Compiègne turned into the most tedious sojourn
for everyone except the imperial couple. Occasionally, it was
enlivened by a hunt in the surrounding woods. The event was
never much fun for Lucia but at least it was an opportunity to
leave the palace and get some fresh air:

Today we rushed through the woods in an open
buggy, though we never actually saw the hunters,
among whom was the Emperor. The Empress followed the hunt in her carriage, and we followed her.
After six hours we stopped for a picnic lunch. I had a
plate of asparagus and drank a glass of champagne.[31]

During her stay at Compiègne, Lucia managed to take two
days off to visit the former empress, Joséphine, in the duchy of
Navarre, sixty miles east of Paris. The small chateau of Navarre,
to which Napoleon had in effect exiled his former wife for the
duration of the wedding celebrations, was very run-down. The
walls needed painting and the rooms seemed to lack proper furniture. There was, all about the house, a melancholy atmosphere of

impermanence. But it quickly dissolved once Lucia stepped out into the gardens, which were nicely kept and very beautiful; she wondered if a caring gardener had made a point of preserving the structure and design of the lawns and the hedges and the flower beds while the chateau was left in a state of semi-abandon.

Joséphine had always seemed younger than her years, but now she looked old and worn, and her teeth were so black she barely opened her mouth when she spoke. Still, she was as amiable and warm-hearted as Lucia remembered her from their previous meeting in Venice in 1797. Soon the two were talking like old friends, and Lucia could not help mentioning how much she missed Alvisetto, and how she hated the idea of sending him off to boarding school in Paris. Joséphine could not have been more sympathetic: she knew what it meant to live separated from one's children, and she told Lucia how much she had relied on Eugène and her daughter Hortense when going through the awful experience of her divorce from Napoleon. "We had the most pleasant time together,"[32] Lucia later wrote to Paolina. The next day Joséphine, escorted by four imperial guards, took Lucia to Louvieux, six miles up the road, to see a textile plant. They spent a few carefree hours looking at new spinning machines and frames and designs, and running their hands over the beautiful fabrics.

After a month in Compiègne, Empress Marie Louise wondered aloud why so many Italian ladies were still following her around, and when she was told they were Princess Augusta's ladies-in-waiting, she let it be known that they were no longer required to stay. To her relief, Lucia moved back to Paris and took rooms with Alvise at the Hotel d'Europe, in rue de Richelieu. Princess Augusta gave her ladies some time off in the city before returning to Italy, and Lucia at last had an opportunity to explore Madame Dupont's Paris. "I want to see where she lived! I have the same curiosity as those visitors who rush to the birthplace of a Voltaire or a Rousseau—only more so since she was so much more important to us."[33]

Lucia's quest was only partially successful: though she reached Madame Dupont's neighbourhood, and wandered in very familiar terrain, she never found rue du Maçon, where her governess had grown up. The names of the streets were the main obstacle: none of them matched the ones Madame Dupont remembered from her youth. The urban landscape had also changed. During the Revolution, buildings had been destroyed, while churches had been turned into stables or barracks. Lucia wrote to Paolina:

> Tell Madame I crossed Pont Saint Michel. She would not recognise it as all the side-buildings on the bridge have been torn down and replaced by two wide pavements. I recognised rue de la Houchette because I remembered Madame describing it as "small and crooked," but today it is called something else. At the church of Saint Severin, I found a ninety-four-year-old man sitting by the front door—they live to a very old age where Madame comes from! He told me the church was reopened in 1802. It is quite beautiful inside, with as many as five naves. I asked about Madame Dupont's family. The old man seemed to remember her father but he said they lived in rue du Foin, not rue du Maçon . . .[34]

Lucia made her way back towards her hotel in rue de Richelieu, which was known as rue de la Loi during the Revolution and the Directoire, and had only just regained its original name. As she passed through the tree-lined esplanade in front of the Invalides, she suddenly recognised the proudly pouting lion of Venice, which the French had taken in 1797, as he looked down at the indifferent passers-by from the top of a fountain. On the spur of the moment, and despite having already walked for several hours, Lucia headed in the direction of Place du Carousel, for she remembered hearing that the great bronze horses Bonaparte had removed from the basilica in Saint Mark's Square had been placed on the top of the new *arc de triomphe*. And sure enough, there they were, cantering awkwardly in the Parisian sky. They seemed small and ungainly from the ground. As Lucia stood there, increasingly indignant, her head turned upwards and her eyes squinting in the glare of the sun, she realised the horses were hitched to a gold-plated chariot. It was driven by two allegorical statues so entirely out of proportion they made the poor horses look rather like dogs.

Later she learnt that a bronze of Napoleon was to drive the chariot—the two allegorical pieces were merely substituting while the statue was completed. *"Le char l'attend"* (the chariot awaits him) was a pun on the word "charlatan" making the rounds in Paris.[35] Lucia had a good laugh when she heard it.

Despite her swollen feet, she was determined to continue what she referred to as the Madame Dupont Paris Tour, and devoted the next day to Saint Denis, the church of the kings of France, which her former governess had described many times to her. The damage from the revolutionary period was still visible on the facade as most of the statues were still headless. Her guide gave her a chilling account of what had occurred inside the church, which she passed on to Paolina.

> The tombs of the kings were destroyed with sledge-hammers and all the lead casings were taken away. The bones were extracted from the debris and scattered haphazardly in the local cemetery. The Jacobins brought heavy wagons into the church to cart off the lead bars that supported the roof, cracking the marble pavement as they came and went. Eventually, the roof crashed to the ground and destroyed the pavement completely.

Napoleon was having Saint Denis restored to its former splendour. He wanted his own mausoleum near those of the great French kings. Dozens of stonemasons, glassworkers and carpenters were at work when Lucia walked in. "The floor of the central nave is covered in shiny white marble while the side walls are black," she described to her sister. "The great gothic windows have been refitted with the most beautiful glasswork. The atmosphere inside the church is again one of great dignity." The Bonaparte mausoleum was below the ground level. "The door to His Majesty's *caveau* [vault] is made of bronze-plated iron. There are three locks, each one covered by the head of a lion. Bumblebees, the emblem of the Bonapartes, are carved everywhere . . ."[36]

Another landmark in Madame Dupont's Paris was the Bois de Boulogne. "Do you remember how she enthused us with her descriptions of a most agreeable park, where the ladies met to ride their horses?" she asked Paolina. It turned out the Bois was no longer a *bois*. "It was reduced to a vast moor during the Revolution as all the trees were cut down to make heating wood. I saw the new shoots coming through, though—for posterity's delight." At the end of her walk, Lucia joined a crowd of Italian friends for a picnic lunch at Bagatelle, an open-air restaurant that had been very fashionable in pre-revolutionary days and that was now struggling to come back into vogue:

> There were sixty of us and we ate under a big tent pitched in a lovely meadow in front of the pavilion commissioned by the Comte d'Artois* during the reign of the last king and built in only forty days. It makes you sad to look at it now: everything is so dilapidated. All the furniture is missing. The walls and ceilings are in a state of utter neglect. The mirrors above the mantelpieces are the only thing left, though I doubt they are the original ones . . .[37]

But the garden outside the pavilion was lovely, and the day was warm and beautiful. Excellent food was served at a buffet *en plein air*. There were tasty cold soups, fresh eggs, mutton chops, roast chickens and Lucia's favourite fowl dish, *pigeon à la crapaudine*, and delicious spring peas, salads and strawberries. Most of the people there would soon be journeying back to Italy and the thought of going home no doubt enhanced the festive mood. As

---

* The Comte d'Artois, the future King Charles X, was Louis XVI's youngest brother.

the wine flowed, the company became louder and Lucia joined a group singing old Venetian songs.

That evening, back at the Hotel d'Europe, Lucia was in her study, still feeling flushed from the day's sunshine, when Alvise came in to announce that he was enrolling Alvisetto in a school in Paris. "I feel as if I had been struck by a thunderbolt," Lucia wrote to Paolina in desperation. Only a few days earlier, Alvise had told her that since Alvisetto was studying well in Milan, he had decided to postpone his transfer to Paris by a year or two. But in the meantime he had received a letter from Monsieur Vérand saying that in fact Alvisetto's grades were not improving at all. Even worse, he was rude to his teachers. She told her sister:

> That fateful letter has changed things around completely and my husband now tells me he has already written to Milan giving instructions to send Alvisetto to Paris without delay. I cannot bear the thought of not seeing him for God knows how many years. He will become a stranger to his own parents. I feel deeply wounded by this whole affair.

Alvise and Lucia spent the second half of May and the first half of June looking at schools, from the smallest ones, where six or seven pupils were taught by a master in the old Socratic manner, to the more structured *collèges* with as many as 500 students, which the emperor strongly supported. They also looked for lodging arrangements at religious establishments and various *pensionnats*. Lucia complained to Paolina:

> This search is killing me, I can't even imagine how hard it will be to say goodbye to him. Tears are streaming down my face even as I write to you and I'm afraid you will find their trace all over this paper. But you are my sister, and you are a mother, and I know that you understand what I feel.

Lucia wanted to enlist the help of a person who might yet dissuade Alvise. "It is hard to find the right man, though. The French are not going to embrace my cause, while the Italians, who do not share Alvise's opinion, don't have enough influence over him. And those who have settled here have by now embraced French culture." It occurred to her that the one person who had "considerable sway" over Alvise and might yet dissuade him was Joséphine, who had returned from Navarre and was spending a few days at Malmaison before leaving for the waters at Plombières, in Savoy. Lucia went over for lunch and the former empress agreed to talk to Alvise. In the afternoon, they walked in the park and visited the exotic animals that Joséphine had collected in her private zoo. Lucia winced as she caught sight of Joséphine's two black swans swimming in the pond. She feared they were a bad omen, but kept her mouth shut.

A few days later Lucia told Paolina that "the [former] Empress has spoken to Alvise, and apparently Princess Augusta has also talked to him. But I don't know what will come of all this. Alvise has not said a word to me about these attempts to dissuade him, and he is not aware that I know about them."[38]

In the end, Joséphine's behind-the-scenes diplomacy helped to find a solution that was more acceptable to Lucia: Alvisetto would not go to boarding school but would lodge in a private house with Monsieur Vérand, and enrol in the prestigious Lycée Napoléon as a day student. "The separation will be painful but I shall be less anxious if Vérand is here," Lucia conceded.[39] Alvise agreed to a two-year trial period instead of the full eight years of secondary education; and he promised Alvisetto would return to Italy if the experiment was not a success. A pleasant room for him and Vérand was found in rue Chanoineuse, near Notre Dame, in the apartment of Monsieur Humbert, a professor at the Lycée, and his Alsatian wife. "She seems like a good woman and Alvisetto will be able to practise his German with her," Lucia observed, trying to make the best of the situation.[40]

At the end of June, a dazed and travel-weary Alvisetto arrived in Paris with Vérand. Lucia was overjoyed to have him with her, and did not stop hugging and kissing him even though she already felt the pain of their imminent separation. A few days later, Princess Augusta informed her ladies-in-waiting they were all free to return to Milan. "She wants us to arrive in Italy before her, so it means we must leave right now," Lucia explained to Paolina.[41] As she helped Alvisetto settle in with the Humberts and prepare his school material, she noticed Alvise was growing agitated as the separation approached, though of course he tried not to show it. They were off in mid July, headed for the Swiss Alps. "I said goodbye to Alvisetto last night after putting him to bed," Lucia wrote to her sister from the village of Morais, in the mountains near Geneva. "My poor little boy was in a terrible state, and wouldn't stop crying." Alvise insisted that it was all for Alvisetto's own good, and reminded Lucia that when *he* was a little boy, his parents had sent him away to Rome for six years. Lucia found the comparison odd considering how miserable her husband had been as a child, but she let it go at that. "As I write," she added, "the full moon is shining over this small village where we shall be spending the night but my heart is broken . . ."[42]

Lucia took to her bed as soon as she reached Milan. She had felt progressively worse during her journey from Paris and she did not improve when she reached home. A persistent nausea settled over her, and she developed stomach pains which did not go away despite frequent bouts of vomiting. A rheumatic fever complicated her general condition. In the autumn, she also suffered a prolapse of the uterus which made it very uncomfortable to move around.

The doctors in Milan were confounded by Lucia's mysterious ailments. She was prescribed the usual remedies: waters, mud cures, a meatless diet, no exercise. There was little improvement. The *palazzo* assigned to Princess Augusta's ladies-in-waiting was temporarily unavailable and she ended up having to rent a "horrid" small apartment in Corso di Porta Rienza, on the road to Villa Bonaparte, from a man ominously called Signor Scorpioni. Alvise was away in the countryside and was not there to help with the move. Contributing to her general discomfort was the guilt she felt for leaving Alvisetto behind: it never went away, just like the nausea. Each letter she received from him tore her heart to pieces, and she longed to make the trip back to Paris even if she felt so awful. The doctors, however, were adamant: she should not even contemplate the idea of such a trip in her condition.

It was a miserable time made sadder by the death of Signora Antonia, the woman who had raised Alvisetto in Venice during the first years of his life. "I shall never forget how much I owe her for the loving way in which she took care of you when you were a little child," she wrote to her son. "In death one cannot pray for oneself, you know that; but remember that the soul of the dead can draw relief from the mortification of those who remain behind. You can show your own attachment to Signora Antonia by offering her your tears and your prayers."[43]

Princess Augusta and Marchioness Litta came to Lucia's rescue, reducing her duties at the royal palace to a minimum. The other ladies-in-waiting agreed to pick up the slack and substitute when it was her turn to be on duty. Princess Augusta regularly exempted her from the afternoon walk. In the evening, whether at *Petit cercle* or *Grand cercle*, Lucia usually sat in the back seats so she could make an early exit. "They all cooperate for my well-being," Lucia assured an increasingly worried Paolina. When she was not at work she stayed at home. "I rarely take a coach, I don't call on people, I don't go shopping and never go out after lunch or dinner. Today I came home early, had lunch, rested. I went back to the palace in the evening for *cercle* but I was home by ten thirty. I ate a bowl of soup, undid my hair, undressed and am now in bed."[44]

A whole year passed without any serious signs of improvement. After going through a long list of Milanese and Venetian physicians, Lucia decided to consult Cavalier Paletta, a medicine man who was frowned upon by mainstream doctors for his unorthodox remedies. Paletta argued the prolapse of the uterus was caused by the weakness of the muscles and ligaments sustaining it, and recommended Lucia "insert a dose of iron-rich ochre" into her vagina.[45] She was to drink great quantities of the "acidulous" mineral water of Recoaro, near Vicenza, and apply to her loins the ferruginous deposits of that water. Lucia started the cure immediately, making frequent trips to Vicenza. For good measure she started rubbing her loins with holy water of the Blessed Virgin which Paolina had sent from a sanctuary near the town of Caravaggio. Within weeks she started to feel better. "The uterus is rising at last," Lucia was relieved to notice.[46] She was uncertain as to the cause of her general improvement but she did not miss the opportunity to tell her sister that it was surely due to the miraculous water she had sent her. Her appetite returned, and she was able to hold her food down—except, of course, when she over-indulged, as when she ate "a plate of mushrooms, some fried fennel and grilled perch, in addition to various meat dishes and wine." Not surprisingly, she spent the night "vomiting in great abundance." "I know you are scolding me," she sheepishly told her sister. "You are right to do so."[47]

Lucia's health problems did not keep her away from her "little transactions"—Alvise's affectionate but somewhat dismissive term for the small farming investments she had been making over the past decade. Every year, she made a small profit by selling potatoes she grew in two fields she rented from the agency in Alvisopoli. She also raised a few pigs for *prosciutto* and she kept a flock of sheep for their wool. Her earnings were enough to pay Madame Dupont's stipend, to make a few charitable donations, to help Paolina when she was in need, and to spend a little on herself without having to ask Alvise for money.

In addition to her pigs and sheep, she now invested in a pair of six-month-old calves. Alvise, without showing great enthusiasm for Lucia's commercial activity, had never openly discouraged it, allowing his impatience to grow until it erupted over the matter of the two calves. Signor Locatelli, the agency's general manager, had rather innocently suggested to Lucia that she send her two calves to pasture over to the Valli Mocenighe, the large estate near Este where most of the cattle was raised, so she could feed them at no cost. Now a year had passed and Alvise told Lucia he did not want her doing business outside of Alvisopoli, adding that he wanted to buy the two calves from her at the same price for which she had purchased them since they had been fed on his land. Lucia answered curtly that she was selling on the market. One of Alvise's agents sold the two calves for her, at zero profit, later admitting that he had sold them to the agency. Lucia told her sister that she was furious:

> The way Alvise sided with the agent and against his own wife really stung me; he should show more respect for me—especially in our own house. He has completely humiliated me. I never would have thought that my own husband would turn out to be my worst enemy . . . Oh, I get so mad when I am put down like this. If only you knew how angry I have been all day over this matter![48]

The atmosphere did not improve during the following months. Alvise led his own life, which revolved around Alvisopoli and the other Mocenigo estates; he made occasional forays into Milan only if the Senate was in session. Lucia was stuck in the paralysing routine at court, where her schedule returned to normal as her health improved. To make matters more unpleasant between them, Alvise instructed the family banker in Milan not to make any disbursements to his wife without his written approval. Lucia had always been very careful with the money entrusted to her. Now she suddenly found herself short of cash for household expenses not covered by her stipend—Alvise was often travelling and was hard to reach at short notice. So Lucia was forced to pawn her silverware and her gold just to get by and to pay her bills. She felt humiliated, of course, but also annoyed by the sheer inefficiency of this method.

Lucia did not understand why Alvise was being so unkind to her. She assumed that her husband was seeing other women during his constant travels in the provinces; new friendships as well as old flames. But there did not seem to be any serious attachment undermining their relationship. She felt her marriage, which had

already endured so much, was entering a new, perilous phase—
and for no clear reason. More baffling to her was the fact that
Alvise was no longer his usual self with their son.

Alvisetto was spending the summer of 1812 on a farm in
Annières with Vérand. The boy had not seen his parents in two
years, and his letters were becoming more poignant each month.
"Oh darling mother," he wrote from the countryside south of
Paris, "have pity on me and give me news about you. I would
give everything I have to receive a letter from you now . . ."[49]
Lucia did not have the courage to tell him it was going to be
another year until they could be reunited, as she had been placed
on duty at court for the duration of the winter trimester. Even if
her health permitted, she would not be able to make the journey
to Paris before April of the following year. Alvise had promised
his son a trial period of two years. The two years had passed, yet
he showed no sign of wanting to confront the issue, let alone
journey to Paris; and he lost his patience for very little.

Alvisetto was assembling a small library and he wrote several
times to his father asking him if he could post him a few history
books he had in Milan. There was one book in particular he was
very keen to have: a classic account of the travels of Niccolò and
Antonio Zen, two Venetian navigators who had explored the
North Atlantic in the fourteenth century. Alvise complained to a
bewildered Lucia:

> [Our son] is so insistent. He's asked me a thousand
> times about these books, and a thousand times I've told
> him that the cost of sending them would be greater
> than their value. I'm determined not to let him have
> them. For the following reasons: 1) to punish him for
> his insistence, 2) to force him to be more compliant,
> 3) and to be more obedient, 4) and to be more tolerant,
> 5) I spend all I spend and still it's not enough?[50]

Alvise no longer spoke to his mother, Chiara. Their relationship had deteriorated over the ownership of some properties, and

though a financial settlement was reached after a long and hurtful litigation, a reconciliation did not follow. Lucia regretted this state of affairs. She was no longer close to Chiara, as she had been as a young daughter-in-law, but she had remained in touch with her throughout the dispute between mother and son. She had also encouraged Alvisetto to keep up a correspondence with his grandmother. When Alvise learnt what was going on behind his back, he became enraged:

> Alvisetto is still of an age in which he is not allowed to send letters that are not read by his parents. I must remind you that [the boy is Chiara's] grandson because he is my son. This means I stand between him and her. However much she hates me and tries to harm me, I shall always respect and love my mother because that is an immoveable law of nature. But [Alvisetto] is not her son. He is bound to me, and he must not try to get on with someone who is so obviously and so powerfully my enemy.[51]

What was gnawing at Alvise? His conflict with his mother surely cast a shadow over his life, making him short-tempered and intolerant with the people he was closest to. He was also under extreme pressure to find money to pay the huge taxes the Napoleonic government was levying on property to finance its military expenditures. Increasingly, Alvise was forced to use the profits from his other estates to sustain his very expensive projects at Alvisopoli. Nor did it cheer him to see more and more farm hands—boys he had seen grow into strong young men and who thought of themselves as *alvisopolitani* above all else—recruited by the army and dragged off to some faraway battlefield on the eastern front. By 1812, Alvise was losing his early enthusiasm for Napoleon's Kingdom of Italy. His mood may well have been coloured by an increasing pessimism about the future.

. . .

At the end of the summer, Prince Eugène left Italy at the head of his Armée d'Italie to join forces with Napoleon, who was on his way to Moscow. Joséphine arrived in Milan and settled in Villa Bonaparte to be with her three grandchildren and to assist Princess Augusta in the birth of her fourth child. (Napoleon had personally approved the journey to Milan in an affectionate letter he wrote to Joséphine from a village in Eastern Prussia, adding that Eugène was already with him and managing fine.)

Lucia was still in Vicenza, completing a cycle of Paletta's cure, but she returned to Milan to pay her court to Joséphine shortly after Princess Augusta's successful delivery. The two had a lot of catching up to do. Joséphine told her about her quiet life at Malmaison, surrounded by her rare animals and her exotic plants. She saw little of the emperor, she said, but he occasionally made a surprise visit when he was in Paris. He was always kind to her and to her children, whom he loved as his own, and he wrote to her regularly. Joséphine asked after Lucia's health, for Prince Eugène and Princess Augusta had informed her that she had not been well. Lucia told her about her medicine man and the mineral waters of Recoaro, adding that in truth the greatest cause of her suffering was being so far away from Alvisetto—she had even drawn up a secret plan to meet him halfway, in Lyon . . . Joséphine was a sympathetic listener, and in a moment of intimacy, Lucia mentioned the difficulties she was having with Alvise. There were times, she said, in which the tension was so high she thought she would not be able to stand it any more.

The latest incident had occurred over dinner the night before—Alvise was in town for a Senate session. Lucia's stomach pains had given her a little trouble during the day so she had asked for some broth and a slice of bread. As she waited for the food to be served at the table, she began adding up a few figures on a piece of paper—small sums she owed—while Alvise started his usual litany against his mother. When he saw Lucia was not giving him her full attention, he blew his top. "I realise now that it was a mistake to appear so thoughtless [when he was talking about his mother]," Lucia conceded, "but my momentary distraction caused him to utter such awful words against me that I burst into tears. I continued to cry in silence for the rest of the meal..."[52]

By early winter, the news from Russia had become disheartening. "In just a few days, more than 30,000 horses perished from the cold," Lucia reported to her sister in Venice, relaying whatever information she could pick up at court.

> All our cavalry is now reduced to marching in the snow. There are no more mules to transport our artillery, and most pieces had to be abandoned or destroyed . . . Our men, whom nature has not made strong enough to face the challenges [of the Russian campaign], are struggling on, exhausted and utterly disheartened.[53]

Napoleon's army suffered a devastating rout. The Italian contingent—27,000 men—was wiped out. Only a handful of officers and soldiers made it back home. Often Lucia's reports were little more than lists of the dead and the missing: "Lauretta Mocenigo's son died with a bullet in his chest . . . The young Widman boy is dead . . . The Giustinians have lost their child and are so crushed with grief they will not leave the house . . . Alemagna's son has returned disfigured after losing his nose to frostbite . . ."[54]

It was the gloomiest winter in a long time. Lucia could not wait to leave Milan at the first signs of spring and join her son in Paris. Her health was on the mend. "My stomach has definitely recovered," she assured Paolina in early March. "I am feeling well." A few weeks later she announced that her "u-t-e-r-u-s is in good shape, exactly where it is meant to be."[55] There was nothing holding her back any more. She completed her duties at court at the end of March, and left for Paris in April with the intention of spending several months with Alvisetto, who was now thirteen— a young adolescent. She chose the road of the Simplon Pass because it was the quickest way to reach Paris, only to find the pass was still snowbound. The passage on sleds was hazardous and would have taken much too long. She turned around, and headed for the safer route of Mont Cenis, by way of Turin. "Obstacles always appear when you least expect them," Lucia scribbled to her sister as she hurried along. Tucked among her clothes in one of the trunks was the travel book about the two Venetian navigators that Alvise had refused to send to his son. "I shall read it during the journey so I can give it to Alvisetto when I see him."[56]

Chapter Nine

A YEAR IN PARIS

Lucia thought Alvisetto had grown "prodigiously" since she had last seen him. When he rushed to embrace her, clutching a bouquet of fresh flowers in one hand and a small portrait of Napoleon in the other (it was originally intended for Alvise), she was shocked to see that he was quite a bit taller than her. At close range, she also noticed the jumble of new teeth that crowded his mouth and had slightly altered his facial expression. After more hugging and kissing before a fretful Vérand and an over-excited Teresa, Lucia dragged Alvisetto off to the nearby church of Saint Sulpice for a prayer of thanksgiving; then the two went off, hand in hand, to the Tuileries Gardens.

On closer inspection, she realised her son had twice as many canines as he should, and they were growing one on top of the other. "One only notices when he opens his mouth or laughs," she later assured Paolina. Still, the extra teeth were going to have to be pulled out. "I feel for the poor boy, and of course I worry the irons will damage the enamel on his other teeth."[1] The light dimmed on the way back home, and Lucia also noticed her son's vision was not very good. He was probably a little short-sighted, she guessed. He would have to have his eyes checked for glasses.

Alvisetto and Vérand no longer lodged with the Humberts. In view of Lucia's arrival, they had moved to an apartment in a *petit hotel* on a quiet street in Faubourg Saint Germain. The house belonged to Monsieur Minier, an etcher of some repute who lived on the ground and first floors with his wife. The Mocenigos were on the second and third floors. It was not a large apartment by any means. The antechamber was used as a dining room. On the southern side, a small living room overlooked the pretty garden tended by Madame Minier. Opposite to the living room, separated by a narrow corridor, was Lucia's bedroom, which had a rather glamorous view of Jacques-Louis David's house-studio (she occasionally glimpsed the great artist as he got in or out of his carriage). A staircase led to Alvisetto's bedroom on the upper floor, next to which was Vérand's room. Teresa, who had come to Paris with Lucia, slept in the maid's room on the same floor. Despite the size, Lucia found the apartment to be adequate. One problem bothered her, however: the lack of shutters at her bedroom windows. Also, the gratings could not be secured, and banged when the wind picked up in the evening. She resolved the matter by sleeping in the living room, where it was quieter.

Once the joy of their reunion had worn off, Lucia focused on Alvisetto's manners. She did not like what she saw. "He doesn't hold himself well at the table," she complained to her sister. "He tends to slouch or lean his head on his open hand. And he eats much too quickly."[2] She was disappointed by Vérand, who seemed entirely self-absorbed and fretted about mysterious ailments during much of the day. Alvisetto had lost respect for his old tutor, and teased him no end. Vérand, on his part, made no effort to engage the boy in conversation or stimulate his mind in any way. They had grown into an odd couple, and Lucia wondered what their daily *tête à têtes* could possibly have been like during all the time they had lived together.

One evening—Lucia happened to be out on a visit—Alvisetto came to the table with the penknife he used to sharpen his pencils, and left it open, beside his plate. At some point during dinner, Vérand asked him to pass him a lemon, and Alvisetto, rather rudely, told him to get it himself. Vérand lost patience and leaned over brusquely to grab the lemon. Fearing Vérand was about to strike him, Alvisetto jerked to the side. In the general confusion, the penknife found its way down Vérand's sleeve. Within a matter of seconds, blood gushed out from his arm, his shirt turned crimson and a large stain spread on the tablecloth. Luckily the local surgeon was able to rush over and stop the haemorrhaging. Still, Vérand's arm was a dreadful mess of yellows and blues. The next day Lucia called Professor Dubois, the Imperial Surgeon, to make sure a main artery had not been seriously punctured. "It cost me a gold *louis* but at least it has taken away the awful anxiety." Vérand took to his room to nurse his blemished limb and did not come out for days. "You can imagine how Alvisetto was frightened by the whole incident," she wrote to Paolina, ever the protective mother.[3]

Lucia was unhappy with the way Vérand had arranged Alvisetto's schedule. Her son had to get up at five o'clock in the morning in order to study for two hours with one of his teachers before going off to school. In the afternoon, he crossed the Jardin du Luxembourg to attend riding class at the Manège Impérial. He was home by dinnertime, and then hung sleepily over his homework until ten or eleven o'clock. Lucia was not surprised to learn that his grades were poor: he was probably dozing off during most of his classes. She cancelled his early-morning tutorials at home so he could sleep an hour later and still have time for morning mass. She had to drag him to church: "My son is not very devout," Lucia admitted to her sister, "and doesn't appreciate long services at all." He was always tugging at her sleeve, and whispering "Let's go, let's go."[4]

During her first weeks in Paris, Lucia called on few people, mostly friends from Milan who worked for the government in one capacity or another. She did not feel at all compelled to make her way into society; she certainly did not have a leather notebook in which to annotate the names and addresses of the families she called on, as she had had in Vienna back in 1801. "The purpose of my visit here is to be with my son," she told Paolina. "Thus I spend most of my time at home."[5] That was true only in part. Lucia had no intention of living as a recluse in Paris. She had plenty of time to explore the city when Alvisetto was at school. She loved walking through the Jardin du Luxemburg, where the roses were in full bloom. And she would use any excuse to cross the Tuileries Gardens and spend a couple of hours in the busy shops of the Passage Feydau or the Passage Panorama. After a session with her hairdresser, Monsieur Guillaume, she often stopped for a lemonade at the Café de la Foi or an ice cream at Tortoni's, and if the sun was out she sometimes prolonged her little excursion by having lunch at Martin Restaurateur, a popular restaurant near the Palais Royal. "For only two francs," she boasted, "I can have a soup, an entrée, a roast of some kind and vegetables and dessert."[6] She never neglected her daily devotions, usually going to mass at the local parish, Saint Jacques, or to Saint Sulpice, the most beautiful church in Faubourg Saint Germain, where she sometimes saw the formidable Madame de Genlis absorbed in prayer. The first time Lucia glimpsed her at her pew, she was dressed in black and wore a little straw hat, also black, and a red scarf over her shoulders. "I had been told she was tall, as tall as Madame Dupont; she may have been, but now she stands with a stoop and is very thin."[7] If Lucia was away from her neighbourhood at the time of prayer, she walked into the first church she encountered. She stopped by at weddings and funerals, mixing with strangers just to observe the faces around her; later she would jot down a description of the trembling young bride of a rich *parfumier* or the eighty grieving relatives of a wool merchant.

Lucia kept a diary in Paris which she filled with brief, factual entries. She described herself wandering around the tombstones at the Père Lachaise cemetery, or looking at the pictures at the Louvre, where she once worked herself into a fit of indignation at the sight of a painting of Palazzo Mocenigo which had once hung in the Chiesa della Carità in Venice. If Alvisetto had a free afternoon, she sometimes took him to the carousel at Place Vendôme or else to play ball under the great chestnuts in the Jardin du Luxembourg.

Although Lucia was on leave from her position as lady-in-waiting to Princess Augusta, she was nevertheless expected to pay her court to Empress Marie Louise at Saint Cloud—a duty she fulfilled with no enthusiasm, dropping by when she had nothing better to do, and possibly at a time when she knew the empress would not be receiving and she could simply leave a card. It did not always work, though, and several times she got stuck having to watch the king of Rome, Napoleon and Marie Louise's two-year-old son, play in his imperial pen or make a mess of his dinner. Even less appealing than the visits to Saint Cloud were those to Madame Mère, Napoleon's temperamental mother. Fortunately, a liveried servant usually ushered Lucia away saying the old lady was busy— *"Madame est en affaires."*[8] In contrast, Lucia was always glad to visit Empress Joséphine (Napoleon had allowed her to retain the title). She drove over to Malmaison a week after arriving in Paris, and took Alvisetto with her—Joséphine had heard so much about him she had told Lucia to bring him along so that he might play with her grandchildren (her daughter, Queen Hortense of Holland, was trapped in a miserable marriage with Napoleon's younger brother, Louis, and often came to seek comfort at Malmaison). The empress received Lucia, Alvisetto and the trailing Vérand in the billiard room. A small parrot with the most colourful plumage was perched on her breast. The greetings had to be interrupted when the bird started to peck the flowers of a little bouquet fixed on Joséphine's head, forcing her to remove three strings of pearls from her neck lest the parrot take aim at them next. Despite the confusion, Lucia did not overlook the exceptional quality of the pearls, estimating they were possibly worth 100,000 francs.

Lemon ices and biscuits were served in the garden-room, where other visitors were assembled. There were several relatives from the island of Martinique, and Madame d'Ahremberg, one of the empress's faithful ladies-in-waiting. The large room gave out on to a terraced lawn with bushes of creamy-coloured roses bursting all around it. Beyond the formal garden and the greenhouses, fields of young wheat swayed in the afternoon breeze. One of the charms of Malmaison was the way it combined the intimacy of a garden, the grandeur of an English park and the rusticity of a working farm. Joséphine took Lucia to see the rhododendrons she had planted along the main alley and the elaborate new waterworks. Back at the house, they visited the refurbished apartment upstairs. "The bedroom is magnificent," Lucia wrote:

> The tapestry is a crimson velvet decorated with the most beautiful gold embroidery. The bed-cover is made of a delicate Indian muslin, also embroidered with gold filaments. The dressing table is in gold and vermilion. It's worth at least 200,000 francs.[9]

Lucia had an open invitation to visit Joséphine, and the following months, Malmaison became a second home to her in Paris. She went once or twice a week, sometimes for lunch, sometimes for afternoon tea and a walk in the park, sometimes for dinner and a few hands of Boston. The company was always an interesting mix of Joséphine's older friends from the periods of the Revolution and the Directoire and members of the new imperial aristocracy who had remained loyal to her even after the divorce from Napoleon. The atmosphere was relaxed, the entertainment very simple: billiards, cards, parlour games. It was not an especially brilliant society, nor did it have the presumption to be so. Still, Joséphine's good taste, her languorous elegance, gave Malmaison a stylishness that was entirely absent from the pompous court at Saint Cloud.

It was mostly through her Malmaison connections that Lucia's social life in Paris picked up and gained a sense of direction. In any other European city, being a single woman and a foreigner would probably not have worked to her advantage; but it did in Paris. Her company was sought after, and she began to move with ease in circles that were fairly typical of the twilight years of the Empire, where politicians and old soldiers mixed with the literary set in an atmosphere of general disenchantment.

General Baraguey d'Hilliers, whom she had not seen since their meeting in Vienna in the aftermath of Napoleon's triumph at Austerlitz, and his wife, *la Générale*, welcomed her in their house as a long-lost friend. Retired General Sérurier invited her to his country estate outside Paris. "He's a very good person, very hospitable," she wrote to Paolina about the man who had handed Venice over to the Austrians on that cold and drizzly morning in January of 1798. "He recently bought a farm and lives there with his wife and brother."[10] At a small dinner given by Jean-Jacques Cambacérès, the former second consul, Lucia received the attentions of none other than Joseph Fouché, the ruthless minister of the interior.

Soon Lucia found her way into the literary salon of her long-time heroine, Madame de Genlis. There she met René de Chateaubriand, the great Romantic author. She was surprised by his "odd appearance"—the big head covered with black curls so out of proportion with the small, wiry body. He appeared very concentrated all the time, and Lucia was quite intimidated by "the intense look in his eyes."[11] But she did manage to hold his attention by telling him *The Genius of Christianity* had been the vicereine's favourite reading during *Petit cercle* in Milan. Another frequent star guest was the geographer Alexander von Humboldt, who enthralled Lucia with his fascinating tales of exploration in South America.

Her most touching encounter in Madame de Genlis's salon was with Dominique Vivant Denon, the artist, archaeologist and art connoisseur who had made his name in Egypt with Napoleon and was now the powerful director of the Louvre. Denon had been a close friend of Lucia's father back in the 1790s in Venice, and when Andrea Memmo was confined to bed by his illness, he had come by every day to sit with him and give him the comfort of good conversation. At the time, Lucia's difficult pregnancy was keeping her in Vienna, away from her dying father, and she always harboured a feeling of gratitude towards the young Frenchman who had kept him company until the end. Twenty years later, Lucia finally had a chance to meet Denon—the man everyone knew as "the Eye of Napoleon." He welcomed Lucia warmly into his house-cum-museum, and gave her a tour of his cabinet, a treasure trove of "Egyptian objects, paintings, drawings, bronze sculptures, porcelains and even Indian furniture" that he had gathered during his travels.[12] Of course, Lucia was not unaware that Denon was Napoleon's principal adviser in the looting of artworks across Europe, most of which adorned the rooms of the Louvre. It was probably for the sake of her father's memory that she chose not to dwell on this point—there is not a critical word about Denon in her diary or in her letters, even though she felt strongly about the issue of stolen art; especially art stolen in Venice.

It was Denon who introduced Lucia to David, her neighbour across the street and the most celebrated artist of his age. He had always been famous, as far as she could remember. In fact he was already famous back in the 1780s, when Angelica Kauffmann used to take her around to the ateliers of the major painters in Rome. Now he was Napoleon's favourite artist, and had put his stark, neoclassical imprint on the aesthetics of the Empire. At the age of sixty-five, he was still working on a majestic scale. When Lucia went to see him at his studio, she was completely overwhelmed by the powerful painting he was completing, which was bursting with naked soldiers preparing for battle. She recognised the famous scene from antiquity: Leonidas and his 300 Spartans on their way to meet the Persian army at Thermopylae. Strong Leonidas, the saviour of Greece, stood among his men, sword drawn, staring straight into Lucia's eyes. She wondered whether the artist was drawing a parallel between Leonidas and Napoleon. France's system of alliances had come unhinged after the disastrous Russian campaign and the Empire was under threat everywhere in Europe. Was Napoleon, like the bearded Leonidas, the heroic defender of civilisation against the advance of the barbarians?

Lucia had never felt so free to organise her life as she did in the late spring of 1813, after settling in her Paris apartment. The combination of her independence and her exposure to so many people of talent energised her; at the age of forty-three she yearned to engage her mind more fruitfully. Conversations in prominent salons, however agreeable and stimulating, no longer seemed enough. She was attracted by the rigour that only an academic community could provide, and she eventually found what she was looking for at the Jardin des Plantes, the botanical gardens where many of the great French scientists gave public lectures.

It all started quite by chance. One afternoon, Lucia went to the Collège Duplessix to hear Jean Charles de Lacretelle, a renowned historian of the French Revolution, only to be turned away by an unpleasant clerk who told her the lecture was "for men only." Instead of going home in a huff, she walked over to the nearby Jardin des Plantes, where women were evidently welcome. She heard Geoffroy de Saint Hilaire, an eminent zoologist, give a fascinating talk on quadrupeds. Lucia was hooked. Soon she was attending Saint Hilaire's courses on fish, butterflies, shells and corals. Next, she enrolled in Jean-Baptiste Lamarck's course on invertebrates, learning all she could possibly want to know about molluscs and giant squids. Professor Havy introduced her to mineralogy, and Professor Des Fontaines to botany. She became an assiduous and attentive student, took copious notes and revised every evening at home, while Alvisetto struggled with his homework.

Lucia chose not to share this part of her life with Paolina—there is no mention of lectures in her letters to her sister. It is hard to understand why she was secretive about an experience that was obviously so important to her, especially with her sister, whom she usually kept informed about every detail of her life, down to her bodily functions. But she evidently felt protective about this new development. In reading her brief diary entries, one senses a coyness about the whole enterprise of a late education, as if she did not want people to know about it back in Italy because she feared their condescending remarks.

By mid summer, Lucia was a familiar figure at the Jardin des Plantes, hurrying to her lectures, staying on after class to make a query or ask for some clarification, fetching a sample in the herb garden or checking the mushroom beds in the dank underground cellars. Professor Havy grew so fond of her he gave her a small collection of his quartzes. Professor Des Fontaines took her for educational walks in the garden, pointing out the most exotic trees and telling her their history. Professor Saint Hilaire called on her to assist him each time a shipment of specimens—reptiles, butterflies, insects—arrived from the Americas.

Every morning Lucia took Alvisetto to early mass, saw him off to school, then headed to the Jardin des Plantes following the banks of the Seine. She had given up her carriage soon after arriving in Paris to reduce her running costs, and she actually enjoyed the long walks along the river. In the afternoon, on her way back, she took the habit of stopping at the flower market to pick up some buttercups and bluebells, and popping into Félix's, her favourite *pâtisserie*, to buy a small pastry or two. On those rare occasions when she headed home earlier than usual, she idled in the streets of Faubourg Saint Germain, gathering along the way the most eclectic collection of goods: a set of drawing pencils, for example, or a *sou* of nails, a set of candles, a pair of socks, a couple of pigeons to roast for dinner, some bottled water and always a good supply of dried figs and prunes to help her bowel movements.

She occasionally broke her routine in the city with a day-trip to the porcelain factories at Sèvres, or to Montmorency—she picnicked under the great chestnut tree where Jean-Jacques Rousseau used to take his meals. "They say it is 500 years old," she noted in her diary. "The trunk is so large it takes four men to wrap themselves around it."[13] She spent a sunny day at Versailles, inspecting the restoration work on the palace, which had been devastated during the Revolution. She wandered over to Marie Antoinette's Petit Trianon, also entirely restored. An old Swiss guard, in his harlequin-like uniform, appeared from nowhere and offered to take her around. It was getting late, but Lucia followed her kindly guide through the royal apartments, then out in the gardens. "He took me to the grotto, the garden theatre, the wood full of tall, leafy trees; finally we reached the make-believe farming village." Lucia had heard so many descriptions of the Petit Trianon and the surrounding grounds, including Marie Antoinette's whimsical "village," that her visit took on a dreamy quality. The melancholy Swiss guard had come to France with Marie Antoinette in 1770 and had miraculously survived the years of turmoil. Having nowhere to go, he had stayed on as the unofficial custodian of the Petit Trianon, keeping the queen's memory alive with little anecdotes and recollections he shared with visitors.

At the end of the tour, Lucia saw the old man fade in the gloaming as mysteriously as he had appeared. "It was a beautiful night," she wrote in her diary, "and I made my way back [to the town of Versailles] by the light of the moon."[14]

Lucia could not remember feeling so at peace with herself as she felt in that summer of 1813. "I sleep well," she assured Paolina, "and my friends say I've even put on weight. I have a pleasing complexion and I feel good."[15] She only wished Alvisetto were more diligent in his studies, and more engaged in his spiritual life. "Oh, the boy has a good heart, and he does his prayers, and confesses, and takes communion, and that is all very well but it is not enough," she complained to her sister. She found his attitude towards religion to be too perfunctory. "Devotion to the Creator needs a great deal of work, but [Alvisetto] lacks the necessary spiritual nourishment, and I worry that when he will reach the age of overwhelming passions he will not have the strength to hold on to his faith."[16]

Father Laboudrie, his confessor, was having a hard time with Alvisetto as well. He did not find it easy to absolve him from his sins and allowed him to take communion only after serious penance—he was made to read for eight or fifteen days in a row, depending on the gravity of his sins, from the *Imitation of Christ* of Thomas à Kempis. But from what we can guess, Alvisetto's sins could not have been that terrible. They probably ranged from needling poor Vérand to doing sloppy homework.

At the end of the summer, Alvisetto faced his final examinations at the Lycée. Lucia suggested he pray for the intercession of Saint Ignatius "since his Jesuit schools were the best ever"[17] but her son cheekily replied he had already done so on his own initiative. For his French essay, the mighty *dissertation*, Alvisetto was asked to draw "a comparison between a wounded soldier who devotes his last thoughts to his beloved general, and a man devoted to God, who willingly submits himself to a preordained destiny." Alvisetto was not inspired. "He turned in a poor composition because he did not understand the question properly," Lucia noted with annoyance.[18] Saint Ignatius had not come to the boy's rescue after all, leaving her to wonder whether he had, in fact, prayed to the great Jesuit scholar.

Alvisetto's teachers showed unexpected mercy despite his poor showing in French, and allowed him to pass to the next grade, *troisième*. The school year started in early October, after a short break, and Lucia enlisted the help of the assiduous and ever-present Father Laboudrie to make sure his new teachers were not anti-clerical hangovers from the period of the Revolution. "They don't have to be zealous Catholics," she explained. "I just want to make sure that when they speak of religion, or things related to religion, they do so with respect." Father Laboudrie assured her that Alvisetto's principal teachers were "very pious."[19]

Lucia had not planned to remain in Paris another full academic year, but Alvise urged her to stay on because travelling to Italy was risky. In August 1813, even Austria, France's main ally, had declared war against her, immediately heading south to recover its Italian provinces. Prince Eugène was in no position to defend the Kingdom of Italy: after the Russian campaign, it had become very hard to enlist new conscripts, and what little remained of the Armée d'Italie was ridden with desertions. He had retreated to the enclave of Mantua, leaving the enemy to advance unopposed into northern Italy. The Austrians had taken Trieste, gaining access to the Adriatic, and by October, just as Alvisetto was starting his school year, they lay siege to Venice.

Alvise, meanwhile, was stuck in Milan: the Senate was back in session, though nobody knew for how long. He was also cut off from his estates, now under Austrian control, and could no longer draw an income from them. As he explained to Lucia, once he went through the savings in his account in Milan, he would not be able to send her money in Paris. "My advice to you is that you should stay where you are," he wrote. "I must also impress upon you the need to make only the most necessary expenses from now on."[20]

Napoleon came back to Paris for a few days in October, preparing to lead his tired army into yet another battle. Lucia went to court at Saint Cloud to be introduced to the emperor as lady-in-waiting to his stepson's wife. When she was finally ushered before him, she found him slouching in his throne, looking listless and overweight. He perked up just a little when Lucia's name was read out. "Ah, a Venetian lady,"[21] he said, as if trying to summon some vague memory from the misty past. He said a few words in Italian to her before his gaze drifted again.

The emperor left town some days later. Lucia was at Malmaison, playing a game of Boston with Joséphine, when the news arrived that the Grande Armée had been torn to pieces at the battle of Leipzig by the coalition forces of Austria, Prussia, Russia and Sweden. Joséphine had stayed in bed late and had not come down until after lunch. She looked tired, Lucia noticed, and was hardly able to concentrate on her game.

In November the weather turned cold and windy. Lucia asked Monsieur Minier to put in shutters to stop the constant rattling and the icy draughts. He answered she would have to pay half the costs or else sign a longer lease. Lucia declined both offers: she was already short of money, and she could no longer count on regular remittances from Italy. Besides, it was not clear how long she would be staying in Paris and it made no sense to commit herself to a long lease just to get some shutters on the wall. She decided to look for another apartment. During the next four weeks she scoured the Faubourg Saint Germain, checking out leads, climbing up hundreds of stairs, visiting apartments that were either too dark or too small, too dirty or too expensive. She visited everything there was to rent around Place de la Sorbonne, rue de Vaugirard, rue de l'Enfer and rue de Sainte Geneviève—nearly thirty apartments according to her count—before she found suitable lodgings at number 13, rue de l'Estrapade, next to the church of Sainte Geneviève. It was a sunny, comfortable second-floor apartment. More importantly: there were shutters at the windows. The owners lived downstairs; *madame* did the washing for a fee, and prepared excellent meals that could be brought upstairs. The apartment came with stables, which Lucia did not need but might sublet to friends who had horses, and a small coach-house where she could park her *bastardella*, the old gig Checco had brought from Italy and which they used to drive out to Malmaison, when they could borrow a horse.

There was, however, one drawback to the apartment: three sisters "of loose morals" lived next door, and attracted a constant flow of visitors. Lucia went to the Saint Germain police station to ask if there was any way to have the ladies evicted from the building. The officers looked at her as if she were a "madwoman."[22] She thought of turning down the apartment for the sake of Alvisetto. As she wrote to Paolina, it was hard enough steering him away from preying prostitutes in the streets in broad daylight, let alone on the same landing. One day, they were shopping near Palais Royal, when a woman in flashy clothes, her face covered by a veil, appeared from nowhere and accosted her fourteen-year-old boy, took his hand and whispered in a husky voice: *"Voilà le jeune homme que j'adore"*—"Look here at this adorable young man." Lucia tore him away, casting a savage look at the face behind the veil. "I tell you, these street-women are out of control," she complained to her sister. "They take no notice whatsoever of the prohibition to approach men in broad daylight."[23]

In the end, Lucia took the apartment because winter was quickly setting in. Besides, she had already missed too many classes at the Jardin des Plantes, and she was eager to get back to her regular study pattern. She arranged to have the furniture and luggage moved, and by December, she and the rest of the household were settled in at rue de l'Estrapade.

The first snow fell early that year, and turned the streets and squares of the sprawling city into a sea of slush and mud. The Tuileries Gardens were immersed in a dense fog most of the day, and one barely made out the leafless trees lining the alley like spidery sentinels. Ice began to form in the two large basins. A young boy about Alvisetto's age was usually in one of them, dangerously treading the thin surface. Passers-by stopped and threw coins at him to keep him on the ice and see if he would crash in the freezing water.

A feeling of resignation hung over the city, as if Parisians were conscious of the impending catastrophe and wished it would pass as quickly as possible. "They say carts filled with dead and wounded soldiers are already clogging the roads to Paris," Lucia told her sister. "I don't think it's true. These rumours are surely the product of fear alone."[24] In a way, she was right: Napoleon was still fighting in the Rhineland, still winning some battles. But the official bulletins announcing more French victories were received in gloomy silence. It was no use trying to fool the people any more. A tattered army of young conscripts was not going to turn the tide against the enemy when the enemy was the rest of Europe. The Parisians were tired of war, and they were tired of Napoleon. And so was the once ultra-loyal Legislative Assembly. While the emperor led his men to Pyrrhic victories, back in Paris the ground was being prepared for his downfall.

The news from Italy was even more depressing for Lucia. Venice was still under siege by the Austrians, and she had not heard from her sister since October. Rumours spoke of widespread disease and starvation. Communications were still open between Paris and Milan, but Alvise's letters were of little comfort. "For the most part," she complained, "they are filled with reproaches to me."[25] He accused her of spending too much and paying scant attention to Alvisetto's studies. Lucia could take "a little ill-humour" from her husband in such difficult times. She knew it was frustrating for him to be separated from his beloved Alvisopoli; she knew it was hard to witness the foundering of a kingdom in which he had invested so much. But why did he have to take it out on her? She was doing her best to lead a respectable life in Paris with minimum resources and no great help from him; and all of this to satisfy his obsessive desire to turn their son into a loyal subject of an Empire that was now collapsing.

Lucia was stung by the accusation of having been slack in supervising Alvisetto's studies, perhaps because she felt it was at least partially true. She had been so busy looking for new lodgings, organising the move and keeping up with her heavy course load at the Jardin des Plantes that she had not immediately noticed Alvisetto's rapidly declining performance at school. At the start of the year he had been sixth in the class, a very respectable ranking considering he was not a native French student; the second week he had already slipped into twelfth place, and by the third he was down to twenty-ninth, at the very bottom of his class, where he remained. One day she found her son in tears over his homework and finally woke up to the situation.

"This reversal has truly mortified him,"[26] Lucia told her sister, blaming herself for being so distracted by other matters. But she was mostly angry with Vérand, who should have been the first to alert her to Alvisetto's difficulties. Instead, he had taken to his bed, debilitated by the boy's poor showing, and he remained out of commission pretty much until Christmas, complaining about sweats, fevers, aches and a whistling noise in his head. "He moans all day and forces the help to wake up in the middle of the night to attend to his needs," Lucia protested:

> We all know he is just a victim of his own anxiety. Still, I had two doctors come to visit him. They told him, of course, that nothing was the matter, and to get out of bed and have some food. Monsieur Vérand is an angel when he is up and about, but he is pretty heavy going when he takes to his bed. And a useless financial burden, I might add.[27]

Monsieur Rougement, Alvise's banker in Paris, had to turn Lucia away several times because not even a trickle of money was coming from Milan any more. The small additional savings from Lucia's agricultural commerce had dried up. The stipend she was still entitled to as lady-in-waiting reached her with increasing irregularity. She was already running the household on a shoestring, and the prospects were not good. Encouraged by Alvise, she drew up a list of objects to be put up for sale: furniture and jewellery, for the most part, including a beautiful necklace of gold shells which she tried to sell to various jewellers. At the end of the list, she added Alvise's gala Senate uniform which had surfaced, like old family flotsam, from one of the trunks after the move to the new apartment. It now hung in the entrance hall at rue de l'Estrapade, cumbersome and useless. It was the one item she was eager to get rid of.

On Christmas Eve, Lucia had a quiet dinner at home with Alvisetto, Vérand, Teresa and Checco. A boiled fish arrived from the landlady downstairs. Later, Vérand and Alvisetto read a few pages of the Zen brothers' travels in the North Atlantic while Lucia curled up in the living room with a book she had picked up at Monsieur Foucault's, one of the booksellers she visited regularly on rue Jacob. It was a guide for improving one's marriage, written by a German pastor, Goliath Werner. The book had recently been translated in French and was selling briskly in the Paris bookstores. The full title was *Peaceful Marriages: a key to forestall, prevent and even put an end to all divorces, quarrels and all matter of domestic woes.* Whether she found Father Werner's suggestions of any use Lucia does not say, but her choice of reading material is as good a measure as any of how frustrating her long-distance relationship with Alvise had become.

Shortly before midnight all books were put aside. Everyone bundled up and, braving the snow flurries, scurried over to the church of Saint Sulpice to attend Christmas mass.

The new year began on a subdued note. The news coming from the war area portended a vast and imminent catastrophe. Yet it was received with no great alarm; or so it seemed to Lucia, who sensed a strange torpor around her, and a widespread feeling of resignation. "It is very quiet," she noted in her diary. "Parisians go out very little. People seem to prefer staying at home these days."[28] Lucia's professors at the Jardin des Plantes were her principal companions. Her workload became heavier. She had classes every day. In the evening she ate with Alvisetto and Vérand, then revised her notes until she was too tired to go on.

On her way home from the Jardin des Plantes, on the last day of Carnival, Lucia walked over to the *boulevards* hoping to see the masked revellers rushing by in open carriages—she thought it might remind her of the Venice carnival. But she only caught sight of a single *cabriolet* carrying three masked passengers, "and I heard they were paid by the police to display a little good humour." That night, breaking her stay-at-home routine, she went to the masked ball at court in Saint Cloud. "I stayed until two," she jotted down later. "The ladies wore a domino [cloak], the men wore tails. There were not many people at all."[29] Coming home she passed by the Barrière du Trone, one of the main Paris gateways into the city. "Sixteen cannons have been placed in addition to the usual two. I also counted fourteen ammunition carts."[30]

She wondered whether Napoleon was already making preparations to defend the city.

Her visits to Joséphine were the one regular social engagement Lucia did not give up in the winter of 1814. At least once a week, she had Checco hire or borrow a horse, harness the gig and take her out to Malmaison. The empress often looked weak and she tired very quickly. One day—it was early February and the grounds were covered with snow—Lucia went over for dinner and they played their usual game of Boston. They talked about the terrible situation in Italy: there were uprisings in Milan and Joséphine worried about what might happen to Prince Eugène, his wife and the children, and whether they might make it safely back to Paris. She also asked after Alvisetto and was sorry to hear about his difficulties in school. She told Lucia to bring him with her on her next visit.

The following Sunday, Lucia and Alvisetto went to Malmaison for lunch. Queen Hortense's children were also there and he played with them in the afternoon. The sun came out and Lucia took a short walk with Joséphine, but after a few minutes the empress was exhausted and they made their way back. A week later, Lucia went back alone: "She was unwell and received me in her beautiful bedroom. She was lying on the muslin bedspread and had drawn a white silk blanket over her, with gold braids and frills. The window curtains were also drawn."[31]

Lucia did not return to Malmaison until a fortnight later, when she was received by the principal lady-in-waiting and the chamberlain: Joséphine's breathing difficulties had apparently worsened and she was not seeing anyone. On the way home, Lucia and Checco were caught in "a column of twenty to twenty-five carts carrying wounded soldiers and headed for Saint Germain."[32] The rumour was that the French army was falling back on Paris and that the final battle might take place just outside the city.

That night—the night of 29 March—Lucia was kept awake by the constant beating of drums as Napoleon's troops entered Paris and marched through Faubourg Saint Germain and then headed south, in the direction of Fontainebleau. Around half past three in the morning, Alvisetto came into her room sleepy-eyed, asking what was the matter. He settled by the windowsill until dawn, watching the exhausted, poorly clad soldiers marching down the street.

The allied armies had by then reached the eastern city limits. Only days before, Austria, Russia, Prussia and Great Britain had signed the Treaty of Chaumont which bound them to fight on until the final overthrow of Napoleon. Even at this hopeless hour, the emperor was convinced he could outmanoeuvre the much stronger enemy by moving south and east, to Fontainebleau, and attack the allies from the rear. But while he laid out his military strategy, Talleyrand, the wily survivor of so many political seasons, was again taking charge of France's destiny, secretly negotiating with the enemy to save Paris from an allied attack and prepare the ground for the emperor's deposition.

At seven in the morning, Lucia left the house in rue de l'Estrapade with Alvisetto as she did every day, and went to early mass at the church of Saint Jacques. The last soldiers had marched out of town and the streets were strangely quiet. When they emerged from the church, the street was again filled with troops, but they belonged to the National Guard. Lucia heard the rumble of cannon shot; she pointed out to Alvisetto the flashes of cannon-fire to the right of Montmartre, and the tall columns of smoke rising at Vincennes.

The Lycée was closed that morning. Instead of returning home, Lucia and Alvisetto joined the stunned crowd that was gathering silently in the street and followed the aimless flow. The stores were bolted and shop-signs were erased or painted over to mislead looters on the prowl. Lucia spotted a few bedraggled soldiers making their way home from the battlefield near Vincennes. There was great confusion but not chaos. Well-organised police patrols maintained order. The women wore little black hats as a sign of mourning and several frowned at the flowery headgear Lucia had put on unthinkingly when she had left the house early in the morning. Alvisetto was too embarrassed to continue, and insisted they go home.

Cannon-fire boomed all day in the distance and subsided in the evening. Lucia stayed up all night, too anxious to fall asleep. Next morning, she learnt the French authorities had signed the capitulation of Paris. By midday the allied vanguard entered the city. Lucia went back to the street with Alvisetto. The atmosphere had changed overnight, and a new, unbridled energy was spreading very fast. Within minutes she spotted "at least twenty men and women wearing the white cockade," the symbol of the royalists. "Excited young men on horseback shouted, 'Long live the Bourbons!' "

As soon as the allied vanguard had taken control of the city, the high command marched into Paris at the head of a well-disciplined army. Emperor Alexander of Russia led the convoy, with King Frederick William of Prussia and Prince Schwartzenberg, who was standing in for Emperor Francis of Austria, still several days away from Paris. "Ninety thousand soldiers marched in perfect order," Lucia reported in her diary, frankly impressed by the glittering parade. "The cavalry looked superb, the horsemen in high uniform riding beautiful steeds. They wore a green sprig in their helmet and a white band around their arm. The mighty Cossacks came next, and then an endless column of carriages and carts carrying weapons and munitions."

The contrast with the tattered French army that had left town on its way to Fontainebleau could not have been sharper.

Foreign soldiers marched to Place Vendôme and then gradually filled the Champs Elysées. Thousands of Parisians lined the avenues to watch the spectacle. "Many shouted 'Bravo! Long live the Bourbons!' and waved their white handkerchiefs." Lucia noticed that the same men were inciting the crowd at different points in the streets. They were most certainly Bourbon agents "still gauging the size of royalist support." Someone in the swelling crowd attracted Lucia's attention to the long rope that was being passed down the line towards Place Vendôme, where Napoleon's statue stood atop the great bronze column. "Everyone started to follow the rope with their eyes. After a while, word came back that the noose had already been placed around Napoleon's neck, and the statue was going to be pulled down."[33] Lucia was suddenly afraid of being caught in a wave of street violence. She took Alvisetto's hand and turned around to go home.

The allied troops were still filling the Champs Elysées. Lucia and Alvisetto walked against the flow, stopping briefly in front of the Palais des Tuileries, where a small crowd was waiting for something to happen: rumour had it that one of the allied leaders might come out to salute the Parisians. But no one came out, and after a short rest, mother and son moved on, their slow trek home occasionally interrupted by the nervous canter of a stray horse on the cobblestones.

Napoleon was in Fontainebleau when he learnt that Paris had capitulated. It was too late to outmanoeuvre the enemy. There was nothing more to be done. The emperor handed himself over to the French Provisional Government. It fell to its president, Talleyrand, to proclaim the deposition of Napoleon and the end of the Empire, and to ensure a smooth transition of power. The next day, 31 March, Lucia transcribed in her diary the announcement made by Baron Pasquier, chief of the Paris Police:

> The events of the war have brought to your doorstep the armies of the coalition. Their number and their strength made it impossible for our troops to continue defending the capital, and the commanding officer was forced to capitulate. It has been a very honourable capitulation. A longer resistance would have endangered the safety of people and properties. At this momentous time, I beseech you to remain calm and peaceful . . .[34]

Lucia, however, continued to be restless; she felt the pull of the street, the need to witness the extraordinary metamorphosis taking place in Paris. On 1 April, two days after the final allied victory, she ventured with Checco past the eastern Barrière Saint Martin, on the road to Meaux. They reached Belleville Heights, left the carriage on the road and clambered up the hill until they came upon a wide-open plain. Clusters of curious onlookers were picking their way among the charred and still smoking remains of the battle. The bulky carcasses of dead horses were scattered in the field and the air was filled with the stench of rotting flesh. Mercifully, dead and wounded soldiers had been carried away, but a band of Cossacks was still guarding a group of disgruntled, worn-out French prisoners who had been crammed into a makeshift corral.

Lucia saw a sudden commotion near the prisoners' camp. A woman had been looking for her husband; she had brought a bundle of civilian clothes she hoped to pass on to him so that he might try to escape. The other prisoners started pulling and tearing at the bundle, and eventually they grabbed the poor woman and manhandled her savagely until the guards intervened. Frightened by the violence, Lucia backed off and hurried down the hill with Checco.

On the way back to town, hundreds of carriages and carts were caught in an endless traffic jam. In the noisy, dusty confusion, Lucia saw "white cockades and kerchiefs everywhere." To avoid being stuck in traffic all the way into Faubourg Saint Germain, she and Checco made a wide detour passing by Place Vendôme. "The statue [of Napoleon] was still standing and there were no ropes dangling from its sides,"[35] she jotted down in her diary when she got home.

The energy released by the sudden collapse of the Empire spent itself peacefully in the streets of Paris. Except for isolated incidents, the city remained relatively calm. There were few excesses on the part of the occupation forces, and no major outbreaks on the part of the Parisian crowd. The initial surge of vindictive feelings against Napoleon had subsided fairly quickly. Indeed, not only was the emperor's statue still standing on the bronze column in Place Vendôme when Lucia drove by, but "many people had climbed up the spiral staircase inside the column and had stepped out on to the capital to enjoy the view."[36]

The Lycée reopened after a two-day interruption. Every reference to Napoleon had been taken down and replaced by the words "Public School." "In times of Revolution we can do no better than to get back to our studies,"[37] one of Alvisetto's teachers, Monsieur Leclerc, told Lucia as he welcomed her son back to class. She followed his dictum, and resumed her own courses at the Jardin des Plantes, happy to be back in the company of her erudite professors.

In the days immediately following the armistice, Emperor Alexander was the principal guarantor of peace and security in Paris. As Baron Pasquier, the chief of police, confirmed in his proclamation of 31 March, "[the emperor of Russia] has given the municipal authorities every assurance of his benevolent protection of the people of this capital city." It could not have been otherwise: the city teemed with Russians. Hundreds of officers were put up in private houses, many in the elegant streets of Faubourg Saint Germain. They were flush with cash; indeed,

Lucia was still unable to retrieve money from the bank because all the money available went to pay the salaries of Alexander's officers. In those early spring days, as Paris regained its colours, Russian soldiers filled the cafés and restaurants and theatres. The proprietor of the fashionable Restaurant Véry boasted to Lucia he was making "10,000 francs a night off General Platow's Cossacks."[38]

Emperor Alexander, the "benevolent protector," was a popular attraction in Paris. Among the victorious allied leaders, Frederick William of Prussia was only a king, while the other emperor, the dour Emperor Francis of Austria, reached the capital long after every one else. But Alexander's stardom was not merely a question of rank. There was a genuine curiosity among Parisians for the liberal emperor who had conquered Napoleon. Lucia was not immune to it, and on the way home from class, she often mingled with the ogling crowd stationed under the emperor's windows. "Today I saw him come home on horseback, dressed in a simple green uniform, with only a small escort,"[39] she wrote in her diary, quite taken by the emperor's simple ways. She was even more impressed when Alexander put an end to his soldiers' high-flying lifestyle with the start of Holy Week. Easter and Orthodox Easter happened to coincide in 1814. According to Lucia, the Russian emperor was "a model of piety." He abstained from eating "not just meat but also eggs, milk and butter, out of respect for Catholics."[40] After having indulged their palates at Véry's, his officers were limited to a diet of "potatoes, beans, dried prunes, etc . . ." and were forbidden to go to the theatre.

At first, Alexander lived with his retinue on the top floors of Talleyrand's large mansion on Place de la Concorde because the palace of the Elysée, which he would eventually occupy, was still being refurbished. Talleyrand was quite happy to move down to the mezzanine floor with his staff in exchange for the privilege of having the emperor and his principal advisers at such close quarters. He and Alexander dined together most evenings. Their associates collaborated closely.

With one eye on France's best interests and the other on his own political survival, Talleyrand had quickly concluded that the preferable outcome of Napoleon's debacle was a return to Bourbon authority, this time held in check by a parliamentary constitution which he immediately set about drafting. Alexander was not at all keen to see a Bourbon back on the throne in France, and especially not the arch-conservative pretender Louis XVIII, younger brother of the decapitated Louis XVI, who was on his way to Paris and making large claims already. It was only because Talleyrand waved before Alexander the draft of his liberal constitution that the Russian emperor finally resigned himself to a Bourbon restoration.

On 12 April, two days after Easter, Lucia was again in Place Vendôme to see the Comte d'Artois, Louis XVIII's brother, make a triumphant entry in Paris. He was "dressed up" as a National Guard, Lucia pointedly wrote, with the royal blue cordons as the only embellishment. From Place Vendôme, the Bourbon vanguard moved directly to the Palais des Tuileries, and soon the Comte d'Artois came out to greet the very large crowd from deposed empress Marie Louise's balcony. The crowd refused to go away after he had gone back inside, but continued to clap and cheer, demanding that he come out again. Lucia found the scene rather distasteful: "It reminded me of the theatre."[41]

Talleyrand had accurately read the mood of the people, who seemed to welcome the idea of a return to the monarchy. Lucia was never a royalist, let alone a Bourbon sympathiser, yet she had always felt a deep sorrow for the fate of Louis XVI and Marie Antoinette. She went looking for the common grave at the old Cimetière de la Madeleine where the decapitated bodies of the king and queen had been dumped twenty-one years earlier. The cemetery had long been abandoned, but some years previously the owner of the house next door had managed to purchase a plot of land which included the burial ground. Since then, he had tended the two graves, pulling out weeds, planting flowers and growing a protective hedge. "The owners are a very nice family, and they gladly take around those who ask to see the enclosure,"

Lucia wrote to Paolina. "The proprietor also showed me the diamond-studded box the King of Prussia gave him as a token of his esteem and appreciation for what he had done."[42]

At the time of the burial, two young weeping willows had been planted over the graves as markers. Over the years, the trees had grown considerably, one towards the other, until their upper branches had joined. But now the willow on top of Marie Antoinette's grave was losing its leaves. As the proprietor explained to Lucia, the roots, having grown eight feet deep, had reached the lime in which her body was thrown.

Louis XVIII arrived in Paris on 3 May. He was a supercilious sixty-year-old, overweight and overbearing; but he was also a stubborn negotiator, and not at all inclined to wear the constitutional straitjacket Talleyrand was fashioning for him. The draft constitution went back and forth between the new monarch and the president of the provisional government. By the time Louis XVIII installed himself at the Tuileries, he had curtailed the powers of Parliament and individual freedoms considerably. Talleyrand lamented the changes to his original draft, but in the end he was satisfied that sufficient guarantees ensured that France would not see a return to absolute monarchy. On the other hand, Emperor Alexander, who had moved from Talleyrand's mansion to the Elysée palace, did not take the changes at all well, and thereafter refused to speak to his former host.

On 16 May Lucia went to court for a formal presentation to Louis XVIII. The point of this otherwise futile exercise was to attract the king's attention during the brief moment when one was face to face with him—not always an easy task given the soporific atmosphere that usually hung over this ceremony. She described herself on her card as the wife of the former captain of Verona, remembering that Alvise, despite the Directoire's vociferous protests, had treated the future king well back in 1795, when he was living in exile in Italy as the Comte de Lille. "The King receives like our dear old uncle Lorenzo, sprawled in his throne," Lucia wrote to her sister. "The ladies shuffle by him in a long line; they are only allowed a curtsey. The King nods without saying a word, except to those whom he knows personally." It turned out Lucia's little trick with her card worked beyond her expectations. She could not resist showing off a bit to her younger sister:

> The King saw me, examined me for a short while, and then exclaimed "Ah Lucietta! How are you! It's been so long!" The tone of his voice was so cordial and his expression so friendly that he seemed genuinely pleased to see me after nineteen years. And fancy him remembering my Venetian nickname![43]

In reality, the atmosphere at the new court was anything but cheerful. The king and his royal siblings were rather advanced in age, and soured by many years of exile. The haughty Duchess of Angoulême, daughter of Louis XVI and Marie Antoinette and the king's sister, restored stuffy rules of etiquette at the Tuileries that were a throwback to the ancien régime. "I really do not like the way we get pushed out of the room by the ushers after we have presented ourselves,"[44] Lucia grumbled. There was no place to mingle, and the ladies were left to mill about with the servants outside the receiving chamber until their carriage appeared.

Leaving court one evening she overheard a lady say that Joséphine had died. "I could not bring myself to believe it," she wrote in her diary. "I left in a hurry and came home immediately."[45] She could not sleep at all that night. The next morning, she sent word to Queen Hortense "to learn whether the Empress had in fact passed away." When the news was confirmed Lucia was overcome with sorrow. An air of mystery had surrounded Joséphine's illness from the beginning. Lucia had seen the empress fade but the topic of her health was always left untouched, and now suddenly she was dead—apparently after taking a chill during a walk in the garden with Emperor Alexander. When Lucia arrived at court in the evening, she was late and the doors to the king's apartments were closed. Other ladies were waiting outside. She joined two old friends of Joséphine, both in tears. The three of them wondered whether Napoleon, who was living in exile on Elba, had been informed.*

The following day Lucia, dressed in mourning, gathered the final draft of her letter of condolences to Prince Eugène—she had stayed up late writing several versions—and drove out with Alvisetto to Queen Hortense's palace, where Eugène was staying before returning to his wife and children in Bavaria. It was a very emotional leave-taking; both Hortense and Eugène were crushed by the death of their mother. For Lucia, it was also the last formal act of her brief career as lady-in-waiting to a court that had vanished under the ruins of Napoleon's Empire.

In the darkest hour, just before the final collapse, Napoleon had ordered Eugène to cross the Alps and come to the defence of France. Eugène had resisted the call from his stepfather because his wife was about to give birth again. Furthermore, by remaining in the Kingdom of Italy at the head of a much reduced Armée d'Italie, he had hoped to lay a claim to the kingdom, or at least a portion of it, in any redrawing of the European map. But during the preliminary talks held by the great powers in Paris in April and May 1814 after Napoleon's demise, it became clear that northern Italy would fall under Austria's control in one form or another. By the time Eugène hurried back to Paris to assist his dying mother, his kingdom had disintegrated. Mob violence in the streets of Milan culminated on 20 April with the gruesome lynching of Eugène's unpopular finance minister, Giuseppe Prina. Lucia learnt that Alvise had managed to leave Milan safely and reach Alvisopoli, but she knew little else, and communications remained very fragmented.

During the following weeks Lucia became obsessed with one question: what future lay in store for Venice? At the end of April the Austrians finally lifted the siege but the city was prostrate after six months of isolation, hunger and disease. The death of

---

* He had not. One of Napoleon's servants, returning to France from Elba, read about the death in a newspaper in Genoa. He sent a copy of the paper to the former emperor.

the Republic seventeen years earlier, Lucia confided to her diary, was still "a thorn in my heart." There was, she knew, very little chance of resurrecting it. But she felt it was wrong to give up all hope. "Surely this is the time to try," she told her sister, "what with all the European sovereigns gathered here [in Paris] at once." If the Bourbon monarchy had been restored—so went her argument—why not imagine that the Republic of their elders might also be? In a moment of enthusiasm, she wrote to her Venetian friends still in Milan begging them to underwrite a petition to the allies "for the rebirth of our Republic." She reminded them that the Genoese had already taken a similar step. "It will perhaps prove useless, but at least [we] will not have to blame [ourselves] for not having made every possible effort."[46]

It was a valiant but doomed endeavour. The allies did not have the slightest interest in reviving the Republic of old. "Everywhere I am told that Venice will be ceded back to Austria," she observed sadly. Clearly, Emperor Francis was the person she should try to see: she asked for an interview and was received on 24 May. Lucia lobbied hard on behalf of Venice, reminding the emperor that the city had greatly suffered and would need special attention to get back on its feet. Indeed, why not make it an important administrative centre, a regional capital of the Austrian Empire? Why not make it the official residence of a Habsburg archduke? Lucia pressed on, carried away by her own arguments. "But all the Emperor did, after each suggestion I made, was to repeat: 'Please stay calm, Madam, have no fear.' "[47]

Shortly after her useless meeting with Emperor Francis, Lucia ran into a Milanese acquaintance who had lost no time in converting to the Habsburg cause. He congratulated her on the happy prospects of Venice under Austrian rule. Lucia replied with indignation that she was a republican. "I will certainly adapt to the new situation," she wrote in her diary. "But I remain inconsolable."[48] Frustrated at her inability to do something for Venice, she went to the foreign ministry's archives to see whether she could not at least retrieve stolen documents that had belonged to her family. With the help of a friendly archivist, she found stack upon stack of letters and parchments pertaining to the history of the old Venetian Republic. Rummaging through the mouldy papers, she pulled out her father's correspondence with the doge when he was ambassador to Constantinople. She asked the complicit archivist if she could take the letters, and hurried home with her prize. Emboldened by this stroke of good luck, she wrote to Talleyrand, now Louis XVIII's foreign minister, asking for an interview to discuss what steps should be taken to have all the archives taken by Napoleon shipped back to Venice. There was no reply. Talleyrand was busy preparing the Congress of Vienna and had very little time on his hands. "He probably thought I was just another foreigner asking for a favour,"[49] Lucia concluded. She made one more attempt. This time, however, she added to her name the old Austrian titles she had never used, not forgetting the Starred Cross of the Habsburg Empire she had received just before leaving Vienna in 1806, and sent in the request, curious to see whether Talleyrand would pay her more attention.

The Treaty of Paris was signed at the end of May, formally ending hostilities with France, which was now reduced to its pre-Revolution frontiers. The allied troops withdrew from the capital, and a long line of kings, chancellors, diplomats and generals flowed back to the various European capitals. Emperor Alexander left town in a huff, so peeved was he at the way things had turned out (though not without having made arrangements to purchase Joséphine's fabulous art collection).

"London, Vienna, Milan: these days everyone seems to be going somewhere,"[50] Lucia observed, capturing the end-of-season atmosphere. It was time to begin planning her own departure. There was no longer any point in staying in Paris for Alvisetto's education after Napoleon's fall—even Alvise conceded as much. Besides, their son was not exactly shining at school. His teachers worried about his lack of zeal and his indifference to his studies. Lucia, on her part, had lost all patience with him: it was a struggle to get him up in the morning (and she had her own classes to attend!), he was slow with homework and she was always having to go fetch him at the Jardin du Luxembourg, where he stopped to play ball on his way home from riding school. "I don't know how to educate Alvisetto," she burst out in frustration to Paolina. "What he needs is a man of knowledge and authority"[51]—an obvious dig at Alvise, so absent from their lives, but also at Vérand, who had been of such little use around the house and rather a weight on her. "What with all his ailments, cures, convalescences, I hardly ever see him out of bed." It was, she concluded, "very, very, very necessary"[52] to send Alvisetto off to boarding school once they were back in Italy, possibly somewhere near Venice, like Padua.

Unlike her listless son, Lucia was ever more diligent in the pursuit of her studies at the Jardin des Plantes, as if determined to soak up as much knowledge as possible, no matter how haphazardly, before returning to Italy. When crates arrived from overseas, carrying all manner of reptiles, birds and insects, she was always on hand to help Professor Saint Hilaire sort out hundreds of specimens. He taught her the art of vivisection and how to handle live animals, including snakes—a requirement for the certificate in anatomy she was working towards. She passed her chemistry course with Professor Laugier and her mineralogy course with Professor Havy with flying colours. But botany was the subject she grew passionate about, and Professor Des Fontaines's course absorbed her more than any other.

Lucia got up before dawn every morning and walked down the still deserted *quais* along the Seine to be at the Jardin des Plantes in time for Des Fontaines's class at six o'clock. After the lecture, she usually went to collect samples and cuttings on the grounds, carrying a tin tray slung over her shoulder. Jean Thonin, the legendary chief gardener, helped her select the seeds of trees that had recently arrived from North America and which he thought might do well at Alvisopoli: silver maple and red maple, canoe birch, Easter red cedar, American sweet gum and other fast-growing species. Professor Des Fontaines compiled a list of plants and shrubs for Lucia to take to Italy and sent her to Monsieur Noisette, who oversaw the nursery in rue Jacob. She assembled a considerable botanical collection in boxes that were piling up in the entrance at rue de l'Estrapade. Her 200 rose cuttings covered an eclectic variety: she mentions the pinkish Anemone Rose, the tie-dyed Rose Panachée (*Rosa variegata*), one she calls "Rose Bissone" ("with its sweet smell of pineapple and raspberry *gelée*") and the fashionable *Rosa multiflora*, a prolific shrub with white and pink flowers "that grows like a vine."[53] It had come from China only two years before and was already very popular among Parisian rose-lovers.

She completed her botany requirements with Monsieur Dupont, the Serviteur des Roses at the Jardin des Plantes. He was a cheerful man who tended to his 457 species of rose with great devotion. In his extraordinary garden, which was just then reaching its fullest profusion, Dupont taught Lucia the art of grafting. His wife, Louise, had died twelve years earlier, and he had buried her heart in a corner of the garden where low ivy now grew, in the shape of a heart. Dupont added in a whisper that he wanted his own heart to be buried next to that of his wife.

Lucia secretly hoped that once Alvise had taken care of the most urgent tasks on his estates, he would travel to Paris and help her organise the family's trip back to Italy. She even fantasised that the two might steal a quick trip to London: "It would be wonderful to make a dash," she confided to her sister. "The opportunity is unique as we are so close and, for once, at peace."[54] But Alvise was too tied up with his affairs, what with the harvest coming up and the perennial threat of summer rains. The accounts were in such disarray that he could not send her money for the journey and instructed her to finance the trip by selling everything she could: furniture, jewellery, clothes, and even his old Senate uniform—if she could find a buyer for it.

It was a tough task. The Russians had left town, and the English tourists who were starting to arrive in Paris were much more careful with their money. She made the rounds of all the jewellers she knew hoping to sell the set of shells she had been trying to get rid of for months. She finally sold it to an Englishman through the concierge of the Hotel de l'Europe for 700 francs. Lucia was quite pleased with herself as that style of jewellery was no longer fashionable and she would never have sold it to a Parisian. She was also able to sell the beds, two chests of drawers and a cupboard. But she had no luck with Alvise's Senate uniform, not even among Bonaparte die-hards. She instructed Alvisetto to undo the embroidery so she could at least sell the gold thread and the silver buttons; then she had Mademoiselle Neppel, her seamstress, unmake the uniform and she sold the pieces of cloth to the tailor, Monsieur Robert. With the proceeds from the sale she bought ten pairs of gloves, a box of dried figs and one of dried apricots.

In the end, Lucia raised enough cash to purchase two horses for the gig, which Checco would be driving back to Italy with Teresa, and to hire a carriage. The coachman, Signor Maccari, a genial Florentine, was to manage the trip, providing meals and lodgings along the way. There was still a little cash left for one last shopping spree. Socks, shoes, shirts, fabrics, dried foods: Venice had been under siege for six months and Lucia had heard there still was a penury of the most basic goods. She longed to be home. "I can't wait to sleep in my own room," she told Paolina, "though I fear there will be many rats as the apartment has been empty for so long. Make sure that proper stops are put into cracks and holes." As much as she loved Paris, she felt the constant pull of her Venetian roots. "This is a great city but I prefer the one I was born in, and I hope to spend the few years of life I still have surrounded by our beloved lagoons."[55]

In the midst of last-minute preparations, Lucia received a call from the foreign ministry: though very busy preparing for the Congress of Vienna, Talleyrand was willing to see Lucia for a *petit quart d'heure d'entretien*, the note said—a brief fifteen-minute interview. Two elderly generals were already sitting in the waiting room when she arrived. A few minutes later, they were joined by the Prince de Rohan, a wrinkled gentleman from the oldest house of Brittany, who engaged Lucia in amiable chit-chat—his daughter had apparently been escorted by a

Mocenigo in Venice at the time of the Republic—until it was her turn to go in. Talleyrand was polite but distant, and he made it plain he was a very busy man. Right away Lucia asked him how he thought Venice should proceed in its petition to obtain the papers belonging to the Republic, which, she added pointedly, "I know to be in France."

Talleyrand: Ah, but when Venice and Milan were joined [in the Kingdom of Italy] the papers were assigned to Milan.

Lucia: Sir, I saw them in the archives here in Paris.

Talleyrand: Well, they are merely in consignment.

Lucia: But they are here . . .

Talleyrand: In consignment . . .

Lucia: May I at least put in a petition to retrieve the papers?

Talleyrand: They belong to Milan, and since they are here only in consignment it really is not possible to do so. Milan belongs to Vienna now.

Lucia: So Venice should eventually make the request to Vienna?

Talleyrand: Everything to Vienna . . . (Changing subject) Your father must have known [French ambassador] Choiseul Gouffier in Constantinople . . .

Lucia: He might, though I remember he was there at the time of [Ambassador] Saint Priest . . .

Talleyrand: Of course, Saint Priest . . .[56]

The old diplomat had steered the conversation on to a dead track. Lucia's fifteen minutes were up. "I realised he wanted me to take my leave, so I left." She walked home feeling low and decided to make a detour to see if Alvisetto was still in the park. The sight of her gangly teenage son chasing the ball like a little boy put her in better spirits. The evening was warm and they tarried under the great leafy chestnuts, going over their latest sales, adding up figures and looking ahead to their long journey back to Venice. Later she wrote to her sister that on the way home from the Jardin du Luxembourg, Alvisetto gave her his arm for the first time.

The apartment was bursting with boxes and crates and trunks. All was ready. Lucia made her farewell rounds: Madame Sérurier, Madame Baraguey d'Hilliers, Madame Chateaubriand, Madame de Genlis, who gave her the four-volume biography of Henry IV. And then, of course, her new professor friends: Saint Hilaire, Laugier, Havy...Professor Des Fontaines came to rue de l'Estrapade to present Lucia with her well-earned certificate of botanical studies. He too gave her a book as a parting present: *Le Jeune Botaniste*, by Auguste Plée. An indispensable read, he said with emotion, for any aspiring botanist.

On 24 August, she took her leave from the king. "I was in such a rush I had to change in the carriage," reads the last entry in Lucia's Paris diary.

> He seemed pleased to see me when I came up to him and curtsied. He said: "I thought you had left already. How are you?" I replied cheekily: "I would not have left before your saint's day." And His Majesty: "Well, then, I thank you very much."[57]

The party left Paris on a sunny morning at the end of August (one day later than planned because Teresa objected to leaving on a Friday). Lucia, Alvisetto and Vérand travelled in the carriage with Signor Maccari; Checco and Teresa followed in the gig. In Fontainebleau, Lucia called for a stop to visit the chateau where Napoleon had abdicated. The next day they toured the cathedral of Sens. There were many more stops along the way, in Auxerre, Chalons, Macon. It took them ten days to reach Lyon; they travelled across the lush French countryside at a pleasant pace, never straining the horses. Occasionally Signor Maccari let Alvisetto take the reins; Checco and Teresa cheered him on from the gig. Lucia was pleased with the coachman, who was able to provide comfortable lodgings and plenty of good food along the way (she had asparagus nearly every day!). When the inn was crowded, Signor Maccari himself served the meal in the rooms.

After a rest in Lyon, they headed for the Alps. The air became cooler and crisper. In Chambéry they stopped for their last French meal: onion soup, beef *à la mode,* roast chicken with peas and potatoes, fricassée of lamb, cheese and pears and biscuits, and two bottles of good wine. They arrived rather stuffed at the border station after the village of Lanslebourg, where their papers were checked by Austrian guards—the Austrians had temporary control over Piedmont until the House of Savoy was reinstated. Lucia produced old documents showing she was an Austrian countess, and the party breezed through. They left at dawn the next day for the last climb up through the Mont Cenis Pass. Three mules pulled the carriage and one the gig. Lucia recognised the muleteer, a well-known figure to travellers. He had once carried Napoleon piggy-back after his carriage had crashed in the snow; the emperor had rewarded him with a pension and eighteen gold *napoléons.* The crossing was much easier now: there was a wide esplanade at the pass, and a good road leading down to Italy. It was a beautiful, clear day; Lucia and Alvisetto got out of the carriage to stretch a little and decided to walk down the mountain, carefully picking their way on the gravel. They reached the old frontier town of Susa in time for a hearty Piedmontese lunch, their first Italian meal in a long time: vermicelli soup, mushrooms from the neighbouring woods, roasted eels and spinach, *mascarpone* and grapes.

It took another ten days to cross northern Italy from the Alps to the Adriatic. On 25 September, four weeks after leaving Paris, the little convoy was met in Padua by Alvise, Paolina, her two boys, Venceslao and Ferighetto, and her youngest daughter, Marietta (Cattina, the eldest, was married and living in Bologna; Isabella had died while Lucia was in Paris). Alvise invited them all to lunch at the Croce d'Oro, the fancy restaurant in town; afterwards, they ambled over to Caffè Pedrocchi for ice creams.

They spent the night in Padua before making the last leg of the journey home. Lucia got up early the next day, went to wake all the children and took them out for breakfast. Everyone went to mass while Alvise made arrangements for their passage. Then they all piled up in a *peotina*, the typical flat-keeled Venetian transport vessel, and made the familiar journey down the Brenta Canal before heading out to Venice across the lagoon. It was a merry passage. "Paolina sang a lovely little aria."[58]

Chapter Ten

BYRON'S LANDLADY

The happiness of seeing Venice again faded rapidly as Lucia entered the Basin of Saint Mark and glided up the Grand Canal. An eerie silence had replaced the customary din across the waterway. There was no traffic, no busy confusion. A tenebrous gleam shone off the mournful palaces. Many were empty and in disrepair, as if the owners had fled leaving them to crumble slowly in the brackish tidal waters of the lagoon. After passing the first bend, the party moored at the rickety dock and clambered out of the gondola. Palazzo Mocenigo looked rundown and inhospitable: the walls were peeling, the air was dank, the plants in the courtyard were going to seed. Entire floors of the *palazzo* were still shut, and the forlorn gaze of the staff betrayed the vicissitudes suffered during the siege.

Later, Lucia went out with Alvisetto looking for familiar places—it seemed like the easiest way to lift their spirits. They went over to Ca' Memmo at San Marcuola, walked down the Frezzeria to Saint Mark's Square and made their way home passing by the church of San Moisè and Campo Santo Stefano. It was hardly a cheerful tour. Many shops were boarded up. The streets were filthy and malodorous, and a querulous moan rose from the beggars lining the walls. Mangy mongrels and skinny cats roamed the back alleys fighting for miserable scraps of food. Several times they ran into Austrian soldiers patrolling the streets and yelling orders in German.

.   .   .

Alvisetto remained in Venice but a few weeks before it was time for him to enrol in Father Ménin's seminary in Padua. He took lodgings with Vérand in a private house within walking distance from the school. Lucia helped him settle in, making sure he had proper clothes and shoes for the winter, a new pair of eyeglasses and the necessary school material. Sensitive as ever to shifting political circumstances, she reminded her son that it would be wise "to set aside a few hours every day to practise German." She urged Vérand to speak to him in that language as often as possible, suggesting they read out loud in the evening from a good German play "so as to enhance his familiarity with dialogue."[1] But there she stopped, whereas Alvise was already making enquiries about the best German universities for his son: Gottingen, Leipzig, Berlin . . . There were, of course, a number of excellent institutions in Prussia and in the Austrian Empire; but there was plenty of time to make a decision—it was going to be another two years before Alvisetto graduated from school— and Lucia saw no reason to rush things. As in the past, she wondered whether it was really necessary to send him so far away to further his studies.

Lucia soon started to miss their life in Paris—the freedom they had enjoyed, their cosy routine, their walks at the Jardin du Luxembourg. Venice, her beloved Venice, now seemed so restrictive and isolated from the rest of the world. A few brave hostesses, like her old friends Isabella Teotochi Albrizzi and Marina Benzoni (who had danced half-naked under the Liberty Tree in 1797), still kept their houses open and did their best to create an air of intellectual vivacity and cosmopolitanism. But their salons were run on a shoestring, with stale biscuits and bad wine served as refreshments. And the conversation sounded inevitably provincial compared to the exchanges Lucia had had at her Parisian soirées.

Alvise was rarely in Venice, spending nearly all of his time travelling to his estates. The Mocenigo properties on the mainland were in dreadful condition. The floods had devastated the harvest of 1814. Famine and disease were crippling the farming system and causing terrible human loss. The situation at

Alvisopoli was especially dismal because of the high water-levels there. The sheep flocks had been wiped out and most of the cattle had died of starvation. The fields, so recently reclaimed, were reverting to marshland. The town had deteriorated to unspeakable squalor. Ghostly crowds of starving labourers, their wives and children in tow, roamed the land begging for work and food. Alvise's utopian project was collapsing. If the Austrians did not reduce the crushing fiscal burden imposed on Alvisopoli during Napoleon's rule, allowing a little breathing space to get the agricultural cycle going again, Alvise would be forced to declare bankruptcy and lose the property—a prospect that darkened his mood considerably.

To Lucia, it felt as if she had regressed to that earlier period of her marriage when she lived a lonely life at Palazzo Mocenigo, fighting to save her pregnancies while her mother-in-law came down from her apartment to watch over her. The difference was that Lucia was now the mistress of the vast and mostly empty house: Chiara had moved out of Palazzo Mocenigo after quarrelling with Alvise and lived across town, at Santa Maria Formosa, with a monthly stipend from her son.

There were times, Lucia complained to her sister, when she felt her only reliable, if unpleasant, company were the rats in her apartment. While Lucia was still in Paris, Paolina had come over to Palazzo Mocenigo to fill in the holes, but evidently the paper fillings had not been enough. Every night, bands of famished rodents scurried across the bedroom floor and scratched the crumbling wooden legs of the bed. "A very large one kept me up all night,"[2] Lucia complained to her sister in a typical note.

On the few occasions when Alvise was at home, he could be very impatient with Lucia; but she had reached a point in her life when she was weary of taking the extra step to accommodate her husband's surliness. They had lived apart for so much of their married life that neither had learnt to live with the other's moods and rhythms and habits, and they no longer had the energy to try to make things better between them. Tempers flared easily, and the arguing was fairly constant.

The tension between them was deepened by a new revelation:

Alvise had an illegitimate daughter living on the mainland. When Lucia and Alvisetto were in Vienna, Alvise had had an affair with Carolina Faldi, wife of Piero Faldi, a family friend. Carolina had given birth to a girl who was christened Luigia in honour of Alvise—Alvise being the Venetian equivalent of Luigi. She was now a boarder at a school for girls in Montagnana (incidentally, the same town near which Colonel Plunkett's regiment was encamped when he had met Lucia sixteen years earlier). Alvise cared deeply for his daughter. He often went to see her, and he made sure she and her family were well provided for.

One night, the shouting at Palazzo Mocenigo became so loud, the words uttered by husband and wife so awful, that Alvise felt compelled to call in Paolina to try to bring back a minimum of civility to his marriage. Paolina rushed over, and on her way in she was shocked to see the frightened looks on the faces of the staff. Alvise and Lucia seemed shaken. Paolina heard them out separately, and grew even more dismayed when she realised how deeply they could still hurt each other after nearly thirty years of marriage. Lucia had criticised Alvise for his ceaseless womanising, and Alvise had lashed back by attacking her own morality and by bringing up a past they had both worked so hard to bury. They had lost control over themselves, hurling insults to each other in a vortex of mutual recrimination. How could she possibly bring true peace between them, Paolina wondered. "In the beginning, it was not my sister's intention to offend you," she wrote the next day to Alvise, "nor do I think you wished to offend her by giving your humiliating reply." But they had gone too far to resolve matters by simply telling each other they were sorry: an exchange of perfunctory apologies would be meaningless at this stage. There was only one way of putting such awfulness behind them, Paolina concluded: "To erase all memory of what happened."[3] They should try to look into each other's eyes, she said, as if they had never spoken those words.

The winter of 1814–15 turned out to be especially harsh. The cold brought more hunger and disease and a deadly air hung over the lagoon. Lucia's old governess, the beloved Madame Dupont, died of pneumonia. And Paolina lost little Marietta to tertian fever—her third daughter to die after Isabella and baby Lucia. "Big" Lucia was heartbroken for her sister. She commissioned a tall marble cross from the funerary sculptors over on the Fondamenta Nuove, the embankment that faced the new cemetery on the island of San Michele, and asked Alvisetto to compose an inscription in Latin verse to honour his ten-year-old cousin. "Please avoid a generic composition," she pleaded. "Write about her real virtues and qualities. And don't rush through this: set some time aside to concentrate on the task."[4] To inspire him, Lucia sent him a page filled with ideas. Alvisetto tried his best, or so he assured his mother; but the proper words would not come to him. He eventually gave up the task and she had to do it for him.

Lucia worried about Alvisetto. She felt he was becoming nonchalant and lazy at a time when everyone should be giving all they had. He showed little interest in his studies and seemed to waste much of his spare time. Would he get any work done—she wondered—if he were not so closely supervised by Father Ménin at school and Vérand at home? Alvise, who had ambitious plans for him, was clearly disappointed. And Lucia, wishing to avoid a new confrontation with her husband over their son's education, urged Alvisetto to shape up:

> It upsets me that your father should have reason to complain about your aversion to study. You are sixteen, old enough to understand that the displeasure you give to your parents will ultimately be to your own detriment. What will you reap from so much idleness?[5]

Evidently Alvisetto enjoyed his relative autonomy in Padua from his loving but sometimes overbearing mother. When classes were over, he loitered about town, often joining other fellow students at the smoke-filled coffee shops, and incurring Vérand's ineffectual reproaches. He was a gregarious type, and probably devoted a little too much time to leisure and too little to his studies. It was all fairly innocent. Lucia, however, insisted in micromanaging her son's life from Venice. "I must discourage you from spending money at the coffee shop," she nagged in one letter. "*One* ice cream a day is quite enough," she told him in another. "Lingering at the coffee shop longer than is necessary to eat it is clearly not to a young man's advantage."[6] And so on.

Lucia's fretfulness turned into discomfiture when she learnt, from an unusually watchful Vérand, that Alvisetto's sheets were covered with sticky spots. She told Vérand he should not shy away from lecturing her son at length against masturbation: "There will never be enough words with which to inspire real horror in him for those dreadful spots."[7] If Vérand carried out the task—and there is no reason to believe he would disregard such a strong injunction from Lucia—he must have elicited quite a few guffaws from the over-excited teenager in his charge.

At the end of the winter, Lucia's excessive preoccupation with Alvisetto subsided momentarily because, like everyone else, she was distracted by the news that Napoleon had escaped from Elba. The fallen emperor reached the south of France on 1 March, headed north to Paris and three weeks later was back in power. For three months, Europe teetered between past and future. Once again the allies amassed their troops along the French border. Napoleon struck first, marching into Belgium and defeating the Prussians on 16 June. But two days later his army was beaten decisively by Wellington at Waterloo and he was forced to abdicate a second time. The nightmare of a Bonapartist resurrection receded as Napoleon was sent off to Saint Helena, a tiny speck in the southern Atlantic.

During Napoleon's brief return to power the Austrians did not sit still. On the contrary, they accelerated their formal takeover of northern Italy. On 7 April, the newly formed Kingdom of Lombardy–Venetia was integrated into the Habsburg Empire. Archduke John, brother of Emperor Francis, arrived in Venice to mark Austria's assumption of power with the proper solemnity—

yet another high mass in the basilica of Saint Mark took place on 7 May. The archduke hosted a masked ball at La Fenice and the next day he headed for Padua.

Vérand had written to Lucia warning that Alvisetto was so eager to show his Austrian heart he wanted to ride out on horseback to greet the archduke. "Don't do it," Lucia pleaded in a late-night note to her son:

> Dear Alvisetto, I am just now back from the *bal masqué* at La Fenice and I beg you not to expose yourself to danger. Find a good spot from which to watch the imperial cortège, but please don't ride out in the confusion of carriages and horses. I am counting on you. I don't want to have to worry about this.[8]

After some grumbling, Alvisettto relented and watched the archduke's cortège from a safe place, with Vérand at his side.

Spring turned into summer on a hopeful note. The rain that year did not spoil the wheat and corn, and the harvest season looked more promising than it had in a long time. Then, in early July Alvise received the news he had been hoping for: the payment of property taxes on Alvisopoli was suspended, pending the completion of a new cadastral survey ordered by the government. It was a huge relief. Perhaps the worst was over; if there were no more rains during the rest of the summer Alvisopoli might yet be saved. Lucia urged her son to "pray that Heaven hold back the scourge that will otherwise cause famine and disease."[9]

Heaven, it turned out, struck in a wholly unexpected way.

In late August Alvise was suddenly ill, with terrible pains in his stomach. His condition deteriorated very rapidly. He was rushed back to Venice and the best doctors were called in to see him, but nothing seemed to stop or even slow down the disease—probably a tumour. Alvise felt life slipping away from him: he called in the family notary and asked that he take down a new will. He was so weak he hardly had the strength to sign his name.

Quite mysteriously and to everyone's relief, he suddenly recovered and was soon back on his feet—a pale wraith with lingering pains, but so surprised to be alive as to be in relatively good spirits.

Alvise made a triumphant return to Alvisopoli, and Lucia was genuinely moved by the display of affection shown to him by the *alvisopolitani*. She reported to Paolina:

> His carriage was escorted into town by a large crowd amid cries of hooray. The throng of cheering labourers was led by Alvisetto on horseback. The town itself looked lovely, as everyone had put flowerpots and festoons at their windows. At the big house, Alvise was greeted with bouquets and sonnets. Mass was held in the small, beautifully decorated church. A few verses on his recovery were recited with a musical arrangement. Alvise sat in the front pew with Alvisetto, while I was seated to the side. After the Te Deum, Alvise walked out into the cheering crowd. A big lunch was served at the house. Alvise ordered that another table be laid out for twenty-six poor people, and Alvisetto served them food and gave each one a few coins. There were fireworks in the evening and the *alvisopolitani* danced late into the night.[10]

Although Alvise diligently took the ounce of quinine the doctors prescribed him, the pains never really left him and soon increased, especially in the middle of the day. He returned to Venice towards the end of the autumn, in time for Emperor Francis's first official visit. But he was too ill to participate in the many functions and festivities. He was especially disappointed not to be in Saint Mark's Square to witness the return of the four bronze horses taken to Paris by Napoleon. In December the illness spread again very quickly and this time there was nothing much to be done. Alvise died on Christmas Eve 1815. His body was taken to Alvisopoli. He had wanted a small, private ceremony at his estate rather than a grand funeral in Venice. On a cold and bleak winter morning, family and close friends gathered in the little church. The town square was filled with a silent and stunned crowd of *alvisopolitani* who had come out to mourn the estate's founding father.

Alvise's will was unsealed two days after his death. He urged Lucia "to forget all the displeasures I may have caused [you] and for which I am truly sorry." Henceforth and until her death, she was to receive a generous monthly stipend from his estate. As a proof of his affection and esteem, he named her sole guardian of Alvisetto, "my most beloved only child, universal heir of all my movable and immovable properties, stores, capitals, credits, moneys and stocks."[11] In writing his signature at the bottom of the page, Alvise had scratched the paper so weakly with his quill there was only the faintest trace of ink, and his name was a barely legible scrawl.

Lucia was moved by Alvise's unexpected words of contrition, and even more so by the unconditional embrace of Alvisetto as his own son. In a way, his love for the boy had led him back to the love he had once felt for the young girl he had married so many years ago. Before dying, he did what Paolina had asked him to do: he forgot "the displeasures" of their life together, and asked Lucia to do the same. More surprisingly, he asked her to take up his life-work. Lucia had seen how Alvise had struggled over the years. Now it was suddenly her turn to take charge and the task ahead must have seemed daunting.

"I have already been to see Mama's portrait, and those of all the aunts and uncles and cousins, and ancestors,"[12] Lucia wrote to her sister shortly after arriving at Castel Gomberto. In the spring following Alvise's death she took Alvisetto and Vérand to the big house near Vicenza that belonged to her mother's family, the Piovene. She had to get away from Alvisopoli—from the vociferous crowd of creditors, petitioners, agents and labourers that besieged her all day long. "I want things to be run as if my husband were still here," she had repeated over and over after taking charge of Alvise's affairs.[13] But it would not do: every day dozens of decisions needed to be made that would affect the future of the estate and the people who worked and lived on it. Crushed by her new responsibilities, Lucia had escaped to Castel Gomberto, a place filled with memories, good feelings and domestic comforts. "It has warmed my heart to find the house as it always was . . . There are plenty of good beds, many guests, no shortage of linen and silverware."[14]

Every morning she drove out to Valdagno to take the waters. The skies were often stormy, with lightning and thunder, but the atmosphere in the house was always merry. In the large drawing room, there were games of billiards, draughts, cards and bingos of every possible kind. Vérand usually played the piano, Lucia caught up with her numerous relatives and Alvisetto received the undivided attention of his Piovene cousins. Lucia was relieved to see that he was in much better spirits than he had been after his father's death.

Not long after Alvise's funeral, Alvisetto had returned to Padua with Vérand to resume his studies. It had not been easy for him. He had struggled with his grief and had started to act out of character. "I went to visit him in Padua," Lucia later told Paolina. "At first he seemed anxious to be with me; but then he became distant, as if to underline his independence from me . . . He was bossy and uncaring. Everything had to be done his way and for his pleasure . . . I was hurt but I noticed he, too, often cried."[15] After a few days at Castel Gomberto, Lucia was happy to report, Alvisetto was again his old self, "respectful of his mother and her authority over him."

Lucia continued to be haunted by some of the words in Alvise's will, especially by his plea to forget all those "displeasures" he had caused her. He was not asking her for Christian forgiveness—it would not have been like him. Indeed, his words had nothing to do with religion. This was a matter between Alvise and Lucia alone, between husband and wife. Going through his papers, Lucia found many packets of letters written to him by different lovers over the course of several decades—

there were hundreds of letters, notes, small pieces of paper, and in many handwritings. She knew some of the women who had written them, especially those from the early years of their marriage; but many were complete strangers. At certain times—when she had been away, in Vienna, in Milan, even in Paris—he clearly had had more than one relationship going on. How did he manage all those parallel lives? How did he distribute his feelings? There was a genuine wonder mixed in with the pain caused by all that correspondence. So much of his life had been unknown to her.

Lucia did not return the letters, but neither did she throw them away. Instead, she put them in order, catalogued them by "author" and tied them in neat little bundles before storing them away in the attic of Palazzo Mocenigo. However, there is at least one set of letters missing from the collection: those of Carolina Faldi, the mother of Alvise's daughter, Luigia. In his will, Alvise spoke very tenderly about Luigia and showed an enduring attachment to her family. He left 12,000 gold sequins for her dowry, provisions for her education and for living expenses if she did not marry. Alvise entrusted Lucia with the responsibility of carrying out this part of his will. During their dealings, Carolina Faldi may have asked to have her letters back, in which case Lucia probably obliged her.

Lucia stayed at Castel Gomberto until the end of June, when her curative cycle at nearby Valdagno was completed. She did not look forward to the difficulties and complications that awaited her at Alvisopoli and the other Mocenigo estates. But there was no more time for delay. Harvest season was nearing and she was determined not to let the agents and farmers undermine her authority at the beginning of her tenure. She ordered all the wheat cut by the end of July and had it spread out under the sun until it was time to sell it at auction at the local fairs. She decided the selling price and approved every contract after careful review. "Soon I will have the linen seeds laid out in the sun too," she wrote to Paolina. "The silk is being treated and will shortly be ready for market."[16] In August she supervised the corn harvest;

in September she moved to the estates further south for the grape harvest. After three years of crippling disruptions, the sprawling Mocenigo farming empire was beginning to function again, albeit at reduced capacity. Lucia was perfectly aware this was only the start of a long and uncertain struggle. She had the weather to thank if the harvest was not spoiled that year, and she knew it. But in her letters to Paolina she showed a new confidence, and a barely disguised satisfaction with her initial accomplishments.

Lucia remained very active in the early autumn, during the tilling and sowing season. When the autumn rains began, the water had to be drained immediately to save the new crops and avoid the unwholesome stagnation. More ditches were dug, existing levees were reinforced. She laid out plans to plant more poplars and willows along the roads and canals, and to embellish the town with catalpas and acacias, laurel hedges and flower beds. She invested in a mulberry plantation to revamp the silk-producing factory. She started work on a rose garden in the back of the main house, planting the many specimens brought back from Paris, and she surveyed the park begun years earlier with Alvise to see where to place the exotic trees she had picked out with Professor Des Fontaines.

All this activity, she knew, was forcing her to neglect Alvisetto, who had started his last year at the seminary in Padua. Fearful that her son might not understand why she was suddenly so absent, she entreated Vérand to explain to him "how busy I have to be here at Alvisopoli, making sure all the work proceeds as it should and plans are laid out for the future." She was so taken up by her work that even her letters to Vérand—not an especially useful adviser on agricultural matters—became excuses to ramble on about "the general inertia" that slowed everything down in the fields or her doubts about whether this or that agent was running things as well as he should. "We have honest but not very enterprising workers," she complained. The agents and stewards were weak, she said, while she was still looked upon with too much suspicion to be truly effective. "If only we had a person of real authority here, who could act as a permanent spur, then we might obtain, if not all we should, at least half of it, which would be enough to turn the tide." She was endlessly frustrated by the wastefulness and lack of organisation. "Our agents want the oxen to work all day long except when the men in the fields take a long break for lunch and have a rest. Why don't they break up the hours so the animals also have a chance to rest but the work in the fields is not interrupted for so long?" There was no risk in confiding her thoughts to Vérand; but in Alvisopoli she kept them to herself for she felt, quite understandably, that her position was still too tenuous to impose her views on men who were perhaps set in their ways but were far more experienced than her. With the frustrations, however, came moments of exhilaration as well. Again, to Vérand: "Yesterday I went to supervise the sowing of corn seeds. All the labourers lined up and then advanced together. It was a beautiful sight." And later that day she walked over to the main granary to make sure no one had removed supplies before they went to market. She caused quite a commotion by suddenly ordering that all the stocked wheat be weighed in her presence. The process took several hours, and not everyone was happy. But it was a way of showing that she cared and that she could be taken seriously. "Despite the clouds of dust, I decided to stay until it was over. It was dark when we finished, but I was still there, holding up the lamp for them."[17]

In the winter of 1817 Alvisetto received his patents of nobility from the Imperial Court in Vienna. He was now Count of the Austrian Empire and Magnate of Hungary, the twin titles granted to Alvise during the first period of Austrian rule in Venice (1798–1805). These were heady documents for an impressionable seventeen-year-old, and they no doubt strengthened his sense of loyalty to the Habsburg crown. Vienna, not Paris or Milan, was the powerful and alluring capital of his new world.

Emperor Francis named one of his younger brothers, Archduke Rainier, viceroy of the Kingdom of Lombardy–Venetia. In the spring Rainier came to Venice on his first official visit. Alvisetto was eager to be seen in a flashy new Austrian uniform on that occasion, and he enlisted his mother to help him find the proper one. Lucia was still recovering from a long and debilitating bout of tertian fever: perhaps the stress of the previous summer and autumn had weakened her more than she realised, for she was bedridden during much of the winter, and even suffered a dangerous relapse in March. Still, she understood more than anyone else how important it was for Alvisetto to have the right attire. She wrote to friends in Vienna asking for a book she remembered which had figurines wearing all the uniforms of the Habsburg Empire. Once she had identified the right uniform she had it copied "with the precise colours, the embroidery properly highlighted . . . the headgear with all its embellishments, as well as the épée and scabbard."[18] The sketch was rushed off to the tailor just in time for Alvisetto to make his good impression on the imperial delegation.

The harvest in the summer of 1817 was very poor compared to the previous year. Rainfalls caused large-scale floods that seriously harmed the crops. The levee along the main canal at Alvisopoli burst and it took weeks to rebuild it, while hundreds of acres remained under water. Travelling from one estate to another was problematic because the roads and tracks were muddy. And every new drop of water made things worse. Lucia was so fearful of more rainfall she hardly slept any more. "I pray the Lord Almighty he will free me of the anxiety the weather is causing me," she told Paolina, adding that the agents were taking it out on her.[19] Even Giovanni Lazzaroni, general manager of the Mocenigo Agency and Alvise's right-hand man for many years, "is no longer well-disposed towards me and thinks ill of what I do."[20]

In his will, Alvise had requested that a specific number of masses be celebrated in his memory in the little church of Alvisopoli. Now Lucia discovered with dismay that his wish had been disregarded. Lazzaroni explained there was simply not enough money in the Agency's coffers to pay for the extra services and offerings. Lucia reacted with anger and guilt. "It fills me with sor-

row," she told Lazzaroni, "to learn that our income is not sufficient to do things the way my poor husband had laid out, and to
have to remain silent..."[21]

Alvisetto did not improve the general atmosphere when he
graduated rather ingloriously from the seminary at the end of the
summer. "He could easily have distinguished himself more,"
Lucia snapped, clearly irritated by her son's lack of diligence.
What was she going to do with him now? "God willing he will
keep away from poisonous occasions," she wrote to Vérand, "[as
you know] his youthful fervour is so much greater than his
strength of character."[22] After briefly considering the possibility
that Alvisetto join her in running the Agency, Lucia returned to
the original plan of sending him to university. She was encouraged in this choice by Mattia Soranzo Mocenigo, a distant cousin
with a reputation for wisdom whom Alvise had named "consul-
tant" to his wife in his will. Alvise's old project of sending
Alvisetto to a prestigious university in Germany was quickly dis-
carded. Lucia wanted him to be close at hand so that he could
visit her often and gain familiarity with Alvisopoli and the other
estates. It was decided he would study law at the university of
Padua. "Alvisetto too seems comfortable with the idea,"[23] she
observed.

Vérand felt this was the right moment to make a long-delayed
journey to France to attend to pressing family business of his
own. After all, Alvisetto was eighteen years old and out of
school; he could easily do without his supervision for a few
months. But Vérand underestimated the degree to which Lucia,
so completely absorbed by work, had come to rely on him with
regard to Alvisetto. She nipped Vérand's plan in the bud:

> You well understand how important your continued
> assistance to my son is at an age in which proper coun-
> selling is especially needed. The supervision on the
> part of an honest and wise educator is necessary to
> keep him away from all those dangers and enticements
> that lurk in the path of a young man . . . To aban-

don him at this early stage would be tantamount to losing at once all the gains obtained by your good governance.[24]

Lucia was under tremendous pressure. The summer's poor harvest at Alvisopoli meant more resources would have to be transferred from the other Mocenigo estates to avoid sinking further into debt. She received an even harder blow in February, when the government rejected Alvise's petition to have the fiscal burden on Alvisopoli reduced. Lucia spent the rest of the winter with lawyers and family advisers trying to reverse the decision. "I find myself absolutely unable to submit myself to such an excessive burden," she declared in her final statement to the authorities, adding that if the order were not repealed she would be "forced to give up the estate."[25]

Alvisopoli was not her only worry. The situation in Venice continued to deteriorate. The combination of trade barriers and the rise of Trieste as Vienna's favoured port in the Adriatic had crippled the local economy. During his visit to the city, Archduke Rainier had written back to Vienna that he was stunned to find such poverty and squalor. Shops were still closed. Housing and health conditions were appalling. The active population was declining quickly. The streets were filled with beggars, rubbish and debris from crumbling buildings. Four years had gone by since the end of the siege. The Austrians had been running the city ever since, yet they had done little to lift Venice out of its dismal situation.

Lucia, who relied on her income from family properties in the city to run Palazzo Mocenigo, could no longer afford the maintenance costs and living expenses. The sprawling *palazzo* was falling into disrepair. She had already closed off entire floors because she could not afford to heat them in the winter, giving up room after room in her losing struggle with rats. She would soon have to start dismissing the staff; she might even have to abandon Palazzo Mocenigo, as so many families had already done with their palaces. But this depressing state of affairs was shaken up by an unexpected business opportunity.

Lucia had met Lord Byron a few times at the soirées given by Albrizzi and Benzoni, but their acquaintance had remained superficial. Byron had arrived in Venice in November of 1816, and for a year and a half he had led a dissolute and extravagant life, mostly, though not exclusively, in the arms of Marianna Segati, the "light and pretty"[26] young wife of the draper in the Frezzeria in whose house he was lodging. During the same period, Lucia was completely preoccupied with the running of her affairs on the mainland and was seldom in town.

By the early spring of 1818, however, Byron's year-long affair with Marianna Segati came to an end. Word was that he wished to leave the house in the Frezzeria and was seeking more substantial quarters, possibly with a view of the Grand Canal. A wealthy foreign tenant was just what Lucia needed to ease the crushing financial burden and hold on to Palazzo Mocenigo. When she heard Byron was looking for spacious lodgings on the Grand Canal, she pricked up her ears. But it turned out that Fabio Gritti was already arranging the lease of a *palazzo* on the Grand Canal beyond the Rialto bridge, at San Marcuola. The deal was practically sealed, and Byron was already writing to his friends in London that he was moving into Palazzo Gritti.

How Lucia managed to unthread Byron's deal with the Grittis is not entirely clear. It appears that Mattia Soranzo Mocenigo, the family adviser, played a central role in bringing about the new arrangement. Mattia was one of the poet's few Venetian friends. He knew, of course, that Lucia was in dire financial straits, and he persuaded Byron to reconsider his agreement with the Grittis, reminding him, no doubt, that Palazzo Mocenigo was more prestigious and better located on the Grand Canal. The Grittis did not put up much resistance to protect their lucrative lease. Fabio Gritti was a cousin of Lucia's on her father's side, and a close friend. He had helped and advised her during the most difficult times after Alvise's death, and he bowed out gracefully.

On 1 June, Byron settled into the *piano nobile* of Palazzo Mocenigo. Months later, when his relationship with Lucia soured, he complained about having been "seduced"[27] by Mattia Soranzo Mocenigo into making a deal with her. But in the late spring of

1818 he was enthralled by the prospect of living in such a fabled *palazzo*. "It is four, and the dawn gleams over the Grand Canal and unshadows the Rialto," he wrote soon after moving in. "I must go to bed; up all night . . . it's life, though, damn, it's life."[28]

Expensive life, to be sure. Lucia asked a very high price: 4,800 francs a year—roughly the equivalent of 200 pounds sterling. It was a large amount as it was, but a huge one relative to the depressed Venetian economy. Byron was undeterred: he signed a three-year lease—a considerable commitment on the part of such a restless traveller. Further, he agreed to pay each year's full rent in advance every month of June. For Lucia, this was manna from heaven. She was going to keep Palazzo Mocenigo after all. Her famous and very wealthy new tenant also agreed to hire several members of the house staff, including Tita, one of the family gondoliers.*

Lucia gladly moved her belongings into a small apartment on the mezzanine floor and, much relieved by the way matters had resolved themselves in Venice, travelled back to the mainland, where more good news awaited her. Her desperate appeal regarding the excessive taxes on Alvisopoli had been granted: "The royal government"—she read—"is pleased to inform you that the suspension of tax payments will continue until further notice."[29] With a lightened heart, she went off to Valdagno for her yearly water cures and then settled in Alvisopoli during the long, hot months of July and August to supervise the wheat and corn harvests. Towards the end of the summer, she moved to Este, from where she took care of affairs at the nearby estates.

Lucia saw little of her son during his first year at university. When the summer term was over, Vérand left for France while Alvisetto travelled south towards Ferrara with other fellow students. It was his first taste of real freedom. He seldom gave news of himself, though he was occasionally spotted in one town or

---

* Giovanni Battista Falcieri (1798–1874), known as Tita, became one of Byron's most trusted servants. A tall, strong man, with a long black beard, he was also very gentle and kind. He was with Byron in Missolonghi, and held the poet's hand as he lay dying; he accompanied the corpse back to England, and settled there, eventually finding employment in the house of Benjamin Disraeli in Buckinghamshire.

another by friends of the family who were thoughtful enough to inform Lucia. All the same, she worried that he might fall in with "a band of oafs" and wondered how he got by since "he doesn't have any money to travel."[30]

Lucia was still in Este, making last-minute arrangements for the grape harvest, when Alvisetto reappeared at last, and very much in a hurry to meet the enrolment deadline for the new academic year. They went to Padua together for the start of the term, both of them staying at the run-down old Memmo *palazzo* on Prato della Valle, which Lucia and Paolina had recently inherited upon the death of their uncle Lorenzo. Lucia headed to Venice in late October, in time to tuck herself into her mezzanine apartment before the cold season set in. She asked Paolina to make sure her rooms were ready and her bed made. "Most importantly, check to see if all the holes in my bedroom have been properly filled in—and not just with paper . . ."[31]

Lucia found Palazzo Mocenigo transformed by Byron's colourful menagerie. Inside the porch he had set up a noisy little zoo: several types of bird, dogs, two monkeys, a fox and a wolf. All of them lived in large cages that cluttered the access to the canal and terrified anyone passing by. The atmosphere was even more chaotic upstairs, on the *piano nobile*. Byron had collected up to fourteen servants, including his cook, Stevens, and his valet, William Fletcher. A former clerk at the British Consulate, Richard Edgecombe, managed the household: he paid salaries, bought groceries and kept the accounts. He was always rushing, always very obsequious every time Lucia ran into him in the courtyard. Byron's two-year-old daughter, Allegra, and her shy governess, Elise, were the latest additions to this eclectic and very rambunctious little court.

The lady of the house, as it were, was Margherita Cogni, the illiterate young wife of a country baker, whom Byron had met while summering at La Mira, on the Brenta Canal, the year before. Byron's torrid affair with the very sensual Margherita had accelerated the break-up with Marianna Segati. After the poet moved to Palazzo Mocenigo, Margherita, known as *La Fornarina* (the baker's wife), left her husband, came to Venice and joined the crowded ménage living on the *piano nobile*. Margherita had a fiery temperament, was loud and theatrical, and made hysterical scenes over the merest trifle. Byron explained to his friends that she had forced herself into the household without his consent, but that every time he angrily told her to leave "she always finished by making me laugh with some Venetian pantaloonery or another."[32]

By the time Lucia returned to Palazzo Mocenigo in the autumn of 1818, however, Margherita had worn out Byron's patience. She took her leave with a final, pyrotechnical performance, shrieking and yelling and slicing the air with a large knife. Alerted by the racket, Lucia went to her balcony and saw the frenzied Margherita leap into the freezing waters of the Grand Canal. "All of this was for the sake of effect and not real stabbing or drowning," Byron observed coolly. "She was fished out without much damage except throwing Madame Mocenigo into fits."[33]

Lucia did not usually intrude upon Byron's life nor did she comment on his style of living—not in her letters at least. A certain distance, she felt, was the prerequisite for keeping their relationship on a sound, business-like footing. She kept an eye on him discreetly and limited herself to appropriate enquiries about beds and mattresses, linen and silverware. During the first year of the lease, every thing went smoothly despite the noise, the confusion, the constant coming and going, not to mention the wild cawing and barking in the porch. But the atmosphere changed in the spring of 1819, and what had been a perfect landlady–tenant relationship soon turned into a fierce confrontation.

One evening in late April, at Marina Benzoni's, Byron met Teresa Guiccioli, the young and beautiful wife of Count Guiccioli from Ravenna. Byron became completely besotted by the manipulative, twenty-year-old Teresa, and a few weeks later, at her beckoning, he followed her and her husband to Ravenna. Before leaving, he made sure Richard Hoppner, the British consul who had negotiated the lease with Lucia and took care of Byron's business affairs in Venice, had enough cash to pay the second instalment of his three-year rent at Palazzo Mocenigo. But by early summer, the rumour was that Byron was so taken by his new love that he did not want to return to Venice, and was looking for an early release from his contract. Lucia became alarmed: she was counting on the income for the entire three years to put her accounts in order in Venice. The law was on her side and she was not about to offer any favours.

Alvisetto, meanwhile, had again disappeared. Lucia had approved a trip to Rome and Florence on the grounds that it would help him build up useful connections, on condition that Vérand go with him. Now she regretted sending them off. Alvisetto's rare letters were vague and not very reassuring. What was he up to? Who was he seeing? "He never mentions any prominent Roman family and I hope he has not been negligent in forming honourable and useful relationships," she wrote to Vérand. "Surely he must understand that such connections are useful in times of difficulty."[34]

Vérand was not in the mood for Lucia's long-distance lecturing. He complained to her that Alvisetto considered his presence a weight, and that he often excluded him from his social engagements and his amusements. Also, his brother was dying and he wished to travel to Lyon as soon as possible. Could he please be released of his duties? "Such hurry to go to Lyon is understandable," Lucia replied with impatience, "but grant me the favour of going there after my son's return to Venice (somehow my ears don't like the sound of your proposal to leave him before bringing him back to me)." Alvisetto, unbeknownst to his mother, took it upon himself to grant his tutor a leave. Lucia was furious. "I cannot and will not consent to this," she wrote to Vérand, who was already in Florence. "I expect to see my son returning as he left—I would be offended if it were otherwise. To change plans that were agreed to at the moment of separation is simply not right."[35] Vérand stopped in his tracks, fearful of incurring Lucia's wrath; he suggested that *she* take a brief vacation and join Alvisetto in Florence. "It would be very pleasant to join him for at least part of the journey," she replied with irritation, "but how could I possibly entertain a project that would take me away [from Alvisetto's] business affairs, which are neither few nor easy to tend to. The voice of reason tells me that I must manage his properties as best I can. Let me be clear: if I go, who stays?"[36]

It was time for them to come back, Lucia insisted. They had been away three months; it was long enough. Alvisetto needed to be in Padua to prepare for his last year at university and his final exams. "Besides, he has completed the tour of all the beautiful cities in Tuscany; to linger would mean that he is staying only to amuse himself, which he can do at any time and in any place . . . I am alone here and I need assistance."[37]

With Alvisetto safely back in Padua and Vérand off to France, Lucia finally focused on the pressing problem presented by her glamorous but unreliable tenant. Under Teresa Guiccioli's influence, Byron was growing critical of, even hostile to, the decaying city that had seduced and inspired him for more than two years. In Ravenna, removed from the vortex of dissipation, he was like a reveller waking up in the diaphanous early morning mist. He had lived too crazily; he had spent far too much money. The huge staff, the gondola, the horses he kept at the Lido, the *casini* (small pleasure houses) he rented in Venice and on the Brenta: such an extravagant set-up did not make sense to him any more. The most urgent step was to leave Palazzo Mocenigo and the two *casini*.

Byron asked his friend Alexander Scott, who was in Venice, to give notice to Lucia, adding that she could keep the entire rent for the second year, which had already been paid, if she rescinded the contract and he did not have to pay her the third and final instalment. Scott balked at the prospect of a legal brawl with one of Venice's most prominent ladies: "Give up your houses! Discharge your servants! Oh my! I will wait for your second thoughts—a few days can make no difference, the less so as Mme Mocenigo is out of town."[38]

Byron did indeed have second thoughts during the course of the summer. The ambiguity of his role in the odd arrangement with the Guicciolis was making his stay in Ravenna increasingly uncomfortable: he was in love with Teresa but he resented being turned into a gallant, a *cavalier servente* in the old and most decadent Venetian tradition. He decided to return temporarily to Venice until matters were cleared between Count Guiccioli and Teresa: after all, the rent at Palazzo Mocenigo was paid, the apartment was fully staffed and waiting for him. "I shall take it as a favour," he wrote to Henry d'Orville, Hoppner's assistant, "if you will have the goodness to inform my landlady that I (having changed my mind) do not intend quitting or giving up my house and establishments at present—and that they and the servants will continue to be present on the former footing . . . You will oblige me infinitely by keeping a tight hand over my ragamuffins."[39]

Lucia found Byron installed again at Palazzo Mocenigo when she returned to Venice in late October from Este. She made it clear to Hoppner that, while Byron was free to leave at any time, she was not going to forsake 4,800 francs—the amount of the third instalment—just because her tenant had fallen for a trouble-making countess in Ravenna.

Lucia's firmness added to Byron's sombre mood. He wanted to leave Venice, but he felt trapped in it. He told friends different things: that he was going back to London, that he was leaving Europe, that he was joining Simón Bolivar in South America. "Alas! Here I am in a gloomy Venetian *palazzo*, never more alone than when alone," he wrote to John Cam Hobhouse, his closest friend. "Unhappy in the retrospect—and at least as much in the prospect."[40]

Matters between Byron and Lucia were further complicated by the "Gnoatto Affair," as it became known in the small English community. In his happier Venetian days, Byron had been very generous with his money, giving to charity and helping out the many in need with whom he came into contact. He had lent a considerable sum to a staff member at Palazzo Mocenigo named Gnoatto, who had been unable to pay him back (though he had offered to return the money in monthly instalments). Byron transformed this minor episode into a telling example of Venetian trickery and became obsessed with it. He warned Lucia he would deduct the sum owed to him by Gnoatto from the third and final payment due in June 1820 if she did not either force him to pay it back or fire him. He threatened to take her to court and "to give her as many years work of it" as he could. "I am not even sure I will pay her at all," he told Hoppner, "till she compels her scoundrelly dependent to do me justice—which a word from her would do." Lucia saw no reason to send away a member of the staff because he had borrowed money from her tenant. Byron became cocky: "If Mother Mocenigo does as she ought to do—I may perhaps give up her house—and pay her rent into the bargain—if not—I'll pay nothing and will go to law—I love a *lite*."[41] He used the Italian word for lawsuit.

The brawl was becoming a little too heated for the cautious Hoppner, who hoped Byron would recover his money "without having recourse to the violent measures you propose with Madame Mocenigo and which, to say the truth, I do not think would altogether accord with your accustomed justice and liberality."[42] Byron, however, was determined to press on. On 22 April he wrote from Ravenna, where he had returned, to explain that "with regard to Gnoatto—I cannot relent in favour of Madame Mocenigo, who protects a rascal and retains him in her service." But he was no longer so keen on a *lite*, he told Hoppner, as Venetian tribunals were corrupt and sentences never carried out. He would seek his own justice. "I repeat, not one farthing of the rent shall be paid until either Gnoatto pays me his debt—or quits Madame Mocenigo's service . . . Two words from her would suffice to make the villain do his duty."[43]

At the end of April, a month and a few days before the rent was due, Byron asked his lawyer, Castelli, to state his ultimatum to Lucia in person. Nothing came of it: Gnoatto did not reimburse the money and Lucia did not dismiss him. Hoppner ran through Byron's instructions one more time, hoping the poet might change his mind *in extremis:* "I shall not pay Madame Mocenigo's rent, which I believe comes due next month, without an order from you."[44] Byron was more fired up than ever: "we'll battle with [Mother Mocenigo]—and her ragamuffin."[45]

Two weeks later Byron backed down. His relationship with Teresa and Count Guiccioli had become so entangled—he was now living in Palazzo Guiccioli!—that he was anxious to ship his furniture and his animals to Ravenna and close the Venice chapter for good. He instructed Hoppner to pay Lucia the rent:

> You may give up the house immediately and licentiate the servitors, and pray, if it likes you not, sell the gondola . . . Mother Mocenigo will probably try a bill of breakables . . . [I reckon] the new Canal posts and pillars, and the new door at the other end, together with the year's rent, and the house given up without further occupation, are ample compensation for any cracking of crockery . . . She may be content, or she may be damned; it is no great matter which. Should I ever go to Venice again, I shall betake me to the Hostel or the Inn.[46]

An unexpected twist in the plot turned the finale of this whole affair into an *opera buffa*. On 1 June, Lucia sent her agent to collect the rent over at the English consular office. Hoppner went to fetch the sack with Byron's cash and realised with horror that most of the money was gone and that he did not have enough to pay the rent. "We can only conclude that it was stolen,"[47] he wrote to Byron, mortified. Byron found himself consoling the disheartened consul for the "disagreeable accident," but insisted he "examine into the matter thoroughly, because otherwise you [will] live in a state of perpetual suspicion . . . in Venice and with Venetian servants anything is possible that savours of villainy."[48]

Thus Lucia's agent returned to Palazzo Mocenigo empty-handed. She sent a note back asking to know the cause of the delay, warning that she was going to sue if any difficulty arose. Hoppner answered that Byron had left insufficient funds with him, but that he would gladly pay part of the rent immediately—there was enough in the sack to pay half; he would then write to Byron asking for more money with the first post to Ravenna. Lucia stiffened and said that would not do. Hoppner, feeling partly responsible for the imbroglio, offered to pay the entire amount with his own money hoping Lucia would demur. Instead, she immediately accepted. Hoppner was taken aback: "I actually expected she would prefer waiting, but on the contrary she replied she wanted the money."[49]

Lucia was not finished with the flustered British consul. She sent her agent over to Hoppner's with a bill for 4,862 francs instead of the 4,800 agreed to in the contract, arguing the value of the gold *louis*, the currency in which the contract was stipulated, had increased. Hoppner was indignant. He refused to pay the extra sixty-two francs and hurled "considerable abuse" at the agent. But he soon regretted drawing his sword against Lucia to defend Byron's interests: "In consequence of the affront put upon her . . . She will revenge herself by giving us as much trouble as she can, and I shall therefore leave her as little as possible of what does not belong to her before I make the house over to her."[50] He sold Byron's gondola with great difficulty, and at a loss. "What is to be done? There is no money and in lieu of it plenty of misery and discontent."[51]

There was a squalid little coda to the dispute. At the end of July, Lucia sent Byron a list of broken or missing items, including two valuable silver coffee pots. Hoppner, summering in Bassano, did not have the heart for another battle in the long war with Lucia. Whereas Byron was quitting Venice for good, the consul was staying on, and had nothing to gain from protracted warfare. "I do not like to expose myself unnecessarily to the old lady's scurrility or the ill opinion she may express of me to others," he admitted. "I am at wits' end as well as the end of my money & little able to withstand the shock of the Mocenigo battery."[52]

Byron felt sympathy for Hoppner and insisted he make clear to Lucia that he was merely acting as go-between: "State my words as my words; who can blame you when you merely take the trouble to repeat what I say?"[53] He argued Lucia had no business asking to be reimbursed for breakables a year before the lease was up—a rather disingenuous position to take since he was telling everyone he was leaving Venice and did not intend to return. But

Lucia's relentlessness exasperated him. In his view, she was needlessly hounding him:

> I have replenished three times over, and made good by the equivalent of the doors and canal posts any little damage to her pottery. If any articles [were] taken by mistake, they shall be restored or replaced; but I will submit to no exorbitant charge nor imposition. What she may do I neither know nor care: if they like the law they shall have it for years to come, and if they gain, what then? They will find it difficult to "shear the wolf" no longer [in Venice]. They are a damned, infamous set . . . a nest of whores and scoundrels.[54]

Lucia was in Padua attending to preparations for Alvisetto's graduation. And with Byron away in Ravenna, Hoppner felt there was no point in pressing the matter of the breakables right away. He would take his time and deal with the problem in the autumn. By then, Alvisetto, a doctor in law, was sure to start taking charge of Mocenigo affairs. "I will settle personally with the young Count, the bastard, any disputes which may arise,"[55] he assured Byron nastily.

Lucia took possession of Palazzo Mocenigo in the autumn, after Alvisetto's graduation. She was glad Byron and his exotic ménage had left: however glamorous, his stay had caused a lot of ill feeling. Still, she was far from regretting that he had come to live in Palazzo Mocenigo. His valuable English pounds had brought succour to the house at a time of hardship and uncertainty. Life was not going to be easy in the years ahead. She had learnt enough to know that Alvisopoli, which she once described to Paolina as "that most wretched estate,"[56] would continue to drain energy and money. But the period of emergency she had lived through after Alvise's death seemed behind her.

Alvisetto decided to surprise Lucia by secretly renovating her apartment during the summer, when she was in the country. Lucia got wind of the changes—of course she would—and she wrote to Paolina that she was reminded of when she was a young bride-to-be, living in Rome with her sister and their father, and Alvise was busy with masons and carpenters and painters preparing her apartment in Venice. "[Alvisetto] wants it to be more functional [but] I have not been told what instructions he has given—I hope he is not spending too much money."[57]

There was one more pressing matter to attend to which Lucia had put in the back of her mind during the trying times following Alvise's death but which now required her full attention: what to do with the monumental statue of Napoleon which her husband had commissioned ten years earlier from Angelo Pizzi with the intention of placing it in the main square at Alvisopoli. Pizzi had died in 1812, leaving the statue unfinished in a studio at the Accademia delle Belle Arti, a short way down the Grand Canal. After the return of the Austrians to Venice, the directors of the Accademia had started to pressure Lucia to take charge of the embarrassing sculpture. It now occurred to her that her friend Canova might come to her rescue for the sake of old times, and she wrote to him asking if she could not by any chance interest him "in a piece of the purest marble of Carrara." She never mentioned the word "Napoleon" in her letter, trusting Canova, who had initially been approached by Alvise for the job, knew very well what she was talking about. Obliquely, she reminded him the statue could easily take on a different profile "from the one initially pursued." And if he was not interested himself, would he not show it to someone he could recommend? "As my son's guardian," she added at the end of her pitch, "it would give me great pleasure to enter into negotiation with you. We would be exchanging favours, as it were. For I am certain that if you were to look for a nice piece of marble you would not find a finer one as this. Furthermore, the work was already begun, and rather well. My son is not eager to see it finished, though, and he has left me free to sell it for a sum which I am sure will be agreeable to you."[58]

Canova, however, was not a taker, and Lucia resigned herself to have the statue (which was rather more finished than she had led Canova to believe) transported the short distance up the Grand Canal to Palazzo Mocenigo, and placed in a shadowy corner at the far end of the *androne*. It made no sense to attract the attention of the Austrian authorities any further by shipping the disgraced colossus all the way to Alvisopoli; its bulky presence in Venice was cumbersome enough.

Alvisetto obtained a cadetship with the Austrian army and left for his military service, unaware he was following in his real father's footsteps. He had matured during his last year at university, growing into an affable young man, with a good mind and a solid education. He was eager to do well in the world, and looked forward to a successful career in the Austrian administration after his tour of military duty. His loyalty to Vienna was unquestioned, but, like Lucia, he felt his Venetian roots very strongly. Soon his mother would cease to be his legal guardian. As head of the Mocenigo dynasty, he would take over from her the responsibility of running the family estate. Would he be up to the task? To Lucia, of course, he remained in many ways a boy. "He is young and I fear he is still a little green," she reasoned with Paolina, "but he has no bad habits and no major character flaws so I suppose there is reason to be hopeful."[59]

Epilogue

Lucia and Byron parted on very unfriendly terms, yet in a way the poet never really left Palazzo Mocenigo, or Venice for that matter, and still today his spirit hovers over the city he helped to resurrect. Venice was dead when he arrived in 1816, and the Austrians had no intention of spending money or effort to revive it—certainly not during the early years, when the policy in Vienna was to favour the port city of Trieste and let Venice go to ruin. It was Byron, a stranger to Lucia's Venetian world, who gave the city a new life by turning those sinking ruins into an existential landscape—an island of the soul. Despite his dissolute lifestyle, he was an inspired and extremely prolific writer during the happier days of his Venetian sojourn, composing beautiful lyrics and poems about Venice, not to mention hundreds of letters to his friends that were an unbridled torrent of words and imagery and feeling.

For much of the nineteenth century, artists and poets drew on the romantic myth Byron had forged, and nourished it. In the new Venice that travellers came to see, Lucia had a small part to play, a cameo as it were, as Byron's landlady (how the poet would have fumed!). But she was also a living connection to the fabled lost Republic of the doges. An invitation to Palazzo Mocenigo became a coveted prize on the Venice Grand Tour. Foreign visitors lined up to see her, and according to the accounts left to us by diarists and letter-writers, she enjoyed playing her role and always made an effort to turn these brief encounters into special occasions.

In his *Mémoires d'outre-tombe*, Chateaubriand describes a

courtesy call he paid to Lucia in 1833. They had not seen each other since meeting in Paris in the twilight days of the Empire nearly twenty years before. As his gondola pulled up to the landing at Palazzo Mocenigo, Chateaubriand had a haunting vision: Byron's old mooring pole was still planted there, his coat of arms "half erased" by wind and saltwater. Lucia was waiting for him upstairs:

> Madame Mocenigo lives retired in a tiny corner of her own private Louvre, overwhelmed by its vastness. The desert advances daily into the inhabited parts. I found her sitting across from Tintoretto's original sketch of his *Paradise*. Hanging on the wall right above her was Madame Mocenigo's own portrait, painted in her youth . . . Madame Mocenigo is still beautiful, the way one is beautiful in the shadow of old age. I covered her with compliments, which she returned. We were lying to each other and we both knew it: "Madame, you've never looked so young."—"Monsieur, you haven't aged a bit." We lamented the ruin of Venice so as not to mention our own . . . The time came to take my leave, and I respectfully kissed the hand of the Doges' Daughter whilst casting a lingering glance at the same beautiful hand in the portrait, which now withered at my lips.[1]

Lucia was certainly getting on—she was sixty-three when Chateaubriand went to see her—but she was hardly a relic from the past. Indeed, she was still running the Mocenigo Agency, battling daily with inefficient agents, litigious neighbours, stern tax-enforcers and greedy moneylenders. The 1820s had been especially hard. She had been forced to take out more loans, and when there had been nothing left to mortgage, she had sold one by one the Memmo properties she had inherited from her father's family. It had been a painful choice, each new sale "a sacrifice I make for my son,"[2] but Lucia had made it her mission to preserve the Mocenigo estate intact during her watch. Fortunately, by the early 1830s, the economic outlook of the region improved, with the abolition of anachronistic trade barriers and the development of steam-driven industry. As the agricultural sector picked up, the Agency gained a sounder footing. Even Alvisopoli became less of a drain on the family holdings.

Alvisetto came of age in 1824, majority being reached at twenty-five, and though Lucia gave him regular updates and never made major decisions without consulting him, he did not really take charge of the family business until the late 1830s. Lucia's willingness to stay at the helm well beyond her guardianship enabled Alvisetto to pursue a diplomatic career in the Austrian government. After his military service, he obtained a post as secretary in the Austrian embassy in Naples. He later moved to the embassy in Rome, still in a rather junior position and rather anxious to move up the ladder at a faster clip. Despite his occasional frustration at the slow pace of his career, he remained an enthusiastic Austrophile, wary of the growing opposition against the conservative governments of Europe. When protests erupted in France, Belgium, the Netherlands and even Spain, he was "deeply troubled by the folly"[3] of progressive liberals, and told his mother he hoped it did not spread to the territories in the Habsburg Empire.

Alvisetto's loyalty was rewarded. He was made Chamberlain of His Majesty the Emperor and King, and Chevalier of the Order of Saint George. He was also promoted, at last, to the position of Legation councillor in the Austrian embassy in Florence. Emperor Francis received him in Vienna "with the greatest kindness," he reported glowingly to Lucia. "His Majesty is well, thank God. He asked how you were. He told me of the importance of my position and promised to think of me if other opportunities should arise, confident that I shall continue to serve with as much zeal as ever."[4] Alvisetto was eventually appointed Austrian chargé d'affaires to the Prince Elector of Hesse. His assimilation into the Habsburg administration was by now complete, yet he must have felt a little disappointed at his less than sparkling achievements, especially in the light of his father's ambitions for him. On the other hand, spectacular careers were rather rare during the grey, ultra-conservative years of the Restoration.

As Alvisetto neared his fortieth birthday, Lucia nimbly stepped in to find a suitable wife for her over-aged bachelor son. He had shown little inclination to marry and have children and ensure the Mocenigos did not become extinct, and he evidently needed a little prodding from his mother. Lucia set her aim very high, on Clementina Spaur, young daughter of Johann Baptist Spaur, governor of Lombardy–Venetia. After months of careful manoeuvring, the two sides reached an agreement—the long and detailed marriage contract bearing testimony to very elaborate negotiations. On 24 November 1840, at the age of forty-one, Alvisetto married Clementina. It was a notable match, which brought together wealth and political power.

The newly-weds settled into the large apartment on the *piano nobile* adjoining Lucia's. Alvisetto retired from his career as a civil servant in the Austrian administration to take full charge of the Agency. He turned out to be an imaginative businessman, no doubt anxious to prove himself after his lacklustre career in diplomacy. He diversified the Mocenigo holdings, taking advantage of the economic expansion which had started in the thirties, investing heavily in property, railways, energy, steamships, and founding his own shipping line, the Società di piroscafi Mocenigo. He had a hand in many of the high-profile business ventures started in the forties, foremost among them the Venice–Milan railway, which reached across the lagoon and connected the city to the mainland. Although some of his investments turned out to be only moderately profitable, Alvisetto became a driving figure in the rapid development of the region. "From salt mines to rice fields," one historian has written, "from land redevelopment to gas lighting, from steamships to railways, there is not a single area in which Mocenigo did not participate in one form or another from 1840 to 1848."[5]

Indeed, Alvisetto's transformation from mid-level career

diplomat to enlightened industrialist is quite astonishing. He became widely respected and sought after for his entrepreneurial advice. "The man is notable for his intelligence and ready eloquence," remarked Niccolò Tommaseo, a leading intellectual and political figure in Venice who was seeking influential allies in the drive for emancipation from Vienna. "He has the composed and courteous elegance, if not the dignity, of our gentlemen of old."[6]

By the early forties, Alvisetto's loyalty to the House of Habsburg was wavering. The frustrations he accumulated over the years in the Austrian administration probably played a role in his growing resistance to Vienna's heavy-handed rule. His father-in-law's retirement from the governorship no doubt made it easier for him to challenge the government. More importantly, Alvisetto's wide-ranging business activities brought him face to face with an obtuse system of government which was limiting the economic and political development of the region. At a time of growing national aspirations, Vienna continued to rule the Kingdom of Lombardy–Venetia like a colony.

Many activists saw Alvisetto as a potential political leader, an ideal bridge between the lawyers and intellectuals who opposed Vienna's rule and the land-owning liberal aristocracy. "He is an effective speaker," one observer noted, "and he is sufficiently ambitious to be drawn to the glamour of a political role."[7] But those who looked to Alvisetto as a potential leader of a movement against Austria underestimated the complex nature of his ties to Vienna. He was not ready to be drawn into a fully fledged opposition and he saw himself more as a man of dialogue, a facilitator in a gradual process of emancipation from Vienna, certainly not as a revolutionary leader.

There is a telling episode in this respect. Two young Venetian officers in the Austrian navy, Emilio and Attilio Bandiera, had formed a secret society, Esperia, with strong ties to Giuseppe Mazzini, the Republican leader living in exile in London, and to his organisation, Giovine Italia. The Bandiera brothers were betrayed by a spy and went into hiding on the island of Corfu. Emilio, who was trying to generate support for the Mazzinian cause in Italy, wrote to Alvisetto, whom he had never met, declaring him to be the man in whose hands "the destiny of Venice should be entrusted once our democratic revolution will have taken place."[8] Alvisetto was startled by the letter, and frightened. The last thing he wanted was to be associated with the radical revolutionary Mazzini. In a moment of panic, he handed the letter over to the Austrian police.

A few months later, in July 1844, the Bandiera brothers were arrested after a landing in Calabria, summarily tried and shot. They became the first martyrs of the Italian Risorgimento. Alvisetto's little act of treachery was not divulged at the time so it did not lessen his standing in the liberal camp, and he was soon to become a player on the revolutionary stage in Venice.

Lucia settled into grandmotherhood, with its joys and sorrows. The first granddaughter, born in 1842, died in infancy. Three years later a boy was born; predictably, he was given the name Alvise and christened in the neighbourhood church of San Samuele, where a long line of Alvise Mocenigos had been christened before him. As customary, food was distributed to 300 poor families. The following year another boy was born, Giovanni. There was now a busy traffic between Lucia's apartment and the adjacent one, occupied by Alvisetto's family. The door separating the two was usually left open, as Lucia enjoyed dropping in on her daughter-in-law, Clementina, the way Chiara stopped by to see her after she had moved into Palazzo Mocenigo as a young bride.

The ghostly Venice of the twenties was a faded memory. The city was relatively prosperous again. The population was increasing. The shops were filled with goods from all over Europe. The canals were crowded with boats and the coffee shops were packed until late at night. The landscape of the city was changing: the Austrian administration approved plans to fill in and pave many side canals to improve circulation, and to build garden areas and promenades. Yet Venice remained a divided city, with the Venetians and the Austrians leading separate lives.

In no place was the separation more evident than in Saint Mark's Square, where Austrian officers sat at the tables of Quadri sipping coffee and listening to the orchestra play waltzes, while the Venetians crowded the smoke-filled rooms at Florian's, across the square.

Although officially retired, Lucia led a busy life: she was very active on the board of La Fenice, the Venice opera house, she took care of her residual rental properties, she entertained small parties of younger friends*—most of her contemporaries having passed away—and she went out of her way to maintain good relations with Austrian officials.

Her lingering joy in her declining years was the company of Paolina, who still lived at Palazzo Martinengo, old Ca' Memmo, up the Grand Canal from her. They saw each other as often as they could, and wrote daily, mostly about the vicissitudes of old age: sores, stomach seizures, discharges, regurgitations, throat lumps. Was the footbath giving relief? Was the magnesia having effect? The tone was sometimes caustic, sometimes humorous, always tender. When Lucia lost a blackened canine, she slipped it in an envelope and sent it to her sister "so that you may have the first fragment of my mortal spoils."[9]

The winter in 1842 was especially harsh. "Stay where you are," Lucia entreated her sister, who wanted to go to church despite having caught a chill. "This bitter cold will damage your health even inside the house. It says in the papers it is worse than in 1812, the year the French armies were forced to retreat in Russia . . . Promise me you'll stay covered warmly, don't go up and down the stairs unless you must . . . And take your meals near your [warm] bedroom. Adieu my dearest sister."[10]

---

*Lucia's closest friend was Giovan Battista Foscolo. He was fifteen years younger than her and a bachelor. He had taken on the duties of a *cavalier servente* when Lucia had returned from Vienna in 1806, escorting her around town and to the theatre when Alvise was away. He did chores for her and helped her with financial and legal matters. There is nothing to suggest they ever became lovers, but they grew very close, especially after Lucia helped him find work during the Austrian administration. She bequeathed him 9,000 ducats in her will, but she did not leave enough funds behind and in the end Alvisetto supplied the sum.

It is the last letter between the sisters to have come down to us. Paolina died shortly afterwards, leaving her sister completely bereft.

Lucia began preparing for her own death. She put her affairs in order, paid her outstanding debts, arranged her correspondence. She wrote her will. There was not much she could leave any more, not after having sold most of her properties to save Alvisopoli; but she made sure the house staff was taken care of after she was gone, and she set aside small sums and valuable objects for relatives and close friends to remember her by. She was very meticulous about her funeral arrangements, and specified everything from the number of torches to be lit, to the number of gondolas (only two) for the funerary procession, to the number of services to be celebrated after her death for the benefit of her soul. Her body was to be laid in a casket made of cypress wood (which her carpenter made for her), enclosed in a box of cheaper larchwood. She purchased a burial plot in the cemetery on the island of San Michele—she did not want to be buried at Alvisopoli, although she gave Alvisetto permission to transfer her remains there at a later date if it was important to him.[11]

Everything was ready, only the time to die had not come, and Lucia was to live through one more great upheaval.

Alvisetto's opposition to the Austrians hardened in the face of Vienna's reactionary politics, and by 1847 he was a strong supporter of Daniele Manin, the brilliant lawyer and scholar who was leading the nationalist movement in Venice. The Austrian police imprisoned Manin for seditious activities, but was forced to release him in January 1848 because of public protests. Alvisetto was at the prison gates to greet him and led the cheering crowd that carried him to Saint Mark's Square.

Revolution was breaking out across Europe. In Vienna, Prince Metternich, the symbol of Austria's repressive rule, was forced to resign. Anti-Austrian pressure continued to build in Venice.

Fearing a popular insurrection, the military commander, Count Ferdinand Zichy, capitulated and withdrew his forces. On 23 March, Manin formed a provisional government and proclaimed a democratic Republic—an inheritor state of the Republic Napoleon had buried in 1797 at Campo Formio.

Vienna, however, had no intention of losing Venice. Austrian forces regrouped under Field Marshal Radetzky and marched back into northern Italy to recover the lost provinces. Manin's government had two choices: join forces with Charles Albert, the ambitious king of Piedmont and Sardinia, or become the magnet for a more radical and democratic revolution in Italy. The liberal camp favoured joining the Piedmontese. Alvisetto, breaking with Manin, organised a public rally in support of this policy. The liberals won the day, and on 7 August the union between Venice and Piedmont was signed. However, it never took effect: the Austrians crushed the Piedmontese army at Custoza and took control of Lombardy and the Venetian mainland. The Venetian Republic stood alone, isolated in the lagoon. Manin was called back to lead the new emergency government. One of his first acts was to expel Alvisetto and other leaders of the liberal camp. At the end of August, Alvisetto, Clementina and the two boys, left Palazzo Mocenigo and sailed to Ravenna, and from there travelled on to Florence.

Lucia did not go with them—could not go, actually. Weeks earlier she had taken a tumble and badly damaged her hip. She was still trussed up and bedridden when Alvisetto and the rest of the family were forced to leave Venice, and travelling was out of the question. She grudgingly stayed behind, tended by the faithful Teresa, and a few other members of the house staff at Palazzo Mocenigo. It must have felt strange to see her son head for the same city where she and Alvise had been exiled half a century before.

In early September she was relieved to learn that Alvisetto and his family had settled into a pleasant Florentine house. "The air is excellent, we have a nice garden, and there is peace and quiet," her son wrote, his only worry being "the damage the children might cause to the beautiful furniture."[12] But it did not take long for the news to get worse. Alvisetto, in constant touch with his agents on his estates, reported to his mother that the Austrian soldiers had ravaged several properties, and some 1,400 Croatian soldiers were encamped at Alvisopoli.

In October, Manin's government imposed a forced loan that hit landowners especially hard. Alvisetto, determined to show himself a good patriot, went deeper into debt to pay his share, borrowing from moneylenders, raising mortgages on everything he owned, signing promissory notes. The weight of "such a disproportionate levy" broke Alvisetto's spirit. He was hurt by "the injustice, the personal hatred, the sheer ingratitude of [his] fellow citizens."[13]

Confined to her apartments at Palazzo Mocenigo, Lucia worried about the family in Florence and the perilous state of affairs the estate seemed to be falling into. Was Alvisetto making the right moves? Was he telling her everything? Often she felt she was being left in the dark. Meanwhile, food and fuel shortages were making life in Venice more uncomfortable each day. Her hip was slowly on the mend, but she had to be moved around in a chaise-longue carried by the gondoliers, who learnt to lower her in her gondola with great dexterity for her daily outings. Friends and relatives came by to keep her company in the evening. And she had a new best friend, an Englishman. Rawdon Brown had settled in Venice some years before and had become very knowledgeable about the city's history (he thrived in Venice's archives). Lucia was always pleased to see him appear at her door: he was amusing, vivacious and kept her well informed on the latest developments in Manin's revolutionary government.

As Christmas approached, Lucia received a melancholy letter from Alvisetto. "In the face of misfortune," he told her, "family ties grow stronger. I cannot tell you how often we speak about you, and how strongly we wish to be reunited with you." He added, revealingly: "In revolutions such as those we are living in, men with great ambitions leap into the fray and either triumph or perish; men with small ambitions, such as myself, withdraw from the stage. One's family becomes the greatest consolation."[14]

Alvisetto was being pressed by moneylenders to whom he had resorted at the time of the forced loan, and had reached the end of his tether. "I have nothing left in Venice, nothing left in the countryside," he wrote in despair to his chief agent, Giovanni Pasqualini. "How is it possible that they cannot see this?"[15] At the end of 1848, he painted a disheartening picture for Lucia: "Dear mother, every time I look at the children I feel a chill as I think about their financial future, so gravely compromised already and at risk of total ruin if the current misfortunes continue."[16] It did not augur well for the new year.

In February 1849, having obtained a short reprieve from his creditors, Alvisetto left Florence and took the family to Alvisopoli. The winter landscape was made bleaker by the devastation that had taken place during his absence. The Austrian troops had turned the fields, neatly tilled and sowed in the early autumn, into choppy seas of hardened mud. They had cut down the poplars along the dirt roads and levees to make fires, looted the grain stores and decimated the cattle stock. After the Austrians had left, moving south towards Venice, bands of marauders claiming to be "communists" had taken over plots of land and now had to be forcefully dislodged. It was hardly a warm return home. "The lack of ready cash and resources is such that we are forced to live in great economy," he wrote in another gloomy letter. "We spend our evenings gathered around a single candle, and I keep sugar and coffee supplies under lock and key."[17]

In Venice, the situation was no better. The isolation of Manin's infant Republic quickly brought on a collapse of living conditions. Food supplies disappeared from the stores. Public health worsened dramatically. Manin assumed dictatorial powers to maintain public order. In April, Radetzky's army lay siege to the city by blockading the port and placing heavy artillery along the coastline. Manin, still naively hoping for help from France or England, enforced a policy of "resistance at all costs." All through the spring and summer, the Austrians bombarded the city with tens of thousands of projectiles, and even dropped bombs with the aid of air balloons. The Venetians showed extraordinary strength of character and valour and resisted for nearly five months. But by the end of the summer they had no ammunition left. The famine was devastating the population. The water supply had long been exhausted and families were drinking directly from the canals. Sanitary conditions were ghastly. A cholera epidemic broke out and in a few weeks killed more than 3,000 people. The rotting corpses were literally piling up in the streets. Neither France nor England were going to lift a finger to rescue the besieged Republic. Manin finally capitulated on 22 August and sailed to exile in London. Radetzky's troops entered the city. Venice had been the last bastion of resistance; Austria now regained full control of the Kingdom of Lombardy–Venetia.

Lucia hardly recognised her son when he returned to Palazzo Mocenigo: he had grown a thick beard and was much thinner than when he had left. She was glad to have little Alvise and Giovanni scampering about the house again—how the two boys had grown in a year! Clementina, on the other hand, looked tired and drawn—in Alvisopoli she had had a very late miscarriage.

Alvisetto's litany about his financial woes tapered off as the estates in the countryside resumed full production and the Agency started to generate more cash thanks to the Austrian reconstruction effort. Lucia was too old to start planning for the future, but she was relieved to see Alvisetto regain his enthusiasm for new business ventures. He wanted to invest in the food and drink business—"restaurants, coffee houses, wine shops and beer halls" for the Austrian clientele. The Mocenigo Agency owned many apartments and houses to rent in Venice and though money was still scarce among Venetians, Alvisetto was determined not to lower rents because, he said, "Very soon Venice will be extremely busy with foreigners."[18]

Among the first foreigners to reach Venice after the siege were John Ruskin and his pretty young wife, Effie. They arrived in November 1849 by boat—the railway bridge was badly damaged during the revolution—and took rooms at the Danieli on the Riva degli Schiavoni. Ruskin took off on his architectural explorations, while Effie organised her own visits, normally in the company of the lively Rawdon Brown. "He has promised to present us to [Madame] Mocenigo whom he is very intimate with," she wrote to her mother.[19] Effie was curious to meet Lucia, if a little intimidated. "She considers herself a sort of Queen in Venice as she is the last of the great Venetian Dames." Lucia hardly thought of herself as a queen, though evidently this was how Mr. Brown was advertising her on his tours of the city. Effie gives a vivid account of her visit with Lucia:

> It was in this Palace that Byron lived when in Venice . . . The walls of the rooms are covered with full length pictures of Doges of the family in their ducal robes, admirals and statesmen . . . We were received by some well dressed servants and conducted through a number of cold, grand marble and frescoed apartments, to some nice warm well furnished ones where sat the Lady on a small couch. She received us very kindly and considering her age, 80 years, she was extremely well looking and upright . . . As she can no longer go out she receives visitors all day or relations. Her manners were quite beautiful and took away from your first impressions caused by the absurdity of her dress which though excessively rich was not becoming for her age . . . Generally speaking her features were marked and fine and [she has] still sparkling black eyes her hair grey but false curls of jet black at each side of her face, the hair surmounted by a blonde cap with blue artificial flowers, a brown loose satin Polka cloak lined with white,

hanging open and showing her neck very bare, pale yellow kid gloves and exquisite point lace collar and handkerchief, a fan and dress of purple & green silk . . . After we were seated she rang for the men servants and they entered instantly bearing on massive silver plate & cups, black coffee, cake and iced lemonade in tumblers. The latter I took and found delicious. She was very affectionate to me and kissed me on both cheeks speaking French, and presented me with a work written I suppose a century ago by her father . . . We took leave of the old Lady and walked through her sleeping apartment by her permission. Here I was much astonished by the toilette table; I had never seen anything like it before; there was the mirror frame, two little other mirrors, essence pots, rouge pots, perfume bottles and boxes of various kinds, everything in wrought silver. It was very beautiful.[20]

A few days later, Effie was introduced to Alvisetto at La Fenice. She was not pleased by what she saw, innocently remarking: "He is very like his old mother in appearance, but extremely dark, and certainly to look at him you never could believe he was a descendant of the doges who lie entombed in [San] Giovanni e Paolo, each Mocenigo face finer & more beautiful than the other, even in old age."[21]

Mr. Brown brought visitors around to Palazzo Mocenigo for a few more years. Lucia always rose to the occasion, dressing up for her guests and offering cake and iced lemonade in heavy silver tumblers. But in truth she was only waiting to join her beloved Paolina, her "other me." She died on 7 March 1854, a month shy of her eighty-fourth birthday, and was buried, as she had wanted, in her cypress casket, on the island of San Michele.

In the end, Alvisetto decided not to transfer Lucia's remains to the family chapel in Alvisopoli, where he and his children were later buried, next to Alvise, the founding father of the estate. There are no other tombs in the chapel. Despite the strenuous efforts to ensure a male line, the Mocenigos of San Samuele did not survive beyond the next generation.*

Palazzo Mocenigo was sold many years ago and is now a prestigious condominium on the Grand Canal. There are no visible traces of Lucia, save for a plaque on the facade commemorating Byron's stay and the mystifying statue of Napoleon hidden away at the end of the entrance hall. I recently visited the cemetery on San Michele to pay homage to my great-great-great-great-grandmother, but I discovered she no longer rests there: a century ago some of the older tombs were destroyed to make place for a wider mooring berth. Her bones, I was told, have long since dissolved in the silty waters of the lagoon.

Alvisopoli, the estate that caused Lucia so many worries over the years, was also sold, in the 1930s, and broken up in separate properties. But the hamlet of Alvisopoli still exists—a few houses, a general store, and the Bar Mocenigo are scattered along a sleepy back-road west of Portogruaro. After years of neglect, the main villa was recently restored and turned into a low-cost housing project. The park Lucia designed behind the house has miraculously survived the encroaching urban sprawl, and now borders the noisy *autostrada*. The local branch of the World Wildlife Fund tends it; paths and bridges and benches have been added to attract the local population, but visitors are rare. Few of the plants and trees Lucia brought from Paris in 1814 still grow there, but in the springtime a beautiful white and pink

---

*Alvisetto's two boys, Alvise and Giovanni, died very young. A later son, Andrea, married Olga Windish-Graetz, and had a daughter, Valentina. Alvisetto's youngest daughters, Maria Amalia and Amelia, died without children. Valentina, the last of the Mocenigos, married Edmondo di Robilant, a Piedmontese. Their son, Andrea di Robilant, my grandfather, inherited the Mocenigo estate with the proviso that he take on the name. He never got around to doing it, and the Mocenigos became extinct.

rose blossoms randomly in the sunnier parts of the wood. The gardeners do not know its provenance and call it the *Rosa moceniga;* but it is probably a variety of the *Rosa multiflora* that Lucia brought from Paris, and now grows wild in the garden of Alvisopoli.

Sources

ABBREVIATIONS

AdR Papers   Author's Private Papers
AM   Archivio Memmo, Biblioteca Mai, Bergamo
ASF   Archivio di Stato di Firenze
ASV   Archivio di Stato di Venezia
JMA   John Murray Archive, National Library of Scotland,
    Edinburgh
LPD   Lucia's Paris Diary

CHAPTER ONE: ROME

1. Andrea Memmo to Giulio Perini, Rome, 25 April 1786, ASF, Acquisti e doni 94, filza 146.
2. Lucia to Alvise, Naples, 21 February 1786, AdR Papers.
3. Lucia to Alvise, Naples, 28 February 1786, AdR Papers.
4. Lucia to Alvise, Naples, 7 March 1786, AdR Papers.
5. Ibid.
6. The medical report signed by Professor Perlasca is in the Biblioteca Civica Correr di Venezia, Manoscritti, misc. IX, 1138. On the death of Lucia's mother, see *A Venetian Affair*, by Andrea di Robilant, New York: Knopf, 2003.
7. Andrea Memmo to Giulio Perini, Rome, 30 April 1785, ASF, Acquisti e doni 94, filza 146.
8. Andrea Memmo to Giulio Perini, Rome, 17 September 1783, ASF, Acquisti e doni 94, filza 146.
9. Andrea Memmo to Guglielmo Chiarabba, Rome, 22 May 1784, AdR Papers.
10. Andrea Memmo to Guglielmo Chiarabba, Rome, 12 March 1785, AdR Papers.
11. Andrea Memmo to Guglielmo Chiarabba, Rome, 16 October 1784, AdR Papers.
12. On Memmo's election to Procuratore di San Marco, see Andrea Memmo to Giulio Perini, Rome, 9 July 1785, and Rome, 13 August 1785, ASF, Acquisti e doni 94, filza 146.

13. Andrea Memmo to Giulio Perini, Rome, 30 April 1785, ASF, Acquisti e doni 94, filza 146.
14. On the arrest of Sebastiano Mocenigo by the Inquisitors, ASV, Archivio Mocenigo, B 120–122.
15. Sebastiano Mocenigo to Alvise, Brescia, 19 November 1778, ASV, Archivio Mocenigo, B 122.
16. Pisana Mocenigo to Alvise, undated, ASV, Archivio Mocenigo, B 124.
17. Alvise to Sebastiano Mocenigo, 13 March 1781, ASV, Archivio Mocenigo, B 120.
18. Andrea Memmo to Giulio Perini, Rome, 20 May 1786, ASF, Acquisti e doni 94, filza 146.
19. Andrea Memmo to Guglielmo Chiarabba, Rome, 13 May 1786, ASV, Archivio Mocenigo, B16.
20. Alvise Mocenigo to Sebastiano Mocenigo, undated, ASV, Archivio Mocenigo, B 120.
21. Lucia to Alvise, Rome, 18 March 1786, AdR Papers.
22. Ibid.
23. Lucia to Alvise, Rome, 1 April 1786, AdR Papers.
24. Lucia to Alvise, Rome, undated, AdR Papers.
25. Lucia to Alvise, Rome undated, AdR Papers.
26. Lucia to Alvise, Rome, 8 April 1786, AdR Papers.
27. Ibid.
28. Lucia to Alvise, 27 May 1786, AdR Papers.
29. Andrea Memmo to Guglielmo Chiarabba, Naples, 17 January 1786, ASV, Archivio Mocenigo, B 16.
30. Andrea Memmo to Guglielmo Chiarabba, Rome, 2 February 1786, ASV, Archivio Mocenigo, B 16.
31. Andrea Memmo to Guglielmo Chiarabba, Rome, 22 April 1786, ASV, Archivio Mocenigo, B 16.
32. Lucia to Alvise, Rome, 1 April 1786, AdR Papers.
33. Lucia to Alvise, Rome, April 1786, AdR Papers.
34. Lucia to Alvise, Rome, May 1786, AdR Papers.
35. Lucia to Alvise, Rome, 27 May 1786, AdR Papers.
36. Lucia to Alvise, Rome, 3 June 1786, AdR Papers.
37. Lucia to Alvise, Rome, 27 May 1786, AdR Papers.
38. Lucia to Alvise, Rome, 1 and 15 July 1786, AdR Papers.
39. Lucia to Alvise, Rome, 17 June 1786, AdR Papers.
40. Lucia to Alvise, Rome, 10 June 1786, AdR Papers.
41. Andrea Memmo to Guglielmo Chiarabba, Rome, 10 June 1786, ASV, Archivio Mocenigo, B 12.
42. Andrea Memmo to Guglielmo Chiarabba, Rome, 18 March 1786, ASV, Archivio Mocenigo, B 12.
43. Andrea Memmo to Guglielmo Chiarabba, Rome, 7 July 1786, ASV, Archivio Mocenigo, B 12.
44. Ibid.
45. Lucia to Alvise, Rome, 10 June 1786, AdR Papers.
46. Andrea Memmo to Guglielmo Chiarabba, Rome, 12 August 1786, ASV, Archivio Mocenigo, B 12.

47. Lucia to Alvise, Rome, 24 June 1786, AdR Papers.
48. Chiara Zen Mocenigo to Lucia, Venice, 22 June 1786, ASV, Archivio Mocenigo, B 122.
49. Lucia to Alvise, Rome, 1 July 1786, AdR Papers.
50. Ibid.
51. Ibid.
52. Lucia to Alvise, Rome, 15 July 1786, AdR Papers.
53. Andrea Memmo to Guglielmo Chiarabba, Rome, 17 August 1784, AdR Papers.
54. Lucia to Alvise, Rome, 26 August 1786, AdR Papers.
55. Lucia to Alvise, Rome, 2 September 1786, AdR Papers.
56. Lucia to Alvise, Rome, August 1786, AdR Papers.
57. Ibid.
58. Lucia to Alvise, Rome, 23 September 1786, AdR Papers.
59. Lucia to Alvise, Rome, 2 September 1786, AdR Papers.
60. Andrea Memmo to Giulio Perini, Rome, 7 July 1786, ASF, Acquisti e doni 94, filza 146.
61. Lucia to Alvise, Rome, 14 October 1786, AdR Papers.
62. Ibid.
63. Lucia to Alvise, Rome, 23 September and 7 October 1786, AdR Papers.
64. Andrea Memmo to Guglielmo Chiarabba, Mira, 13 November 1786, ASV, Archivio Mocenigo, B 122.
65. Andrea Memmo to Guglielmo Chiarabba, Florence, 28 October 1786, ASV, Archivio Mocenigo, B 122.
66. Lucia to Alvise, Florence, October 1786, AdR Papers (torn, mud-splattered note).

CHAPTER TWO: PALAZZO MOCENIGO

1. Lucia to Alvise, Venice, undated, AdR Papers.
2. Lucia to Alvise, Venice, March 1787, AdR Papers.
3. Lucia to Alvise, Venice, April 1787, AdR Papers.
4. Andrea Memmo to Giulio Perini, Venice, 11 August 1787, ASF, Acquisti e doni 94, filza 146.
5. The quotes in this paragraph are taken from undated, hand-delivered messages from Lucia to Alvise, AdR Papers.
6. Andrea Memmo to Giulio Perini, Venice, 20 February 1787, ASF, Acquisti e doni 94, filza 146.
7. Andrea Memmo to Giulio Perini, Venice, 7 April 1787, ASF, Acquisti e doni 94, filza 146.
8. Andrea Memmo to Giulio Perini, Venice, 27 September 1788, ASF, Acquisti e doni 94, filza 146.
9. Andrea Memmo to Giulio Perini, Venice, 24 March 1787, ASF, Acquisti e doni 94, filza 146.
10. The quotes in this paragraph are taken from undated, hand-delivered messages from Lucia to Alvise, AdR Papers.
11. Ibid.
12. Lucia to Alvise, Venice, 7 September 1788, AdR Papers.

13. Andrea Memmo to Giulio Perini, Venice, 10 March 1787, ASF, Acquisti e doni 94, filza 146.
14. Lucia to Alvise, Dolo, 9 September 1788, and Lucia to Alvise, undated, AdR Papers.
15. Lucia to Alvise, Dolo, 18 July 1788, AdR Papers.
16. Ibid.
17. Andrea Memmo to Giulio Perini, Padua, 27 September 1788, AdR Papers.
18. Ibid.
19. Andrea Memmo to Giulio Perini, Venice, 28 July 1787, ASF, Acquisti e doni 94, filza 146.
20. Andrea Memmo to Giulio Perini, Rome, 13 August 1785, ASF, Acquisti e doni 94, filza 146.
21. Unsigned letter, 23 February 1788, ASV, Archivio Mocenigo, B 120.
22. Attributed to Pietro Gradenigo, ASV, Archivio Mocenigo, filza 120.
23. Andrea Memmo to Giulio Perini, Venice, 14 March 1789, ASF, Acquisti e doni 94, filza 146.
24. Letter to the Inquisitors, 1 March 1788. On Sebastiano Mocenigo and Andrea Memmo's campaigns in the election of 1788, see ASV, Archivio Mocenigo, B 122.
25. Andrea Memmo to Giulio Perini, Venice, 27 September 1788, ASF, Acquisti e doni 94, filza 146.
26. Andrea Memmo to Giulio Perini, Venice, 27 September 1788, ASF, Acquisti e doni 94, filza 146.
27. Lucia to Alvise, Venice, undated, AdR Papers.
28. Lucia to Alvise, Valdagno, 7 August 1789, AdR Papers.
29. Lucia to Alvise, Valdagno, 8 August 1789, AdR Papers.
30. Lucia to Alvise, Valdagno, 29 July 1789, AdR Papers.
31. Lucia to Alvise, Valdagno, 10 and 13 July 1789, AdR Papers.
32. Lucia to Alvise, Valdagno, 14 August 1789, AdR Papers.
33. Lucia to Alvise, Valdagno, undated, AdR Papers.
34. Lucia to Alvise, Valdagno, 29 August 1789, AdR Papers.
35. Lucia to Alvise, Valdagno, 28 August 1789, AdR Papers.
36. All the quotes by Foscarina come from hand-delivered, undated notes, AdR Papers.
37. Sebastiano Mocenigo to Alvise, Venice, undated, ASV, Archivio Mocenigo, filza B 122.
38. Lucia's quotes relative to her first stay in Cordovado are in letters from Lucia to Alvise over the summer of 1790, AdR Papers.
39. Lucia to Alvise, Cordovado, 28 July 1790, AdR Papers.
40. Lucia to Alvise, Dolo, 27 July 1791, AdR Papers.
41. Lucia to Alvise, Dolo, 16 and 27 June 1791, AdR Papers.
42. Lucia to Alvise, Dolo, 16 June 1791, AdR Papers.
43. Lucia to Alvise, Dolo, 8 July 1791, AdR Papers.
44. Chiara Zen Mocenigo to Lucia, Venice, 17 January 1792, ASV, Archivio Mocenigo, B 122.
45. Alvise did not burn the letters. They were found in a neat bundle among Lucia's correspondence, AdR Papers.

46. Chiara Zen Mocenigo to Lucia, Venice, 23 March 1792, ASV, Archivio Mocenigo, B 122.
47. Lucia to Alvise, Venice, undated, AdR Papers.
48. Dinda Petrocchi Orsini to Alvise, undated letters and notes, AdR Papers.
49. Lucia to Alvise, undated, AdR Papers.
50. Ibid.

CHAPTER THREE: VIENNA

1. Caspar von Riesbeck, *A General Collection of Voyages and Travels*, edited by John Pinkerton, vol. VI, London: Longman, Hurst and Rees, 1809; see his description of Frankfurt.
2. Lucia to Paolina, Frankfurt, 16 July 1792, AM, Lettere di L.M.
3. Lucia to Paolina, on the Rhine, 22 July 1792, AM, Lettere di L.M.
4. Lucia to Paolina, Munich, 11August 1792, AM, Lettere di L.M.
5. Lucia to Paolina, Mainz, 28 July 1792, AM, Lettere di L.M.
6. Riesbeck, op. cit., p. 20.
7. Ibid. p. 35.
8. Ibid. p. 47.
9. Lucia to Paolina, Vienna, 29 September 1792, AM, Lettere di L.M.
10. Lucia to Paolina, Vienna, 27 October 1792, AM, Lettere di L.M.
11. Chiara Zen Mocenigo to Lucia, Venice, 29 September 1792, ASV, Archivio Mocenigo, B 122.
12. Lucia to Paolina, Vienna, 29 September 1792, AM, Lettere di L.M.
13. Lucia to Paolina, Vienna, 3 November 1792, AM, Lettere di L.M.
14. Lucia to Paolina, Vienna, 27 October 1792, AM, Lettere di L.M.
15. Lucia to Paolina, Vienna, 3 November 1792, AM, Lettere di L.M.
16. Lucia to Paolina, Vienna, 14 November 1792, AM, Lettere di L.M.
17. Lucia to Paolina, Vienna, 24 November 1792, AM, Lettere di L.M.
18. Lucia to Paolina, Vienna, 14 November 1792, AM, Lettere di L.M.
19. Lucia to Paolina, Vienna, 15 December 1792, AM, Lettere di L.M.
20. For a discussion on delivery "in the chair," see Lucia to Paolina, Vienna, 22 and 26 December 1792, and 5 and 16 January 1793, AM, Lettere di L.M.
21. Lucia to Paolina, Vienna, 19 January 1793, AM, Lettere di L.M.
22. Lucia to Paolina, Vienna, 26 January 1793, AM, Lettere di L.M.
23. Lucia to Andrea Memmo, 12 December 1792, AM, Lettere di L.M.
24. Lucia to Paolina, Vienna, 22 December 1792, AM, Lettere di L.M.
25. Ibid.
26. Lucia to Paolina, Vienna, 26 December 1792, AM, Lettere di L.M.
27. Lucia to Paolina, Vienna, 5 January 1793, AM, Lettere di L.M.
28. Lucia to Paolina, Vienna, 6 February 1793, AM, Lettere di L.M.
29. Lucia to Paolina, Vienna, 27 February 1793, AM, Lettere di L.M.
30. Lucia to Paolina, Vienna, 5 January 1793, AM, Lettere di L.M.
31. Lucia to Paolina, Vienna, 5 March 1793, AM, Lettere di L.M.
32. Lucia to Paolina, Vienna, 26 December 1792, AM, Lettere di L.M.
33. Lucia to Paolina, Vienna, 27 March 1793, AM, Lettere di L.M.
34. Lucia to Paolina, Vienna, 20 March 1793, AM, Lettere di L.M.
35. Lucia to Paolina, Vienna, 3 April 1793, AM, Lettere di L.M.

36. Lucia to Paolina, Vienna, 20 March 1793, AM, Lettere di L.M.
37. Lucia to Paolina, Vienna, 27 March and 3 April 1793, AM, Lettere di L.M.
38. Lucia to Paolina, Vienna, 20 March 1793, AM, Lettere di L.M.
39. Lucia to Paolina, Vienna, 3 April 1793, AM, Lettere di L.M.
40. Lucia to Paolina, Vienna, 10 April 1793, AM, Lettere di L.M.
41. Lucia to Paolina, Vienna, 20 March 1793, AM, Lettere di L.M.
42. Lucia to Paolina, Vienna, 17 and 20 April 1793, AM, Lettere di L.M.
43. Lucia to Paolina, Vienna, 24 April 1793, AM, Lettere di L.M.
44. Chiara Zen Mocenigo, Venice, 24 April 1793, ASV, Archivio Mocenigo, B 122.
45. Lucia to Paolina, Vienna, 24 April 1793, AM, Lettere di L.M.
46. Lucia to Paolina, Vienna, 29 May 1793, AM, Lettere di L.M.
47. Chiara Zen Mocenigo to Lucia, Padua, 9 July 1793, ASV, Archivio Mocenigo, B 122.
48. Chiara Zen Mocenigo to Lucia, Padua, 4 July 1793, ASV, Archivio Mocenigo, B 122.
49. AdR Papers.
50. Chiara Zen Mocenigo to Lucia, Venice, 20 August 1793, ASV, Archivio Mocenigo, B 122.
51. Alvise to Sebastiano Mocenigo, Verona, 9 March 1795, ASV, Archivio Mocenigo, B 122.
52. Chiara Zen Mocenigo to Lucia, Venice, 3 April 1795, ASV, Archivio Mocenigo, B 122.

CHAPTER FOUR: THE FALL OF VENICE

1. ASV, Delibere del Senato (Secreta), Ca. Mil., T.F., filza 23.
2. Alvise to the Senate, 29 May 1796, ASV, Delibere del Senato, Ca. Mil., T.F., filza 23.
3. Ibid.
4. From a letter by General Berthier, received by Alvise on 30 May 1796, ASV, Delibere del Senato, Ca. Mil., T.F., filza 23.
5. Alvise to the Senate, Udine, 5 April 1797, ASV, Archivio militare, T.F., filza 45.
6. Alvise to the Senate, Udine, 11 April 1797, ASV, Archivio militare, T.F., filza 46.
7. Alvise to the Senate, Udine, 15 April 1797, ASV, Archivio militare, T.F., filza 46.
8. From the Senate to Alvise, 17 April 1797, ASV, Archivio militare, T.F., filza 46.
9. George McClellan, *Venice and Bonaparte*, Princeton: Princeton University Press, 1931, p. 192, and Amable de Fournoux, *Napoléon et Venise 1797–1814*, Paris: Editions de Fallois, 2002, p. 89.
10. de Fournoux, op. cit., p. 100.
11. Lodovico Manin, *Memorie del Dogado*, Venice: Ongania, 1886, p. 24.
12. Alvise Mocenigo et al. to the Senate, Codroipo, 10 May 1797. Quoted by Giovanni Di Stefano e Giannantonio Paladini in *Storia di Venezia 1797–1997*, Venice: Supernova-Grafiche, 1997.
13. de Fournoux, op. cit., p. 102.

14. Alvise to Chiara Zen Mocenigo, Vienna, 22 May, 1801, ASV, Archivio Mocenigo, B 119.
15. *Il Monitore*, 7 June 1797, Collezione Biblioteca nazionale marciana.
16. Ibid., 16 and 18 September 1797.
17. Ibid., 18 September 1797.

CHAPTER FIVE: COLONEL PLUNKETT

1. From an undated entry in Alvise's Cahier de Lettres begun on 5 November, 1800, ASV, Archivio Mocenigo, B 119.
2. The passports are dated 28 June 1798, ASV, Archivio Mocenigo, B 28.
3. Lucia to Paolina, Florence, 27 July 1798, AM, Lettere di L.M.
4. Ibid.
5. Ibid.
6. Lucia to Paolina, Florence, 5 August 1798, AM, Lettere di L.M.
7. Lucia to Paolina, Florence, 12 September 1798, AM, Lettere di L.M.
8. Lucia to Paolina, Florence, 2 August 1798, AM, Lettere di L.M.
9. Maximilian Plunkett to Paolina, Florence, undated, AM, Lettere di L.M.
10. Lucia to Paolina, Florence, 12 September 1798, AM, Lettere di L.M.
11. Lucia to Paolina, Florence, 2 August 1798, AM, Lettere di L.M.
12. Lucia to Paolina, Florence, 13 October 1798, AM, Lettere di L.M.
13. Alvise's travelling papers, dated 23 March 1799, are in ASV, Archivio Mocenigo, B 28.
14. For a description of Colonel Plunkett's role in the 1799 campaign in Switzerland, see *Geschichte des K. und K. Infanterie-Regiments Freiherr von Appel n. 60*, Erlau, Vienna: Kriegs Archiv, 1898.
15. Lucia to Paolina, undated, AM, Lettere di L.M.
16. See *Geschichte*.
17. Undated entry, Cahier de Lettres, ASV, Archivio Mocenigo, B 119.
18. Entry of 26 July, 1801, Cahier de Lettres, ASV, Archivio Mocenigo, B 119.
19. Ibid.
20. Ibid.

CHAPTER SIX: VIENNESE CAROUSEL

1. Entry of 5 November 1800, Cahier de Lettres, ASV, Archivio Mocenigo, B 119.
2. Undated entry, Cahier de Lettres, ASV, Archivio Mocenigo, B 119.
3. Lucia to Paolina, Baden, 6 September 1801, AM, Lettere di L.M.
4. Ibid.
5. Lucia to Paolina, Baden, 10 September 1801, AM, Lettere di L.M.
6. Lucia to Paolina, Baden, 11 September 1801, AM, Lettere di L.M.
7. Lucia to Paolina, Baden, 14 September 1801, AM, Lettere di L.M.
8. Lucia to Paolina, Baden, 9 September 1801, AM, Lettere di L.M.
9. Ibid.
10. Lucia to Paolina, Baden, 8 September 1801, AM, Lettere di L.M.
11. Lucia to Paolina, Vienna, 30 September 1801, AM, Lettere di L.M.
12. Lucia to Paolina, Toeplitz, 6 August 1802, AM, Lettere di L.M.

13. Lucia to Paolina, Teschen, 7 August 1802, AM, Lettere di L.M.
14. Lucia to Paolina, Vienna, 4 September 1802, AM, Lettere di L.M.
15. Lucia to Paolina, Vienna, September 1802, AM, Lettere di L.M.
16. Lucia to Paolina, Baden, 14 September 1803, AM, Lettere di L.M.
17. Lucia to Paolina, Vienna, 23 October 1802, AM, Lettere di L.M.
18. Lucia to Paolina, Vienna, 8 October 1801, AM, Lettere di L.M.
19. Lucia to Paolina, Vienna, September 1802, AM, Lettere di L.M.
20. Lucia to Paolina, Margarethen, 12 November 1802, AM, Lettere di L.M.
21. Lucia to Paolina, Margarethen, 11 October and 12 November 1802, AM, Lettere di L.M.
22. Lucia to Paolina, Margarethen, 12 November 1802, AM, Lettere di L.M.
23. Lucia to Paolina, Abano, 14 April 1804, AM, Lettere di L.M.
24. Lucia to Paolina, Magarethen, 8 January 1803, AM, Lettere di L.M.
25. Lucia to Paolina, Vienna, 25 December 1802, AM, Lettere di L.M.
26. Ibid.
27. Lucia to Paolina, undated, AM, Lettere di L.M.
28. Lucia to Paolina, Vienna, 4 January 1803, AM, Lettere di L.M.
29. Lucia to Paolina, Vienna, 12 February 1803, AM, Lettere di L.M.
30. Lucia to Paolina, Vienna, 13 March 1805, AM, Lettere di L.M.
31. Lucia to Paolina, Vienna, 26 May 1804, AM, Lettere di L.M.
32. Lucia to Paolina, Vienna, 25 December 1802, AM, Lettere di L.M.
33. Lucia to Paolina, Vienna, 19 February 1803, AM, Lettere di L.M.
34. Ibid.
35. Lucia to Paolina, Vienna, 23 February 1803, AM, Lettere di L.M.
36. Lucia to Paolina, Vienna, undated, AM, Lettere di L.M.
37. Lucia to Paolina, Vienna, 4 February 1803, AM, Lettere di L.M.
38. Lucia to Paolina, Vienna, undated 1803, AM, Lettere di L.M.

CHAPTER SEVEN: THE EDUCATION OF ALVISETTO

1. The contents of this letter were kindly provided to me by Marco Leeflang and are quoted by Lolo Clary in his diary (entry of 6 September 1803). See Lolo, *Le journal du Comte Charles Joseph Clary-Aldringen*, Tome 2 (1803–1814), ed. Marco Leeflang, Utrecht: Marco Leeflang 1998, p. 92.
2. Baptismal Registry in the Archivio Patriarcale di Venezia.
3. Ibid.
4. Lucia to Paolina, Alvisopoli, 20 November 1803, AM, Lettere di L.M.
5. Ibid.
6. Lucia to Paolina, Alvisopoli, 24 November 1803, AM, Lettere di L.M.
7. Lucia to Paolina, Vienna, May 1804, AM, Lettere di L.M.
8. Lucia to Paolina, Vienna, 5 January, AM, Lettere di L.M.
9. Ibid.
10. Lucia to Paolina, Margarethen, 24 October 1804, AM, Lettere di L.M.
11. Lucia to Paolina, Vienna, 31 March 1805, AM, Lettere di L.M.
12. Lucia to Paolina, Vienna, 7 September 1804, AM, Lettere di L.M.
13. Ibid.
14. Maria Contarini to Alvise, Vienna, 24 February 1804, ASV, Archivio Mocenigo, B 126.

15. Ibid.
16. Lucia to Paolina, Vienna, 31 October 1804, AM, Lettere di L.M.
17. Lucia to Paolina, Vienna, 22 September 1804, AM, Lettere di L.M.
18. Lucia to Paolina, Vienna, 19 April 1805, AM, Lettere di L.M.
19. Lucia to Paolina, Margarethen, 30 October 1804, AM, Lettere di L.M.
20. Lucia to Paolina, Vienna, 22 June 1805, AM, Lettere di L.M.
21. Details on Robertson's projects were drawn from *Wonderful Balloon Ascents* by Fulgence Marion, translated from the French, London 1870 (etext also available on the Project Gutenberg website). See in particular Chapter VII.
22. Lucia to Paolina, Vienna, 31 October 1804, AM, Lettere di L.M.
23. Lucia to Paolina, Vienna, 21 November 1804, AM, Lettere di L.M.
24. Ibid.
25. Lucia to Paolina, Vienna, 5 January 1805, AM, Lettere di L.M.
26. Lucia to Paolina, Vienna, 16 January 1805, AM, Lettere di L.M.
27. Lucia to Paolina, Vienna, 5 March 1805, AM, Lettere di L.M.
28. Ibid.
29. Lucia to Paolina, Vienna, 31 March 1805, AM, Lettere di L.M.
30. Lucia to Paolina, 26 August 1805, AM, Lettere di L.M.
31. Lucia to Paolina, Vienna, 26 April 1805, AM, Lettere di L.M.
32. Lucia to Paolina, Vienna, 6 and 21 April, AM, Lettere di L.M.
33. Ibid.
34. Lucia to Paolina, Vienna, 19 April 1805, AM, Lettere di L.M.
35. Lucia to Paolina, Vienna, 21 April 1805, AM, Lettere di L.M.
36. Lucia to Paolina, Vienna, 17 April 1805, AM, Lettere di L.M.
37. Lucia to Paolina, Vienna, 15 and 16 February 1805, AM, Lettere di L.M.
38. The contract is in ASV, Archivio Mocenigo, Carte di Alvisopoli, B 105.
39. Lucia to Paolina, Margarethen, 9 August 1805, AM, Lettere di L.M.
40. Lucia to Paolina, Vienna, 6 July 1805, AM, Lettere di L.M.
41. Lucia to Paolina, Margarethen, 1 July 1805, AM, Lettere di L.M.
42. Ibid., and Lucia to Paolina, 27 July 1805, AM, Lettere di L.M.
43. Ibid.
44. Lucia to Paolina, Margarethen, 19 July 1805, AM, Lettere di L.M.
45. Lucia to Paolina, undated, AM, Lettere di L.M.
46. Lucia to Paolina, Margarethen, 9 August 1805, AM, Lettere di L.M.
47. Lucia to Paolina, Margarethen, 2 August 1805, AM, Lettere di L.M.
48. Lucia to Paolina, Vienna, 7 August 1805, AM, Lettere di L.M.
49. Lucia to Paolina, Margarethen, 9 August 1805, AM, Lettere di L.M.
50. Lucia to Paolina, Margarethen, 2 August 1805, AM, Lettere di L.M.
51. Lucia to Paolina, Margarethen, 15 August 1805, AM, Lettere di L.M.
52. Lucia to Paolina, Margarethen, 22 August 1805, AM, Lettere di L.M.
53. Lucia to Paolina, Vienna, 1 October 1805, AM, Lettere di L.M.
54. Lucia to Paolina, Vienna, 13 November 1805, AM, Lettere di L.M.
55. Lucia to Paolina, Vienna, 3 December 1805, AM, Lettere di L.M.
56. Ibid.
57. Lucia to Paolina, Vienna, 5 December 1805, AM, Lettere di L.M.
58. Lucia to Paolina, Vienna, 13 December 1805, AM, Lettere di L.M.
59. Lucia to Paolina, Vienna, 31 December 1805, AM, Lettere di L.M.
60. Lucia to Paolina, Vienna, 18 June 1806, AM, Lettere di L.M.

CHAPTER EIGHT: LADY-IN-WAITING

1. Lucia to Paolina, Novara, 18 December 1806, AM, Lettere di L.M.
2. Lucia to Paolina, Novara, 8 January 1807, AM, Lettere di L.M.
3. The notes of Monsieur Vérand are in ASV, Archivio Mocenigo, B 146.
4. Lucia to Paolina, Novara, 10 March 1807, AM, Lettere di L.M.
5. Lucia to Paolina, Novara, 17 March 1807, AM, Lettere di L.M.
6. Lucia to Paolina, Novara, 14 April 1807, AM, Lettere di L.M.
7. Lucia to Paolina, Vienna, 6 January 1806, AM, Lettere di L.M.
8. Lucia to Paolina, Novara, 29 December 1807, AM, Lettere di L.M.
9. Lucia to Paolina, Milan, 29 January 1808, AM, Lettere di L.M.
10. Ibid.
11. Lucia to Paolina, Milan, 8 February 1808, AM, Lettere di L.M.
12. Lucia to Paolina, Milan, 27 January 1808, AM, Lettere di L. M.
13. Alvise to Paolina, undated, AM, Lettere di L.M.
14. Lucia to Paolina, Milan, 27 January 1808, AM, Lettere di L.M.
15. Lucia to Paolina, Milan, 17 December 1809, AM, Lettere di L.M.
16. Lucia to Paolina, Milan, 21 January 1809, AM, Lettere di L.M.
17. Lucia to Paolina, Milan, 13 February 1808, and 3 March 1810, AM, Lettere di L.M.
18. Lucia to Paolina, Milan, 16 April 1808, AM, Lettere di L.M.
19. Lucia to Paolina, Milan, 22 April 1809, AM, Lettere di L.M.
20. Lucia to Paolina, Milan, 6 December 1809, AM, Lettere di L.M.
21. Lucia to Paolina, Milan, 21 January 1809, AM, Lettere di L.M.
22. Lucia to Paolina, Milan, 6 December 1809, AM, Lettere di L.M.
23. Quoted in *Joséphine*, by Ernest John Knapton, Milan: Mondadori, 1992, p. 284.
24. Lucia to Paolina, Milan, 4, 13 and 19 March 1810, AM, Lettere di L.M.
25. Lucia to Paolina, Paris, 13 April 1810, and Compiègne, 20 April 1810, AM, Lettere di L.M.
26. Lucia to Paolina, Paris, 28 March 1810, AM, Lettere di L.M.
27. Ibid.
28. Ibid.
29. For details on Empress Marie Louise's first days at Compiègne, see *Trois mois à Paris, lors du mariage de l'Empereur Napoléon I et de l'Archiduchesse Marie Louise*, by Prince Charles Clary-Aldringen, Paris: Plon, 1914.
30. Lucia to Paolina, Compiègne, 20 April 1810, AM, Lettere di L.M.
31. Ibid.
32. Ibid.
33. Lucia to Paolina, Paris, 14 May 1810, AM, Lettere di L.M.
34. Lucia to Paolina, Paris, 28 May and 6 June 1810, AM, Lettere di L.M.
35. *Trois mois à Paris,* p. 59.
36. Lucia to Paolina, Paris, 14 June 1810, AM, Lettere di L.M.
37. Lucia to Paolina, Paris, 7 May 1810, AM, Lettere di L.M.
38. Lucia to Paolina, Paris, 14, 28 May 1810, AM, Lettere di L.M.
39. Lucia to Paolina, Paris, 11 June 1810, AM, Lettere di L.M.
40. Lucia to Paolina, Paris, 8 July 1810, AM, Lettere di L.M.

41. Lucia to Paolina, Paris, 11 June 1810, AM, Lettere di L.M.
42. Lucia to Paolina, Paris, 14 July 1810, AM, Lettere di L.M.
43. Lucia to Alvisetto, Milan, 19 January 1811, ASV, Archivio Mocenigo, B 146
44. Lucia to Paolina, Milan, 1 and 6 April 1812, Archivio Memmo, Lettere di L.M.
45. The letter by Doctor Paletta is in Lucia to Paolina, Milan, 31 May 1812, AM, Lettere di L.M.
46. Lucia to Paolina, Milan, 24 June 1812, AM, Lettere di L.M.
47. Lucia to Paolina, Vicenza, 28 July 1812, AM, Lettere di L.M.
48. Lucia to Paolina, Vicenza, 30 July 1812, AM, Lettere di L.M.
49. Alvisetto to Lucia, quoted in Lucia to Paolina, Milan, 6 August 1812, AM, Lettere di L.M.
50. Alvise's comments are transcribed in a letter from Lucia to Paolina, Vicenza, 13 August 1812, AM, Lettere di L.M.
51. Ibid.
52. Lucia to Paolina, undated, AM, Lettere di L.M.
53. Lucia to Paolina, Milan, 23 December 1812, AM, Lettere di L.M.
54. Lucia to Paolina, Milan, December 1812, AM, Lettere di L.M.
55. Lucia to Paolina, Milan, 23 September 1812, and 3 March 1813, AM, Lettere di L.M.
56. Lucia to Paolina, Vercelli, 7 April 1813, AM, Lettere di L.M.

CHAPTER NINE: A YEAR IN PARIS

1. Lucia to Paolina, Paris, 25 April and 27 May 1813, AM, Lettere di L.M.
2. Lucia to Paolina, Paris, 25 October 1813, AM, Lettere di L.M.
3. Lucia to Paolina, Paris, 20 May 1813, AM, Lettere di L.M.
4. Lucia to Paolina, Paris, 26 July 1813, AM, Lettere di L.M.
5. Lucia to Paolina, Paris, 19 April 1813, AM, Lettere di L.M.
6. Lucia's Paris Diary (LPD), ASV, Archivio Mocenigo, B 33.
7. Lucia to Paolina, Paris, 8 July 1810, AM, Lettere di L.M.
8. LPD, January 1814, ASV, Archivio Mocenigo, B 33.
9. LPD, 4 June 1813, ASV, Archivio Mocenigo, B 33.
10. Lucia to Paolina, Paris, 20 June 1813, AM, Lettere di L.M.
11. LPD, 12 May 1814, ASV, Archivio Mocenigo, B 33.
12. LPD, 18 June 1813, ASV, Archivio Mocenigo, B 33.
13. LPD, 18 August 1813, ASV, Archivio Mocenigo, B 33.
14. LPD, 1 August 1813, ASV, Archivio Mocenigo, B 33.
15. Lucia to Paolina, Paris, 16 July 1813, AM, Lettere di L.M.
16. Lucia to Paolina, Paris, 21 June and 16 July 1813, AM, Lettere di L.M.
17. Lucia to Paolina, Paris, 3 August 1813, AM, Lettere di L.M.
18. Lucia to Paolina, Paris, 5 October 1813, AM, Lettere di L.M.
19. Ibid.
20. Alvise's letter is quoted in Lucia to Paolina, Paris, 16 October 1813, AM, Lettere di L.M.
21. LPD, 14 November 1813, ASV, Archivio Mocenigo, B 33.
22. Lucia to Paolina, Paris, 30 November 1813, AM, Lettere di L.M.
23. Lucia to Paolina, Paris, 17 October 1813, AM, Lettere di L.M.

24. Lucia to Paolina, Paris, 16 December 1813, AM, Lettere di L.M.
25. Lucia to Paolina, Paris, 26 December 1813, AM, Lettere di L.M.
26. Lucia to Paolina, Paris, 25 October 1813, AM, Lettere di L.M.
27. Lucia to Paolina, Paris, 7 and 16 December 1813, AM, Lettere di L.M.
28. Lucia to Paolina, Paris, 10 March 1814, AM, Lettere di L.M.
29. The quotes in this paragraph are taken from LPD, 22 February 1814, ASV, Archivio Mocenigo, B 33.
30. LPD, 15 March 1814, ASV, Archivio Mocenigo, B 33.
31. LPD, 13 February 1814, ASV, Archivio Mocenigo, B 33.
32. LPD, 4 March 1814, ASV, Archivio Mocenigo, B 33.
33. LPD, 29 March 1814, ASV, Archivio Mocenigo, B 33.
34. LPD, 31 March 1814, ASV, Archivio Mocenigo, B 33.
35. LPD, 1 April 1814, ASV, Archivio Mocenigo, B 33.
36. Ibid.
37. Ibid.
38. LPD, 10 April 1814, ASV, Archivio Mocenigo, B 33.
39. LPD, 5 April 1814, ASV, Archivio Mocenigo, B 33.
40. Lucia to Paolina, Paris, 13 April 1814, AM, Lettere di L.M.
41. LPD, 12 April 1814, ASV, Archivio Mocenigo, B 33.
42. LPD, 26 June 1814, ASV, Archivio Mocenigo, B 33.
43. Lucia to Paolina, Paris, 17 May 1814, AM, Lettere di L.M.
44. LPD, 26 June 1814, ASV, Archivio Mocenigo, B 33.
45. Lucia to Paolina, Paris, 29 May 1814, AM, Lettere di L.M.
46. Lucia to Paolina, Paris, 3 May 1814, AM, Lettere di L.M.
47. Lucia to Paolina, Paris, 27 May 1814, AM, Lettere di L.M.
48. LPD, 16 April 1814, ASV, Archivio Mocenigo, B 33.
49. Lucia to Paolina, Paris, 29 July 1814, AM, Lettere di L.M.
50. LPD, 23 June 1814, ASV, Archivio Mocenigo, B 33.
51. Lucia to Paolina, Paris, 20 June 1814, AM, Lettere di L.M.
52. Lucia to Paolina, Paris, 22 June 1814, AM, Lettere di L.M.
53. LPD, 17 June 1814, ASV, Archivio Mocenigo, B 33.
54. Lucia to Paolina, Paris, 6 May 1814, AM, Lettere di L.M.
55. Lucia to Paolina, 10 March and 12 June 1814, AM, Lettere di L.M.
56. LPD, 16 August 1814, ASV, Archivio Mocenigo, B 33.
57. LPD, 24 August 1814, ASV, Archivio Mocenigo, B 33.
58. LPD, 25 September 1814, ASV, Archivio Mocenigo, B 33.

CHAPTER TEN: BYRON'S LANDLADY

1. Lucia to Vérand, 28 January 1815, and Lucia to Alvisetto, 2 December 1814, ASV, Archivio Mocenigo, B 146.
2. Lucia to Paolina, 8 August 1815, ASV, Archivio Mocenigo, B 146.
3. Paolina to Alvise, undated, ASV, Archivio Mocenigo.
4. Lucia to Alvisetto, 18 August 1815, ASV, Archivio Mocenigo, B 146.
5. Lucia to Alvisetto, 28 August 1815, ASV, Archivio Mocenigo, B 146.
6. Lucia to Alvisetto, 9 March 1815, ASV, Archivio Mocenigo, B 146.
7. Lucia to Vérand, 28 January 1815, ASV, Archivio Mocenigo, B 146.
8. Lucia to Alvisetto, undated, 1815, ASV, Archivio Mocenigo, B 146.

9. Lucia to Alvisetto, 12 August 1815, ASV, Archivio Mocenigo, B 146.
10. Lucia to Paolina, 15 October 1815, AM, Lettere di L.M.
11. Alvise's will, Venice, 15 September 1815, ASV, Archivio Mocenigo.
12. Lucia to Paolina, Castel Gomberto, 28 May 1816, AM, Lettere di L.M.
13. Lucia to Carlo del Prà, 13 March 1816, ASV, Archivio Mocenigo.
14. Lucia to Paolina, Castel Gomberto, 28 May 1816, AM, Lettere di L.M.
15. Ibid.
16. Lucia to Paolina, Alvisopoli, 26 July 1816, AM, Lettere di L.M.
17. Lucia to Vérand, Alvisopoli, 9 October 1816, ASV, Archivio Mocenigo, B 146.
18. Lucia, undated, 1817, ASV, Archivio Mocenigo, B 146.
19. Lucia to Paolina, Alvisopoli, 7 October 1817, AM, Lettere di L.M.
20. Ibid.
21. Lucia to Giovanni Lazzaroni, 3 July 1818, ASV, Archivio Mocenigo, various letters.
22. Lucia to Paolina, 5 September 1817, B.M. Archivio Memmo, Lettere di L.M. and Lucia to Vérand, Alvisopoli, 22 October 1816, and 7 October 1817, ASV, Archivio Mocenigo.
23. Lucia to Vérand, Alvisopoli, 22 October 1816, ASV, Archivio Mocenigo, B 146.
24. Lucia to Vérand, 7 October 1817, ASV, Archivio Mocenigo.
25. Lucia's petition is dated 19 February 1818, ASV, Archivio Mocenigo, B 105.
26. Byron to Thomas Moore, Venice, 17 November 1816, in Leslie A. Marchand (ed.), *Byron's Letters and Journals*, London: John Murray, 1973–94.
27. Byron to Richard Belgrave Hoppner, Ravenna, 20 July 1820, in *Byron's Letters*.
28. Byron to Thomas Moore, Venice, 1 June 1818, in *Byron's Letters*.
29. The suspension is dated 22 June 1818, ASV, Archivio Mocenigo, B 105.
30. Lucia to Paolina, Este, 6 November 1818, AM, Lettere di L.M.
31. Lucia to Paolina, Este, 3 November 1818, AM, Lettere di L.M.
32. Byron to Murray, Ravenna, 1 August 1819, in *Byron's Letters*.
33. Byron to Douglas Kinnaird, 19 January 1819, in *Byron's Letters*.
34. Lucia to Vérand, 23 April 1819, ASV, Archivio Mocenigo, B 146.
35. Lucia to Vérand, 30 April 1819 and 7 May 1819, ASV, Archivio Mocenigo, B 146.
36. Lucia to Vérand, 26 May 1819, ASV, Archivio Mocenigo, B 146.
37. Lucia to Vérand, 2 June 1819, ASV, Archivio Mocenigo, B 146.
38. Alexander Scott to Byron, 27 July 1819, JMA.
39. Byron to Henry d'Orville, 9 August 1819, in *Byron's Letters*.
40. Byron to John Cam Hobhouse, Venice, 20 November 1819, JMA.
41. Byron to Hoppner, Ravenna, 31 March 1820, JMA.
42. Hoppner to Byron, Venice, 15 April 1820, JMA.
43. Byron to Hoppner, Ravenna, 22 April 1820, in *Byron's Letters*.
44. Hoppner to Byron, Venice, May 1820, JMA.
45. Byron to Hoppner, Ravenna, 20 May 1820, in *Byron's Letters*.
46. Byron to Hoppner, Ravenna, 12 June 1820, in *Byron's Letters*.
47. Hoppner to Byron, Bassano, 21 June 1820, JMA.
48. Byron to Hoppner, Ravenna, 12 June 1820, in *Byron's Letters*.

49. Hoppner to Byron, Bassano, 21 June 1820, JMA.
50. Ibid.
51. Hoppner to Byron, Venice, 12 July 1820, JMA.
52. Ibid.
53. Byron to Hoppner, Ravenna, 20 July 1820, in *Byron's Letters*.
54. Ibid.
55. Hoppner to Byron, Bassano, 21 June 1820, JMA.
56. Lucia to Paolina, Alvisopoli, 16 October 1827, AM, Lettere di L.M.
57. Lucia to Paolina, Padua, 9 September 1820, AM, Lettere di L.M.
58. Lucia to Antonio Canova, Venice, 10 July 1821. Manoscritti Canoviani. Museo Civico di Bassano del Grappa.
59. Lucia to Paolina, Padua, 7 July 1820, AM, Lettere di L.M.

EPILOGUE

1. René de Chateaubriand, *Mémoires d'outre-tombe*, Les Livres de Poche, Garnier, vol. 4, pp. 620–1.
2. Lucia to Paolina, Alvisopoli, 30 October 1826, AM, Lettere di L.M.
3. Lucia to Paolina, 13 November 1830, AM, Lettere di L.M.
4. Quoted in Lucia to Paolina, undated, AM, Lettere di L.M.
5. Adolfo Bernardello, La prima ferrovia, Venezia, 1996, p. 279, n. 131.
6. Paolo Prunas (ed.), *Venezia negli anni* 1848 *e* 1849, Florence, 1931, vol. 1, p. 21.
7. Anatole de la Forge, *Histoire de la République de Venise sous Manin*, quoted by Piero Del Negro in *Storia di Venezia, L'Ottocento e il Novecento*, Rome: Enciclopedia Treccani, p. 119.
8. Marco Meriggi, *Il Regno Lombardo-Veneto*, Turin: Utet, 1987, p. 324
9. Lucia to Paolina, Castel Gomberto, 28 May 1816, AM, Lettere di L.M.
10. Lucia to Paolina, Venice, 5 November 1842, AM, Lettere di L.M.
11. Lucia's will, dated Venice, 7 March 1854, is in ASV, Archivio Mocenigo, B 41.
12. Alvisetto to Lucia, Florence, 7 September 1848, ASV, Archivio Mocenigo, B 150.
13. Alvisetto to Lucia, Florence, 1November 1848, ASV, Archivio Mocenigo, B 150.
14. Alvisetto to Lucia, Florence, 10 December 1848, ASV, Archivio Mocenigo, B 150.
15. Alvisetto to Lucia, Florence, 22 December 1848, ASV, Archivio Mocenigo, B 150.
16. Alvisetto to Lucia, Florence, 30 December 1848, ASV, Archivio Mocenigo, B 150.
17. Alvisetto to the agent Pasqualini, Alvisopoli, 26 March 1849, ASV, Archivio Mocenigo, B 150.
18. Alvisetto to Lucia, 3 September 1849, ASV, Archivio Mocenigo.
19. Mary Lutyens (ed.), *Effie in Venice*, London: Pallas Athene, 1999, p. 98.
20. Ibid., pp. 116–20.
21. Ibid., p. 122.

Select Bibliography

Acton, Harold, *The Bourbons of Naples* (2 vols). London: Methuen, 1956–61.

d'Alméras, Henry, *La vie parisienne sous le Consulat et l'Empire*. Paris: Albin Michel, 1909.

Altan, Mario Giovanni Battista, "Alvisopoli: la mitica città di Alvise Mocenigo." *Itinerari*, September 1974, pp. 21–30.

Alberti, Annibale, et al., *Verbale delle sedute della municipalità provvisoria di Venezia nel 1797*. Bologna: 1928.

Andrieux, Maurice, *Daily Life in Papal Rome in the Eighteenth Century*. London: Allen & Unwin, 1968.

Antonielli, Livio, *I prefetti dell'età napoleonica*. Bologna: Il Mulino, 1983.

Asprey, Robert, *The Rise and Fall of Napoleon Bonaparte*. London: Little, Brown, 2000.

Bellicini, Lorenzo, *La costruzione della campagna: ideologie agrarie e aziende modello nel Veneto, 1790–1922*. Venezia: Marsilio, 1983.

Berengo, Marino, *L'agricoltura veneta dalla fine della Repubblica all'unità d'Italia*. Venice: Banca commerciale italiana, 1963.

————, *La società veneta alla fine del Settecento*. Milan: Sansoni, 1956.

Bergami, Giuseppe (ed.), *Napoleone a Campoformido*. Milan: Electa, 1998.

Bernardello, Adolfo, *La prima ferrovia tra Venezia e Milano*. Venice: Istituto Veneto di Scienze, 1996.

Busiri-Vici, Andrea, "Andrea Memmo, un ambasciatore veneziano a Roma." *Strenne dei romanisti*, pp. 121–28. Rome: 1974.

Capra, Carlo, et al., *Napoleone e la Repubblica italiana, 1802–1805*. Milan: Skira, 2003.

Casanova, Giacomo, *History of My Life* (12 vols). Translated by William Trask. Baltimore: Johns Hopkins University Press, 1997.

du Casse, André, *Mémoires et correspondances politiques et militaires du Prince Eugène de Beauharnais*. Paris: Michel Lévy, 1859.

Cessi, Roberto, *Campoformido*. Padua: Tipografia Messaggerie, 1914.

de Chateaubriand, René, *Mémoires d'outre-tombe* (4 vols). Paris: Garnier, 1998.

Clary, Charles Joseph, *Trois mois à Paris lors du mariage de l'Empereur Napoléon I et de la duchesse Marie-Louise*. Paris: Mitis et Pimodan, 1914.

Del Negro, Piero, "Il 1848 e dopo." *Storia di Venezia: l'Ottocento e il Novecento* (3 vols). Rome: Enciclopedia Italiana Giovanni Treccani, 2002.

Di Stefano, Giovanni, and Giannantonio Paladini, *Storia di Venezia, 1797–1997* (3 vols). Venice: Supernova, 1997.

Eisler, Benita, *Byron: Child of Passion, Fool of Fame*. New York: Knopf, 1999.

Erickson, Carolly, *Joséphine, a Life of the Empress*. New York: St. Martin's Press, 1999.

de Fournoux, Amable, *Napoléon et Venise, 1796–1814*. Paris: Editions de Fallois, 2002.

Fugagnolo, Ugo, *I dieci giorni di Napoleone I a Venezia*. Venice: 1982.

Fugier, André, *Napoléon et l'Italie*. Paris: J.B. Janin, 1947.

Georgelin, Jean, *Venise au siècle des Lumières*. Paris: Ecole des Hautes Etudes de Sciences Sociales, 1978.

Gesani, Luigi, *Storia dei funerali e delle elezioni del doge di Venezia nell'anno 1789*. Manuscript in the Museo Civico Correr in Venice.

Ginsborg, Paul, *Daniele Manin and the Venetian Revolution of 1848–49*. Cambridge: Cambridge University Press, 1979.

Goethe, Wolfgang, *Italian Journey*. London: Penguin, 1982.

Goetz, Robert, 1805, *Austerlitz: Napoleon and the Destruction of the Third Coalition*. Greenville, SC: Greenville Books, 2005.

Gottardi, Michele, "Da Manin a Manin: istituzioni e ceti dirigenti dal 1797 al 1848." *Storia di Venezia, l'Ottocento e il Novecento* (3 vols). Rome: Enciclopedia italiana Giovanni Treccani, 2002.

Gross, Hanns, *Rome in the Age of the Enlightenment*. Cambridge: Cambridge University Press, 1990.

Guiccioli, Teresa, *Lord Byron's Life in Italy*. Translated by Michael Rees; edited by Peter Cochran. Newark: University of Delaware Press, 2005.

Gullino, Giuseppe, "La congiura del 12 ottobre." *Critica Storica*, XVI, n.4, 1979.

————, "Nobili di Terraferma e patrizi veneziani di fronte al sistema fiscale delle campagne." *Venezia e la Terraferma*. Milan: 1981.

Hermanin, Federico, *Il Palazzo di Venezia*. Rome: La libreria dello Stato, 1948.

Hibbert, Christopher, *The Grand Tour*. New York: Putnam's Sons, 1969.

Junot, Laure, duchesse d'Abrantes, *Mémoires de Madame la Duchesse d'Abrantes ou souvenirs historiques sur Napoléon, la Révolution, le Directoire, l'Empire et la Restauration* (18 vols). Paris: 1831–35.

Knapton, Ernest John, *Empress Joséphine*. Cambridge: Harvard University Press, 1963.

de La Forge, Anatole, *Histoire de la République de Venise sous Manin*. Brussels: Amyot, 1853.

Lane, Frederic, *Venice, a Maritime Republic*. Baltimore: Johns Hopkins University Press, 1973.

Lawday, David, *Napoleon's Master: A Life of Prince Talleyrand*. London: Jonathan Cape, 2006.

Leeflang, Marco (ed.), *Lolo: le journal du comte Charles Joseph de Clary* (2 vols). Private edition.

de Ligne, Charles-Joseph, *Mémoires du Prince de Ligne*. Paris: Mercure de France, 2004.

Lisini, Alessandro, *La visita di Giuseppina Bonaparte a Venezia nel 1797*. Venice: 1939.

Lutyens, Mary (ed.), *Effie in Venice: Mrs. John Ruskin's letters home between 1849 and 1852*. London: Pallas Athene, 2001.

MacCarthy, Fiona, *Byron, Life and Legend*. London: John Murray, 2002.

Manin, Lodovico, *Memorie del Dogado*. Venice: Ongania, 1886.

Mansel, Philip, *Prince of Europe, the Life of Charles Joseph de Ligne*. London: Weidenfeld & Nicolson, 2003.

Marchand, Leslie A. (ed.), *Byron's Letters and Journals* (13 vols). London: John Murray, 1973–94.

Masson, Frédéric, *Joséphine, impératrice et reine*. Paris: Goupil, 1899.

———, *Joséphine répudiée*. Paris: Ollendorf, 1901.

McClellan, George, *Venice and Bonaparte*. Princeton: Princeton University Press, 1931.

Memmo, Andrea, *Elementi dell'architettura lodoliana. Edizione corretta e accresciuta dall'autore* (2 vols). Zara: 1833–4.

Meriggi, Marco, *Il regno lombardo-veneto*. Turin: Utet, 1987.

Molmenti, Pompeo, *Carteggi casanoviani*. Milan: Remo Sandron, 1920.

———, *Epistolari veneziani del secolo XVIII*. Milan: Remo Sandron, 1914.

Monitore Veneto, *Anno I*. Venice: 1787.

Norwich, John Julius. *A History of Venice*. New York: Knopf, 1982.

———, *A Paradise of Cities*. New York: Doubleday, 2003.

Nuzzo, Giuseppe, *Venezia tra Leoben e occupazione austriaca*. Salerno: Spadafora, 1937.

Pasquali, Susanna, "Scrivere di architettura intorno al 1780: Andrea Memmo e Francesco Milizia tra il Veneto e Roma." *Arte Veneta* 59. Milano: Electa, 2003.

Pavanello, Giuseppe, *Venezia nell'Età di Canova 1780–1830*. Venice: Electa, 1978.

Pemble, John, *Venice Rediscovered*. Oxford: Oxford University Press, 1995.

Pillepich, Alain, *Milan capitale napoléonienne, 1800–1814*. Paris: Lettrage Distribution, 2001.

———, *Napoléon et les Italiens*. Paris: Nouveau Monde Editions/Fondation Napoléon, 2003.

Pinkerton, John (ed.), *A General Collection of Voyages and Travels*. London: Longman, Hurt, Rees, 1809. The travels of Caspar von Risbeck are in vol. VI.

Potocka, Anna, *Mémoires de la Comtesse Potocka*. Paris: Stryienski, 1897.

de Rémusat, Claire, *Mémoires*. Paris: Calmann-Lévy, 1879–1900.

di Robilant, Andrea, *A Venetian Affair*. New York: Knopf, 2003.

Romanelli, Giandomenico, "Alvisopoli come utopia urbana." *L'Abaco*, May 1983, pp. 9–25.

———, *Venezia Ottocento: l'architettura, l'urbanistica*. Venice: Marsilio, 1988.

Roworth, Wendy Wassyng, "The Residence of the Arts: Angelika Kauffman's Place in Rome." *Italy's Eighteenth Century: Gender and Culture in the Age of the Grand Tour* (edited by Paula Findlen, W. W. Roworth and Catherine Sama; forthcoming).

———, "Rethinking Eighteenth Century Rome." *Art Bulletin*, March 2001, vol. lxxxiii, n.1.

Santalena, Antonio, *Napoleone I a Venezia*. Venice: 1907.

Silvan, Gianmaria, "Una nota in più per il Campanone di San Pietro." *Sculture romane del Settecento: la professione dello sculture* (edited by Elisabetta Debenedetti). Rome: Bonsignori, 2001.

Sorel, Albert, *Bonaparte en Italie*. Paris: Flammarion, 1933.

Spinosa, Antonio, *Napoleone, il flagello d'Italia*. Milan: Mondadori, 2003.

Tassini, Giuseppe, *Curiosità veneziane*. Venice: Filippi, 1990.

Thompson, J. M, *Napoleon Bonaparte*. London: Sutton, 2001.

Torcellan, Gianfranco, "Andrea Memmo." *Illuministi italiani*, vol. 7. Milan: Ricciardi, 1965.

———, *Settecento Veneto e altri scritti storici*. Turin: 1969.

———, *Una figura della Venezia settecentesca: Andrea Memmo*. Venice: 1963.

Trevelyan, George Macaulay, *Manin and the Venetian Revolution of 1848*. London: Longmans, 1923.

Tulard, Jean, *Le Grand Empire, 1804–1815*. Paris: Albin Michel, 1982.

Vianello, Nereo, *La tipografia di Alvisopoli e gli annali delle sue pubblicazioni*. Florence: Olschki, 1967.

Wynne, Giustiniana, *Pièces morales et sentimentales*. London: J. Robson, 1785.

———, with Bartolomeo Benincasa, *Les Morlacques*. Modena: 1788.

Zaghi, Carlo, *L'Italia di Napoleone*. Turin: Utet, 1985.

Zamoyski, Adam, *Moscow 1812: Napoleon's Fatal March*. London: HarperCollins, 2004.

Zorzi, Alvise, *La Repubblica del Leone, storia di Venezia*. Milan: Rusconi, 1979.

———, *Venezia austriaca*. Rome-Bari: Laterza, 1985.

———, *Venezia scomparsa* (2 vols). Milan: Electa, 1971.

Index

ALSO BY ANDREA DI ROBILANT

"*Splendidly engrossing. . . . [An] extraordinary story.*"
—The New York Times Book Review

A VENETIAN AFFAIR
*A True Tale of Forbidden Love
in the Eighteenth Century*

In the waning days of Venice's glory in the mid-1700s, Andrea Memmo was scion to one of the city's oldest patrician families. At the age of twenty-four he fell passionately in love with sixteen-year-old Giustiniana Wynne, the beautiful, illegitimate daughter of a Venetian mother and British father. Because of their dramatically different positions in society, they could not marry. And Giustiniana's mother, afraid that an affair would ruin her daughter's chances to form a more suitable union, forbade them to see each other. Her prohibition only fueled their desire and so began their torrid, secret seven-year affair. Eventually, Giustiniana found herself pregnant, and for help she turned to the infamous Casanova—himself infatuated with her.

Biography/978-0-375-72617-0

VINTAGE BOOKS
Available at your local bookstore, or visit
www.randomhouse.com